Logic for Beginners

A Skills-based Introduction

Second Edition

Michael J. Monge

Archimedes Publishing
Irvine, California

ALSO BY MICHAEL J. MONGE

Concealed Within Scripture: The Diary of Jesus
Why I'm Not A Democrat: And Why You Probably Shouldn't Be Either

Printed in the United States of America

ISBN 978-0-9831884-2-1

Archimedes reportedly declared that given a long enough lever and a place to stand, he could move the Earth from its position.

Visit us at www.archimedespublishing.com

Cover design by Mike and Heidi Monge.

The analogy between dominoes and logic is intentional and illustrative. In dominoes, when each domino is placed in the proper position the correct distance from the next, striking the first domino will result in the entire chain falling, all the way to the last domino. In logic, for a chain of reasoning, when each step in the chain is valid, the truth of the first premise flows down the chain, guaranteeing the truth of the final conclusion. A similar idea is captured in the gears of a clock. When each gear is correctly positioned, turning the first gear results in the rotation of the hands of the clock.

Dedicated to my wife Heidi and daughter Jordan,

The two great loves of my life

Contents

List of Skills to Be Honed

What is Logic About?

Many students have heard of Socrates, Plato and Aristotle, and some may even know that they are philosophers, but very few have any idea why these thinkers are considered so important. There are a great many reasons, but one of the most central reasons is the impact they had on the development of what we today call logic. Much of it has to do with the relationship between Socrates and the so called "Wise Men" of his day, or Sophists.

One would think that people would respect those they call Wise Men, but the Sophists in Socrates' day were looked down upon in a way, at least by Socrates and many others. Judging by the writings of Plato, a student of Socrates, the sophists used arguments not to justify their beliefs, but to win any debate in which they found themselves. Think about the word "lawyer" today. Lawyers garner some respect for their accomplishments, but often the word is used almost as a pejorative. The word "sophist" had a similar dichotomy of connotations. Perhaps that is why Pythagoras, when asked what he did, refused to say he was a sophist, and instead replied that he was a philosopher. He was one who loved wisdom, but was aware of how elusive it might be.

If one wanted to win in a court case, it was great to find a Sophist who would help. They would argue anything you were paying them to argue. They understood logic in a mercenary fashion. Logic was getting the jury to side with you, regardless of your actual guilt or innocence.

Socrates and his followers were very disturbed by this view of logic. Socrates did not use argument and debate as a method of winning just to prove his opponent wrong, but of actually trying to figure out which side was most justified by the evidence and reason. One problem was that at the time no one had systematized what counted as a good or bad reason. Socrates, at least as he is portrayed by Plato in numerous dialogs, would do so in a piecemeal fashion, dealing with certain issues as they arose, but such an approach required a keen insight and analysis in each case. The problem was that the Sophists were always willing to twist language in some new way which hadn't been considered.

To counter the power of the sophist, Aristotle devised techniques which would now be called logic. He developed the categorical syllogism, which involves statements which assert a relationship between classes, or groups of things. Using categorical logic, it becomes much easier to analyze and recognize mistaken reasoning and to distinguish good reasoning. He also developed the recognition of fallacies, or common patterns of poor reasoning.

Forever afterward, people would have these tools, and others in the writings of Aristotle, and many developed since then, to refute the audacious arguments of the sophists. In fact, to the early followers of Aristotle, these tools in Aristotle's writings were known as the Organon, which is Greek for "organ" or "tool." Modern logic may have taken a dramatic transformation around the turn of the twentieth century, which we will see when we get to truth-functional logic, but its goal is still the same: to determine which statements are supported by the evidence and by reason, and to refute arguments which are defective and manipulative.

Before we get to logic proper, however, it may be instructive to get a glimpse of Socrates and the sophists at work. The passage below was written by your author, but it was based on an actual dialog written by Plato over two thousand years ago. I have attempted to be fairly representative of both Socrates and the sophists, at least as they are portrayed by Plato. In the spirit of seeing reasoning and argumentative discourse pre-Aristotle, I include the following dramatically simplified version of the dialog "Euthydemus." Pay particular attention to several things: the nature of the arguments the sophists make, the purpose the sophists have in arguing, and the way Socrates is able to use their answers to refute them. Finally consider, if possible in this small passage, the excellence at which the sophists are aiming, and that at which Socrates is aiming.

With all that in mind, imagine that you are wandering around ancient Greece, and you come across the following exchange.

Dionysodorus: Hello fair youth of Athens. I am here to teach you, to make you into excellent young men. My brother, Euthydemus, and I are teachers, and we are here to teach you what we can.

Ctessipus: What do you charge for this service?

Dionysodorus: I assure you it is a fair price. When you think about it, though, what could be more valuable? Imagine how much you would pay for a new cell phone, or an Ipad, and ask whether they could possibly be of more use to you than perfecting your soul.

Ctessipus: That sounds great. What do you think Socrates?

Socrates: That does sound great. I just wonder how we can be sure that these gentlemen can do what they say. It is a difficult business, perfecting one's soul.

Dionysodorus: I am sure you have your doubts, but I assure you that my brother and I can teach you better than all men.

Ctessipus: That is an astonishing claim. I know enough to be doubtful of it. How can you possibly hope to convince me that it is true?

Dionysodorus: I can see that Socrates here has been an influence on you. This is exactly one of the things I will be able to teach you: the use of rhetoric in order to persuade people. Let me put it this way. You are doubtful that the two of us are better teachers than all men. But imagine, if all men were teaching you, then how could you possibly hear all of them at once? You couldn't even hear, none the less comprehend, everything they were all saying. And you certainly can't claim to be taught well if you cannot even comprehend what you are being taught. Or would you disagree?

Ctessipus: Of course not.

Dionysodorus: It follows, then, that we are better teachers than all men.

Ctessipus: Wait a minute, I'm having a hard time following. I feel as though I am being tricked in some way.

Dionysodorus: Only if you think that you can be tricked by reasoning.

Ctessipus: It's not the reasoning that I am worried about, but perhaps there is something I am overlooking.

Socrates: There certainly does seem to be something disconcerting in your presentation, Dionysodorus. Are you saying that reasoning and persuasion are identical?

Dionysodorus: Of course, they are. How could they be any different?

Socrates: Well, it seems to me that someone might be persuaded of something even when they haven't been given good reasoning.

Dionysodorus: Ah, you are one of those old-fashioned believers, aren't you? One who claims that there is some standard of reasoning beyond what men think. I follow Protagoras in holding that man is the measure of all things. If men believe something to be good reasoning, then it is, and if one has been persuaded by reasoning, then one holds it to be good.

Socrates: I must disagree with you. There must be some standard of good and bad reasoning that doesn't just depend on the whims of the day.

Dionysodorus: You old-timers really make me laugh. It sounds to me like the people of one generation telling the people of the next generation that they can't figure out things on their own. You are saying that the forms of reasoning which you judge to be good, are the same ones everyone must adhere to, regardless of what they think.

Socrates: I by no means said that the ones I think are good are the ones to which everyone should adhere, but we should all adhere to the ones that are in fact good.

Dionysodorus: There you go again with the claim that there is some standard above human judgment. Aren't you simply arguing in a circle?

Socrates: My dear, you are a wise man, one who understands my own argument better than I. It seems to me that if you are right, then no one could ever speak falsely. Could you tell me how I am mistaken?

Dionysodorus: I don't follow you.

Socrates: If any process of reasoning that seems good to someone is by that fact actually good, then whatever anyone believes will be right, since no one believes anything on the basis of reasoning they take to be bad.

Dionysodorus: Absolutely right!

Socrates: So, then, no one can ever speak falsely?

Dionysodorus: That is where our reasoning has led us, so that is what we must accept.

Socrates: But, that's just it. I do reject it.

Euthydemus: Then you are right.

Socrates: So, then you disagree with your brother.

Euthydemus: I said no such thing.

Ctessipus: What?! But what you just said contradicted what he just said.

Euthydemus: My dear boy, you will never convince me that I did, since there is no such thing as contradiction.

Ctessipus: That's just ridiculous. Everyone knows that there is such a thing.

Euthydemus: So, you would appeal to the crowd to support your case. Very bad reasoning indeed. Let me ask you, can something exist and not exist?

Ctessipus: Of course, not.

Euthydemus: Because that is a contradiction?

Ctessipus: Yes.

Euthydemus: And contradictions cannot exist?

Ctessipus: Exactly. Wait. What?

Euthydemus: So, then you agree with me; there is no such thing as a contradiction.

Socrates: I can see that Ctessipus is getting upset. Let me ask you something, Euthydemus. Are you just playing with language, or are you truly giving us your thoughts?

Euthydemus: What do you mean?

Socrates: Sometimes someone will present an argument as a foil, so to speak, in order to get an audience to think in a different way, or for some other instructive point, even though they do not agree with the argument. Is this what you are doing?

Euthydemus: Isn't it up to you to refute me, if you think my argument is mistaken?

Socrates: Let me be clear. I think that it is possible for people to speak falsely. Your brother stated that no one could ever speak falsely. Would you agree with him?

Euthydemus: I always agree with my brother.

Socrates: Fine. I just want to make sure that your skill is not simply the manipulation of language, so I will ask you: when I say that someone speaks falsely, what sense do the words have?

Euthydemus: Why do you ask me what sense words have, when words cannot have any sense?

Socrates: Please, elaborate.

Euthydemus: Answer me this: things that can sense, are they alive or dead?

Socrates: Things that can sense are certainly alive.
Euthydemus: And are there any words that are alive?
Socrates: Certainly not.
Euthydemus: Then, again, why did you ask me what sense my words had, since everything that has sense is alive?
Socrates: Perhaps I misspoke. But doesn't that in fact establish my claim. For if I misspoke, then it is possible to speak falsely. But if I spoke correctly, then it is possible for words to be alive, and I spoke falsely when I denied it.

If you are like most people, you found something deeply unsettling about the arguments of Euthydemus and Dionysodorus. It seems as if they have no real beliefs, but will say anything in order to win the argument. Socrates is looking for truth, whereas the Sophists are looking to win. One well-known Sophist bragged that he could make the stronger argument sound like the weaker one, and the weaker one sound like the stronger.

At the heart of the view of Socrates, Plato, and later Aristotle is that people can't believe anything they feel like believing. The concern is not one of political authority or morality, but of ordinary sense. One cannot believe that all dogs are mammals while at the same time believing that there is a dog somewhere which is not a mammal. One or the other of these beliefs must be wrong. So, something is going very wrong in someone's reasoning if he is willing to assert both of these two contradictory statements.

Furthermore, we should have reasons for the beliefs which we do have, and not just any reasons, but good reasons. The study of logic aims at uncovering why some reasons are good and some are not. Throughout the textbook we will learn many additional techniques, but one very important principle I hope you will learn is exemplified in the dialogue above. When we use a reason to justify our beliefs, then we cannot consistently deny the use of that reason to anyone else. I call this principle the Fundamental Principle of Reasoning.

Fundamental Principle of Reasoning
If one uses a reason to justify one's belief, then *ceteris paribus* (all things being equal), one cannot deny the use of that reason to anyone else.

Reasons are objective, at least in some sense. We may disagree about how a reason is applied, but if we use a process of reasoning, then we are accepting it as legitimate. If someone else then uses that same process of reasoning in the same way but on a different subject matter, then we are bound by intellectual consistency to accept their conclusions. Either that, or abandon the process of reasoning as illegitimate and admit that we may have no good basis for our beliefs. What is wrong is to use a reason ourselves, but deny the use of that reason to anyone else, as long as it is used in the same way.

In the original "Euthydemus,"Plato shows that when one adopts the reasoning processes and goals of the Sophists, then one can believe patently false things. Ctesippus eventually uses their reasoning to get Euthydemus to admit that his father is a dog, and his mother is the mother of sea-urchins, gudgeons, guppies and pigs. He uses that as a basis to reject the use of those processes and assumptions. The only alternative, as adopted by the two Sophists, is to believe anything and everything whatsoever.

If one can believe everything and nothing, then I can throw you in prison for wiping your nose, and then deny that I threw you in prison. In fact, when you say that you are in prison, I can deny that you are in prison, and think that I am perfectly justified in believing it. None of us wants this kind of reasoning used against us, and so, if we are intellectually consistent, we will not use it against others.

The examples of Euthydemus and Dionysodorus may be extreme, and unlikely to convince anyone today, but there are much subtler forms of rhetoric. By studying logic, we learn about the kind of arguments which can be presented, determining which ones are good (and what good means in this context) and which ones are not.

That is logic, in a nutshell. For a deeper understanding, you'll have to read the rest of the book.

CHAPTER

1

Truth, Logic, and the Difference

What is Truth?

Skill 1.1

Identifying Statements

Not everything is true. That is not to say only that some things are false, but some things are neither true nor false. In fact, most things are neither true nor false. Think about this book which you are reading. No one would call it "true". Nor is it a false book. To say so would be to commit what is commonly referred to as a category mistake. Books simply are not in the category of things which can be said to be true or false.

Consider other physical objects. Can a ball be true? Have you ever seen a false telephone? It does not seem that ordinary physical objects are the kinds of things which can be true or false.

Sometimes we say that a person is true to his beliefs, or to his sweetie, and arrows are sometimes said to be "true". Yet these ascriptions do not mean "true" in the ordinary sense, or at least not the sense with which we are concerned in logic. When referring to people, it means they are faithful, and when applied to arrows, it means that they fly straight.

What is it then that can be called true or false in a literal sense? If ordinary physical things cannot be true, perhaps abstract concepts will fit the bill. Can justice be true, or love? Can the number two be a true number, but the number *i*, the imaginary square root of negative one, be false? Even these abstract concepts don't work.

Could other ideas be true or false? If I imagine an image of a unicorn, there is a sense in which that image is unreal, but I still can't imagine calling it a false image. I have heard of false hopes, but never true hopes. False hopes are hopes which will never be realized, I suppose, but that seems like a more figurative use of the word.

There must be some things that are literally true or false. Perhaps you have already figured it out, but if not, see if looking at the linguistic objects in the following table will help you to do so.

A	B
Go to sleep. Singing Yabba Dabba Doo Are you going to eat that? Can you hear me now? Holy Guacamole! Under the sink	Water is composed of hydrogen and oxygen. Strawberries are in the rose family. Great White sharks are dangerous. No one knows everything. There are eight days in a week. Aristotle first formalized categorical logic. I exist.

Table 1.1

Perhaps you had already suggested sentences. Sentences can be true or false. 'The Earth orbits the Sun' is a true sentence, while 'the Earth orbits the moon' is false. Yet not every sentence is true or false. Look at the sentences under A in the preceding box, and consider the following exchange:

Jonathan: "Go close the door."
Isabella: "False."

Isabella's response just doesn't make sense. We would rightly think that she didn't understand what Jonathan said, maybe because she misheard him, or maybe because she doesn't speak the same language, or speaks it very poorly. If you ask me "What time is it?" and I respond "Wrong," you would be confused. It is not possible to be wrong when one is asking a question.

We distinguish these types of sentences, which can be true or false, by calling them **statements.** Any sentence which can be true or false is a statement. Statements are sometimes called propositions or claims, and when a person makes a statement, proclaiming that the statement is true, we will call it an assertion.

Statement
A sentence which can have the property of being true or false.

It is not necessary for someone to know whether a statement is true or false in order recognize it as a statement. All that is required is that we can see that there is a possibility that the statement can be true or false. For example, consider the statement "Over the past 100 years throughout the world, more people were born on August 10th than any other day of the year." I have no idea whether this statement is true, but that doesn't mean it fails to be a statement, nor does it mean that I cannot rightly call it a statement. There have been a certain number of people born on every day of the year over the past one hundred years, and the number born on August 10th is either higher than any other day, or it is not. The sentence *IS* either true or false, regardless of my knowing which one it is. That fact is enough to make the sentence a statement.

Statements are very important things. Without statements, communication would be very difficult, if not impossible. I have asked a few questions and given a few imperatives, but mostly what I have been doing, if you haven't noticed, is to write statements. I have certain beliefs, and I am communicating them to my readers using statements. When I have an idea, I use a statement to express the thought to someone else. I could instead use a picture, or maybe point at something, but we all know how easy it is to misinterpret those (if you're unsure, play a game of Pictionary). We all owe a great deal to whomever it was who invented statements.

Tell me your opinion about something. You will use a statement. Tell me a fact about the world, or about anything else. You will also use a statement. Whatever the difference between facts and opinions is (which it a great deal more complex than most people think), one big similarity is that they are both expressed using statements. Try to answer someone's question. You will have a difficult time doing so without using a statement. ("Answering a question with a question" is responding to someone, but it is not answering their question.)

True
A property of those statements which comport with reality.

Statements, like other sentences, have a multitude of properties. They are composed of a certain number of words, they are written in a certain language[1], they have either a single clause or multiple clauses, they may be written or spoken, etc. But there is one very important property of statements which is critical to their function, and that is whether they are **true**.

---

[1] To be very precise, some philosophers use the term "statement" to refer to a claim in a particular language, and the term "proposition" to refer to the information content contained within a statement, so that a statement in English which expresses the same information as a statement in French, is seen as a single "proposition." In this introductory text, we won't have occasion to be that precise.

Do we have class today? "Yes, we have class today." Supposing that this statement is uttered on a day on which we have class, then the statement is true. That tells me something about the way the world is, and I care about the way the world is. I am thirsty, and I see a glass on a counter with a clear liquid in it. I want to know whether the statement "There is water in the glass on the counter in front of me" is true. If so, I might drink it, if I'm not too finicky, or I'm very thirsty. It might depend on whether I believe the statement "I can easily get a fresh glass of water nearby" is true.

It might be very unusual to actively identify statements. Generally, we just think, or speak. We don't catalog all the statements which are true around us. Just start making such a list, and you will quickly see how difficult that would be. Think of all the things you are wearing, all the things you are doing, all the things which are in the same room as you, and you will begin to see the difficulty. Fortunately, we just concentrate on the things around us in which we are interested.

There are many more important things to learn about statements, but we will spread much of it out throughout the rest of the book. We will learn about categorical statements and truth-functional statements and many other things. But you should always keep in mind that what we care most about is whether a clear, unambiguous statement is true.

How do we go about figuring out whether a statement is true? If there were an easy answer to that question, we wouldn't need schools. The question is actually so difficult that some philosophers have given it up, and hold that there is no reliable method of deciding whether a statement is true. I disagree with that extreme skeptical position, but I have to agree that in some cases they have a point. In some cases, it is practically impossible to be certain about the truth of a statement, such as those dealing with the size of the universe, or from where it came. Many of the statements dealing with these kinds of issues are called philosophical statements. In any case, I do believe that I hold many statements to be true, and I hold many statements to be false, and I believe that there are many statements which I don't have a belief one way or the other. And, most importantly, I am very interested in believing all statements which are true, and not believing those statements which are false.

To believe a statement is to think that it is true. To believe that Barack Obama is the President is to believe that the statement "Barack Obama is the President" is true. We can't separate belief from truth. That is not to say that one cannot believe a statement when that statement is actually false; that is a situation which occurs all too regularly. What I mean is that the concept of belief in a statement wouldn't make any sense without the concept of truth. Nor could we make sense of the concept of truth without having beliefs. The two concepts are interconnected and depend upon each other.

So, another way of getting at my earlier question is to ask "When should I believe a statement?" The answer is, at least in general, "When it is true." When a statement is true, I should believe it, although this condition is not very useful. Perhaps, although this is a substantive philosophical viewpoint, we should sometimes believe a statement even when it is not true, or more precisely, even when I don't have a reason to believe it is true. This view is controversial; those philosophers and scholars who reject it are called evidentialists, while fideists and pragmatists reject it, although for different reasons.

For our purposes, the concept of truth will be taken for granted throughout the rest of the textbook. I don't know that I could improve on our intuitive understanding in any case. Philosophers do of course argue about the nature of truth, and what truth means, but we do have an intuitive understanding which should be enough for our purposes. The nature of belief can also be questioned and examined, but again, for our purposes, we will simply take for granted that people know what they believe. When I examine a statement, I can tell for myself whether I believe it.

Enough about statements (for now).

What is logic?

I suspect everyone reading these words has heard of **logic**. We undoubtedly think of it as a positive, good thing. Calling someone's words illogical is a derogatory claim. None of us aim deliberately to be illogical. But what is it exactly that we are trying to avoid? If we could clearly understand what being "illogical" meant, we would probably have a good idea of what being "logical" meant.

Logic
The study of the relevance between statements, and everything that is connected to it.

Unfortunately, in the real world, the answer may be very vague and uncertain. Many of us probably mean different things, or several things, and we are often unable to articulate them. An easy answer is that a "logical" statement or process of reasoning is one that "makes sense". Sadly, this expression does us no good. It is probably less clear than the one we are trying to understand. What does it mean for a statement to "make sense"? Does it mean that a person uttering it is not speaking gibberish, or that we agree with what he is saying? Let's not add words that we need to define and understand, but stick to one at a time.

So, what do people mean when they say something is illogical? Some other possibilities are that they think the statement made is silly, or dumb, or that it is unsupported, or that it is bizarre, or that the reasoning employed is faulty, that it contains faulty assumptions, or is odd in some other way. Sometimes, when people call other people illogical, it means no more than the person vigorously disagrees with them. It could be that some combination of these is meant, or some other mixture. It seems that in general, it is nearly impossible to say what someone means when they say something is illogical.

Fortunately, in the broader philosophical community, something much more definite is meant by "logic". Many of us may take no notice of the process of belief formation and revision, even within ourselves, but what else could be more important? We should at least attempt to determine whether the processes inside us which lead to beliefs are reliable. The study of logic is that attempt. Logic is the study of the relevance between statements and everything related to that relevance. This definition may not seem all that clear right now, but the rest of the section, and indeed this textbook, will be aimed at clarifying it.

Relevance
Connection or relation to.
A statement is relevant to another when their truths are intertwined.

Logic is the study of determining whether one statement, or group of statements, is relevant to another statement. **Relevance** is a challenging concept, but hopefully everyone reading this text has some understanding of it. One thing is relevant to another thing if it has some effect on or importance to it. If a thing has no relevance to me, then it cannot affect me and has no importance or connection to me.

When we say that one statement has relevance to another, we don't mean that the first statement cares in any way for the other statement. The relevance we mean involves that fundamentally central property of statements: truth. If one statement is relevant to another, we mean that the truth of the one statement is related to the truth of the other statement. If the first statement is true, then it is more or less likely that the other one is true.

Let's consider an example. The statement "Jake has a pet which can talk" is relevant to the statement "Jake owns a parrot." If the first statement is true, it is more likely that the second statement is true. Two statements can also have no relevance whatsoever to each other. The statement "The moon affects the tides" seems to have no relevance to the statement "No human being is over ten feet tall."

Once we learn more about the specific terminology of logic, we will stop using the term logical to describe a process of reasoning. We will have more specific and precise terms to use. But to offer a basic analysis of what people mean when they describe a statement as logical, the closest thing to how we use the term is that it is relevant to, or follows from, some other statement which we take to be true. A process of reasoning is logical when the steps involved have a sufficient level of relevance between them. Keep in mind that we will soon learn better and more precise ways to express our judgments of relevance.

What is the difference?

Although it may be clear already, I want to draw attention to the differences between truth and logic. Truth is a concept which applies to single statements. We can have a set of statements, all of which are true, but they are true individually, not collectively or as a whole, just as they would be false individually. A true statement is a way of characterizing the world as it is. Sets of statements, on the other hand, are not true all together. They may each be true individually, but it doesn't make sense to call them true as a whole, unless one just means that they are all individually true.

Sometimes people will say of a statement that it sounds logical to them, but strictly speaking, no individual statement can be logical, since logic always involves the relationship between statements. Logic only applies when we have two or more statements. Logic involves truth, but it is not the same thing. Logic addresses the question of whether the truth of one statement is relevant to the truth of another.

It is important to recognize that whether a statement is relevant to another is independent of the actual truth of the statements. In general, we need not know whether a statement is true in order to determine whether it is relevant to another statement. For example, in cultures where a married male wears a ring on his left ring finger to signify that he is married, the statement "Mardell is wearing a ring on his left finger" is relevant to the statement "Mardell is married" regardless of whether it is true that Mardell is wearing a ring on his left ring finger. Since most of us don't know who he is, we don't know whether he is wearing a ring or not, yet we can still assert that if he were wearing such a ring, then it would have some bearing on whether he were married.

This situation is generally the case, although there are exceptions. Many of these exceptions have to do with limited knowledge. For example, can you tell me whether the fact that I get my gas in California would be relevant to the fact that my spark plugs are misfiring? I'm not even sure myself. I do buy my gasoline in California, but that doesn't mean that it is relevant to my spark plugs misfiring. If it were relevant, I would have to believe that it is more likely that my spark plugs are misfiring because I buy gasoline in California. Presumably, one who knows much more about cars and/or gasoline would know whether it is relevant. This truth holds generally. We may be unaware that one statement is relevant to another, but the more understanding we have of the context and the causal, definitional or other connections between the statements, the more likely it is that we will know whether they are relevant to each other.

Fortunately, by the time most of us get to college, we are aware of a great many connections and causes in the world. And even more fortunately, for the most part we will be discussing very general statements, where no specialized knowledge is required to determine the relevance with which we are concerned.

Ultimately, the important thing to understand is that it doesn't make sense to call a statement "logical", as logic deals with the relevance between statements. A single statement cannot be said to be relevant to or by itself. It needs to be relevant to something else, and in the context of logic, it needs to be relevant to another statement. As we proceed, we will also see that a group of statements can be relevant to another statement. Sometimes groups of statements are relevant as a whole to another statement, even when none of the individual statements makes the truth of that other statement more likely.

What counts as a statement?

As we said before, a statement is a sentence which can be true or false. One need not know whether the statement is true or false, but only recognize that the sentence can be true or false. For example, consider this sentence: There are currently more than twenty thousand ants under my house. I don't know whether this sentence is true. Sometimes I suspect that it is true, and I'm sure my wife once thought it was true. But I don't really know. What I am very confident of, however, is that it *is* either true or false, which means that it is a statement.

There are several kinds of sentences, or strings of words, which are not statements, some of which can be seen in Table 1.1 under A. Imagine that you ask someone a question such as "What time is it?" and he responds "That's false." You would probably think that he had either lost his mind or didn't know English. The sentence "What time is it?" is just not the kind of thing that can be true or false. What this means is that straightforward questions are not statements.

Consider a command: "Raise your hand." Can this sentence be true? What would it mean to call this sentence "true"? Nothing. Commands are not statements, since they cannot be either true or false.

Think about this string of words: "to the movies." By itself, this string of words cannot be true or false, and so cannot be a statement. It is important to understand, however, that in a given context, the phrase might be a statement. If a friend asks you where you want to go, and you respond "to the movies," then what you are saying can be true, but only if we consider the entire statement "I want to go to the movies." The phrase is elliptical: it really should be "...to the movies." (Those three dots you often see are called ellipses.)

The importance of being able to recognize statements is that logic involves statements. One cannot back up what one is saying using a non-statement. Try it. Try to prove that something is true by asking questions or issuing commands. It won't happen.[2] The way we prove or demonstrate that something is true is by offering statements.

Even when we use evidence, we might just point to the evidence. Let's say you think someone is guilty, and I ask you why. You point to a screen, which has a picture of two fingerprints, and the word "Matching". Now, I think I know what you are trying to say. You are saying that "His fingerprints match the ones which were found at the crime scene." Notice that even here, when I try to articulate the evidence, it comes out in the form of a statement. Of course, you might come back and say "No. He owns the computer, and it turns out that the one who owns the computer is guilty." It is usually more clear to state what the evidence is than simply to point at it.

Some difficult cases

Rhetorical Question
A question which is not meant to be answered, but is used for rhetorical effect.

If only things were that simple. Unfortunately for the beginning student, there are some important exceptions. One of them is the **rhetorical question**. Rhetorical questions should generally be treated as statements. The reason is that rhetorical questions are not really questions at all; they are just indirect ways of asserting something. An actual

[2] In his day, Socrates used questions to great effect to make points, but he was only trying to show how little his opponents understood their own positions. His approach was so influential that it has become known as the Socratic Method, but using the Socratic Method is not the same thing as making arguments.

question is asked with the expectation that it can be answered in multiple ways, whereas a rhetorical question is generally a way to make a point without directly asserting it.

Compare the two examples in the following table:

Example 1.1	Example 1.2
"I hear that you've been married for ten years. Do you have any children?"	"I heard that they were trying to allow single people to adopt children, but isn't it better for children to be raised by two married people?"

The first question in Example 1.1 is truly asking for information. The speaker is asking the question because he doesn't know the answer, and wants the person to tell him the answer. This question is a real question.

The question in Example 1.2 is not really a question at all. It has the form of a question, but it is not eliciting information. The speaker is not asking his audience to consider the answer to the question and then offer a response. Instead, the audience is supposed to just accept the gist of the question without even thinking. When he says or writes "isn't it better for children to be raised by two married people?" one is not meant to consider whether it is true, but instead is just supposed to accept it as true. Perhaps it is true, but the speaker is not really asking whether it is true but instead is actually asserting that it is true. In effect, he is just saying that it is better for children to be raised by two married people.

Skill 1.2

Identifying Rhetorical Questions

Why is it that people use rhetorical questions? (Is that a rhetorical question?) Why would someone avoid actually asserting a point and instead put it in the form of a question? One reason is probably a lack of confidence. Phrasing the point as an assertion seems too certain, or may come across as abrasive. Phrasing one's point as a question makes it sound as if one isn't really making an assertion at all. Rhetorical questions can mask one's insecurity, or they can be a weaselly way to avoid responsibility. After all, one can say "I didn't assert anything, I just asked a question." But a rhetorical question isn't really a question.

Whatever reason people have for using rhetorical questions, they are usually considered bad form, at least in academic writing. In academia, one is expected to make assertions and back them up. One is not supposed to avoid making assertions by hoping one's audience will fail to recognize a question as rhetorical and will just accept the presupposition of the rhetorical question uncritically.

For our purpose here, what is important is that when a person uses a rhetorical question, we should treat it as a statement. By doing so, it is possible that a rhetorical question can be part of an argument, as either a premise or a conclusion. Just make sure to rewrite the rhetorical question as a statement before you identify it as part of an argument.

Ought Imperative
A command which is best seen as a "should" statement.

One other major tangle can be called supported imperatives, or **ought imperatives**. Sometimes commands are issues as real commands, and sometimes not. In any case, if someone offers a reason in support of an imperative sentence, then we should treat it as a statement. Consider the following examples:

Example 1.3	Example 1.4
"Hand me the newspaper when you're done."	"Don't ever give your personal information over the phone to someone you don't know. Some unscrupulous people can use it to steal your identity."

Skill 1.3

Identifying Ought Imperatives

In Example 1.3, the command is unsupported, and probably doesn't have much support anyway. If you asked the person why, they may tell you, but it will probably just be something like "I wanted to read it" or "I was going to use it to line my birdcage".

In Example 1.4, what looks like a command is given support. The fact that unscrupulous people might use your personal information for identity theft is being used as a reason to justify the command. Unfortunately, as stated the command is still not a statement. What we need to do is rewrite it so that it is. One simple way to do so is to add the words "ought" or "should". Instead of "Don't give your personal information over the phone to someone you don't know" we can use "You *should* not give your personal information over the phone to someone you don't know". This sentence can be true or false, at least in pragmatic sense. We can and do say of "should" statements that they are true or false. Our answer will often rely on our judgment in such cases, but that is sufficient to ground the assertion.

Consider the first statement again. It would be unlikely that the person would have said "You should hand me the newspaper when you're done". That's what makes it a straightforward command, and not a statement. In the second case, however, it is reasonable to think that the author would be perfectly comfortable using the "should" phrase.

Perhaps people use imperatives to express moral or rational "oughts" because it sounds stronger. It's harder to disagree with a command than with a "should" claim. Perhaps it is because they've bought into a kind a relativism where "should" statements cannot be supported, completely oblivious that commands as such cannot be supported either. Whatever the reason is, when a person issues a command which is supported by a claim, we should treat the command as a statement by using "should" or "ought".

Keep in mind that when I present rules to you, they are not intended to be followed mindlessly. You must always use your judgment. If someone offers reasons to defend something he has said, you should treat what he says as an argument, which means that you must treat what he says as if it could be true. You must treat his sentences as statements, even if they don't look like statements.

CHAPTER ONE EXERCISES

Basic Concept Exercises

Decide whether each item is a statement. If it can be interpreted as a statement in some contexts, say what they are, or give an example of one.

1. The moon orbits the Earth.
2. How much does this cost?
3. Close the door for me.
4. Please close the door for me.
5. In a minute.
6. What time is it?
7. Galileo was the first man to point a telescope up to the stars and planets.
8. Statements are sentences which can be either true or false.
9. Oh my gosh!
10. The number three is a prime number.

Intermediate Exercises

Decide whether each item is a statement. If it can be interpreted as a statement in some contexts, say what they are, or give an example of one.

11. I don't think you know what you are talking about.
12. Can't you give me a break.
13. Only if you get the right answer.
14. Never let them see you sweat.
15. The psychological impulses of the underdeveloped psyche evaluated with an emphasis on potential harm.
16. If you study, then you have a better chance at passing.
17. Comparing these challenging exercises and the ones in the previous categories can prove difficult.
18. It is so.
19. Under the most difficult circumstances, without any coercion or persuasion.
20. The real test is whether you are willing to engage the assignment, and attempt to come to an answer, whether it is right or wrong.

Challenging exercises

Part I: Decide whether each item is a statement. If it can be interpreted as a statement in some contexts, say what they are, or give an example of one.

21. You wanted a coke, right?
22. Water red purple silently.
23. Neither a borrower nor lender be.
24. Pleased to meet you.
25. The happy sentence read the carpet to the number two.
26. If only there were an easy way to distinguish between statements and commands.
27. What do you say we go to the movies?
28. Give us this day our daily bread.
29. My house is your house.
30. You should make yourself at home.

Part II: The following items are questions or commands. For the questions, decide if each one is a rhetorical question and should be treated as a statement, or if it is a straightforward question. For the commands, decide whether each one is a straightforward command, or if it should be treated as an ought imperative. In either case, if you think an item should be treated as a statement, rewrite the item as a statement.

31. Make yourself at home.
32. Make sure you use supreme unleaded gasoline in this vehicle.
33. Make sure you send your aunt a thank you note.
34. Can't you see that the death penalty is murder?
35. Why don't you drop that class that you're getting an F in?
36. Do you even care that she's cheating on you?
37. Don't we all think that the defendant is guilty?
38. How long will it be before you realize that he is guilty?

39. To be or not to be, that is the question.
40. Have you noticed how often that guy talks about Shakespeare?
41. Haven't you noticed how often that guy talks about Shakespeare?

In-Context Exercises

Political cartoons can entertain, but they generally do so by making a point, one which can be articulated (though often only by someone with some familiarity with the situation). Find a political cartoon which has a point that you can identify. Print out or copy the cartoon and bring it with you to class. On a separate page, rewrite the point of the cartoon in a single sentence. When you get to class, share only the cartoon with fellow classmates, and see if they get the same statement from the cartoon as you did.

Logic Puzzle: A Simple Ordering

Logic puzzles can be an instructive and enjoyable way to gain proficiency in logical reasoning. We will start this chapter with a very simple puzzle, and then proceed with progressively more challenging examples in the chapters which follow.

We have five people, and we want to know their ages. Given the information below, determine the ages of all the people.

1) Adam is older than Cynthia.
2) Barney is younger than Delilah.
3) Every person is between 18 and 45 years of age (inclusive).
4) Cynthia is 44.
5) Delilah is 19.
6) Emily is twice as old as Barney.

Chapter

2

Arguments and Their Parts

Let's say you want to inform someone of something, or you want to get them to believe something. How can you get them to believe it? You might just tell them the thing you want them to believe. You could also bring them to a place and just show them, or point to something, or draw a picture. You might also try to tell them other things which will convince them of the original thing you wanted them to believe. In the first place, they will have to rely on your credibility. If they think you are a credible source on the matter in question, then they will believe you. In the second case, they will examine the evidence, and if it is clear and obvious, then they will believe what you wanted them to believe. Lastly, if the extra information convinces them, then they will come away from the encounter believing what you convinced them to believe.

Logicians have a special word for the last of these methods. They call it an **argument**. In this context, an argument is a statement and a reason or reasons to believe that statement. If I simply tell you something to try to get you to believe it, I have not given you any argument, but if I back up what I say with a reason, then I have offered you an argument.

Arguments, then, are groups of statements. As such, they may or may not have the same properties as individual statements. More importantly, arguments are not just any group of statements; they are a group of statements with a direction. Consider a series of thoughts in your head. If they are just random thoughts with no logical connection between them, then you are not arguing, nor are you engaging in reasoning. In a process of reasoning, one statement relies on another statement for support. One or more statements offer a reason to accept another statement, or to believe that the other statement is true. In short, reasoning involves arguments.

Argument
A group of statements, one or more of which is being used as a reason to believe one of the others.

Keep in mind that this is a special, technical meaning to the term argument. Most people are more familiar with the use of the word which means a shouting match, or two people bickering with each other. It is possible that during an "argument" such as this, one or both parties to the dispute may offer "arguments" in the strictly logical sense, but it is by no means required.

Even in cases where one person does not offer actual argument to someone, that doesn't mean that the other party won't necessarily engage in reasoning. In fact, all of the methods for persuasion or informing with which we started out can be subsumed under the concept of argument. If one person merely asserts something to another, the second person can ask themselves if they have been given any reason to believe the assertion, and they will include as one of their potential reasons that the person in question asserted it. Their reasoning can take the form "Person *p* told me *s*, therefore, *s* is true." Although you haven't offered them a reason, the fact that you are the one saying something can be construed as a reason.

In the same vein, offering someone evidence, or a picture, or pointing to something can be construed as an argument. We saw before how this method can be extremely vague and ambiguous, and one way to be more clear is to articulate the evidence in the form of a statement. Let's say that I see smoke, and I want you to believe that there is a fire. I could just say "Look over there." I expect that you will see the smoke, and draw the same conclusion that I did. Or, I could articulate my reasoning, and say that "There must be a fire, because there is smoke there." Perhaps an argument isn't an argument until it is articulated, but

Conclusion
The statement in an argument which is being supported

Premise
A statement in an argument which is being used as support

inherent in any claim of evidence is an argumentative piece of reasoning, which can be drawn out more or less explicitly.

Logicians have given the parts of an argument names. The statement which is being supported or for which reasons are being given is called the **conclusion**. The statements which articulate those reasons are called **premises**. There cannot be an argument without premises, just as there cannot be premises without an argument (we will consider enthymemes in a later chapter). If there is no conclusion in a piece of writing, then there is no argument, and vice versa. So, one way to help understand arguments better is to understands the parts better. (In case you missed it, that was an argument!)

What is a Conclusion and how does one identify one?

Skill 2.1

Identifying Conclusions

As we saw earlier, a conclusion is a statement for which a reason to believe is offered. A conclusion is a statement, and thus has all the properties of statements, including being true or false. Generally we don't know beforehand whether the conclusion is true or false, or else we wouldn't be considering an argument which supports it. Of course there will be cases where someone argues for a conclusion which we already believe is either true or false. Generally, in these cases it is even more important to disregard our prior intuitions about the conclusion if we want to evaluate the argument properly.

It is very important to realize that a conclusion is just a statement because there is nothing inherent in the conclusion to mark it as a conclusion as opposed to any other unsupported statement. Only the context can determine whether a given statement is a conclusion or not. Consider the statement "logic is a difficult subject" in both of the following examples:

Example 2.1	Example 2.2
I took logic last semester. Logic is a difficult subject. I had a good professor, though.	I took logic last semester. Logic is a difficult subject. I barely managed to earn a C, and I usually get A's and B's.

Hopefully, you can already see that the statement is used as a conclusion in the second example, but not in the first. In Example 2.1, neither of the other two statements could be used as a reason to support the claim that logic is difficult. The fact that I took logic last semester by itself is not a reason to think that logic is difficult. Neither is the fact that I had a good professor. In either case logic would just as likely have been very easy.

In Example 2.2, however, the third statement is very clearly used to support the claim that logic is difficult subject. The fact that I did worse in logic than in my other classes is being used as a reason to believe that logic is difficult. In both cases, though, the statement was exactly the same.

Conclusion Indicator
A word or phrase that generally precedes a conclusion

In these cases we were able to determine whether a certain statement was a conclusion only by realizing that one statement actually did offer support for one of the other statements. Fortunately, in many cases there is a much easier way to recognize conclusions: **conclusion indicators**.

A conclusion indicator, or conclusion indicator word (or words), is a word or phrase which indicates that a conclusion is coming, usually right away. The word "therefore" is a common conclusion indicator word, but it is by no means the only one. It would be a difficult task, and perhaps a misleading one, to try to list every possible conclusion indicator, but a few of the most common ones are listed in the box to the right. Just remember that this list is not exhaustive; there are many other ways to introduce a logical conclusion.

Also remember that these phrases are not perfect, either. Some of them may be used in cases where they do not introduce a conclusion. In particular, the word 'so' is not used as a conclusion indicator in the following sentences:

1. I've been studying for so long.
2. So, how are you?
3. I'm doing so-so.

Although not perfect, most of these terms are fairly reliable in indicating conclusions. One must always consider the context, however, to be sure.

Common Conclusion Indicators

Therefore, ________
Thus, _______
Hence, _______
As a result, ______
Consequently, ______
So, _______
which shows that ______
which goes to show ______
which proves that ______
which demonstrates that ___
which establishes that _____

There are also a few words or phrases which are sometimes confused as conclusion indicators. The words 'if', 'then' and 'in conclusion' are ***not*** conclusion indicators. The words 'if' and 'then' are used in conditional statements, which we will examine in more detail shortly, and the word 'then' is commonly used to indicate the order of a sequence of events. The phrase 'in conclusion' is generally used to indicate that one is coming to the end of a speech or piece of writing. It generally refers to a "conclusion" in the sense of the ending of something, and not the conclusion in a logical sense.

Not every conclusion will be preceded by a conclusion indicator. In these cases some other technique must be used to determine the conclusion of an argument. In some of these cases, a straightforward technique which can be employed is the **therefore test**. To apply the therefore test, take a statement from a passage which you suspect to be the conclusion. Read the other statements in the passage, and then read the suspected conclusion, but precede it with the word "therefore". If the addition sounds like it makes sense, then you have a reason to think you have found the conclusion. This technique will not always work, but with practice you will gain proficiency in using it.

Therefore Test
A test to see if a statement is a conclusion by putting the word "therefore" before it

Let's apply the therefore test to an actual example. Consider the following passage:

> The most dangerous part of a cigarette is the tar: the particulate matter which enters the lungs and coats the alveoli. That is why cigarette makers include filters on their cigarettes. Smoking marijuana is far more dangerous than smoking cigarettes, at least when not using a filter. Marijuana produces just as much tar as tobacco.

The first two sentences include an explanation for why cigarette makers use filters: because the tar is dangerous. We will soon examine explanations more, but they are not arguments, so we will focus on the last two sentences.

Consider the following two examples:

Example 2.3	Example 2.4
Smoking marijuana without a filter is far more dangerous than smoking cigarettes with a filter. Therefore, marijuana produces just as much tar as tobacco.	Marijuana produces just as much tar as tobacco. Therefore, smoking marijuana without a filter is far more dangerous than smoking cigarettes with a filter.

Do not continue reading until you really understand this point. In Example 2.3, the "therefore" is at best bizarre, bordering on nonsensical. In Example 2.4, the "therefore" makes perfect sense. This test gives us a good reason to believe that the conclusion in this passage is that smoking marijuana without a filter is far more dangerous than smoking cigarettes with a filter. For this argument, it is important to note that it presumes that the major harm from smoking comes from inhaling the tar

Identifying conclusions can be very easy, as in those cases when a passage includes a basic conclusion indicator, and it can be incredibly difficult, especially in a passage where the writing is unclear and where the conclusion is more implied than stated. Usually it will be somewhere in between. As with all skills, though, the more you practice, the better you will become at it.

What are Premises and how does one identify them?

Skill 2.2

Identifying Premises

Premises are statements, just like conclusions. As with conclusions, there is nothing inherent in the premise which makes it a premise. A statement is a premise whenever it is used in a context to support another statement. If the exact same statement is not being used to support another statement, then it is not a premise. As statements, premises can be true or false. We will consider the truth or falsity of premises in greater detail in the coming chapters.

Identifying premises can be much more difficult than identifying conclusions. The reason that this is so is that often many of the statements used in an argumentative passage are not premises. Some of these statements provide background, flesh out an idea, or are logically irrelevant in other ways. Even more challenging is that some premises are not explicitly stated, but are only implied. It can be very difficult to discern implied premises, but it is essential if we are to truly understand an argument.

Premise Indicator
A word or phrase which generally precedes a premise

As with conclusions, there are some words and phrases which can indicate that a premise is coming. The words "because" and "since" are very common **premise indicator** words. The box to the right shows a few other examples.

Common Premise Indicators

because ________
since _______
as _______
for _______
as shown by ______
which is shown by ______
as proven by ______
as demonstrated by ___
as established by ______

Because of the difficulties mentioned above, one should not take these premise indicators to be mechanistic rules. It is still essential to use one's judgment at all times in deciding whether a given statement supports a conclusion. Also, some words are premise indicators in some contexts, but not others. The word "since" can be used in a temporal sense as well as a logical sense. The sentence "You must have been at school, since you brought your bookbag home with you" captures an argument, while the sentence "I must have been going to school since I was five" does not capture an argument, but merely indicates a length of time. When the word "since" is used in this temporal sense it is not a premise indicator. The word "because" can be a premise indicator, but it can also be used in an explanation. We will consider explanations a little more when we discuss identifying arguments.

Because it can be so difficult to identify premises, we will start out slowly. In this book, we will begin dealing with arguments which are simple and out of context. In these cases, finding premises can be a relatively easy process. Keep in mind, however, that our goal will be to reach a skill level where the reader is capable of identifying premises and conclusions in complex arguments which might be found in ordinary written or spoken passages.

What are inferences and how do we identify them?

Not every set of statements is an argument, as we have already seen. So what is it about certain sets of statements which makes them more, which makes them arguments? The answer is an **inference**.

Inference
The implicit or explicit claim that a statement follows from another statement or statements

An inference is an idea; it is the idea that one statement follows from other statements. It is an arrow or a direction, which goes from the premise or premises to the conclusion. Arguments are ordered sets, where the premises all come logically before the conclusion (though not always in actuality). Whether inferences have some sort of metaphysical existence, or only exist in our minds, is an issue beyond the scope of this text. Whatever the metaphysical status of inferences, arguments do not exist without them. An argument must have an inference, and every inference makes for an argument.

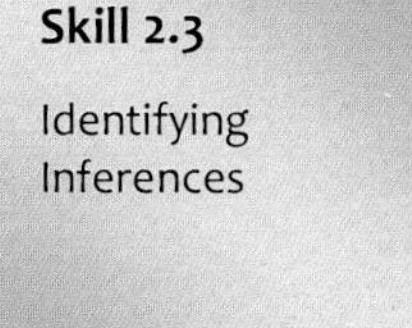

So, an argument is a set of statements with an inference. The inference is the thing which makes the argument more than just a set of statements, and indicates that one or more of the statements supports or is a reason to believe one of the others. This inferential relationship is sometimes explicit, as when an arguer uses indicator words. When an arguer does not use indicator words, the inference is implicit. As long as there is an expectation that a statement is made true, or more likely to be true by another statement or statements, then there is an inference, which means that there is an argument. One can think of an argument as an inference along with the specific statements which make up the premises and conclusion.

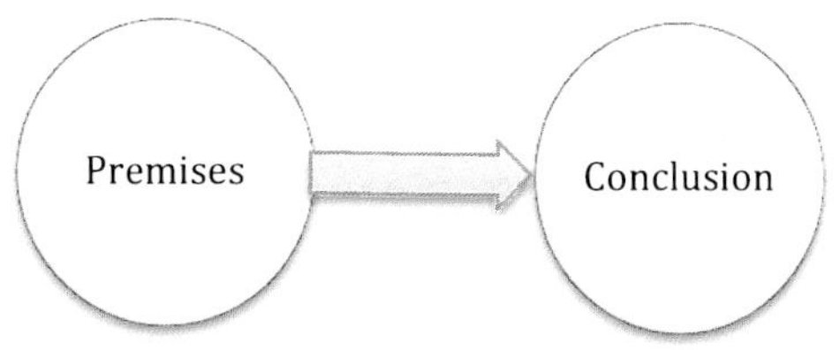

Figure 2.1: The Arrow represents the Inference

Although inferences and arguments may technically be two different things, the relationship between them is so close that in most instances the terms are used somewhat interchangeably. So, identifying inferences is basically the same as identifying arguments.

Here are a few ways to identify an inference or an argument.

1. Look for indicator words
2. Apply the definition
3. Use the "therefore test"
4. Look for common argumentative patterns
5. Look for common non-argumentative patterns
6. Ask!

1. Look for Indicator Words

The simplest way to identify an argument is to look for indicator words. If you see the word "therefore" in a passage, it is a very safe bet that you have an argument. Indicator words are not perfect, however. You must always use good judgment in applying this rule.

2. Apply the definition

The best way to identify an argument is to apply the definition of the word "argument". Anything which meets the definition is an argument, and anything which does not isn't. Unfortunately, this is also in some cases the most difficult test, especially for beginners. An argument is a set of statements where one or more of the statements offers a reason to believe one of the others. So, anytime this situation occurs, there is an argument.

3. Use the "therefore test"

We learned about the "therefore test" earlier. It was used in order to identify the conclusion of an argument. The "therefore test" can also be used to determine whether one is dealing with an argument in the first place. If you can put the word therefore between the statements of the suspected argument, and it makes sense, you have a good reason to think the passage is an argument.

4. Look for common argumentative patterns

In the next chapter we will learn about some common argumentative patterns to help you distinguish deductive from inductive arguments, and you will become more familiar with many basic argument patterns as we go along. Until then, this technique will not be very useful. Once you have learned them, however, this is one of the best techniques there is. Here is a quick list of some of them: argumentative analogies, inductive generalizations, hypothetical syllogisms, *modus ponens* arguments, *modus tollens* arguments, constructive dilemmas, and causal inferences.

5. Look for common non-argumentative patterns

Skill 2.4

Distinguishing Conditionals, Reports, and Explanations from Arguments

Just as there are common argumentative patterns, there are some forms of speech which are often misinterpreted as arguments. Knowing about them may help you recognize them and avoid classifying them as arguments. The following items are not arguments: conditional statements, reports, and explanations.

Conditional Statements

A conditional statement is a claim that something is true under a certain condition. Conditional statements are often expressed in a simple if/then form: If A is true, then B is true. Here is an example of a conditional statement: If you earn 90 points or more on the exam, then you will receive an 'A'.

Notice that this statement does not state that you will earn more than 90 points, nor that you will receive an 'A'. It only states that you will receive an 'A' on the condition that you earn 90 points or more on the exam. This statement is not an argument. It is a single assertion, and not two assertions. It is not the same thing as saying that you will earn 90 points or more, and that therefore you will receive an 'A'. A single conditional statement is not an argument, but it can be a part of an argument. An argument could have a conditional statement as a premise, or as a conclusion, but a single conditional statement by itself is a single compoundstatement.

In some rare cases, a person might express through implication more than they say. A person could utter only a single conditional statement, but imply both an added premise and conclusion. In these cases, we can understand the person as uttering an argument, but the argument must include all of the implied statements; it can't be understood as the conditional statement by itself.

Reports

A report is just like it sounds. A report is length of speech or writing where a person relates information directly, without indicating that there is any inferential relationship between the statements. News reports are not supposed to include any inferential content. The inferential component is traditionally understood to take place before the writing or reporting occurs. The reporter determines what is the case using some logic and critical thinking, and then reports what he takes to be the truth. A chronological report lists events in order of their occurrence.

This distinction will be important for when you are asked to find an argument on your own. The front page of the newspaper would probably be a bad place to look for an argument. The front page is supposed to report information, and in some cases the source of that information, and it shouldn't include any arguments. Of course, a journalist might smuggle an argument in a news report by quoting it from someone else. You should be wary in such cases of examining the argument and not just accepting the conclusion uncritically.

The place to look for arguments is in the section which includes editorials, columns, and letters to the editor, which may be called "Opinion" or "Commentary". This section includes argumentative passages, where someone is trying to make a case to establish a point.

Explanations

Explanations are easy to mistake for arguments. Sadly, although conceptually there is a big difference between the two, in the real world the division is not always so clear. An argument is an attempt to establish **that** something is true or probably true, whereas an explanation is an attempt to explain **why** something is true. In an explanation, a fact is given as being true or accepted, and the explanation provides a reason why the accepted fact is true, but doesn't aim to establish that the fact is true; its truth is taken for granted.

Consider the following examples:

Example 2.5	Example 2.6
Look at the fleas on that dog. It must have fleas because it played with the mangy mutt from next door.	Look at that dog scratching. It must have fleas because it is scratching way more than it would if it just had an itch.

Both examples include the phrase "it must have fleas because", but the function of the passages is much different. In Example 2.5, the presence of the fleas is an accepted fact. The only question is what caused the dog to have the fleas. The example offers a possible explanation: the mutt next door.

In Example 2.6, it is not a given fact that the dog has fleas. An inference is made that the dog has fleas based on the fact that the dog is scratching excessively. Example 2.6 is an argument; it tries to use a true piece of information (that the dog is scratching) to establish that another statement is true (that the dog has fleas).

So the first passage is an explanation and the second one is an argument. When considering whether a given passage is an argument or an explanation, it usually helps to keep a few things in mind:

1. A passage dealing with a past event is usually an explanation.
2. A passage dealing with a claim that is generally accepted is usually an explanation.
3. A passage dealing with a controversial topic is usually an argument.
4. A passage dealing with a future event or possibility is usually an argument.

These guidelines depend upon the fact that we don't usually argue to establish claims which are already widely accepted (such as past events), nor do we try to explain things about which we are not yet sure (such as the future and controversial claims). Of course, we can still argue about the past. When past events are called into question, such as the moon landing or JFK's assassination, people will usually engage in arguments (but then they fall under the controversial criterion).

6. Ask!

If possible, one of the best ways to see whether you should treat a given passage as an argument is to ask the author. If the author intends for one statement to be interpreted as a reason to believe another statement, then we should treat the passage as an argument. If not, then we probably shouldn't interpret it as an argument, either.

There may be exceptions, however. It might be appropriate to treat a passage as an argument even when the author doesn't intend it to be, or vice versa. These would be exceptional cases, such as when the author has no logical background.

Chapter Two Exercises

For each of the following passages, decide whether there is an argument present. If there is, then write down the conclusion. If not, then say what kind of non-argumentative passage it is.

Basic Concept Exercises

1. Ever since the beginning of the universe the same amount of matter/energy has existed.
2. The fact that the suspect's fingerprints were on the murder weapon proves that he committed the crime.

3. The Constitution forbids the establishment of religion, and to include the words "under God" in the Pledge of Allegiance is an establishment of religion, which shows that the Pledge of Allegiance is unconstitutional.
4. Marijuana should be legalized. Nothing should be illegal if there is no criminal intent present, and in smoking marijuana there is no criminal intent.
5. If computers could be made to think like human beings, then they would have rights, and we would have to allow them to vote and give them freedom of speech.
6. Since the Constitution forbids cruel and unusual punishment, the death penalty is unconstitutional.
7. If you do the right thing, it will make you happy, which shows that if you do something and it makes you unhappy, then it is not moral.
8. The Windows Registry file must have certain file associations for windows to run executable files, and your computer is not running executable files, so your registry is probably corrupted.
9. The *Star Wars* movies are the best movies ever. They have an incredible story of freedom and fighting against tyranny, and they inspired generations of movies after them.
10. The explanation for why your car won't start is probably that you don't have any gas.

Intermediate Exercises

11. No one needs logic. It's just another one of those classes that wastes time and has no effect on the real world.
12. I'll bet I can text faster than you can. I don't even have to look at the keyboard.
13. The reason that your car won't start is probably that you don't have any gas.
14. You should invest in a company that pays dividends, like company XYZ.
15. One should never pour any ammonia-based cleaner into a toilet when there is bleach present. Chlorine and ammonia react and can make a toxic cloud.
16. Don't ever pour any ammonia-based cleaner into a toilet when there is bleach present. Chlorine and ammonia react and can make a toxic cloud.
17. Smoking any substance without a filter is far more dangerous than smoking the substance with a filter, so smoking marijuana without a filter (as most people do) is far more dangerous than smoking tobacco with a filter (as most people do).
18. No society can long survive if the people in it are not willing to support it. That's why it is necessary for the government to mandate an income tax.
19. The first paragraph in your essay isn't clear. You should rewrite it.
20. You have Lyme disease because you haven't gotten enough citrus in your diet.

Challenging exercises

21. I don't understand why Republicans are caving on the debt ceiling issue. They support a balanced budget amendment. All that would happen if the debt ceiling weren't raised is that the government would be forced to act as if there were a balanced budget.
22. You haven't put any gas in your car for weeks. I bet it probably won't even start.
23. Your car won't start. I'll bet you don't have any gas in it.
24. The reason you have Lyme disease is that you are going off into the woods and not checking your body for ticks afterwards.

25. The reason you have Lyme disease is that you had a rash, a fever, and fatigue, and now you have swollen joints, Bell's palsy and failing coordination.
26. Your tires are worn excessively in the middle of the tread. It looks like your tires have been overinflated.
27. Telling children that they better believe that the Earth is round because we say it is and we know better and people who disagree with us are ridiculous, is no better than telling them that we ought to burn witches.
28. If mankind were the cause of global warming, then how can you explain the fact that Mars and the other planets are also going through a warming phase.
29. I know you have been saying that kids nowadays are getting out of control, but even Plato complained about children talking back to their parents.
30. If you believe that Nietzsche was a genius and had the right philosophy, and he held that Christianity was a slave religion, then how can you possibly be a Christian?

In-context exercises

A. Construct three simple arguments of your own, and two non-arguments with similar themes. Do not identify their status on the same paper. When you get to class, see if your classmates can identify the arguments correctly.

Logic Puzzle: The Logical Detective

You have three suspects, and you have reason to believe only one of them is guilty, but only one of them is telling the whole truth. Based on the following statements, who is guilty and who is telling the truth?

Albert says: Brian is lying and Charlie is guilty.
Brian says: Albert is guilty and Charlie is lying.
Charlie says: Albert is guilty and Albert is lying.

CHAPTER

3

Diagramming Arguments

Once we have recognized that we are dealing with an argument, the next skill we must hone is the ability to identify the basic structure of the argument. One way to make the structure of an argument immediately apparent is to diagram it. Although we can capture and present the same information in other ways, as we will see in the next chapter, some people absorb information better when it is in a visual form.

Skill 3.1

Diagramming Arguments

Let's start with the very basic idea: Use circled numbers to represent statements, and draw an arrow to represent the flow of the argument. The arrow should begin at the premises, and end at the conclusion. Let's take a simple argument with one premise and one conclusion.

①It is not the case that every mammal gives birth to live young, Therefore, ②there is at least one mammal which does not give birth to live young.

In order for everyone to use numbers in the same fashion, the statements in the above argument have already been assigned numbers. In this case, it should be clear that the second statement is the conclusion, so the proper diagram for this argument is shown below:

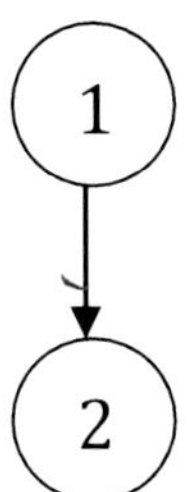

The main conclusion should always be placed at the bottom of the diagram, with an arrow pointing *toward* the conclusion. Students often just draw a line without the arrow head between the circles, but the point is to show the flow of the argument, so that we can see visually what statement is the conclusion and what premises are being used to support it.

Not all arguments will be this straightforward. One complication is that many arguments have **subconclusions**. A subconclusion functions as the conclusion for one argument, but as a premise for another one. A subconclusion functions as both a premise and a conclusion. So, it should have an arrow pointing to it from the subpremise, and an arrow from it pointing to the main conclusion. Once one recognizes that an argument includes a subconclusion, it is a breeze to diagram.

Subconclusion
A statement which functions as a conclusion as well as a premise

Let's see an example:

Skill 3.2

Identifying Subconclusions

①You should end your relationship with your boyfriend. ②He doesn't respect you, since ③He never listens to what you have to say.

Remember that we are not yet considering whether this is a good argument; our focus is only on capturing its structure. The first statement is the main conclusion. The arguer is advising someone to end her relationship, because she has decided that the boyfriend doesn't respect her. This second statement is a premise to the main conclusion, yet it is supported by the third statement, that the boyfriend never listens to her. Ultimately, the argument should be diagrammed as we do here.

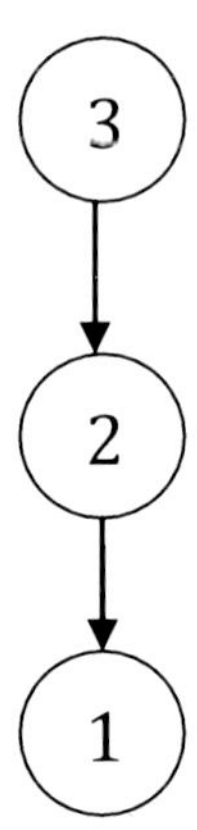

As always, the main conclusion is placed at the bottom of the diagram. There is no limit to how many subconclusions one can have, but it would be impractical to go beyond three or four. If one thought there were more, one would probably pick out the most important ones, and only diagram them. Of course, there isn't much interesting going on if we have only one premise supporting one subconclusion, supporting the conclusion. Things get much more interesting, and useful, when we figure out how to diagram multiple premises. The trick is that one must first decide whether the premises are dependent or independent before one can diagram them.

Skill 3.3

Distinguishing Dependent from Independent Premises

Premises that are **dependent** rely on each other for support. Premises which are independent offer support for their conclusions independently of the other premises which may be present. It is not necessarily the case that there is no relationship whatsoever between **independent premises**. There may be some causal, incidental, or other relationship, but the idea is that there is still support for the conclusion even if the other premise is ignored. Consider the examples here:

Dependent Premise
A premise which requires another premise in order to support the conclusion

Example 3.1	Example 3.2
① You should stop eating eggs. ② Eggs contain cholesterol, and ③ cholesterol is bad for you.	① You should stop eating meat. ② Meat contains toxins, and ③ it is wrong to kill animals just to eat them.

In Example 3.1, the premises each require each other in order to gain support for the conclusion. One premise without the other would simply be unable to support the conclusion adequately. It simply does not follow from the fact that eggs contain cholesterol that one shouldn't eat them, unless it is also true that cholesterol is bad for you. Furthermore, the fact that cholesterol is bad for you wouldn't indicate that you shouldn't eat eggs unless eggs did in fact contain cholesterol. To be clear, if one did think that one of these premises supported the conclusion, it would be precisely because one was assuming the other premise to be true.

Independent Premise
A premise which supports the conclusion by itself

In Example 3.2 something else is going on. Here the conclusion is that one should not eat meat, based upon two premises: one, that it contains toxins, and two, that it is wrong to kill animals just to eat them. In this case, the two premises do not depend on each other for support. Each premise can stand on its own.

We still need to know how to diagram both dependent and independent premises. For dependent premises, add them together using a brace for the arrow, and for independent premises, use an arrow from each one, as in the following table.

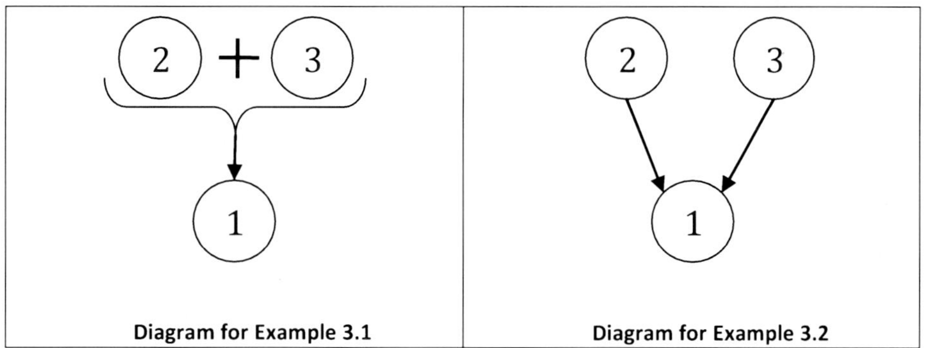

Diagram for Example 3.1	Diagram for Example 3.2

Notice that in the Diagram for Example 3.1, there is actually only one arrow. The arrow represents the inference, and there really is only one inference here. In the diagram for Example 3.2 there are two inferences, each represented by its own arrow. Often, one can think of each independent premise, and its subpremises, if there are any, as separate **lines of argument**. There are as many lines of argument as there are independent groups of premises.

Line of Argument
A set of premises and possibly subpremises which work together separately from other premises

Just to see a detailed example, we will consider Example 3.2. If one were interested in a deeper analysis, one could recognize that each premise actually depends on unstated or assumed premises. The first explicit premise relies on the unstated premise that we should not eat toxins, and the second premise relies on the unstated premise that we shouldn't do anything that is wrong, as well as the premise that one cannot eat meat from animals killed for other purposes.

There are various techniques for including assumed premises. Some authors will use numbers, some use letters. One might use a dotted circle. Here, we will simply assign each new statement a number, and include them in the diagram as any other statement.

① You should stop eating meat. ② Meat contains toxins, and ③ it is wrong to kill animals just to eat them.

Assumed premises:

4 – One should not eat things containing toxins.

5- One shouldn't do anything that is wrong.

6- One cannot eat meat from animals killed for other purposes.

Skill 3.4

Identifying Implicit Premises

Recognizing assumed premises can be a difficult task. Here, it helps to realize that one might kill animals for other reasons, such as thinning of a herd, or because the animal is humanely put to sleep. As stated, the conclusion is very broad and doesn't admit of any exceptions, but the premise only applies to killing animals solely for the purpose of eating them. One might want to revise the argument and say that it is wrong to kill animals for any purpose, but that would be a revision of the argument. Here we will analyze the argument as it is. This fact will also help demonstrate that three premises can all be dependent on each other.

With all our premises laid out, the entire diagram is captured here:

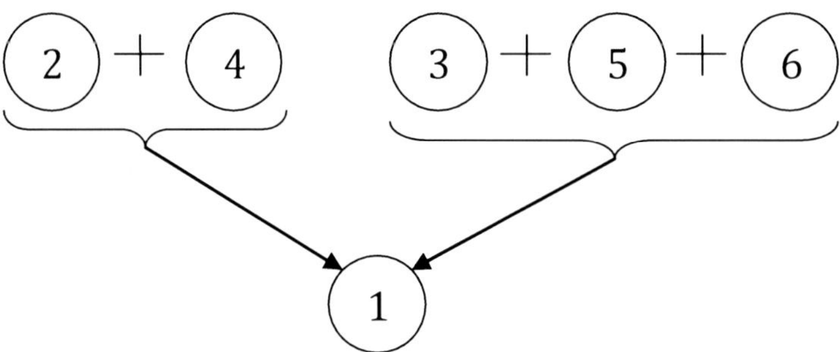

As one can see in the diagram, there are two lines of argument represented. Premises two and four constitute one line of argument, which we could call the "toxin argument" and premises three, five and six represent a separate line of argument, say the "moral argument". The reason it is important to understand when premises are dependent or independent is that it can dramatically affect the criticism one has of the argument. Each independent line of argument stands or falls on its own. All we need to do to undermine the "toxin argument" is to show that one of its premises is false, or cast doubt upon it, but that will leave the other line of argument completely unaffected. In order to fully undermine the argument, it is necessary to criticize all lines of argument. In doing so, one must show either that there is a problem with each inference (that the conclusion does not follow from the given premises), or a problem with one premise from each independent line of argument, or both.

We will learn about evaluating arguments soon enough. For now, keep in mind that each inference can be evaluated separately, and so it is important to know whether given premises are dependent or independent so that we know exactly how many inferences there are. Determining whether premises are dependent or independent can be quite difficult, but here is some advice. Some phrases, when used to connect premises, are strong indicators that the premises are independent, such as "besides" and "in addition". Otherwise, one must consider whether a given premise by itself supports the conclusion. One can try the "therefore test." If the conclusion follows from the premise alone, then the premise is likely independent. If it requires one of the other premises or an unstated assumption in order to have support, then those premises are dependent on each other. When one works with complex arguments, one should be prepared to add premises, then change them, and then maybe add more once one reflects a bit more. Consider your task an ongoing one in a process of revision until you are confident that you have it right.

We have only looked at arguments of limited complexity, but you should realize that with everything you have learned so far, you can handle arguments of unlimited complexity. For example, in the argument diagram below, find the main conclusion, any subconclusions, and subpremises, and decide whether they are dependent or independent.

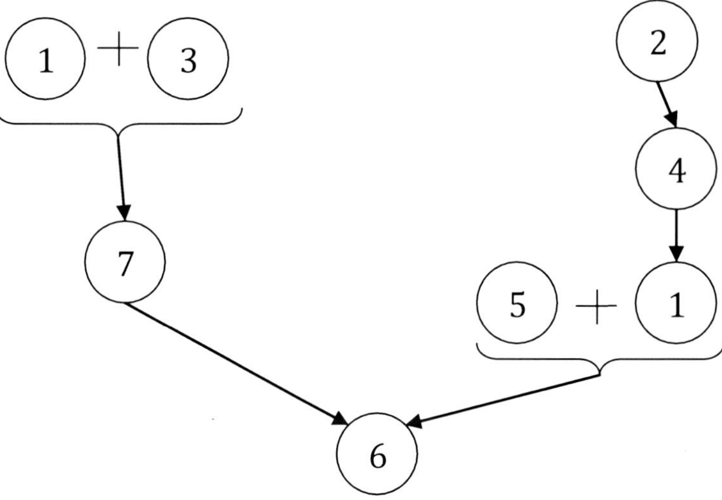

Chapter Three Exercises

For each of the following arguments in all three levels of difficulty, diagram the argument. If necessary, make a list identifying the statements used in your diagram.

Basic Concept Exercises

1. ①Every marsupial is a mammal, and ②every kangaroo is a marsupial, so ③every kangaroo is a mammal.
2. ①The Constitution forbids the establishment of religion, and ②to include the words "under God" in the Pledge of Allegiance is an establishment of religion, which shows that ③the Pledge of Allegiance is unconstitutional.
3. ①Marijuana should be legalized. ②Nothing should be illegal if there is no criminal intent present, and ③in smoking marijuana there is no criminal intent.
4. ①We should eliminate NASA from the federal budget. ②We don't have the money, and ③private enterprise always does a better job than a government bureaucracy.
5. ①All repeating decimals can be written as fractions, and ②all repeating decimals are rational numbers, which goes to show that ③all rational numbers can be written as fractions.
6. ①A Liberal is someone who holds that individuals should make more of their own decisions than the state, but ②people who support universal healthcare want the state to make more decisions than the individual. So, ③supporters of universal healthcare cannot be liberal.

7. ①The *Star Wars* movies are the best movies ever. ②They have an incredible story of freedom and fighting against tyranny, and ③they inspired generations of movies after them.
8. There are two reasons to believe that ①the Big Bang is not the beginning of everything that exists. First, ②if there were nothing that existed, then from where would the energy needed to create the universe come? Second, ③quantum physicists believe that the space in which we exist is only one of numerous "universes", which all together compose what might be called the multiverse.
9. ①I don't think you should go out and party tonight. ②You have a big test tomorrow, and you need your sleep. Plus, ③you know you'll end up spending money that you don't have.
10. ①Without lawyers, big businesses and unions would be able to do whatever they want, and ②what they want to do is consolidate power and control everyone. ③It is a good thing we have lawyers.

Intermediate Exercises

11. ①Lawyers are ruining the country. ②They make everything cost more because of their lawsuits, and ③if you want justice, it will cost you an arm and a leg.
12. Since ①the Constitution forbids cruel and unusual punishment, ②the death penalty is unconstitutional.
13. ①No society can long survive if the people in it are not willing to support it. That's why ②it is necessary for the government to mandate an income tax.
14. ①Figurative language causes all sorts of confusion and miscommunication. ②The point of logic is to cleave through all the confusions of language, not to indulge in them. ③Anyone who studies logic should leave figurative language at the front door.
15. It seems to me that ①people who are presently in jail were much less likely to attend church regularly before they went to prison than the non-prison population. ②If the government is interested in getting people to not break the law, ③which it should be, then ④it should do everything it can to encourage people to attend church regularly.
16. ①The distance between galaxies has been accelerating, ②which, according to Newton's Laws of Mechanics is impossible unless there is some repellent force acting upon galaxies. ③The only repellent forces that are currently accepted in physics are the electromagnetic force and maybe the weak nuclear force, but ④neither of these can explain the acceleration. So, ⑤either there is some previously unknown mysterious force in the universe, or else Newton was wrong.
17. ①There are many reasons why Pluto is not a planet. ②Its orbit is wildly eccentric, at some times crossing the orbit of Neptune. ③It also smaller than the moon. If you need any more evidence, ④it doesn't orbit in the same plane as the other planets, but is angled significantly, more like a comet.
18. ①Republicans always try to deny the ability of minorities and poor people to vote. ②They reject same-day registration for voting, and ③they even want to require voters to show their ID's. ④It's just a fact that minorities and poor people have a more difficult time getting ID's than other people.

19. ①Democrats are not so much interested in voter rights as in gaining political advantage. ②They want to allow people to register the same day that they vote, but that's only because it is much easier to manipulate ill-informed voters. ③They also don't want to require people to show ID's, ④ and minority and poor voters are less likely to have ID's. Everyone knows that ⑤minorities and poor people tend to vote for Democrats.
20. ①Independents are mostly cowards. ②They don't have the courage to take a position and defend it against criticism. ③Independents are far more likely than partisans to say whatever it takes to avoid being attacked. ④It really is pitiful.

Challenging exercises

21. ①Physics is a branch of philosophy. ② Philosophy is the study of truth and the use of reason to resolve rational dilemmas, ③which is what physics does in relation to physical phenomena. Moreover, ④Isaac Newton and all the early physicists said they were working in natural philosophy. Finally, ⑤the highest degree in physics is a Ph.D., which stands for Doctorate of Philosophy in Physics.
22. ①Physics is part of science and not philosophy. ②Philosophy deals with subjects that are uncertain, and where there are no right answers. ③All that philosophy can provide is opinion. ④Science involves facts, and things that are straightforwardly right or wrong. Since ⑤physics deals with facts and straightforward truths, ⑥it is a part of science.
23. I'll prove to you that ①God exists. ②The laws of thermodynamics hold that the entropy of a closed system always increases. That means that ③the order in a closed system always decreases, or that the natural state of the universe is decay. Yet, if the evolutionists are right, then ④life is evolving from less ordered creatures to more ordered ones, which ⑤violates the laws of thermodynamics. ⑥The only entity which could violate laws of nature is God, so therefore ①God must exist, and ⑦He must be the driving force behind evolution.
24. ①There is no reason to believe that God exists. ②God never intervenes in the lives of people, ③seeing that devoutly religious people go through the same vicissitudes as everyone else. ④Countless people have prayed for miracles to no avail. ⑤The idea of God is not even required for explaining the universe or the things in it. ⑥Naturalistic evolution is a much better explanation for life, and ⑦the Big Bang is as complete an explanation of the universe as we will probably ever get.
25. ①Without a political philosophy, there is no point to voting. ②When one does not know in what direction they think government should go, or what justifies government in the first place, then there is no way to know for whom to vote. ③Everyone should develop their own political philosophy before they cast their first ballot.
26. ①I don't understand how leftists can support state-sponsored lotteries. Sure, ②they redistribute money around, but ③they are the most regressive sort of "tax" imaginable. ④Poor people are the most desperate to play them, and turn over large portions of their income to the state. ⑤The state then spreads it around—not to everyone, but a few mega-rich people, at least they are after they win. ⑥It's the most disgusting way to take advantage of poor people imaginable.
27. ①The government doesn't have the right to stop people from doing what they want to do, and ②people want to gamble their money. ③If our state doesn't

allow some kind of gambling, then people will spend that money in other states, ④improving those state's economies and hurting our own. Besides, ⑤we can use the money raised to support our schools.

28. ①Have you heard that some people think that the acceleration of the movement of galaxies away from each other proves that there is either a dark or mysterious force in the universe? ②The notion is just silly. ③All that we need to explain the fact that all visible galaxies are accelerating toward the outskirts of the universe is that there is something with a massive gravitational or other force out there toward the edges of our universe, perhaps other universes. ④No dark energy or weird sounding explanation is required.
29. ①In order for us to have free will, then it must be the case that the future is unknowable. This is because ②if anyone can know the future, then our choices would not be free, but instead would be caused. ③If God has omniscience, then he knows everything, and ④nothing, including the future is unknowable. Therefore, ⑤if we have free will, then God is not omniscient.
30. ①It is sex-based discrimination to treat a member of one sex differently because of their sex, and ②sex-based discrimination is always wrong. ③For the state to say that a man can marry a woman, but cannot marry a man is to treat members of one sex differently than another sex. But that all just goes to prove that ④heterosexuality itself is immoral. Think about it. ⑤The whole point of heterosexuality is to treat one sex differently than another, and it has to stop now.

In-context exercises

A. ①There are four different categorical syllogistic standard forms, but ②the terms can be switched around, and term complements used, with 8 possible arrangements. So, ③there are really 32 different categorical assertions which can be made. Yet, ④we must consider the possibility that someone can assert that a statement is false, ⑤which gives us 64 possible statements which can be made using two terms and their term complements. ⑥If we use one premise and one conclusion, then for each of the 64 possible premises, there are 64 possible conclusions. ⑦All in all, there are 64 × 64 possible immediate inferences, or 4096.

B. ① I'm pretty sure I'm gonna get a 4.0 GPA this semester, since ② I plan on getting an A in Monge's class. ③ He said that he curves his exams, and ④ I always get A's in classes with curves. ⑤ I also received an A on my first exam. ⑥ Since Mr. Monge said that the other exams are easier than the first test, ⑦ I know I can get A's on those as well. So, ⑧ I think I can get A's on all of my exams. ⑨ If I do get A's on all exams, then I should get an A for the course. ⑩ Plus, I'm positive I'm getting an A in all my other classes.

Logic Puzzle: The Embezzler

You find out that someone is embezzling from your company. There are five suspects to the crime:

Mike, who is 35

Susan, who is 30
Julio, who is 19
Janice, who is 26
Samuel, who is 23

Use the following clues, each of which is true, to determine who is guilty.

1. The guilty party(ies) is/are either male or older than 28.
2. No more than three people were working together.
3. Each guilty party is either female, or has a name which does not begin with an 'S'.
4. If Mike and Julio are both guilty, then so is Samuel.
5. If Samuel is not guilty, then exactly two people are guilty.
6. If Susan is guilty, then Mike is not.

CHAPTER

4

Standard Form Arguments

Although argument diagrams are an effective and immediately obvious way to capture the structure of an argument, they do not display the content of the argument as readily as one might like. That is because the content of the argument, the actual premises and conclusions, are not placed on the diagram, but only their numbers. Another way to display the content of the argument is to rewrite it in standard form.

Skill 4.1

Rewriting Arguments in Standard Form

When arguments are written in prose form, they can often be unwieldy. Sometimes it is unclear exactly what the conclusion is, and which premises are being used to support it. Often there will be extraneous material which is not being used to support the conclusion but to flesh out a premise or an idea, or material will be repeated. Moreover, the conclusion may be implied. When analyzing an argument with an unstated conclusion, it is especially important to be clear about what we understand as the conclusion.

In a **standard form argument**, the premises are numbered, a line is drawn underneath them, and then the numbered conclusion is written, usually following three dots, representing the word "therefore". This form allows us to quickly see the conclusion, as well as the basic premises that are relevant to that conclusion. It greatly facilitates our analysis and evaluation, and allows us to be clear with others. It also allows them to see whether we are actually capturing the argument as stated, or whether we are twisting the argument into a straw man (We will discuss straw man arguments in the chapter on fallacies).

Let's start out very simply. Take the argument below, and capture it in standard form.

> You should vote for Proposition 34A. It cleans up crime, and it makes it harder for sleazy politicians to make backroom deals.

This is a fairly straightforward argument. There are no indicator words, but it should be clear that the first statement is the conclusion; the other statements offer reasons in support of the claim that one should vote for Proposition 34A. It also seems clear that there are two premises. So, here is the argument in standard form:

1) Proposition 34A reduces crime.
2) Proposition 34A makes it more difficult for politicians to make backroom deals.

---

3) ∴ Citizens should votes for Proposition 34A.

Notice again that all the statements are numbered, the premises are written in complete sentences, and the conclusion is written at the bottom, with three dots before it and a line on top of it. The reader should also notice that we have rephrased some of the statements. We will say more about paraphrasing shortly, but notice here that we have switched to more formal literal language. We use "reduce" instead of "clean up", because that has a more literal sense. In analyzing arguments, logicians do not care how poetic or beautiful the language is. We care about the logic. Metaphorical or figurative language can obscure analysis, which is why we try to avoid it. It might be more difficult to paraphrase the second premise, which is why we left it closer to the original. Perhaps, however, we could have written "Proposition 34A makes government meetings more transparent." If this phrasing is accurate and more clear than the original, we should probably use it. Even in this simple example we can see the importance of making judgments about clarity. We will need it far more when we deal with arguments of more complexity.

There is one addition we can make here which will have the effect of subsuming argument diagrams under our standard form argument. Hopefully, the reader recognized that the premises listed here are independent, and that both of them support the conclusion directly. We could easily draw a diagram to indicate these things, but it would be nice to avoid creating both a standard form argument and an argument diagram. The solution is to take the information we would have in the argument diagram, and put it in the standard form argument. We simply need to write next to each conclusion or subconclusion the premises from which it is derived, as well as whether they are dependent or independent. It may sound complicated, but we will add it to the example above to show how easy it is, at least in straightforward cases.

1) Proposition 34A reduces crime.
2) Proposition 34A makes it more difficult for politicians to make backroom deals.

---

3) ∴ Citizens should votes for Proposition 34A. (From 1 and 2, ind.)

Next, let's see what an argument with a subconclusion will look like in standard form. Let's use the same proposition, but from perhaps an opposing point of view.

> You should vote against Proposition 34A. It violates the First Amendment to the Constitution. The First Amendment guarantees freedom of speech, and Proposition 34A allows the government to punish you for things that you say.

In this argument the conclusion is again the first statement, but this time it follows immediately from the second sentence alone. In turn, the second sentence is supported by the remaining statements. We want to make all of this structure clear, so we write out the argument in standard form.

1) The First Amendment guarantees freedom of speech.
2) Proposition 34A allows the government to punish people for things which they say.

---

3) ∴ Proposition 34A violates the First Amendment to the Constitution. (From 1 & 2, dep.)

---

4) ∴ Citizens should vote against Proposition 34A. (From 3)

As we can see, this argument includes one subconclusion, from which the main conclusion follows. We should notice, however, that the main conclusion only follows from the subconclusion if we assume that one should not vote for propositions which are unconstitutional. It seems a reasonable premise, and the argument relies upon it, so let's include it here. Again, one simply adds the premise to the standard form argument beneath the subconclusion, as we do here:

1) The First Amendment guarantees freedom of speech.
2) Proposition 34A allows the government to punish people for things which they say.

---

3) ∴ Proposition 34A violates the First Amendment to the Constitution. (From 1 & 2, dep.)
4) Citizens should not vote for unconstitutional propositions.

---

5) ∴ Citizens should vote against Proposition 34A. (From 3 & 4, dep.)

It sounds like Proposition 34A is an interesting measure, with lots of debate and disagreement. Unfortunately, we don't have enough information to make even a basic judgment about it. I would hope that when you vote in actual elections, you do a lot more research that we did here.

Skill 4.2

Paraphrasing Statements

Paraphrasing

To **paraphrase** a statement or passage is to rewrite it in other words. Paraphrasing is a very important skill for logic, as well as most other academic areas. A paraphrase does not generally condense the original, at least not much, but tries to convey the same information, only in different words. Summarizing is very similar to paraphrasing, but it generally greatly reduces the size of the original.

Paraphrase
To rewrite something in other words while retaining the same meaning

We will concentrate now on taking a single statement and rewriting it. In general, people paraphrase in order to make things simpler or more clear. In analyzing an argument, one also tries to simplify and clarify, in particular by eliminating figurative or emotive content, when irrelevant to the argument. Logicians also use paraphrasing to help ensure that the structure of the argument is as obvious as possible.

In a given passage, an author may restate one basic idea several times in several ways. If the idea is used throughout the argument, then it would obscure the logic of the argument to rewrite it in each of those different ways. Instead, we should use one formulation, and stick to it throughout the standard form argument. We don't care about redundancy or repetition here; we care that the structure of the argument is as apparent as we can make it.

Let's take a look at a quick example. Consider the argument below.

> We have good reason to think that the Earth revolves around the Sun. The simplest explanation has the greatest claim to truth, as long as it can account fully for the phenomena. The idea that the Earth orbits the Sun involves way less complicated physics than the alternative.

If we didn't do any paraphrasing, we might get something like the following when capturing the argument in standard form:

1) The idea that the Earth orbits the Sun is less complicated than the idea that the Sun orbits the Earth.
2) The simplest explanation has the greatest claim to truth, as long as it fully accounts for the phenomena.

---

3) ∴ The Earth revolves around the Sun. (From 1 & 2, dep.)

It may seem a little obvious, but revolving around and orbiting mean the same thing, in this context at least, so it makes the argument less complicated, and the logic more clear, if we use the same phrase for both instances where it occurs in the argument. Also, the word "simpler" and the words "less complicated" have the same basic meaning, so it is appropriate to paraphrase one of them into the other. Incorporating these ideas means we can rewrite the argument in the following way.

1) The idea that the Earth orbits the Sun is simpler than the idea that the Sun orbits the Earth.
2) <u>The simplest explanation has the greatest claim to truth, as long as it fully accounts for the phenomena.</u>
3) ∴ The Earth orbits the Sun. (From 1 & 2, dep.)

This example is pretty simple, but hopefully it makes the point. Once you gain some skill in paraphrasing, you will be able to tackle examples much more complicated than this one.

There are two things to keep in mind when paraphrasing. The meaning of the original must always be retained. It is improper to distort the meaning of the author when capturing their argument in standard form, or any other time, for that matter. You wouldn't want other people to do it to you, so try not to do it to others.

In addition, one should ensure that the paraphrase actually accomplishes its job. It must be more clear, or simpler, or more literal than the original, or else there was no point to paraphrasing in the first place.

Improving Style

Ensuring that an argument is in standard form is a fairly straightforward matter. As long as the following conditions are met, the argument is in standard form.

1. Each premise, subconclusion, and conclusion is numbered.
2. Each premise, subconclusion, and conclusion is expressed in a complete sentence.
3. The last premise before each subconclusion is underlined.
4. The statement before the main conclusion is underlined.
5. Each subconclusion and conclusion is preceded by three dots.
6. The last line encapsulates the main conclusion of the argument.

Even though these conditions guarantee that the argument is in standard form, they will not guarantee that the argument accurately captures the original argument. That task is generally much more difficult. Even when it comes to style, however, we can do much better.

A stylistically superior standard form argument will incorporate the following guidelines as well.

Skill 4.3

Creating Stylistically Superior Standard Form Arguments

1. All premises and conclusions should fit together in a logical way.
2. No irrelevant premises will be included.
3. Statements will be paraphrased so that the logical connection between them is clear.
4. There won't be any flashy or figurative language; only concise literal words.
5. There will be no indicator words, or evidence/proof type statements. ("That just goes to prove...").
6. Any implicit premises will be included.

If you follow these guidelines, your standard form argument will be much more clear and helpful when it comes to evaluating the argument. Let's take one last argument. This one will be a little more challenging.

> The fact that we share a large part of our DNA with chimpanzees is often taken to be proof of evolution, but no such connection can be made. All that the similar DNA proves is that we had a common origin, but no creationist ever denied that we had a common origin. Creationists do, in fact, believe in a common origin for humans and chimpanzees. That origin is God. If God made both humans and chimpanzees, it would make sense for him to use the same building materials for both.

This is not a simple argument, but it isn't overly complex, either. Let's begin, as we generally should, by identifying the conclusion. This arguer is rejecting the claim that shared DNA is proof of evolution, so that should be our conclusion. We can reword it this way: "The fact that we share a large part of our DNA with chimpanzees does not prove evolution."

The premises are next. Some of the material seems extraneous, like the claim that no creationist denied that we had a common origin. This information we can leave out. The claim that similar DNA proves a common origin is essential, as is the claim that God is considered a possible common origin for both humans and chimpanzees. The last sentence seems to be a way of bolstering the idea of God as a common origin. As such, we might be able to use it as a premise, but it may be appropriate to leave it out as well. We may not be able to make a firm judgment until we work with the argument a little.

First, we will write the conclusion:

1) ...
2) ...
?

?) ∴ The fact that we share a large part of our DNA with chimpanzees does not prove evolution.

This is the basic structure of the argument in standard form, without any premises added. We don't know yet how many premises there will be, which is why I used the question mark for the third possible premise and for the conclusion.

Let's get the first premise in the argument. In the original, it is stated "All that the similar DNA proves is that we had a common origin." We can word it in the following way:

1) Similar DNA proves only that two creatures have a common origin.
2) ...
?

?) ∴ The fact that we share a large part of our DNA with chimpanzees does not prove evolution.

Next we will write in the second premise:

1) Similar DNA proves only that two creatures have a common origin.
2) Creationists believe that God is the common origin for both humans and chimpanzees.
?

?) ∴ The fact that we share a large part of our DNA with chimpanzees does not prove evolution.

This phrasing, however, does not make the logic of the argument as clear as it could be. At this stage, we want to tweak the wording to clarify that structure. Here is one possibility:

1) Similar DNA proves only that two creatures have a common origin.
2) A possible common origin for both humans and chimpanzees is God.
?

?) ∴ The fact that we share a large part of our DNA with chimpanzees does not prove evolution.

We could leave this argument as it is, with only two premises, but it still seems that there is something missing. The two premises listed here together still rely on a principle about when proof is or isn't achieved. We should add this implied premise if we can. Perhaps the final argument written in standard form should look something like the following:

1) Similar DNA proves only that two creatures have a common origin.
2) There are two possible common origins for humans and chimpanzees: evolution and God directly.
3) Evidence only counts as proof of one theory if it rules out every other possibility.

---

4) ∴ The fact that we share a large part of our DNA with chimpanzees does not prove evolution. (From 1, 2 & 3, all dep.)

This version may not be perfect, but it looks like it is fairly clear and straightforward. One standard we should try to live up to is whether the original author would complain, or would accept the version as accurate. We may never know for sure, but that is what we should be striving to achieve. One might wonder why I left out the last statement: "If God made both humans and chimpanzees, it would make sense for him to use the same building materials for both." Partly it was because it is usually only a good idea to defend the claim that something is possible in a situation where someone is claiming that it is impossible. So, we might not even need a reason to assert that God is a possible common origin for humans and chimpanzees. Secondly, I'm not certain that the way it is expressed would be convincing to one who rejected the possibility of God being a possible common origin. It other words, it would only be seen as persuasive by one who already accepted the conclusion, which means that it could be seen as question-begging. I employed the principle of charity, which holds that we should try to state an argument as strongly as we can before we attempt to criticize it.

It is of course acceptable to include the last statement as a premise, but it would require us to revise our standard form argument. The statement in question is a subpremise, it is used to support one of the main premises, so it must come immediately before the main premise it supports. Let's write it first, and then complete the rest of the argument:

1) If God created both humans and chimpanzees, then it is possible that He would use similar materials to create them.

---

2) ∴ It is possible that if there is a common origin for humans and chimpanzees, it is God. (From 1 alone)

3) It is possible that if there were a common origin for humans and chimpanzees, then it is explained through evolution. (The actual common origin would be a pro-simian-like creature, ancestral to both chimpanzees and humans.)
4) Similar DNA proves only that two creatures have a common origin.
5) Evidence only counts as proof of one theory if it rules out every other possibility.

---

6) ∴ The fact that we share a large part of our DNA with chimpanzees does not prove evolution. (From 2, 3, 4 & 5, all dep.)

The fact that so much judgment is involved in capturing an argument (of any significant length or complexity) and writing it in standard form means that not everyone will capture it in the same way. But there are certainly better and worse ways of capturing the argument. It is also important to notice that we have not evaluated the argument at all. We have simply tried to capture its structure. Deciding whether it is a good or bad argument is a skill we will learn in later chapters.

One way to understand standard form arguments, as well as logic in general, is to think of them as a kind of x-ray image. By capturing the argument in standard form, we are looking through the prose argument to view its skeletal structure, though in the case of an argument, the skeletal structure consists in the logical connections present in it. Just like a doctor will look at an x-ray to diagnose an illness or complaint, we need to be able to examine the structure of the argument in order for us to properly diagnose it.

Chapter Four Exercises

For each of the following passages, decide whether there is an argument present. If there is, then rewrite the argument in standard form. If the conclusion is unstated, make sure to include the implied conclusion. Feel free to include any assumed premises. If no argument is present, then say what kind of non-argumentative passage it is.

Basic Concept Exercises

1. The fact that the suspect's fingerprints were on the murder weapon proves that he committed the crime.
2. Every marsupial is a mammal, and every kangaroo is a marsupial, so every kangaroo is a mammal.
3. The Constitution forbids the establishment of religion, and to include the words "under God" in the Pledge of Allegiance is an establishment of religion, which shows that the Pledge of Allegiance is unconstitutional.
4. Marijuana should be legalized. Nothing should be illegal if there is no criminal intent present, and in smoking marijuana there is no criminal intent.
5. All repeating decimals can be written as fractions, and all repeating decimals are rational numbers, which goes to show that all rational numbers can be written as fractions.
6. A Liberal is someone who holds that individuals should make more of their own decisions than the state, but people who support universal healthcare want the

state to make more decisions than the individual. So, supporters of universal healthcare cannot be liberal.

7. If you do the right thing, it will make you happy, which shows that if you do something and it makes you unhappy, then it is not moral.
8. The Windows Registry file must have certain file associations for windows to run executable files, and your computer is not running executable files, so your registry is probably corrupted.
9. The *Star Wars* movies are the best movies ever. They have an incredible story of freedom and fighting against tyranny, and they inspired generations of movies after them.
10. There are two reasons to believe that the Big Bang is not the beginning of everything that exists. First, if there were nothing that existed, then from where would the energy needed to create the universe come? Second, quantum physicists believe that the space in which we exist is only one of numerous "universes", which all together compose what might be called the multiverse.

Intermediate Exercises

11. Since the Constitution forbids cruel and unusual punishment, the death penalty is unconstitutional.
12. No society can long survive if the people in it are not willing to support it. That's why it is necessary for the government to mandate an income tax.
13. Without lawyers, big businesses and unions would be able to do whatever they want, and what they want to do is consolidate power and control everyone. It is a good thing we have lawyers.
14. One should never pour any ammonia-based cleaner into a toilet when there is bleach present. Chlorine and ammonia react and can make a toxic cloud.
15. Figurative language causes all sorts of confusion and miscommunication. The point of logic is to cleave through all the confusions of language, not to indulge in them. Anyone who studies logic should leave figurative language at the front door.
16. Smoking any substance without a filter is far more dangerous than smoking the substance with a filter, so smoking marijuana without a filter (as most people do) is far more dangerous than smoking tobacco with a filter (as most people do).
17. The distance between galaxies has been accelerating, which, according to Newton's Laws of Mechanics is impossible unless there is some repellent force acting upon galaxies. The only repellent forces that are currently accepted in physics are the electromagnetic force and maybe the weak nuclear force, but neither of these can explain the acceleration. So, either there is some previously unknown mysterious force in the universe, or else Newton was wrong.
18. You voted for Barack Obama because you said that President Bush was a moron and had horrible policies like staying in Iraq and being divisive. But Barack Obama has kept the same policies in Iraq, which seems to show that he thinks Bush had the right policy. And President Obama is even more divisive than President Bush.
19. It seems to me that people who are presently in jail were much less likely to attend church regularly before they went to prison than the non-prison

population. If the government is interested in getting people to not break the law, which it should be, then it should do everything it can to encourage people to attend church regularly.

20. In order for us to have free will, then it must be the case that the future is unknowable. This is because if anyone can know the future, then our choices would not be free, but instead would be caused. If God has omniscience, then he knows everything, and nothing, including the future is unknowable. Therefore, if we have free will, then God is not omniscient.

Challenging exercises

21. You voted for Barack Obama because you said that President Bush was a moron and had horrible policies like staying in Iraq and being divisive. But Barack Obama has kept the same policies in Iraq, which seems to show that he thinks Bush had the right policy. And President Obama is even more divisive than President Bush.
22. Republicans always try to deny the ability of minorities and poor people to vote. They reject same-day registration for voting, and they even want to require voters to show their ID's. It's just a fact that minorities and poor people have a more difficult time getting ID's than other people.
23. Democrats always push to make it easier and easier to vote. They want to allow people to register the same day that they vote, which would make it more difficult to verify that they are entitled to vote, and they don't want to require people to show ID's, which makes it much easier to commit voter fraud. That's the real reason they support these reforms.
24. If you don't have a political philosophy, what's the point of voting? If you don't know in what direction you want the government to go, or what justifies government in the first place, how do you know for whom to vote? Everyone should develop their own political philosophy before they cast their first ballot.
25. I don't understand how leftists can support state-sponsored lotteries. Sure, they redistribute money around, but they are the most regressive sort of "tax" imaginable. Poor people are the most desperate to play them, and turn over large portions of their income to the state. The state then spreads it around—not to everyone, but a few mega-rich people, at least they are after they win. It's the most disgusting way to take advantage of poor people imaginable.
26. The government doesn't have the right to stop people from doing what they want to do, and people want to gamble their money. If our state doesn't allow some kind of gambling, then people will spend that money in other states, improving those state's economies and hurting our own. Besides, we can use the money raised to support our schools.
27. I'll prove to you that God exists. The laws of thermodynamics hold that the entropy of a closed system always increases. That means that the order in a closed system always decreases, or that the natural state of the universe is decay. Yet, if the evolutionists are right, then life is evolving from less ordered creatures to more ordered ones, which violates the laws of thermodynamics. The only entity which could violate laws of nature is God, so therefore God must exist, and He must be the driving force behind evolution.
28. There is no reason to believe that God exists. God never intervenes in the lives of people, seeing that devoutly religious people go through the same

vicissitudes as everyone else. Countless people have prayed for miracles to no avail. The idea of God is not even required for explaining the universe or the things in it. Naturalistic evolution is a much better explanation for life, and the Big Bang is as complete an explanation of the universe as we will probably ever get.

29. There are four different categorical syllogistic standard forms, but the terms can be switched around, and term complements used, with 8 possible arrangements. So, there are really 32 different categorical assertions which can be made. Yet, we must consider the possibility that someone can assert that a statement is false, which gives us 64 possible statements which can be made using two terms and their term complements. If we use one premise and one conclusion, then for each of the 64 possible premises, there are 64 possible conclusions. All in all, there are 64 × 64 possible immediate inferences, or 4096.
30. I'm pretty sure I'm gonna get a 4.0 GPA this semester, since I plan on getting an A in Monge's class. He said that he curves his exams, and I always get A's in classes with curves. I also received an A on my first exam. Since Mr. Monge said that the other exams are easier than the first test, I know I can get A's on those as well. So, I think I can get A's on all of my exams. If I do get A's on all exams, then I should get an A for the course. Plus, I'm positive I'm getting an A in all my other classes.

In-context exercises

The following examples are presented in more colloquial language and cadence. For some of them, the conclusion is implied, and there may be several implied premises. Do your best to capture them in standard form.

A. Telling children that they better believe that the Earth is round because we say it is and we know better and people who disagree with us are ridiculous, is no better than telling them that we ought to burn witches.
B. If mankind were the cause of global warming, then how can you explain the fact that Mars and the other planets are also going through a warming phase.
C. I know you have been saying that kids nowadays are getting out of control, but even Plato complained about children talking back to their parents.
D. If you believe that Nietzsche was a genius and had the right philosophy, and he held that Christianity was a slave religion, then how can you possibly be a Christian?
E. Independents are mostly fools. They are so afraid of joining a political party because that party may support something that they don't like. Imagine if they used that principle when it came to families.

For the following exercise, take the excerpt from the original dialog "Euthydemus" and try to capture Dionysodorus's argument in standard form, starting from "Are the things which have sense alive or lifeless?" As a bonus, try to capture Socrates' argument in standard form.

F. **Socrates:** And now, I will ask my stupid question: If there is no such thing as error in deed, word, or thought, then what, in the name of goodness, do you come hither to teach? And were you not just now saying that you could teach virtue best of all men, to anyone who was willing to learn?

Dionysodorus: And are you such an old fool, Socrates, that you bring up now what I said at first-and if I had said anything last year, I suppose that you would bring that up too-but are non-plussed at the words which I have just uttered?
Socrates: Why, they are not easy to answer; for they are the words of wise men: and indeed I know not what to make of this word "nonplussed," which you used last: what do you mean by it, Dionysodorus? You must mean that I cannot refute your argument. Tell me if the words have any other sense.
Dionysodorus: No, they mean what you say. And now answer.
Socrates: What, before you, Dionysodorus?
Dionysodorus: Answer.
Socrates: And is that fair?
Dionysodorus: Yes, quite fair.
Socrates: Upon what principle? I can only suppose that you are a very wise man who comes to us in the character of a great logician, and who knows when to answer and when not to answer-and now you will not open your mouth at all, because you know that you ought not.
Dionysodorus: You prate, instead of answering. But if, my good sir, you admit that I am wise, answer as I tell you.
Socrates: I suppose that I must obey, for you are master. Put the question.
Dionysodorus: Are the things which have sense alive or lifeless?
Socrates: They are alive.
Dionysodorus: And do you know of any word which is alive?
Socrates: I cannot say that I do.
Dionysodorus: Then why did you ask me what sense my words had?
Socrates: Why, because I was stupid and made a mistake. And yet, perhaps, I was right after all in saying that words have a sense;-what do you say, wise man? If I was not in error, even you will not refute me, and all your wisdom will be non-plussed; but if I did fall into error, then again you are wrong in saying that there is no error,-and this remark was made by you not quite a year ago. I am inclined to think, however, Dionysodorus and Euthydemus, that this argument lies where it was and is not very likely to advance: even your skill in the subtleties of logic, which is really amazing, has not found out the way of throwing another and not falling yourself, now any more than of old.[3]

Logic Puzzle: The Highest Scores

The class took two exams, and the highest scores on the exams were earned by either Abigail, Ben, or Christine. Based on the following statements, determine who received the highest scores:

1) Either Abigail had the high score at least once, or Christine did.
2) If Ben had the highest score on one test, then Christine had it on the other.
3) If Christine had the highest score on one exam, Abigail had it on the other.
4) Either Ben had the high score at least once, or Christine did.

---

[3] Plato originally wrote the "Euthydemus" circa 380 B.C. This version is a translation from Benjamin Jowett, written in 1871.

CHAPTER

5

Relevance, Induction and Deduction

So far we have explored the skills involved in identifying and clarifying arguments, but what we really want to know is whether an argument is good. Before we turn to evaluating arguments, however, we need to understand how to classify arguments into those that are deductive and those that are inductive. In order to do that, we need to understand relevance.

Relevance

Skill 5.1

Judging Relevance Between Statements

To say that one thing is relevant to another means that it has a connection, that it makes a difference. An irrelevant concern is one that doesn't matter, one which is not important. Note that one thing cannot be relevant all by itself; it can only be relevant to someone or something else. Your birthday might be relevant to me, but only if it makes a difference to me, perhaps because I would help you celebrate it if I knew.

When it comes to statements, it is also the case that one statement can be relevant to another statement. Relevant doesn't mean similar, or even necessarily having to do with the same issue. We don't say that one statement is relevant to another because it has the same number of words, or because it is written on the same page. Relevance between statements has to do with that most basic property of statements: truth.

Which statement on the right is relevant to the statement on the left?

The Earth orbits the Sun.	The Sun has far more mass than the Earth. The Earth is round.

The statement that the Sun has far more mass than the Earth is relevant to the claim that the Earth orbits the Sun, since a less massive object will always orbit a far more massive one. The truth of the claim that the Sun has more mass than the Earth affects or has to do with the truth of the claim that the Earth orbits the Sun. Whether the Earth is round or not seems to have nothing to do with whether the Earth orbits the Sun. It would seem that the Earth would still orbit the Sun regardless of its shape. Even if the Earth exploded into billions of tiny rocks, those rocks would still orbit around the Sun.

So, one statement is relevant to another when the truth of the one statement is intertwined in some sense with the other statement. If the truth of the one statement makes the other statement more or less likely, then it has some relevance.

A statement can be either positively relevant to another statement or negatively relevant. A statement is positively relevant when its truth makes the other statement more likely to be true, and a statement is negatively relevant when its truth makes the other more likely to be false. The statement that "Albert lives in the United States of America" is positively relevant to the statement that "Albert speaks English". If it were true that Albert lived in the U.S.A., it would be more likely that he would speak English than that he wouldn't speak English. But the statement that "Albert lives in China and speaks only one language" is negatively relevant to the claim that "Albert speaks English." If it were true that Albert lives in China and speaks only one language, that would make it much less likely that he speaks English (let's ignore the issue of his odd name for a Chinese person living in China).

Comprehension Check Exercises

Decide whether the first statement is positively relevant, negatively relevant, or irrelevant to the second statement. The answers are at the bottom of the page.

1. Ishmael is going to celebrate Christmas/Ishmael is Jewish.
2. Samantha is going to celebrate Christmas/Samantha is American.
3. Anthony is going to celebrate Christmas/Anthony is 10 years old.

Degrees of Relevance

Just as we can distinguish positive relevance from negative relevance, we can distinguish degrees of relevance. For any statement, some statements will be more relevant to it than others will be. The fact that a certain person is Christian is more relevant to the fact that he will celebrate Christmas than the fact that he is American. The fact that I left my headlights on is more relevant to the fact that my car won't start than the fact that I left my dome light on. Both have some relevance, but one makes a bigger difference and is thus more relevant.

Maximal Relevance
A statement is maximally relevant to another when its truth completely determines the truth of the other

There is a limit, however, on how relevant a statement can be. If one statement (or group of statements) is so relevant to another statement that its truth guarantees the truth of the second statement, then it leaves no room for other statements to make a difference. In this case, the first statement is maximally relevant to the second. For example, take the statement that Jake is over forty and married. Is that statement relevant to the statement that Jake is a father? I would say it probably is. Most people who are over forty and married have children, though not all. If Jake is forty and married, then it makes it more likely that he is a father than that he is not. But it is not maximally relevant.

Skill 5.2
Distinguishing Degrees of Relevance

The statement that "Jake has children," however, is maximally relevant to the statement that "Jake is a parent." If it is true that Jake has children, then Jake must be a parent. We would know that Jake is a parent, and nothing else would matter. As long as we accept that Jake has children, we have to accept that Jake is a parent. The truth of the first statement makes it 100% likely (or certain) that the second statement is true. It doesn't matter how old Jake is, or what his nationality, or his sexual preference. Nothing else can squeeze in between the two statements, so to speak. The first statement is maximally relevant to the second.

Notice that for partially relevant statements, other statements can "squeeze in" between the two statements. If I know Jake is over forty and married, I will tend to believe that he is a parent, but there are numerous other statements which could still count against his parenthood, which will make a difference. Perhaps he is impotent, or there is a problem with his fertility. Perhaps his wife is infertile. He might have sworn an oath that he would never have children. He might even just tell me that he is not a parent. Partially relevant statements never preclude the possible relevance of some other piece of information. Maximally relevant statements do not necessarily preclude the possibility that other statements have relevance, but if they have positive relevance, they cannot add any additional certainty, and if they are negatively relevant, then they count against both statements equally.

Comprehension Check Answers

1. Negatively Relevant.
2. Positively Relevant
3. Irrelevant

Distinguishing Deductive and Inductive Arguments

Understanding the distinction between partial and maximal relevance will help us to understand the distinction between **deductive** and **inductive** arguments. It is useful to distinguish between arguments which fit a pattern which is capable of maximal relevance and those which are not. It wouldn't be appropriate to hold an argument to a standard of maximal relevance if it fit a pattern which isn't even capable of achieving it.

Those arguments which fit a pattern which is capable of maximal relevance between the premises as a group and the conclusion are called deductive arguments. Those arguments which fit patterns in which the premises as a group are only capable of partial relevance to the conclusion are inductive arguments. It is important to be able to distinguish the two, because we will use different language to evaluate the two different kinds of arguments.

Although, like most logical concepts, partial and maximal relevance can be challenging to recognize in some cases, there are also some cases which are clear, and there are also some guidelines to help the beginning student. There are several kinds of arguments which are categorized as deductive and some which are categorized as inductive. Recognizing them can help you distinguish between deductive and inductive arguments.

Deductive Argument
An argument which fits a general pattern which has the potential to reach maximal relevance between premises and conclusion

Inductive Argument
An argument which fits a general pattern which can only achieve partial relevance between the premises and conclusion

DEDUCTIVE ARGUMENTS

Mathematical Arguments

Arguments based on math are easily seen to be deductive. Mathematical arguments can achieve maximal relevance. Even a mathematical argument which is wrong is classified as deductive. Consider this argument: the variable A is not equal to 4, therefore $A > 4$. In this case, the premise is not maximally relevant to the conclusion, since even when the premise is true, the conclusion is just as likely to be false as true (in this case, it is not relevant at all). Yet, this argument is still classified as deductive because arithmetical arguments in general can achieve such relevance.

Arguments which involve arithmetic, algebra, trigonometry, geometry, calculus, and even the laws of probability will be classified as deductive. Probability can be a tricky area. Arguments where the conclusion follows based on probability will be inductive, but laws of probability are justified through deductive arguments.

Skill 2.3

Distinguishing Deductive from Inductive Arguments

Arguments based on Definition

An argument which is based on a definition is also capable of maximal relevance. Here is an example of an argument based on a definition: Jane is a married, because Jane has a husband. Since the conclusion follows directly from the definition of the words "married" and "husband", this example is an argument based on definition. It also achieves maximal relevance. Given the premise, there is no way possible for the conclusion to be false; no other fact could lead us to reject the conclusion if we accept the premise. If someone gave us inconsistent information, then we could have a reason which would count against the conclusion, but then we would truly be in a rational dilemma. For example, if someone else told me that Jane had never had a marriage ceremony, nor did she have a marriage license, then it might not be that Jane is married (Can one be married without a ceremony or license?), but if not, then we would also have to reject that claim that Jane has a husband. One cannot reject the conclusion without rejecting the premise. In that case, I would know that my information was inconsistent, and both sides couldn't be right.

Categorical arguments

Group membership is a concept which can achieve maximal relevance, as long as we stick to claims involving every member, no members, or at least one member of the group or groups in question. If we start discussing "most members" of a group, we will generally be dealing with inductive reasoning. One of the simplest categorical arguments is this one: All men are mortal, and Socrates is a man, so Socrates is mortal. The two premises together have maximal relevance to the conclusion, which shows that categorical arguments of these kinds should be treated as deductive.

Many arguments which might not look like categorical arguments can still be put into a categorical form. In the Middle Ages, much work was done to formalize these conversions. Fortunately, today we have other techniques to deal with most of these sorts of arguments. Aristotle's systematic approach to logic dealt primarily with categorical arguments, and we will have a great deal more to say about categorical statements and arguments in later chapters.

Hypothetical and Disjunctive arguments

Some of the arguments that those scholars in the Middle Ages would have attempted to capture using categorical logic are arguments which include hypothetical and disjunctive statements. If those terms sound scary, don't worry. A hypothetical statement is just another way to say a conditional statement, and a disjunctive statement is just a statement involving an "either/or". Here is an example of an argument involving a disjunction:

1) I know it is either Monday or Tuesday.
2) It can't be Tuesday, (because I didn't have class today).
3) ∴ It is Monday.

The two premises together are maximally relevant to the conclusion, which shows that these kinds of arguments can achieve such relevance, which makes them deductive.

Inductive Arguments

Predictions

No argument which makes a prediction about the future based on what we presently know can ever achieve maximal relevance. No matter how confident I am that a future event will occur, there is always the possibility that I will be mistaken. Predictions are only capable of partial relevance, and so it is appropriate to classify them as inductive arguments.

This classification does not mean that predictions cannot be good arguments. Many predictions are reasonable arguments. Based upon my understanding of the spin of the Earth, I would say that the Sun will rise tomorrow. I could be wrong; the Earth could stop spinning for some reason, or the Earth or Sun could just explode. But it would still be a very good argument. The fact that it is not deductive just means that we do not hold it to the standard of maximal relevance, and that we realize that other factors might need to be considered.

One note of caution: an argument with a conclusion about the future might fit a deductive pattern *if* there is a premise about the future. In that case, the truth of the premise could guarantee the truth of the conclusion. One should only identify an argument as a prediction and thus inductive when the premises are about the past or present, and the conclusion is about the future.

Analogies

An analogy is not just any comparison, but one which is meant to imply, or is at least suggestive of, a conclusion. In an argument by analogy, there is a claim that two things are similar in ways of which we are aware, and that we can therefore conclude that they will be similar in another way which has not been verified. Here is an example of an analogy: "My dog likes hot dogs. My neighbor's dog is the same breed as mine, and he eats the same dog food, so I would think that my neighbor's dog would like hot dogs, too." In this case, the similarities which are claimed to be known (and so used as premises) are being the same breed and eating the same dog food. The similarity which is not verified is the liking of hot dogs. The conclusion is that my neighbor's dog will like hot dogs.

In the dog and hot dog example, it is clear that the premises do not achieve maximal relevance to the conclusion. Even if the premises are true, other pieces of information would still be very relevant, such as the possibility that I put a hot dog on the floor in front of my neighbor's dog and he turned away from it. What is more important for classification purposes, however, is that no analogy could ever achieve maximal relevance. No matter how similar two things are, there is always the possibility that they are dissimilar on the matter in question. For this reason, analogies are classified as inductive arguments.

Generalizations

Any statement about a group of things can be considered a generalization. "Dogs have four legs" is a generalization, and it is generally true, though sadly there are a few exceptions. A generalization in this context is a statement, and as such can be true or false. Logic is concerned with reasons for beliefs, though, and so the term generalization has a more specific meaning in the context of reasoning. A generalization is a particular way of arguing for a generalized statement. Sometimes these kinds of arguments are called inductive generalizations to distinguish them from statements.

In an inductive generalization, the conclusion that the members of a group have a certain property is made on the basis that the members of a sample of the same group have that property. To say that "all the coins in a jar are pennies because the first ten coins I pulled out of the jar were pennies" is to make an inductive generalization. Since we haven't seen the other coins, it is possible that at least one of the coins is not a penny. If the next coin I pull out is a nickel, that would count against my earlier conclusion. Inductive generalizations are not capable of maximal relevance, and must be counted as inductive arguments. The only way we could be sure that all of the coins in the jar were pennies is to pull out every single one. As long as the sample used is smaller than the entire whole claimed in the conclusion, the argument will be inductive.

Causal arguments

It would be nearly impossible to make our way in the world if we couldn't reason about causation. We use causal reasoning in science, in troubleshooting nearly everything, in building and engineering things, in our relationships, and just about everywhere else. Any argument which attempts to establish a causal principle, or that one thing is the cause of another, is a causal argument.

It can be very difficult to establish that one thing is the cause of another. Think about how difficult it can be to establish that one person is the cause of another person's death, as in a court of law. Proving that a drug is efficacious in ameliorating a person's illness can be incredibly difficult and cost many millions of dollars. The question for us here, however, is whether a causal argument can reach maximal relevance. The answer is that it cannot.

Even if we are very convinced that one event or thing is the cause of another, it is still a possibility that the cause will occur without the effect. If so, that occurrence would be relevant, and we would have to consider it. Of course, it may be very unlikely, but the fact that it could occur and would be relevant shows that causal arguments cannot achieve maximal relevance, and so should be considered inductive.

Statistical/probabilistic arguments

Any argument which depends upon some statistical probability should be considered an inductive argument. Often causal arguments or predictions will be based upon statistical arguments, but not always. Deductive arguments in general involve some kind of guarantee or complete assurance, whereas inductive arguments involve only a likelihood. So, if an argument involves only a likelihood that its conclusion is correct, it would be an inductive argument.

Consider an argument such as this: If I flip a coin once, it has a 50/50 chance of flipping heads, so if I flip that coin twice, it has a 25% of being heads on both occasions. This argument would generally be considered deductive, even though it involves probability in some sense. The reason is that given the actual truth of the premise, the laws of probability dictate that the conclusion will be true. Technically, any coin may have a slight bias in favor of one side, but if the premise were true, then the conclusion would follow. Yet, if I said that the Lakers have beaten the Clippers 80% of the times they have played, and they are playing again tonight, so the Lakers are going to win, then the argument would be statistical and therefore inductive.

The following argument illustrates a typical probabilistic argument which is inductive.

> Your professor was born on one day of the year out of 365. The day you are happening to read this sentence has nothing to do with what day your professor's birthday is, so it is very unlikely that you are reading this sentence on the day of your professor's birthday.

This is a reasonable argument. If the premises were true, then the conclusion is very likely correct. Yet, these premises do not completely "crowd out" other information. For example, your professor could tell you that it is his birthday today, and that fact certainly would be relevant. Of course, relying on what someone says can always be problematic—your professor could be mistaken, which brings us to the next category.

Arguments from authority

Often we do not even require people to provide us with an argument before we accept what they tell us. In the previous example, if your professor told you that today was his birthday, you would probably believe him. It would be perfectly appropriate and reasonable to do so. If we thought about the reason for you to believe that it was your professor's birthday, your reason would simply be that "your professor told you". Any time someone says something, we can consider their statement to be a conclusion, with the premise that "the person is saying that it is true" as the premise. In some cases, though, this style of reasoning is explicitly stated. In either case, this form of argument is broadly called an argument from authority.

In the explicit sense of an argument by authority, an arguer will tell you that you should believe something because someone who has some kind of expertise has asserted it to be true. For now we are only concerned with classification, so the question we must ask is whether a person's asserting a statement can be so relevant to that statement's being true, that it will guarantee that statement's truth no matter what other information is learned. Clearly, that is not the case. No matter what any one person says, we can never consider their words to be the only ones, as well as the only things, that matter.

Certainly this view holds for broad scientific and other positions, but it holds even for more personal statements. If a person says that they prefer chocolate ice cream to vanilla, can't we take that as an absolute guarantee for what he is saying? Even in these cases, it would still be relevant if he followed it up with "Just kidding." Or that he misspoke. It would still be a relevant fact that he was lying. It is always the case that some other information would count against the conclusion being drawn. That information need not undermine support for the conclusion completely. Perhaps we still would have a sufficient reason to accept the conclusion, even with the new information. Perhaps the man saying that he prefers vanilla to chocolate follows it up with the statement that he actually never tried chocolate ice cream, but it just smelled distasteful. This new information would make the conclusion slightly less plausible, but still very likely to be true. What matters here is that one's assertions cannot be an absolute guarantee of their truth, and so argument involving any kind of appeal to authority should be treated as inductive.

We will spend time in a future chapter delving much more deeply into many of these inductive styles of arguments. For now, all that is expected of you is that you can classify them as inductive.

What about other cases?

The preceding list is not meant to be exhaustive; there will be plenty of arguments which do not fit any of the preceding categories, or at least you will not recognize that they do. What should you do in these cases?

There are a few guidelines which you can follow. First, look for the word "probably" or any phrase which indicates less than absolute certainty. People in general are not going to make their argument sound weaker than it is, so if they actually have a deductive argument (especially one which does achieve maximal relevance), then they won't tend to weaken their argument with phrases such as "it likely follows" or "it is *almost* certain". The word "almost" is important here. It indicates that the arguer recognizes that the conclusion does not follow with certainty from the premises. In this case, and any case with weakening phrases, it is a safe bet that the argument is inductive.

Unfortunately, this guideline doesn't work the other way. People often try to make their arguments sound stronger than they are, and so even when they are dealing with an inductive argument, they will sometimes use strength-enhancing phrases, such as "so it must be the case that" or "so is has to follow that". These sorts of phrases are not reliable indicators that the argument is deductive, so other techniques must be used.

Another way to determine whether an argument is deductive is to ask whether it does indeed achieve maximal relevance. If the premises actually do guarantee the conclusion to be true regardless of any other information, then the argument is deductive, and you should treat it as such. Unfortunately, if it does not, then it is either a defective deductive argument, or else an inductive argument, and you would need some other way to determine which one it is.

Another rule of thumb is that arguments involving states of mind or psychological dispositions should be treated inductively. Drawing conclusions about a person's motives, for example, or their desires and judgments, even when very conclusive evidence is presented, still generally involves uncertainty, which is the hallmark of inductive reasoning. Also, the fact that a conclusion involves a moral claim, or a "should" does not necessarily make it inductive. If there is a "should" statement in the premises, whether explicit or implicit, the argument can still be deductive, so you will need to rely on other techniques.

If you're still stumped after all of this then in most cases we should use the principle of charity. Treat the argument as inductive. If we are to be mistaken is better to think that the person made a strong inductive argument than to think they made a defective deductive argument.

In this section, you should have learned enough to distinguish between deductive and inductive arguments in many cases. In some cases, there is a real choice that can be made. In cases where there are implied premises, it's up to the reader to figure out which premise or premises should be added. In these cases we will need to determine whether it's more appropriate to add a premise which would make the argument deductive or to add one which would make it inductive. We can use the categories above to help us figure it out. It is often the case that we can add a premise to an argument which would make it deductively valid, but would be false. If we can add a plausible premise which makes the conclusion inductively strong, then we should do so.

For example, the argument "My friend has been a lawyer for over ten years, so he must be rich" should be considered inductive. Even though it is phrased as if it should be deductive, the only way the premise could guarantee the conclusion is if we were to add the premise that all people who have been lawyers over ten years are rich, which is almost certainly false. Even lawyers sometimes go bankrupt, and many lawyers work for non-profit institutions for moderate wages. We could add the premise that most people who have been lawyers for over ten years are rich, which is at the very least much more plausible. Adding this premise would result in a strong inductive argument, and is preferable over a deductive one with a clearly false premise.

Chapter Five Exercises

For each of the following passages in all three difficulty levels, decide whether the argument is deductive or inductive. Include your reason, or the type of argument it is, and a quick judgment about whether the argument is good or bad.

Basic Concept Exercises

1. The fact that the suspect's fingerprints were on the murder weapon proves that he committed the crime.
2. Every marsupial is a mammal, and every kangaroo is a marsupial, so every kangaroo is a mammal.
3. Marijuana should be legalized. Nothing should be illegal if there is no criminal intent present, and in smoking marijuana there is no criminal intent.
4. Every professor I have had has worn glasses. A lot of professors must have eye problems.
5. All repeating decimals can be written as fractions, and all repeating decimals are rational numbers, which goes to show that all rational numbers can be written as fractions.
6. The Windows Registry file must have certain file associations for windows to run executable files, and your computer is not running executable files, so your registry is probably corrupted.
7. Some invalid arguments have true premises, so no valid arguments have false premises.
8. If a student sits at the front of the class, it is easier for him to pay attention, and if it is easier for him to pay attention, then it is easier to get a better grade. So, if a student sits at the front of the class, it is easier to get a better grade.
9. I plugged my hair dryer into this outlet, and it worked, but the light that was plugged in before wasn't working. It must be that the lightbulb is busted, or else there is a problem with the wiring in the lamp.
10. The *Star Wars* movies are the best movies ever. They have an incredible story of freedom and fighting against tyranny, and they inspired generations of movies after them.

Intermediate Exercises

11. The Constitution forbids the establishment of religion, and to include the words "under God" in the Pledge of Allegiance is an establishment of religion, which shows that the Pledge of Allegiance is unconstitutional.
12. Since the Constitution forbids cruel and unusual punishment, the death penalty is unconstitutional.
13. A Liberal is someone who holds that individuals should make more of their own decisions than the state, but people who support universal healthcare want the state to make more decisions than the individual. So, supporters of universal healthcare cannot be liberal.
14. If you do the right thing, it will make you happy, which shows that if you do something and it makes you unhappy, then it is not moral.

15. Smoking any substance without a filter is far more dangerous than smoking the substance with a filter, so smoking marijuana without a filter (as most people do) is far more dangerous than smoking tobacco with a filter (as most people do).
16. It seems to me that people who are presently in jail were much less likely to attend church regularly before they went to prison than the non-prison population. If the government is interested in getting people to not break the law, which it should be, then it should do everything it can to encourage people to attend church regularly.
17. Some fruits are apples, and some fruits are red, so some apples are red.
18. Anyone who comes into the country or stays illegally deserves to be deported. If someone deserves to be deported, then we should not have sympathy for them when they are deported. So, we should not have sympathy for illegal aliens who are deported.
19. It seems that when an argument involves facts, it is deductive, but when it involves opinions, it is inductive. Since this argument I am making right now involves opinions, it must be inductive.
20. Just as the family should never be put in the hands of the children, the government should never be put in the hands of the people. Democracy only invites mob rule.

Challenging exercises

21. The distance between galaxies has been accelerating, which, according to Newton's Laws of Mechanics is impossible unless there is some repellent force acting upon galaxies. The only repellent forces that are currently accepted in physics are the electromagnetic force and maybe the weak nuclear force, but neither of these can explain the acceleration. So, either there is some previously unknown mysterious force in the universe, or else Newton was wrong.
22. Republicans always try to deny the ability of minorities and poor people to vote. They reject same-day registration for voting, and they even want to require voters to show their ID's. It's just a fact that minorities and poor people have a more difficult time getting ID's than other people.
23. Democrats always push to make it easier and easier to vote. They want to allow people to register the same day that they vote, which would make it more difficult to verify that they are entitled to vote, and they don't want to require people to show ID's, which makes it much easier to commit voter fraud. That's the real reason they support these reforms.
24. Abraham Lincoln didn't really care about the slaves. He even said "My paramount object in this struggle is to save the Union, and is not either to save or to destroy slavery. If I could save the Union without freeing any slave I would do it, and if I could save it by freeing all the slaves I would do it."
25. There are many reasons why Pluto is not a planet. Its orbit is wildly eccentric, at some times crossing the orbit of Neptune. It also smaller than the moon. If you need any more evidence, it doesn't orbit in the same plane as the other planets, but is angled significantly, more like a comet.
26. Physics is a branch of philosophy. Philosophy is the study of truth and the use of reason to resolve rational dilemmas, which is what physics does in relation to physical phenomena. Moreover, Isaac Newton and all the early physicists said

they were working in natural philosophy. Finally, the highest degree in physics is a Ph.D., which stands for Doctorate of Philosophy in Physics.

27. Physics is part of science and not philosophy. Philosophy deals with subjects that are uncertain, and where there are no right answers. All that philosophy can provide is opinion. Science involves fact, and things that are straightforwardly right or wrong. Since physics deals with facts and straightforward truths, it is a part of science.
28. If mankind were the cause of global warming, then how can you explain the fact that Mars and the other planets are also going through a warming phase.
29. I know you have been saying that kids nowadays are getting out of control, but even Plato complained about children talking back to their parents.
30. The government doesn't have the right to stop people from doing what they want to do, and people want to gamble their money. If our state doesn't allow some kind of gambling, then people will spend that money in other states, improving those state's economies and hurting our own. Besides, we can use the money raised to support our schools.

In-context exercises

A. Think up a topic you would like to explore. Look online and find arguments involving that topic. Print out several arguments. Decide whether the arguments made are inductive or deductive.

Logic Puzzle: The Party

I invited Abigail, Ben, and Christine to my party. Based on the following statements, determine who, if anyone, attended:

1) Either Abigail or Christine attended.
2) Either Ben or Abigail did not attend.
3) If Abigail did not attend, then neither did Christine.
4) Either Ben or Christine attended.

CHAPTER

6

Evaluating Deductive Arguments

Skill 6.1

Recognizing Maximal Relevance

Many of the chapters following this one will address the skill of evaluating deductive arguments. In this chapter, we will address the preliminary task of understanding the terminology used to evaluate deductive arguments. The most important thing you need to know for the entire course is the distinction between relevance and truth, which is the topic to which we turn now.

We already covered relevance in the previous chapter. The aim of every deductive argument is to reach maximal relevance. If a deductive argument does not reach maximal relevance, it is considered a defective argument. Maximal relevance is not the only criterion used to evaluate deductive arguments, but it is generally the first one to which logicians turn.

The important thing you need to impress deep into your mind is that the truth of a statement is generally irrelevant to considerations of relevance. It may sound paradoxical, but the question of whether one statement is relevant to another does not depend at all on whether either statement is true. Consider the following example, and ask whether the statements are relevant to each other: 1) Salvador has $5,000 in his wallet right now, and 2) Salvador is rich. These statements are clearly relevant to each other (though not maximally), and yet no one reading this textbook knows whether either statement is true or false. Regardless of whether either statement is true or false, the fact that Salvador had $5,000 in his wallet would make it much more likely that he is rich.

So, one need not evaluate the actual truth of premises in order to determine whether they are relevant to a conclusion, either maximally or partially. One only needs to consider the premises and the conclusion in a hypothetical way. One has to ask what would be the case if the premises *were* true. At no time in evaluating the relevance of premises to conclusion is it necessary to determine if the premises are *actually* true.

It is time to start looking at some arguments. Consider the following two arguments:

Argument 6.1	**Argument 6.2**
1) Ivan is older than 21. 2) Esther is younger than 21. 3) ∴ Ivan is older than Esther.	1) Ivan is older than 21. 2) Elizabeth is older than 31. 3) ∴ Elizabeth is older than Ivan.

The question to ask is this: given that both premises were true, what would the conclusion be? There are only three answers. The conclusion will be either guaranteed to be true, guaranteed to be false, or else possibly true and possibly false. There are no other possibilities.

In Argument 6.1, the truth of the premises does guarantee the truth of the conclusion. If Ivan were older than 21, and Esther were younger than 21, then the conclusion, that Ivan is older than Esther, would be guaranteed to be true. There would be no way for the conclusion to be false. None of us knows whether the premises are actually true, but it doesn't matter.

These premises are maximally relevant to the conclusion. Since the truth of the premises guarantees the truth of the conclusion, the premises have positive maximal relevance.

In Argument 6.2, the same situation does not hold. In context, perhaps, the fact that someone chose to say that Ivan is older than 21 might mean that Ivan is close to twenty-one, but that information is not contained in the premise, and we have not been given any information as to the context. All it says is that Ivan is older than 21; he could be 89 and the premise would still be true. According to the premise, Elizabeth may be in her thirties, or she may be in her nineties. Given the truth of the premises, and only these premises, there is no way to determine whether Elizabeth is older than Ivan. She could be older than Ivan, or younger, or even the exact same age. So, the conclusion could be either true or false, and the premises are not maximally relevant to the conclusion.

It may help to see ordering diagrams for each of the premises. Examine the ordering diagram for each of the arguments in the boxes below:

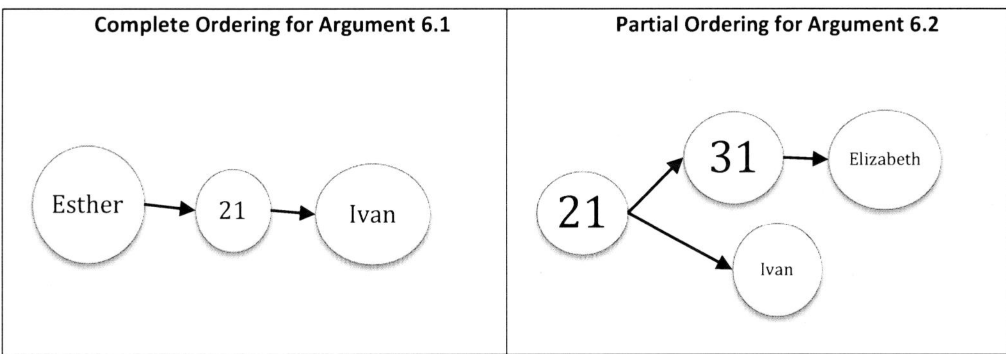

In argument 6.1, the premises can be diagrammed in a complete ordering. Given the truth of the premises, there is only one way to order each person. Esther must come before 21, and Ivan must be put after 21. So, Ivan must be put after Esther. So, for this argument, the truth of the premises guarantees the truth of the conclusion.

For argument 6.2 the situation is different. Obviously, 21 must come before 31. According to the first premise, Ivan is older than 21, which means we must put Ivan after 21 on our diagram. We don't know, however, whether Ivan is older than 31. If he were, he would be put after 31, and if he weren't, we would put him before 31. In order to capture our uncertainty, we place Ivan on another path. The length of the arrows on each path is *not* drawn proportionately. Each arrow might indicate a distance of one year or a distance of a hundred years. All that we know is that along a given path, an object (or "node") on the left is younger than an object to its right. What we cannot do is to compare two objects on different paths. This sort of diagram, where there is more than one path and we don't know the complete order of every object in the diagram, is called a partial ordering.

The final node on the drawing is the circle representing Elizabeth. The second premise tells us that her circle should go to the right of 31, which it does. Even though Elizabeth's circle is placed further to the right than Ivan's circle, the fact that they are on two different paths tells us that we don't know which one is older. The arrow between 21 and Ivan could be 50 years, making Ivan 71. This diagram, which models the premises given, tells us that the conclusion could be true, or it could be false.

Ordering diagrams can be very useful for arguments that rely on rankings or distances, and so it would behoove each student to gain some proficiency in drawing them. We will see that it is often a good idea to try to create a graphic representation of an argument in some way, so that our intuitions can be strengthened and the arguments clarified.

Here is one last example. We will see the argument, as well as a diagram to represent the premises.

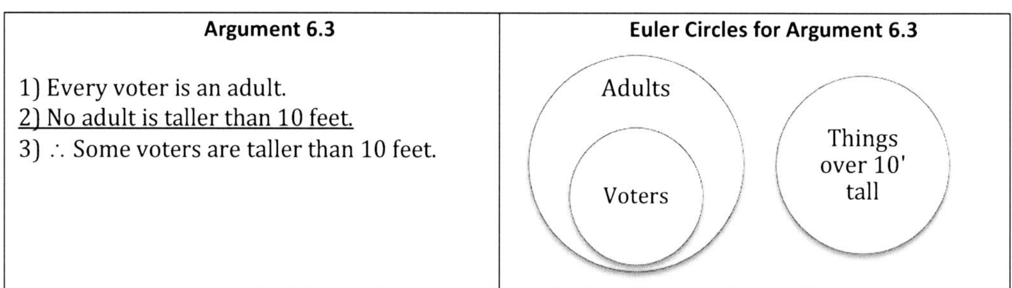

Argument 6.3	Euler Circles for Argument 6.3
1) Every voter is an adult. 2) No adult is taller than 10 feet. 3) ∴ Some voters are taller than 10 feet.	

This argument is very different. It doesn't rely on a simple ordering, but rather several groups and their arrangements. Hopefully, you noticed that it is a categorical argument. Because it has two premises which rely upon each other, it is called a categorical syllogism. To diagram this argument, we are using Euler circles, named after a prominent mathematician who used them. Starting in Chapter 8, we will study categorical reasoning in more detail, and there we will use Venn diagrams, but sometimes Euler circles are more intuitive for beginning students, as in this case.

To model the premise that "Every voter is an adult", we place the circle corresponding to "voters" completely within the circle corresponding to "adults". The premise that "No adult is taller than 10 feet" leads us to draw the circle for "things over 10 feet tall" completely outside the circle for "adults".

Now, with the diagram in place, we can ask ourselves "Given the truth of the premises, what would the status of the conclusion be?" The diagram shows that there is no possibility for the conclusion to be true. Every voter would be an adult, according to the premises, and no adult is over ten feet tall. These premises would guarantee that no voter is over ten feet tall, which in turn would guarantee that it is false that some voters are taller than ten feet tall. So, given these premises the conclusion is guaranteed to be false.

It may seem odd at first, but these premises are actually maximally relevant to the conclusion, but in the opposite direction. These premises guarantee that the conclusion is false instead of true, so they have maximal *negative* relevance. Let's pause here to make sure you understand these distinctions to a sufficient degree by completing the comprehension check exercises below.

Comprehension Check Exercises

For each argument below, determine whether the premises are positively maximally relevant to the conclusion by asking whether the truth of the premises would guarantee the conclusion to be true, guarantee the conclusion to be false, or allow the conclusion to be either true or false. You should pay special attention to two things. First, some of these arguments depend on factual information, yet no knowledge of the actual truth or falsity of the statements is needed in order to determine the answer regarding relevance. Second, whether the premises are maximally relevant or not often seems to depend on the placement of the words in the sentences, and not the nature of the objects themselves.

1. 1) Mercury is less dense than lead.
   2) Gold is denser than lead.
   3) ∴ Gold is denser than mercury.

2. 1) Mercury is less dense than lead.
   2) Gold is denser than mercury.
   3) ∴ Gold is denser than lead.

3. 1) Mercury is less dense than lead.
   2) Gold is less dense than lead.
   3) ∴ Gold is less dense than mercury.

4. 1) Mercury is less dense than lead.
   2) Gold is less dense than mercury.
   3) ∴ Gold is less dense than lead.

5. 1) Cheetahs are faster than giraffes.
   2) Giraffes are faster than turtles.
   3) ∴ Cheetahs are faster than turtles.

6. 1) Cheetahs are faster than giraffes.
   2) Giraffes are slower than turtles.
   3) ∴ Turtles are faster than cheetahs.

7. 1) $a \geq c$
   2) $b \leq c$
   3) $\therefore a \geq b$

8. 1) $a \geq c$
   2) $c \leq b$
   3) $\therefore a \geq b$

9. 1) $a \geq b$
   2) $b \geq a$
   3) $\therefore a = b$

10. 1) $a \geq b$
    2) $b \geq c$
    3) $c \geq a$
    4) $\therefore a \neq c$

You can check your answers in the box at the bottom of the next page. Remember that the premises have positive maximal relevance to the conclusion when, and only when, the conclusion is guaranteed to be true by the truth of the premises.

Validity

Valid Argument
An argument whose premises are positively maximally relevant to the conclusion

Invalid Argument
A deductive argument whose premises are not maximally relevant (positively) to the conclusion

The concept of validity is essential to the study of deductive logic. Unfortunately, the concept as it is used in logic is not the same as the one with which you are probably familiar. Fortunately, you already have been given the concept of validity in logic, only without the label.

Consider how the word "valid" is often used in ordinary conversation. Two people will be engaging in a debate, and one of them will make a point. The other one might respond with "that's a valid point." You should ask yourself what the person, or any person using the word this way, means when they call the point a "valid" one.

Do they mean that it is true? Do they mean that it is a legitimate point? What the heck does "legitimate" mean, here? It doesn't help to define a difficult word using one that is even more unclear. Do they mean that it is inoffensive, or that it is appropriate for the context in some way? Could they mean that it is relevant to the issue at hand? Perhaps they mean some combination of all of these. Or, perhaps, they don't really know which one they mean.

I suspect that they very rarely use the word the way that logicians do. Let's be charitable and not say that they are using the word incorrectly, but rather that logicians use the word in a technical sense. They have a very specific meaning to the word "valid" which is unambiguous and precise, which you need to understand if you hope to do well in logic. For logicians, an argument is valid if and only if the premises of the argument have positive maximal relevance to the conclusion.

That's it.

Skill 6.2

Judging the Validity of an Argument

If the premises of an argument have positive maximal relevance to the conclusion, then the argument is valid. If the premises of an argument do not have positive maximal relevance to the conclusion, then it is invalid. There is no in-between.

As we have seen, the easiest way to determine whether premises are maximally relevant is to ask whether the truth of the premises *would* guarantee that the conclusion would be true. We are focusing on the relevance of premises to conclusion, and not actual truth, so we need not ask here whether the premises are true, but only what would follow if they *were* true. If, given the truth of the premises, the conclusion would be guaranteed to be false, or if the conclusion could be true or false, then the argument is invalid.

Another way to get at the same issue is to ask whether it is at all possible for the premises to be true and the conclusion to be false at the same time. If it is possible, then the argument is invalid. If not, then the argument is valid. In a valid argument, it is not possible for the conclusion to be false while the premises are true, for the very reason that in a valid argument the truth of the premises guarantees the truth of the conclusion.

Comprehension Check Answers

1. True	6. T or F
2. T or F	7. True
3. T or F	8. T or F
4. True	9. True
5. True	10. False

Soundness

It is good to have a valid argument, but it is not the only standard upon which a deductive argument is judged. If we want to evaluate a deductive argument, we also have to ask one other critical question. While the relevance of the premises to the conclusion is an important concern, so is the question of whether the premises are true.

To evaluate something is to make a judgment about something. It is to discern whether it is good or not. The Latin prefix e- means "out of", so in evaluating something, we are "pulling" the value out of it. In evaluating an argument, we are determining whether it has the features which we think will make it a good argument.

It should be clear that one of the features required for a good deductive argument is positive maximal relevance. If your premises do not guarantee your conclusion, i.e. if your argument is invalid, then your argument is defective. But validity cannot be the only feature we value. Consider this argument: All textbooks are on fire, and you are holding a textbook, so what you are holding is on fire. This argument is valid, but there is still something wrong with it. The problem is that although the truth of the premises guarantees the truth of the conclusion, the premises are not in fact true (I hope). In a good deductive argument, the premises must be not only relevant to the conclusion, they also must be true.

Sound Argument
An argument which is valid and has all true premises

A valid argument which has all true premises is a **sound** argument. A sound argument is a very powerful thing. In a sound argument the truth of the premises logically guarantees the truth of the conclusion, and the premises are actually true. So, in a sound argument, the conclusion is logically guaranteed to be true.

Skill 6.3

Judging the Soundness of an Argument

For all its simplicity, students often have a difficult time answering questions about soundness. Does an unsound argument have a false conclusion? If you answered "no" or "not necessarily" then you are right. If you were unsure, or answered incorrectly, then perhaps using a relationship with an analogous structure will help you understand soundness better.

Soundness is a property of arguments, but it is composed of other properties. For an argument to be sound, it must be valid and have all true premises. Compare this structure to eligibility to be President of the United States. According to the Constitution, there are three requirements to be eligible to be President.

Unsound Argument
A deductive argument which is either invalid or has false premises

A person is eligible to be president when and only when
1) that person is 35 or older.
2) that person is a natural-born citizen of the United States.
3) that person has been a resident of the United States for 14 consecutive years.

Let's change the sentences to letters, just for the sake of compressing things:

E is true if and only if	1) T is true 2) B is true 3) R is true

So, E is true if and only if T, B, and R are all true. It should be clear that E stands for "a person is eligible to be president", etc. Let's ask a series of questions.

1. If a person is eligible to be President, do we know that he is 35 or older?
2. If a person is over 35, do we know that he is eligible to be President?
3. If a person is not eligible to be President, do we know that he is 35 or older?
4. If a person is younger than 35, do we know whether he is eligible to be President?

Most students are fairly adept at answering these questions. The answers to 1) and 4) is "yes" and the answers to 2) and 3) is "no". In a sense, truth flows from left to right, and falsity flows from right to left. If the statement on the left is true (that a person is eligible to be President), then all of the statements on the right are true. If the statement on the left is false, then we don't know whether any individual statement on the right is false (although one of them must be). If any statement on the right is false, then we know that the statement on the left is false. If a statement on the right is true, that by itself tells us nothing about the truth of the statement on the left.

I introduce this example because most students are somewhat familiar with it, and it is exactly parallel to the structure of the relationship between soundness and its component properties. Unfortunately, most students have a difficult time understanding the relationship between soundness and validity. Fortunately, it is basically the same as the example dealing with the President, only simpler. There are only two conditions.

Here is how it works:

An argument is sound	when and only when:	1) The argument is valid. 2) All of its premises are true.

If the statement on the left is true, then all the statements on the right are true. If the statement on the left is false, then we do not know whether either of the statements on the right is true or false (although one of them must be false). If one statement on the right is true, we do not know whether the argument is sound (although if both statements on the right are true, then the left statement is true and the argument is sound. If either one of the statements on the right is false, then the left statement must also be false.

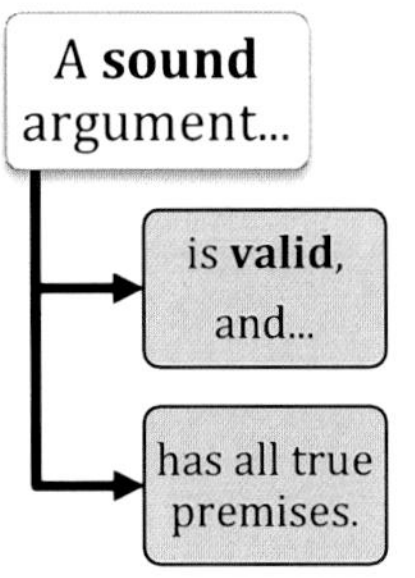

So, if an argument is sound, then the argument must be valid. If an argument is unsound, then it can be valid or invalid. It can also have all true premises or not. An unsound argument cannot both have all true premises and be valid, but we don't know which of the conditions is lacking. Similarly, if an argument is valid, then it can be sound or unsound depending on the truth of the premises, whereas if an argument is invalid, then it is guaranteed to be unsound.

Putting it all together

Let's put all of this together. We have learned how to determine that an argument is valid, and we have learned how to determine that an argument is sound. In order to completely evaluate a deductive argument, we can use a two-step procedure, as outlined in the following flow chart:

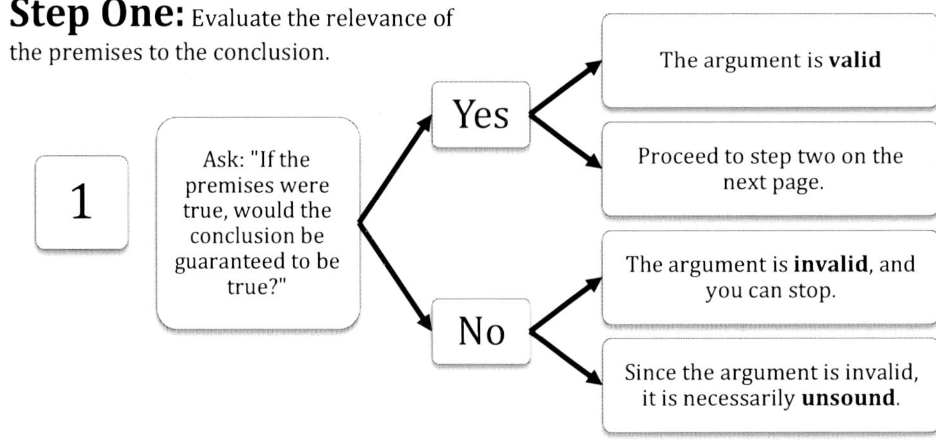

Step Two: Evaluate the actual truth of the premises.

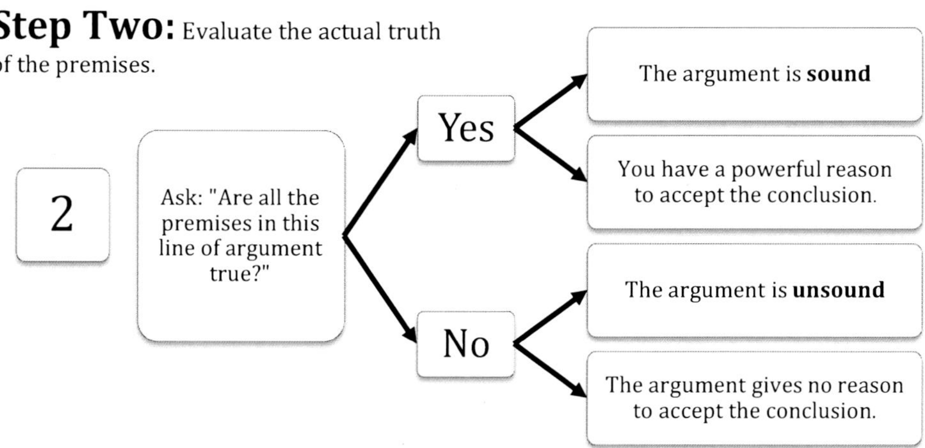
2
Ask: "Are all the premises in this line of argument true?"
Yes
No
The argument is **sound**
You have a powerful reason to accept the conclusion.
The argument is **unsound**
The argument gives no reason to accept the conclusion.

Using this procedure, you will become more and more proficient at evaluating deductive arguments. One might ask whether it is possible to do these steps in reverse order. It is possible, but it's usually a good idea to do them in the order listed here. The reason is that validity is generally a property that can be determined by analyzing the argument itself. Determining whether premises are true or false often requires a lot of research. It's also possible that people strongly disagree on the truth or falsity of the premises. If we can first determine that an argument is invalid, then we can avoid doing all that research, and we can possibly avoid fighting over the truth of the premises if both sides can realize that they are not relevant to the issue at hand.

Criticizing a deductive argument

As we have seen, there are two criteria for deductive arguments. So, if we want to criticize a deductive argument it follows that there are two basic criticisms. We can criticize the argument for being invalid, or we can criticize the argument for having false premises, and we can also do both. You can hear both criticisms when someone says "I disagree with what you're saying, but even if you were right, your conclusion would still not follow."

If you ever find yourself in a situation where you believe an argument is valid, and its premises are all true, but you still think the conclusion is false, then you are in a tight spot indeed. It would be too easy to say that you should just abandon your belief and accept the conclusion, although you should consider that possibility. Technically, you have found yourself in a **rational dilemma**, where you have an inconsistent set of beliefs. You know that something you believe is false, but you don't know what it is. In this case, even when you can't find doubt in the validity of the argument or the truth of the premises, it might still be possible to rationally justify one's belief in the conclusion. All you have to do is construct a deductively sound argument with the opposite conclusion.

Rational Dilemma
A situation where reason seems to pull you in two inconsistent directions

In this case you will have two apparently sound arguments with opposite conclusions. Presumably, we're mistaken about one of the arguments, and it is unsound, but we don't know which one. Technically, introducing a sound counter-argument is not the same as criticizing the original argument, but it does undermine the power that the original argument has.

Chapter Six Exercises

Basic Concept Exercises

For these exercises, determine whether the following deductive arguments are valid or invalid, as well as sound or unsound when possible.

1. Since the moon is smaller than the Earth, it weighs less.
2. If Fox News is controlled by Republicans, then it is not a credible source of news. If Fox News is not a credible source of news, then no one should watch it. So, if Fox News is controlled by Republicans, then no one should watch it.
3. If Fox News is controlled by Republicans then no one should watch it, but Fox News is not controlled by Republicans, so people should watch it.
4. All of the hosts on CNN are respected journalists, and some respected journalists have won Pulitzer Prizes, so some hosts on CNN have won Pulitzer Prizes.
5. Some invalid arguments have true premises, so no valid arguments have false premises.
6. If a person is eligible to be President, then that person is 35 or older. If a person is not a citizen, then that person is not eligible to be President. So, if a person is not a citizen, then they must be younger than 35.
7. Only a legislative body can make laws, and a judge who goes beyond interpreting laws is making the law, so a judge who goes beyond interpreting laws is a legislative body.
8. All tyrants deserve to be removed from power, and all judges which go beyond interpreting the law deserve to be removed from power. Thus, all judges who go beyond interpreting the law are tyrants.
9. If a student sits at the front of the class, it is easier for him to pay attention, and if it is easier for him to pay attention, then it is easier to get a better grade. So, if a student sits at the front of the class, it is easier to get a better grade.
10. No fish can breathe oxygen from the air. Dolphins can breathe oxygen from the air. So, dolphins are not fish.

Intermediate Exercises

For these exercises, decide whether the following statements are true or false.

11. Every valid argument is sound.
12. Every sound argument is valid.
13. If an argument is valid, then it has all true premises.
14. If an argument is invalid, then it has at least one false premise.
15. If an argument is sound, then it has all true premises.
16. If an argument has all true premises, then it is sound.
17. If an argument has all true premises and a false conclusion, then it is invalid.

18. If an argument has a false conclusion, then it is invalid.
19. If an argument has all true premises and a true conclusion, then it is valid.
20. If an argument has false premises, then it is invalid.

Challenging exercises

For these exercises, determine whether the following deductive arguments are valid or invalid, as well as sound or unsound when possible.

21. Everyone who is alive today had two parents, and each of them had two parents. It follows that in our grandparent's day, there were four times as many people.
22. Every integer is either odd or even. Given an integer, x, if x is even, then x^2 is even. But even if x is odd, then x^2 is even. So, no matter what, x^2 will always be even.
23. Anyone who comes into the country or stays illegally deserves to be deported. If someone deserves to be deported, then we should not have sympathy for them when they are deported. So, we should not have sympathy for illegal aliens who are deported.
24. No prime numbers are divisible by seven. Some numbers which are divisible by seven are divisible by four. So, no prime numbers are divisible by four.
25. All numbers divisible by 8 are divisible by 4. No prime numbers are divisible by 8. So, no prime numbers are divisible by 4.
26. Some fruits are apples, and some fruits are red, so some apples are red.
27. Some fruits are apples, and some apples are red, so some fruits are red.
28. A society which allows slavery is unjust. Our society does not allow slavery, so our society is just.
29. The formula for determining the area of a circle is $2\pi r$. This circle has a radius of 4 units, so it has an area of approximately 25 units.
30. In order for us to have free will, then it must be the case that the future is unknowable. This is because if anyone can know the future, then our choices would not be free, but instead would be caused. If God has omniscience, then he knows everything, and nothing, including the future is unknowable. Therefore, if we have free will, then God is not omniscient.

In-Context Exercises

A. Take the dialog below and pull out all the deductive inferences, then decide whether the arguments are valid or invalid, and if possible, sound or unsound.

Anthony: How's it going Drew?

Drew: I just came from the Philosophy Club, and we were discussing capital punishment.

Anthony: That's the death penalty, right? I'm totally against that.

Drew: Really? I was always in favor of it, but I hadn't really seen any of the arguments. Why are you against it?

Anthony: That's easy. Murder is wrong. Any time you kill someone, that's murder. Capital punishment means killing someone, so it's wrong.

Drew: Don't you see a difference between when the state does it or an individual does it?

Anthony: Not at all. The state gets all of its rights from individuals. Individuals don't have the right to kill someone, so the state can't have that right either.

Drew: It still seems to me like you're missing something. I don't have the right to imprison people, or do you disagree? If I use the principle you just stated, then the state wouldn't have the right to imprison people, either. Do you think the state has the right to imprison people?

Anthony: Yes, but it's not the same.

Drew: Why not?

Anthony: It doesn't matter, the Constitution forbids cruel and unusual punishment, and the death penalty is cruel and unusual. Among similar nations, America is the only one that uses it.

Drew: I'm pretty sure the Constitution isn't supposed to be used to consider what other countries do. The death penalty is not unusual in America, but perhaps it is cruel. Why do you think it is cruel?

Anthony: It's obvious! You're killing someone, depriving them of life. What could be more cruel?

Drew: Perhaps depriving them of liberty? Isn't that cruel, in some sense?

Anthony: So, now you're saying that we should get rid of jails, too? Your position is even more extreme than mine.

Drew: All I was saying was that the Constitution doesn't forbid prisons, even though they are cruel in some sense. So even though the death penalty is cruel in some sense, the Constitution may not forbid it. Perhaps we need to clarify exactly what cruel means in the Eighth Amendment.

Anthony: Like I have time for that. I've got to get to class.

Drew: All right, man. Maybe some other time.

Logic Puzzle: Four Suspects

You have four suspects, who make the following statements:

1. Suspect 1 says: Suspect 2 is guilty.
2. Suspect 2 says: Either Suspect 1 or Suspect 4 is guilty.
3. Suspect 3 says: I am not guilty.
4. Suspect 4 says: Either Suspect 3 or Suspect 1 is guilty.

Assuming that there is only one guilty party, who is lying, while the others are telling the truth, determine who is guilty.

CHAPTER

7

Evaluating Inductive Arguments

Evaluating inductive arguments is in some ways more challenging than evaluating deductive arguments. Whereas deductive arguments are either valid or invalid, there is no such stark dichotomy for inductive arguments. The terminology for evaluating inductive arguments is also not as fixed as it is for deductive arguments. Yet, the basic ideas are fairly straightforward and can be learned quickly.

As we have seen it would not make sense to hold up an inductive argument to a deductive standard; it would always fail. Inductive arguments can never achieve maximal relevance, and so are technically always invalid. Logicians tend to refrain from calling them invalid, because they want to emphasize the difference between deductive and inductive arguments, and besides, there would be no point: Saying that an inductive argument is invalid is redundant. So, in evaluating inductive arguments, we must use a less stringent standard.

If we could only use valid arguments to ground our beliefs, we would be forced to live in a very different world. You could never believe anything anyone ever told you, since no matter how strong their credibility, it is always possible that they are wrong, or that they are lying. We could never make any judgments about causation, since no matter how many times one thing has led to another, it is always possible that on the next occasion, it will fail to do so. Inductive arguments are useful; they give us a reason to believe their conclusions, but they do not guarantee that their conclusions are true.

Inductive Strength

Skill 7.1

Judging Partial Relevance

Since inductive arguments only involve partial relevance between their premises and conclusions, they can only support probabilistic inferences. The degree of probability depends upon the degree of relevance. The more relevant the premises are to the conclusion, the more likely it is that the conclusion will turn out to be true (given that the premises are true).

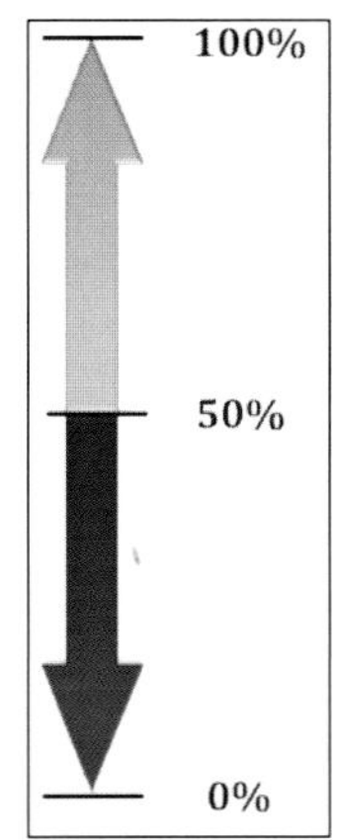

We can think about the range of possibilities here by asking the question, given that the premises of an argument happen to be true, what is the likelihood that its conclusion will also be true? We can arrange the possibilities on a scale from 0% to 100%. Given that one's premises are true, it could be that my conclusion has a 100% chance of being true, which would put the conclusion right at the very top of our scale. Of course, then the argument would be deductively valid. But we could have an inductive argument where the truth of the premises would make it 99.999% likely that the conclusion would be true.

We could also have an argument where the premises literally made no difference to the conclusion. If the premises are irrelevant to the conclusion, then given the truth of the premises, the conclusion would be 50% likely to be true and 50% likely to be false. The conclusion would be right in the middle of our scale. On the other hand, it is also

Skill 7.2

Judging the Strength of Inductive Arguments

possible that the premises could make the conclusion less likely to be true, which would mean the conclusion would be within the red arrow.

We are most interested in those arguments which would place conclusions within the range of the green arrow. If the likelihood of the conclusion is above 50%, even if it is 50.001%, then it can be said that the truth of the premises makes the conclusion more likely to be true. It would be useful to have a general term to apply to such arguments. Logicians, not being the most creative groups, have come to call them **strong**. A strong argument is one in which the truth of the premises makes the conclusion more likely to be true than false. A strong argument has premises which go provide some kind of reason, though not a certain one, to accept the conclusion of the argument.

An argument where the truth of the premises makes the conclusion 50% or less likely to be true is a **weak** argument. Such an argument cannot offer someone a reason to accept its conclusion, regardless of the truth of its premises.

Strong Argument
An inductive argument whose premises are positively relevant to the conclusion, though not maximally so

Unlike deductive validity, inductive strength comes in degrees. Whereas deductive arguments are either valid or invalid, inductive arguments, even strong ones, range from very strong with over 99% probability, to barely strong at all, just over 50% probability. In some cases, it is possible to put a specific percentage probability on an inductive argument, but in general such precision is not possible. Yet, we should have some way to distinguish varying degrees of strength. To do so, we can add qualifiers to the term "strong". We can have an argument which is barely on the strong side, a somewhat strong argument, a strong argument, a very strong argument, and an extremely strong argument.

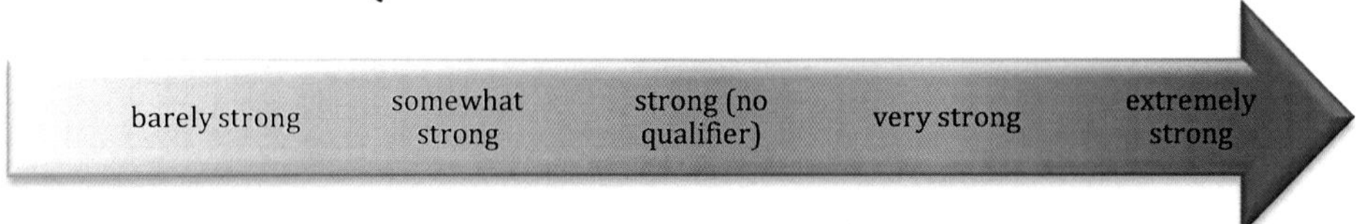

These are not technical categories; they are simply useful distinctions to make. They are also vague; it would be overly rigid to put specific numbers to the categories. You need not even be constrained to use these five categories; feel free to use any other qualifiers as well, to suit your own preferences. The point is not that you only use the qualifiers I mention here, but that you understand that 51% probability is very different from 99% probability, and that you have some way of expressing that difference.

Weak Argument
An inductive argument whose premises are not relevant, or are negatively relevant, to the conclusion

Just as in deductive arguments, mere relevance is not sufficient to make a good argument. Even when an argument is strong, when there is some positive partial relevance between the premises and conclusion, we still need to ask whether the premises are true.

Often, people will hesitate to use the word strong for an argument with only 51% probability. One must keep in mind that we will use the term strong in a somewhat technical sense here. It really just means that the argument has given a reason, not necessarily what we might generally call a strong argument. In actual practice, however, an argument with at least some strength in this technical sense will be generally considered a weak argument. I think the reason is that a statement, even one where it is not known to be true or false, comes with initial plausibility or implausibility. Often, an inductive argument will not be recognized as strong until and unless it can overcome someone's judgment that the conclusion is implausible.

For example, if someone begins thinking that it is highly implausible that human beings and their activity can influence the environment, and someone presents evidence that the global temperature is rising, one might not think that constitutes strong reason to believe that human activity is affecting the environment in that way, whereas someone who thinks it is highly plausible will think the evidence is strong.

These considerations go to show that inductive reasoning is highly sensitive to one's original presuppositions, and so cannot claim the sort of universality that deductive reasoning can. Part of the reason for using the technical meaning of "strong" is to push us to a more universal standard which doesn't depend on any particular point of view. Of course, in evaluating an argument for one's personal use, one should use one's own perspective, but it is useful if we have some objective way to characterize an argument which does not vary from person to person.

Cogent and Compelling Arguments

An argument is **cogent** just in case it is strong (in the technical sense) and it has all true premises. No matter how strongly relevant the premises are to the conclusion, they won't actually support the conclusion unless they are true. Since a cogent argument is strong, and has all true premises, then we do have some good reason to accept the conclusion of a cogent argument.

Cogent Argument
An argument which is strong and has all true premises

Since inductive strength comes in such wide-ranging degrees, so will cogency. It is useful here to have a way to distinguish a cogent argument which has any strength at all from one which has a great deal of strength. We will call such arguments **compelling**. A compelling argument is a kind of cogent argument, where the strength of the argument is very high.

Compelling Argument
An cogent argument whose strength is very high

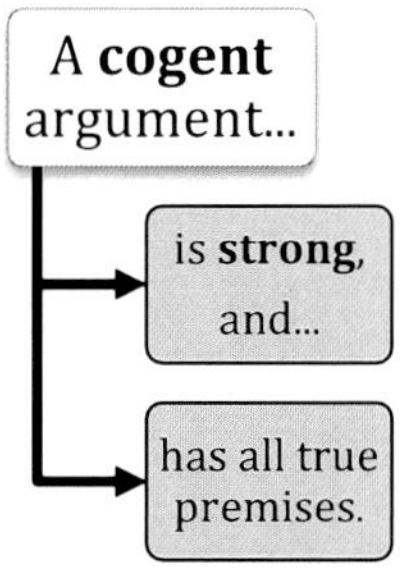

The connection between cogent arguments, strong arguments, and inductive arguments with true premises is exactly parallel to sound arguments, valid arguments, and deductive arguments with true premises. If you know that an argument is cogent, then you know both that it is strong and that it has all true premises. If you know that an argument is not cogent, then you don't know for sure whether the argument is weak or has a false premise (although at least one must be true). On the other hand, if you know that an argument is strong, you still don't know whether the argument is cogent (it depends on whether the premises are all true), but if you know that an argument is weak, then you also know that the argument is uncogent.

A **cogent** argument...
- is **strong**, and...
- has all true premises.

We can also evaluate inductive arguments in a similar two-step procedure as we do for deductive arguments. The difference comes when evaluating the relevance of the premises to the conclusion. Since we are not aiming at deductive validity, we need only ask whether the premises would make the conclusion more likely to be true than not. The terminology is of course different as well.

Skill 7.3
Judging the Cogency and Compulsion of Arguments

Putting it All Together

Just as we did for deductive arguments, we can use a simple two step procedure to completely evaluate an inductive argument. The idea is to become so familiar with this procedure, that it becomes almost a second nature.

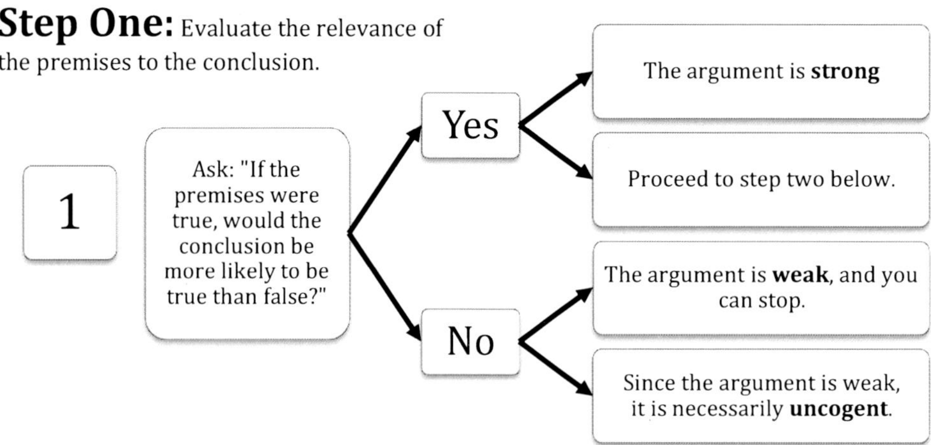
Step One: Evaluate the relevance of the premises to the conclusion.
1
Ask: "If the premises were true, would the conclusion be more likely to be true than false?"
Yes
No
The argument is strong
Proceed to step two below.
The argument is weak, and you can stop.
Since the argument is weak, it is necessarily uncogent.

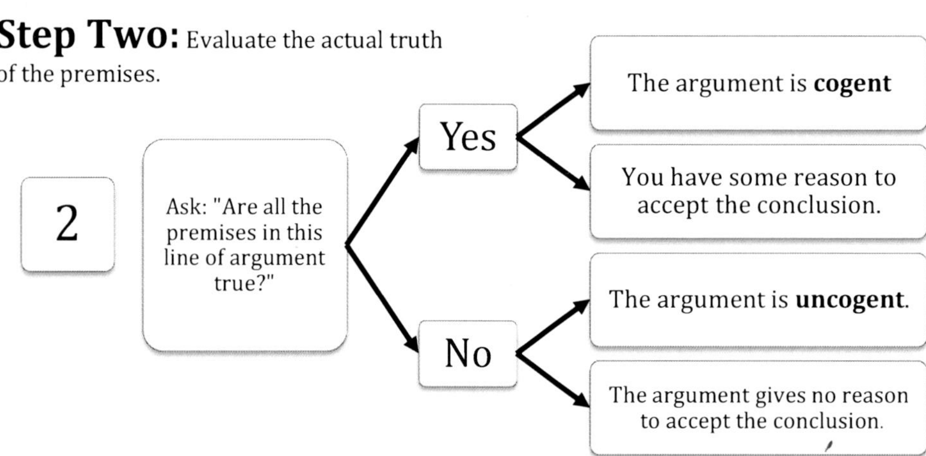
Step Two: Evaluate the actual truth of the premises.
2
Ask: "Are all the premises in this line of argument true?"
Yes
No
The argument is cogent
You have some reason to accept the conclusion.
The argument is uncogent.
The argument gives no reason to accept the conclusion.

This procedure will only help to distinguish between arguments that are strong from arguments that are weak, and not the relative strength of different strong arguments, but if you have the information available to put a more precise probability on the inference, feel free to do so. We will also see in the chapter on inductive arguments that there is a great deal more to evaluating the strength of inductive arguments than we cover here. The more specific information we have about the type of inductive argument, the better our analysis and evaluation can be. For now, however, we will think about inductive arguments in a very general way, and will rely mostly on intuition in judging the strength of the argument.

Criticizing Inductive Arguments

Since there are two basic criteria for inductive arguments, there are two basic ways to criticize such arguments. First, we can make the case that the argument is weak. We can hold that even if the premises were true, they would not be relevant to the conclusion. Second, we can hold that the premises are not true. If there is one false premise, then the argument fails to offer a reason to accept the conclusion.

Yet, even if an argument is cogent (that is, it is strong and has all true premises), there is still a lot of reasoning that can be done. Inductive arguments rely on partial relevance, and so leave room for other information to be relevant. When confronted by an argument which supports its conclusion with 52% likelihood, it would probably still be reasonable to remain agnostic, refusing to accept or deny the conclusion. Yet, most of us would consider a person who rejected the conclusion of an argument involving 99% probability to be irrational, or excessively relying on his feelings.

One complication involves the structure of our beliefs. Can we partially believe things, or does believing something mean we completely accept it? Take an argument with 75% probability. Does this mean that I should, with 75% probability, accept the conclusion, or perhaps that I should accept the conclusion to be 75% true, or does it mean that I should accept the conclusion with 75% certainty? I tend to side with the latter view, but hopefully you understand some of the complexity.

In terms of evaluating inductive arguments, you should just understand that the stronger an argument is taken to be, the more likely it is that I will think you are irrational for not accepting the conclusion. If you do reject the conclusion, I will generally expect that you will try to justify your belief by backing it up with another inductive argument which supports your point of view with at least as much strength as the argument you reject. We will never be able to evaluate every piece of information which might be relevant to a conclusion, but the more information we consider, the more likely we are to reach an equilibrium point, where additional information won't be able to move us away from our conclusion. Such arguments are compelling, and are difficult to refute.

It may help to repeat that point using different terminology. Most people may not be familiar with the term "premise", but they are familiar with a term which captures a particular kind of premise: "evidence". Any time someone presents evidence, they are making an argument, generally an inductive one. We usually restrict the term "evidence" to include only straightforward factual-type statements, but however broadly we use the term, evidence can always be considered to be a premise in an argument supporting a certain conclusion, which is the claim supported by the evidence. Evidence can be very strong, but we never consider evidence in the ordinary sense to reach to deductive validity. After all, the evidence can be faked, or misleading. So, to repeat the point in the previous paragraph using the language of evidence: If I have evidence supporting one conclusion, I will expect you to accept it and my conclusion, unless you can present evidence which is at least as strong for the opposite conclusion. It can be a very challenging task sorting through the evidence and deciding where it points most strongly, but we can all get better at it, if we just keep trying and applying ourselves.

An Argument Evaluation Flowchart

We have learned a great deal of information in the previous two chapters. These two chapters constitute the nucleus of the study of logic. There is of course more complexity, and we have only learned about arguments very generally. Mostly we have only learned the general terminology in dealing with evaluating arguments, and we will see that when we take more specific kinds of arguments, we can say and learn a lot more. The rest of the textbook is devoted to expanding that understanding.

Below is an Argument Evaluation Flowchart. One should understand that this chart is not intended to be followed mechanically, at least not once one internalizes the distinctions it encompasses. Once one develops some proficiency at argument evaluation, one can quickly evaluate an argument without referring to the flowchart at all.

Beginning students, however, might want to have the flowchart available when going through the exercises in this chapter, at least at first. Every student should quickly, however, internalize the flowchart, so that one need not consult it when evaluating an argument.

Chapter Seven Exercises

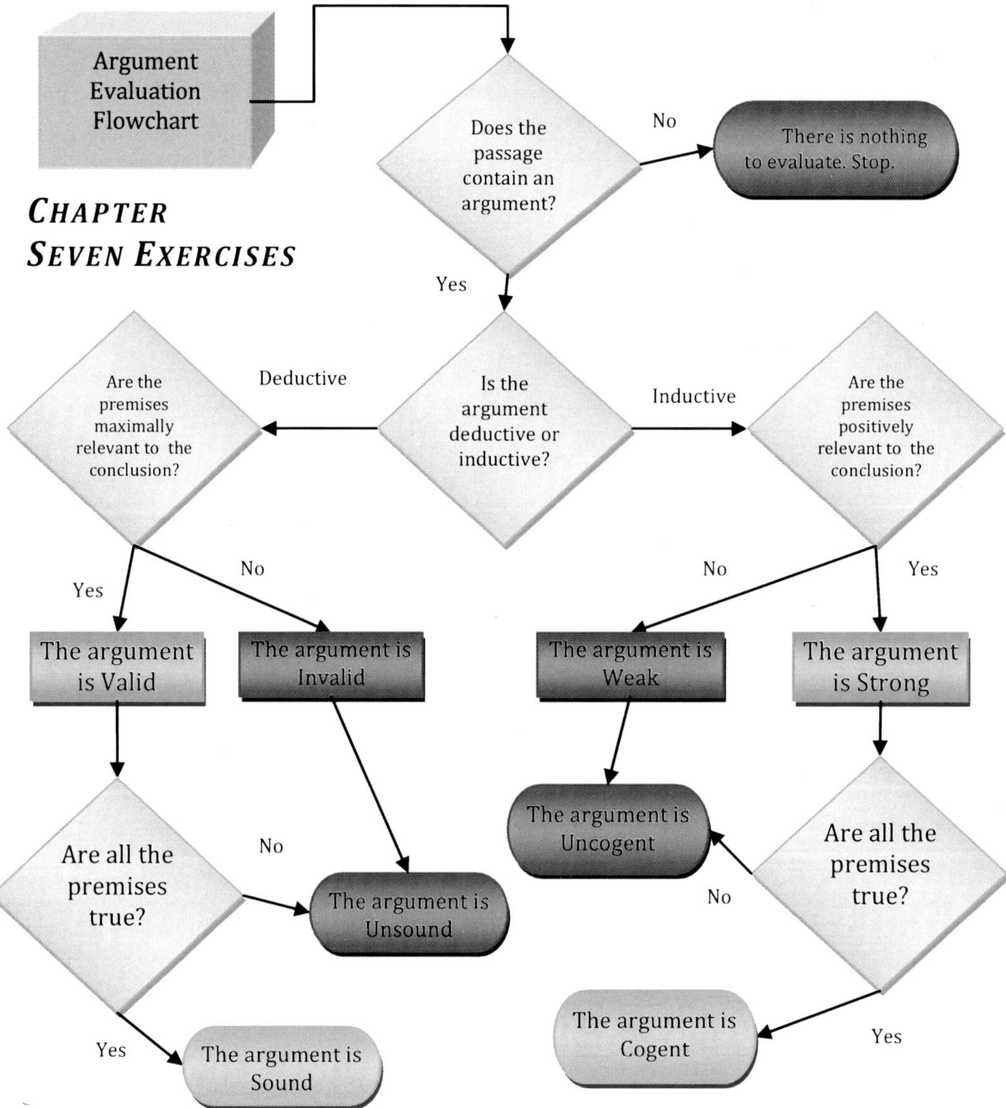

Basic Concept Exercises

For these exercises, determine whether the following inductive arguments are strong or weak, as well as cogent or uncogent when possible.

1. The fact that his fingerprints are on the murder weapon proves that he committed the crime.
2. If mankind were the cause of global warming, then how can you explain the fact that Mars and the other planets are also going through a warming phase.
3. Am I the only one who notices that every time Professor Jones tells us to read the book, she gives us a quiz? She just told us to read the book, so I'm pretty sure we have a quiz in our future.
4. I don't think you should go out and party tonight. You have a big test tomorrow, and you need your sleep. Plus, you know you'll end up spending money that you don't have.
5. The Los Angeles Times conducted a poll where 79% of registered voters said they were going to vote against Proposition 99. I conclude that Proposition 99 will not pass.
6. Most Republicans are opposed to expanding the definition of marriage to include homosexual unions. So, Ron Paul, who is a Republican, is probably opposed to homosexual unions.
7. Most Democrats are in favor of homosexual unions. President Obama is a Democrat, so he is probably in favor of them, too.
8. I was looking through this jar of coins, and of the ones I pulled out, (and I made sure to pull them out randomly), almost three-quarters of them (>75%)were minted in San Francisco. I conclude that, since I pulled out a significant number, at least half of the coins in the jar were minted in San Francisco.
9. I plugged my hair dryer into this outlet, and it worked, but the light that was plugged in before wasn't working. It must be that the lightbulb is busted, or else there is a problem with the wiring in the lamp.
10. Nobody can stay on the internet twenty four hours a day, so there must be some point, at night perhaps, where no one is on the internet.

Intermediate Exercises

For these exercises, decide whether the following statements are true or false.

11. Every strong argument is cogent.
12. Every cogent argument is strong.
13. If an argument is strong, then it has all true premises.
14. If an argument is weak, then it has at least one false premise.
15. If an argument is cogent, then it has all true premises.
16. If an inductive argument has all true premises, then it is cogent.
17. If an inductive argument has all true premises and a false conclusion, then it is weak.
18. If an inductive argument has all true premises and a probably false conclusion, then it is weak.
19. If an argument has all true premises and a true conclusion, then it is strong.

20. If an inductive argument has false premises, then it is weak.

Challenging exercises

For these exercises, determine whether the following inductive arguments are strong or weak, as well as cogent or uncogent when possible.

21. A referee should never be a player in the game in which he is officiating, but the government officiates in the disputes between businesses and individuals. That's why the government should never run businesses or even own them.
22. My economics professor said that the latest Supreme Court decision in favor of Walmart, which held that female employees could not sue as a class action, was a blessing. If the lawsuit were to go forward, it would have devastating effects on the economy. It looks like the Supreme Court made the right decision.
23. The reason you have Lyme disease is that you had a rash, a fever, and fatigue, and now you have swollen joints, Bell's palsy and failing coordination.
24. I know you have been saying that kids nowadays are getting out of control, but even Plato complained about children talking back to their parents.
25. If you believe that Nietzsche was a genius and had the right philosophy, and he held that Christianity was a slave religion, then how can you possibly be a Christian?
26. You voted for Barack Obama because you said that President Bush was a moron and had horrible policies like staying in Iraq and being divisive. But Barack Obama has kept the same policies in Iraq, which seems to show that he thinks Bush had the right policy. And President Obama is even more divisive than President Bush.
27. It seems to me that people who are presently in jail were much less likely to attend church regularly before they went to prison than the non-prison population. If the government is interested in getting people to not break the law, which it should be, then it should do everything it can to encourage people to attend church regularly.
28. If you don't have a political philosophy, what's the point of voting? If you don't know in what direction you want the government to go, or what justifies government in the first place, how do you know for whom to vote? Everyone should develop their own political philosophy before they cast their first ballot.
29. I don't understand how leftists can support state-sponsored lotteries. Sure, they redistribute money around, but they are the most regressive sort of "tax" imaginable. Poor people are the most desperate to play them, and turn over large portions of their income to the state. The state then spreads it around—not to everyone, but a few mega-rich people, at least they are after they win. It's the most disgusting way to take advantage of poor people imaginable.
30. The government doesn't have the right to stop people from doing what they want to do, and people want to gamble their money. If our state doesn't allow some kind of gambling, then people will spend that money in other states, improving those state's economies and hurting our own. Besides, we can use the money raised to support our schools.

In-Context Exercises

A. Take the dialog below and pull out all the inductive inferences, then decide whether the arguments are weak or strong, and if possible, uncogent, cogent, or compelling.

Annabelle: How's it going Drew?

Drew: All right, I guess. I just had a conversation with Anthony about the death penalty.

Annabelle: That leftie nutcake. I just ask him what he believes, and that tells me to believe the opposite.

Drew: That's a pretty odd way to form a belief system.

Annabelle: Take it easy, I was just being facetious. But I'll bet he was against the death penalty, wasn't he?

Drew: Actually, he was. Should I take it that you are in favor of it?

Annabelle: Of course, but I have good reasons for my beliefs.

Drew: What are they?

Annabelle: Well, for one thing, it's not cruel or unusual. The Supreme Court said so.

Drew: They said that it was cruel and unusual when it is arbitrarily applied.

Annabelle: True, but not the death penalty itself.

Drew: That's right, but do you believe everything the Supreme Court says?

Annabelle: Well, no, but the death penalty is only applied in horrendous cases, where someone viciously kills someone else. How cruel is that?

Drew: That is incredibly cruel, but I don't see how that means that the death penalty isn't cruel. I heard an argument in the Philosophy Club that went like this: Most murderers kill their victims quickly, which is still cruel, but the state sits the person in a box, telling them that they will be killed, even setting a time and having a big show of the death. Isn't that more cruel than the killing most murderers do?

Annabelle: So, now you have sympathy for the murderers? They're not people; they're more like animals. When an animal kills a person, we put them down. That's what we should do with these animals.

Drew: Maybe so, but what does that have to do with whether it is cruel?

Annabelle: Where do you stand? It sounds like you're on his side.

Drew: Actually, right now I'm on your side. I just want to make sure that we have good arguments.

Annabelle: Well, I'm confident that I'm on the right side. That's good enough for me.

Drew: Okay, but I'm going to keep thinking about it.

Annabelle: Whatever floats your boat. Later.

Drew: Later.

Logic Puzzle: Right to Life?

If something is not a fact then it is not true. For example, when I say it is not a fact that the Sun orbits the Earth, I mean that it is false that the Sun orbits the Earth. With this in mind, consider the following argument, written in standard form.

1) If it is false that someone has a right to life, then they can be killed for no reason.
2) An opinion is a belief.
3) There is a difference between facts and opinions.
4) ∴ If something is an opinion, then it is not a fact. (from 3)
5) It is the opinion of this author that all people have a right to life.
6) ∴ It is not a fact that all people have a right to life. (from 4 & 5, dep.)
7) If something is not a fact, then it is not true (it is false).
8) ∴ It is false that all people have a right to life. (from 6 & 7, dep.)
9) ∴ All people can be killed for no reason. (from 1 & 8, dep.)

Is there some flaw in the argument above? If so, what is it?

Objective and Subjective Statements

Teachers today have inculcated an almost instinctive tendency for students to see facts and opinions as two diametric opposites. There is, of course, a difference between the two, but there are problems with the unthinking nature that students have been trained to have on this issue. One problem with this view is illustrated in the logic puzzle at the end of Chapter Seven. If one is unable to see the flaw in the argument, it is because of the lack of wisdom imparted in our school system today.

The word "fact" is used in two very different senses. In one sense a "fact" is any true state of affairs in the world. If there is a massive black hole at the center of our galaxy, then it is a fact that there is a massive black hole at the center of our galaxy. If the pyramids were built by aliens, then it is not a fact that the pyramids were built solely by humans. Using this sense of the word, we can never be sure that something is a fact. After all, people will disagree about these issues all the time, and calling something a fact is saying little more than one thinks it is true.

Sometimes the word "fact" only refers to states of affairs which has been "proven" to be true. This sense of the word also has some difficulties, but it is meant to eliminate debate. After all, once something has been proven to be true, it could only be emotional stubbornness for anyone to disagree. This sense of the word is behind the expression that "one is entitled to one's opinions, but not to one's facts." This sense of the word is intended to provide a kind of universal agreement on what counts as a fact, which would be a very cohesive achievement.

The ambiguity arises when one states "It is not a fact that bigfoot exists." Does this statement mean that it is not proven but bigfoot exists, although he might, or does it mean that in fact, there is no such thing as a hairy hominid residing in the United States (besides my brother). The first interpretation uses the metaphysical sort of definition of "fact", and the second relies on the more epistemological definition, the one based on knowledge or proof.

The word "opinion" also seems to have a dichotomy of meanings. In one sense, we use the word "opinion" for any belief someone has, sometimes we use it to refer to factual type beliefs that people have with which we disagree, and sometimes we use it to refer to certain kinds of statements which we don't think it is appropriate to call facts. The first sense is clear enough. The second sense is evident in a situation when someone says "Bigfoot exists" and one responds "That's your opinion." This sense of the word relies on the epistemological definition of "fact" and uses "opinion" as the correlative term. The third sense of the term mentioned above encompasses things like judgments and such claims as "Sublime is the greatest rock band ever."

The most unfortunate part of all of this is that people don't understand the different senses with which these terms are used, and muddle them all together. Sometimes students immediately dismiss an argument because it involves what they take to be statements of opinion. Perhaps on one meaning of "opinion" it would be appropriate to do so, but not on all of them.

In order to cleave through the confusion, we will introduce to other terms, ones with which most students are already familiar, but perhaps not intimately. We introduce the terms "objective" and "subjective". An objective statement is the kind of statement where the individual's interests, desires, or point of view is irrelevant to the truth of the statement. A subjective statement is one whose truth does depend on the interests, desires, or point of view of the subject of experience.

The statement that "the Earth orbits the Sun" is an objective statement. Its truth OR falsity does not depend on whatever anyone thinks. It is either true or false, and whatever people think does not change the matter of fact of whether it is true. Of course, in deciding whether it is true or false, human beings must use their reasoning and observational skills to gather as much evidence as they can, and ultimately they will make a judgment as to whether they believe that it is true, and is thus a fact (def 1), or to turn it into a fact (def 2). Either way, it is an objective statement.

The statement that "Sushi is delicious" does not seem to most people to be an objective kind of statement. It isn't just that people disagree about it; people disagree about clearly objective statements all the time. The idea is that if someone believes it to be true, then for that person it really is true. If I think sushi is delicious, then for me it really is delicious, and if you think it is not, then for you it isn't. Moreover, if I change my mind, then I change the truth of the statement. There really is no matter of fact, or objective reality which decides the issue.

When deciding whether a premise is true or false, then it may be useful to distinguish between whether a statement is objectively true, or subjectively true, but the important point is whether one believes it to be true. Students sometimes have the sense that there can be no reasoning involving subjective statements, but nothing could be further from the truth. We can of course reason from subjective statements, and if we care about logical consistency, to subjective statements.

Imagine if someone said "I love every song ever sung by the Clash." This certainly sounds like a purely subjective statement to me (even though it seems like a simple dichotomy between objective and subjective, moral statements and some other judgments lead some to believe that there must be some kind of middle ground between them). Yet, we can certainly imagine the dialog continuing:

"Don't you hate that song "Should I Stay, or Should I Go?"

"Yeah, it's way too 'pop-py'."

"The Clash sings it."

"Okay, I love most every song that the Clash sings."

There is certainly reasoning occurring here, even though there is both a subjective premise and a subjective conclusion. Logic intrudes even into the purely subjective realm, at least in some cases in some fashion. One cannot avoid logic by retreating into a subjective bubble, unless one thinks it makes sense to say both "I love every Clash song," and "I hate one song sung by the Clash," at the same time.

Ultimately, the point here is to not short-circuit the evaluative process. Don't assume that a passage is not an argument because it involves subjective statements. For one thing, you might be wrong, but for another, subjective statements can be parts of an argument. Also, don't assume an argument cannot be deductive because it has subjective statements. Finally, do not assume that an argument is invalid or unsound because it involves subjective issues. You may be sorely mistaken.

Yes, when evaluating whether a deductive argument is sound or an inductive argument is cogent, one must decide whether the premises are true. You are entitled to make a judgment, whether the issue is a subjective one or an objective one. If it is a purely subjective statement, then people can have different judgments, and each will be equally justified. Just don't avoid making a judgment at all because someone might have a different judgment.

CHAPTER

8

Categorical Statements

So far we've covered the basics in a very general way. You've learned about the distinction between deductive and inductive arguments, and you've learned the basic terminology used to evaluate such arguments. Now we will turn to some specific kinds of arguments where we can begin to apply and expand upon what we have learned.

Skill 8.1

Recognizing Categorical Statements

The first kind of arguments we will examine in detail have a long history. That renowned philosopher Aristotle first examined them in great detail over 2300 years ago. He had heard the Sophists claim that they could make the "weaker argument the stronger one", and he wanted to show that they were mistaken in an objective sense. Aristotle knew that the Sophists could persuade people that a weak argument was a strong one by using rhetorical tricks, but he argued that there were objective features of certain arguments that made one stronger or weaker independently of what a person could be persuaded to think.

Aristotle developed a way of systematizing arguments which is generally called **categorical logic**. Aristotle's writings had such influence in the Middle Ages that people were constrained by his writings. His incredible advances in his day actually hindered logicians over a thousand years later from making the advances they otherwise might have made. Although modern logicians tend not to use categorical logic, it is still useful to learn at least the basics. If an argument is clearly worded in a way amenable to categorical reasoning, it is still often used. One technique for analyzing categorical logic, **Venn diagrams**, is also widely used in many applications today. There are also a few basic ideas which will be introduced here which are important for avoiding mistaken reasoning in a practical sense. For all these reasons, we will still learn a few things from Aristotle.

Categorical Logic
The logic which deals with group membership or exclusion

Venn Diagrams
A way to visually depict the relationship between two or more groups

Let's examine an argument. I am hoping that it will help convince you of the importance of careful thought involving this type of reasoning. Consider the following example:

> A racist is someone who thinks that white people should be treated differently than people in other races. Anyone who supports race-based affirmative action thinks that white people should be treated differently than people in other races. Therefore, anyone who supports affirmative action is a racist.

Skill 8.2

Drawing Basic Venn Diagrams

This is certainly a controversial argument, but the whole point of learning logic is to not let one's preconceived notions dictate whether to accept or reject a conclusion. So, the question here is whether this is a good argument, i.e. a sound argument (since it is deductive). As with all deductive arguments, we need to ask whether the argument is valid, and whether all the premises are true. No doubt many people will intuitively reject the argument, merely because they support affirmative action and don't consider themselves to be racists, or because they believe that racists generally are against affirmative action. Whether these criticisms are helpful or not, they still do not clarify what the problem with the argument is. If the argument is sound, then we have a powerful reason to alter our beliefs. Perhaps some of us really are racists and are unaware of it.

First, let's consider the argument in reverse order. Are the premises true? The first premise says that a racist is someone who thinks white people should be treated differently from people in other races. The first thing to ask is whether the premise is meant to be applied to all racists or to just some particular ones. Even though the article "a" is used, in this context it would seem to be applied to all racists. If it is true, then it is saying that every racist thinks that people should be treated differently because of race. So, is that true?

The question here turns to how we can know whether this statement is true. Would we need to ask every single person who is a racist? Can we know it to be true just based on definitions, or perhaps an intuitive judgment? Without a supporting argument, logic is irrelevant. We can attempt to provide an argument, and analyze it, or perhaps we can just rely on the credibility of the person asserting it. Unfortunately, in this context, we have stripped away the argument from any context, so we don't know the source. We can rely on our background worldview, but then our judgment is only as good as our worldview.

Perhaps we can take a simpler approach. We may not get certainty, but we can get a provisional judgment. If you are familiar with the concept of a "working definition", you'll understand this approach. Can you imagine a person who was a racist who insisted that every person must be treated equally? These two ideas seem incongruent to me. I don't think I would call such a person a racist. This judgment seems enough to me to ground a provisional judgment that the first premise is true. I am open, however, to being disproven, should someone find a person that we agree is a racist who does insist that no one should be treated differently because of race.

The second premise seems to be true as well. Affirmative action programs (at least those which are race-based) imply divergent treatment for people of different races. I can't imagine a person saying they support affirmative action, and yet insisting that every person be treated entirely without regard to race. Treating all races the same is not affirmative action, it is just impartiality. This reasoning leads me to think that all supporters of affirmative action do want to treat people in different races differently.

Does this mean that the conclusion must be true? Are all supporters of affirmative action racist, regardless of their protestations? After all, no one wants to admit that they are racist. Since the premises are true, the only question left is whether the argument is valid. Let's rewrite the argument, trying to make the logic more clear. "All racists are people who think white people should be treated differently than people in other races. All supporters of affirmative action are people who think that white people should be treated differently than people in other races. Therefore, all supporters of affirmative action are racist." Are the premises maximally relevant to the conclusion? If the premises were true, would they guarantee that the conclusion is true?

I hope you can see why it is so important that we come up with a systematic way to deal with such arguments. Otherwise, our emotions may just be too strong for us to deal with the argument fairly. It may be too hard to analyze the argument properly. In this case, supporters of affirmative action can rest easy; the argument is invalid. The truth of these premises does not guarantee the truth of this conclusion. Be careful though; the fact that this argument is invalid does not guarantee that supporters of affirmative action are not racist. It just means that this argument as stated does not guarantee that they are.

If you thought the argument was valid, it could be because you fell prey to the fallacy of illicit conversion. One of the important things to learn from this chapter is that this form of argument is fallacious, and doesn't work logically, because saying that "All A are B" is not the same as saying "All B are A." The second statement could be false even if the first statement is true. We will learn more about this fallacy in the tenth chapter.

Here is a different argument: "All people who think that people in different races should be treated differently are racists. All supporters of affirmative action are people who think that white people should be treated differently than people in other races. Therefore, all supporters of affirmative action are racist." This argument is a valid one. The truth of the premises does ensure the truth of the conclusion. So, if the premises were true, then the argument would be sound. Is it true that every person who thinks that people should be treated differently because of their race is a racist?

I'll leave that question for you to consider either on your own or in your other classes. For now, let's summarize. Arguments which involve groupings of things are called categorical arguments. They are common, and are a good test of one's basic logical skills. To help you develop your skills in categorical reasoning, let's start again with the basics.

Basic Venn Diagrams

Take the names of any two groups of things in the universe; it will always be the case that they will fall into one of five basic categories. They might point out the exact same objects, there may be absolutely no overlap between them, they may have some overlap, or one could be a subset of the other or vice versa. These possibilities are captured using Euler circles in Figure 8.2. The problem is that we may not know into which category the pair fall.

When we know all about the two groups, then it's easy to choose the right diagram. For example, dogs and cats. It's easy to see that the correct diagram is the one in the third box, but what if you were asked to diagram these two groups: philatelists and numismatists. Which diagram would you choose?

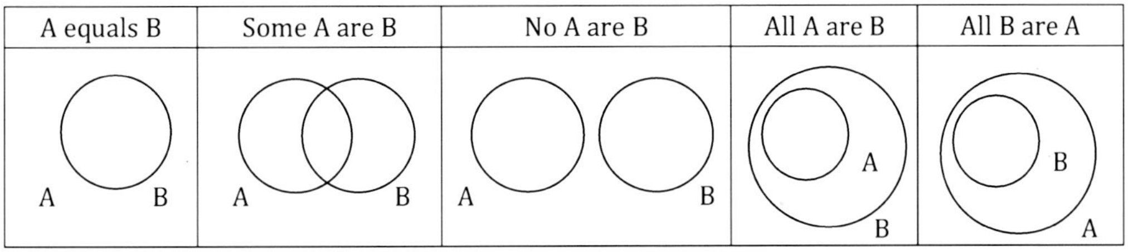

A equals B	Some A are B	No A are B	All A are B	All B are A
A B	A B	A B	A B	B A

Figure 8.1 Euler Circles

In order to avoid this issue, we will always use the same basic diagram for every two groups. Instead of placing one circle within another, we will always draw our diagram with overlapping circles, and we will use shading to indicate that a particular area is empty. This style of graphical representation was developed by John Venn, and these diagrams are commonly referred to as Venn diagrams.

Each of the five diagrams can be drawn using Venn diagrams, as is shown in Figure 8.2. If you look closely, you will see that each Venn diagram and its corresponding Euler circle have the same number of open areas. Both kinds of diagrams are functionally equivalent, but Venn diagrams have the benefit that you don't need to erase and draw a different diagram if you get more information; all you need to do is shade an area if it becomes clear that it is empty.

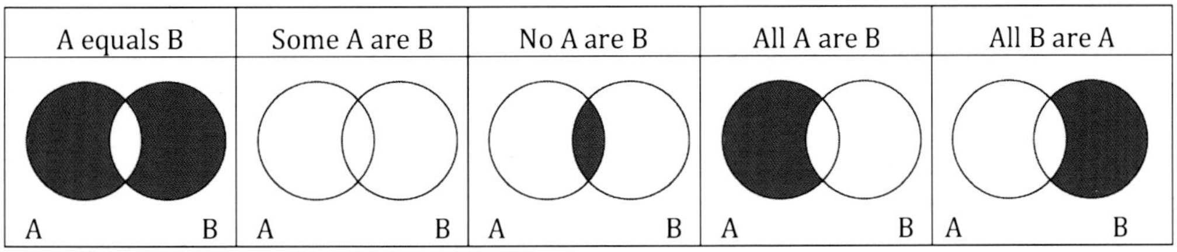

A equals B	Some A are B	No A are B	All A are B	All B are A
A B	A B	A B	A B	A B

Figure 8.2 Venn Diagrams

Students who have already learned about Venn diagrams in a math class may actually be at a disadvantage here, unless they can straighten out one distinction in their minds. In math classes, sometimes an area is highlighted to identify it. For example, say we had a Venn diagram representing even numbers and prime numbers. One might want to point out the region of the diagram where a number is both even and prime. This region is called the intersection of the two groups, and it is written $E \cap P$. If you were asked to highlight the region corresponding to $E \cap P$, you would do so as in the figure 8.3. It just so happens that there is a number in this area: the number 2, which is both even and prime. When we are highlighting, we are not asserting that an area is empty; we are only pointing to a designated area on the diagram.

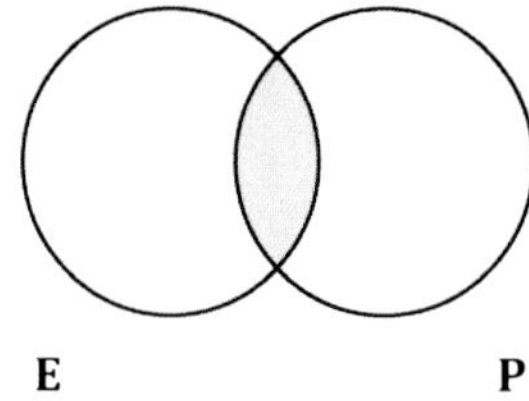

Figure 8.3: $E \cap P$

Another example of Venn diagrams in math is shown in Figure 8.4. To designate the area signified by the expression, E union P, or $E \cup P$, we would highlight any area which is within either E or P. The interior of both circles is entirely highlighted. Again, we are not indicating that these areas are empty; we are only pointing out the area to which we are referring. This use of highlighting is very different from the shading done in logic. In logic, when you shade an area on a Venn diagram, you are asserting that the area is empty; that there is nothing in that area. Leaving an area open does not mean that it definitely does have anything in it, but it does allow for that possibility. Shading an area closes it off, and says that there is definitely nothing in that area. As we will see shortly, to assert that there is definitely something in an area, we will draw an 'x' in that area.

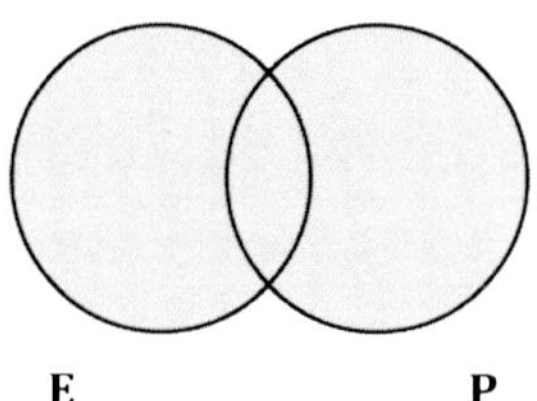

Figure 8.4: $E \cup P$

Complete Venn diagrams

If we knew everything, then we wouldn't need logic. The point of logic is to try to build on what we know (mostly inductive logic), or to ensure that we remain consistent (mostly deductive logic). If we are very familiar with two groups of things we probably wouldn't be arguing about them, and we wouldn't need to draw Venn diagrams. Yet, seeing a Venn diagram in such a situation might help us to understand how useful such diagrams are in other cases.

Let's just use the simple two categories of cats and dogs. Knowing what we know about cats and dogs, it should be very easy to draw a complete Venn diagram for these two groups. We know that there are no such things as animals which are both cats and dogs (unless you are watching Nickelodeon), so the intersection of the two will be empty. We also know that there are some things which are dogs, and that there are some things which are cats. We also know that there are some things which are neither cats nor dogs. If we put all of that together, we will get the Venn diagram in Figure 8.5. As you can see, we mark the known existence of something with an 'x'. This diagram captures the basic information about each area, whether it is empty or has something in it. We don't leave any area blank, because we have knowledge about each area, and can mark it appropriately. We also only use one 'x' for an area with

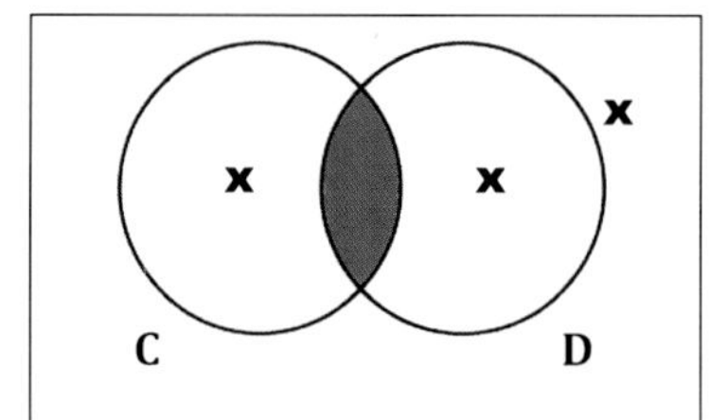

Figure 8.5: Cats and Dogs

something in it because at this basic level we are not interested in the size of each group, or more complicated probability spaces. We just want to know whether the area is empty or not.

Let's try one more. If we decided to make a complete diagram for mammals and dogs, we would get a different picture. It is true that all dogs are mammals, so nothing can be a dog unless it is a mammal. This tells us that one area of our diagram will be empty. Our diagram is displayed in Figure 8.6. We know that the area corresponding to dogs which are not mammals is empty and is therefore shaded. We also know that there are such things as dogs (which are also mammals), that there are such things as mammals which are not dogs (such as cats), and that there are things which are neither mammals nor dogs, such as plants.

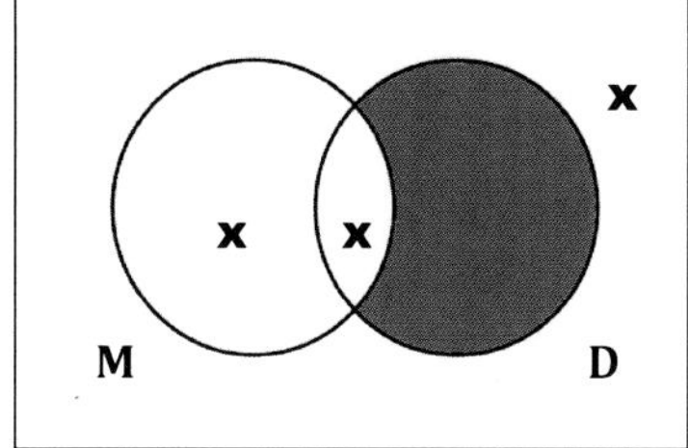

Figure 8.6: Mammals and Dolphins

To say that we understand the logic of some situation or issue is in many cases no more than saying that someone understands what the complete Venn diagram would look like for a group of terms. Not knowing what the complete Venn diagram looks like for any two (or more) groups of things will obviously lead to an inability to assert things about those groups, or perhaps can lead to incorrect conclusions. For example, consider the two groups "fish" and "dolphins". One who has an incorrect picture of the correct Venn diagram for these two groups would hardly be a credible source regarding any statements involving them. The correct diagram is shown in Figure 8.7. There are no such things as fish which are dolphins. They are two different kinds of animals.

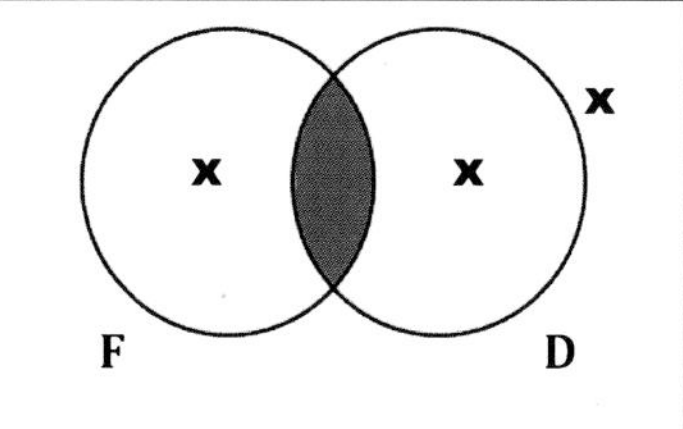

Figure 8.7: Fish and Dolphins

Comprehension Check Exercises

For each of the following pairs of terms, draw a complete Venn diagram. See the box on the next page for the correct answers. Do some quick research if necessary. For the last pair, I constructed a Venn diagram using the following definitions: a fact is a true statement about an objective matter and an opinion is any belief. You may choose other definitions.

a. Sound arguments / Valid arguments
b. Sound arguments / Invalid arguments
c. Mammals / Marsupials
d. Sharks / Fish
e. Smart people / Democrats
f. Smart people / Republicans
g. People whom you love / People whom you will marry
h. Facts / Opinions

The Four Categorical Statements

It is not always the case that we are aware of all the categorical information about two groups. We may only have partial information, from which we would like to know what else

Skill 8.3

Classifying Categorical Statements

term
A word or phrase which represents a group or collection of individuals

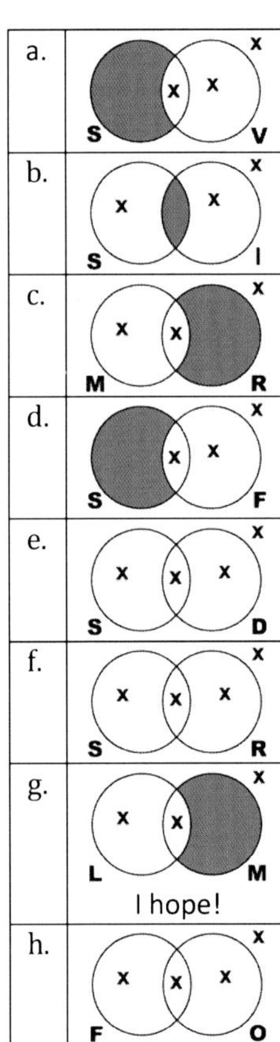

follows. Even when we do know completely about two groups, we may want to focus only on the connections between certain pieces of information, or we may want to concentrate only on the premises which we have been given in an argument. For these reasons, we will refrain from drawing complete Venn diagrams, and will be learning to draw Venn diagrams in situations where we only have partial information. We are given partial information about group membership through the assertion of categorical statements. We will look in particular at four basic patterns.

Let's say that we have two groups of things, and we are saying something about them. One of the groups will be in the subject of our statement, and one will be in the predicate. Let's call the group referred to in the subject the "subject term" and the group referred to in the predicate the "predicate term". When we are discussing the subject term, we can be referring to either all of the members of the group or only some[4] of them, and we can be saying that they are included in the predicate group, or that they are excluded. Combining these dichotomies gives us four possible combinations. We can assert of all members of the subject term that they are included in the predicate term, or that they are excluded, and we can assert that some members of the subject term are included in the predicate term, or that they are excluded. All of this may sound very complicated, but it is really very simple, as hopefully you can see in the following table.

	Included	Excluded
All members	All S are P.	No S are P.
Some members	Some S are P.	Some S are not P.

Let's use some special terminology for each of these possibilities. A universal statement refers to all members of the subject term, whereas a particular statement refers to some of them. An affirmative statement refers to group inclusion, whereas a negative statement refers to exclusion. So, we have four possible types of statements with which to deal. Using the new terminology, our table can be redrawn.

	Affirmative	Negative
Universal	A: All S are P.	E: No S are P.
Particular	I: Some S are P.	O: Some S are not P.

We will follow tradition and use a capital vowel letter to refer to each of the four statements, as you can see in the table above. When we call a statement an A-statement, we will mean a universal affirmative statement. A particular negative statement can be referred to as an O-type statement.

Every statement has a corresponding Venn diagram. For example, "A" statements always have the same diagram. So, there are four specific Venn diagrams which correspond to the four categorical statements. Make sure you understand why each statement corresponds with its Venn diagram. Keep in mind that an area that is shaded is empty; it is blocked so that no individual can be placed inside that area. If we definitely know that an area has something in it, we place an "x" within that area. If an area is not shaded and it doesn't have an "x", then

---

[4] Students should be aware that logicians use the word "some" in a bit of a technical sense. The word "some" can't have a vague meaning if we are to use it in deductive arguments, so logicians define "some" to mean "at least one". So, it is true that "some even numbers are prime", even though the number two is the only even prime number.

we do not know whether that area is empty or not. There might be something in it, or there might not be. Figure 8.9 shows the Venn diagram for each of the four categorical statements. There are no exceptions. *Every* A statement is diagrammed in the following fashion no matter what terms are used, and the same is true of each of the other statements.

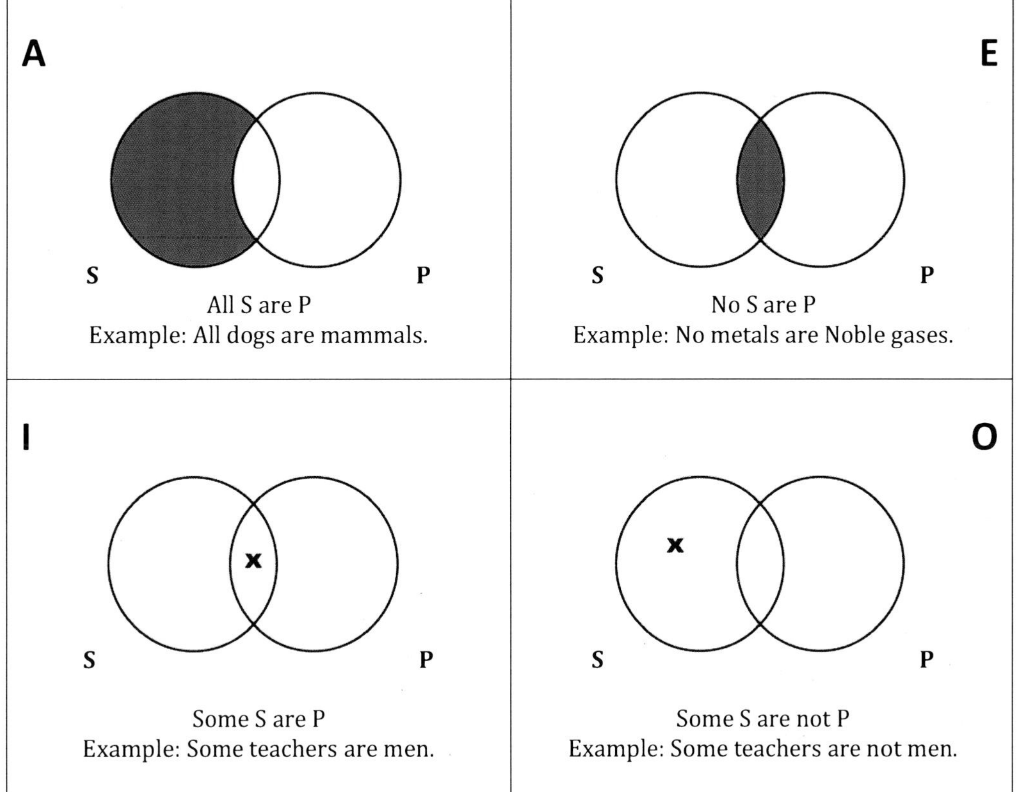

Figure 8.9

Examine the A statement example. The subject term is "dogs" and the predicate term is "mammals". The statement asserts that every member of S is also a member of P, which is true in this case. We show this by shading in the area of S which is outside of P on our diagram. According to the statement, this area is empty, so we can shade it in. For ease of reference, we can call this area the "left crescent", the "S crescent", "S difference P" written S/P, SP-bar written $S\overline{P}$, or simply "area 1", as in Figure 8.10.

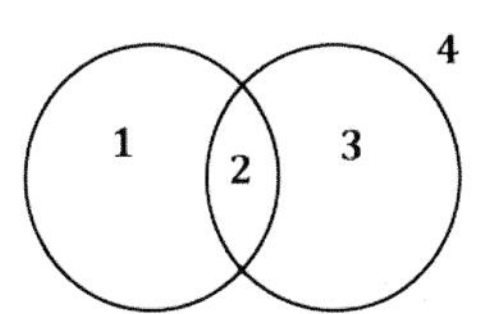

Figure 8.10

The E statement works in the same way. The statement asserts that there are no individuals that are in both S and P, so we shade area 2, which can be called the "middle area" or the "football area". Since the area is empty, according to the E statement, we shade it to show that nothing will fit inside of it.

The I statement works a bit differently. An I statement does not assert that an area is empty, but rather that it is non-empty, or that it has some member inside of it. Since the I statement asserts that there is at least one individual who is both a member of S and a member of P, we draw an "x" in area 2 to mark that individual. Keep in mind that there may be more individuals in the area, but if the I statement is true, there must be at least one member in that area.

An O statement asserts that there is at least one member of S which is outside of P. We have to diagram this individual somewhere on our Venn diagram, and it must be inside of the S circle, but outside of the P circle. The only region which fits these criteria is area 1, so we mark an "x" there.

Meaning versus Implication

There are some clarifications which need to be made in order to avoid a great deal of confusion later on. One distinction to be made clear is that of meaning versus implication. In the strict sense, the meaning of a statement is simply what the words of the statement themselves mean. The implication of the statement is what follows from it. Unfortunately, people often conflate the two. When someone asks "what do you mean by that?" he sometimes is looking for the strict meaning, and sometimes for the implication.

We make this distinction to avoid some confusion regarding particular statements. If we are going to determine whether an I or O statement is true, we need to know what these statements mean. What does someone mean when they say "Some teachers are smart people"? In particular, does this also mean that "Some teachers are not smart people"? It is so easy to slip from the truth of the I statement to the truth of the O statement, but a few examples should make it clear that they do not mean the same thing. They are separable statements, and one should always be careful to ensure that these two statements are always considered separate.

First, it should be clear that some mammals are dogs. The statement asserting that fact, specifically "Some mammals are dogs", is a true statement. We can find at least one mammal which is a dog. Similarly, it should be true that "Some dogs are mammals". Some people seem to balk at this statement. It sounds strange to say that "Some dogs are mammals", presumably because all dogs are mammals. Since it is true that all dogs are mammals, it would be odd to say that some dogs are mammals. Since we are entitled to assert the stronger statement, why would we limit ourselves to the weaker one?

This is a legitimate question, and in ordinary contexts, it is possible that someone who said that some S are P when they knew that all S are P might be misleading someone. But we are interested here in deciding whether the statement is true or false. Is it true or false that some dogs are mammals? It can't be false. Imagine what it would mean to say it is false that some dogs are mammals. That would mean that no dogs are mammals, which is obviously wrong.

To say that some dogs are mammals does not mean, by itself, that some dogs are not mammals. To say that some teachers are smart does not mean that some teachers are not smart. It just means that some teachers are smart. Here is an example which may clarify the distinction. Let's say it is a bit dark, and I reach into my sock drawer and pull out a black sock. I'm not looking for a black sock, so I put it back. I can say for sure that some of the socks in the drawer are black (remember that we limit "some" to mean "at least one"), but that does not imply that all of the socks in the drawer are black, nor does it imply that some of the socks in the drawer are not black. All it means is that some of the socks in the drawer are black.

There is a big difference between the two statements "some dogs are mammals" and "only some dogs are mammals". The word "only" changes the meaning of the statement. When we say "only some dogs are mammals" we are saying that some dogs are mammals and some dogs are not mammals. That turns out to be false, but it is true that only some mammals are dogs, since some mammals are not dogs.

Remember that we are considering partial Venn diagrams. We are not necessarily bringing every piece of information that we know to the table. We can do that separately, but when we are evaluating an argument, we need to look at the premises given. We can add premises that are true and that we happen to know independently, but we must recognize that those premises are added, and that no matter what S and P represent, the statement that "some S are P" by itself does not mean "some S are not P", nor does it mean "only some S are P" or "it is false that all S are P".

There is one other clarification that must be made. What does it mean to say that "All S are P"? Obviously, it means that there are no members of S which are outside of P, but there is a fundamental ambiguity here. Do the words "All S are P" necessarily mean that there is actually an S that is a P? Does the statement "All S are P" necessarily imply that "Some S are P". The answer is that it doesn't, at least not all by itself. If you don't understand why, don't worry, you are in good company. Aristotle himself, and many generations of philosophers after him, did not recognize this distinction, but it exists, and it marks a major difference between traditional and modern logic.

Consider the statement "All students over seven feet tall in my class who earned over 90% on the exam received an A." Is this statement true or false? The important issue is if I claim the statement is true, am I implying that there is a student in my class who is over seven feet tall, and who also received over 90% on the exam? Modern logicians think not. They hold that an A statement can be true even when the subject term is non-existent.

The question here involves whether the truth of an A statement necessarily implies the truth of the corresponding I statement. Can an A statement be true even when its corresponding I statement is false? The answer is that it can be, but only on the condition that the subject term does not exist.

For example, I would say that it is true that "All students over seven feet tall in my class who earned over 90% received an A." The fact that there are no such students doesn't seem to be enough to make the statement false. The statement is true because it captures the condition under which someone would receive an A. It doesn't matter whether anyone actually meets that condition. So, this universal statement can be true even if there are no students who earned above a 90% or received an A.

On the other hand, particular statements do require their subject terms to exist in order to be true. The statement that "Some students over seven feet tall in my class who earned over 90% on the exam received an A" cannot be true unless there is such a student. If there are no such students then the statement is false.

This example shows that it is possible, when the subject term does not exist, for an A statement to be true, and the I statement which matches it to be false. Technically, the inference from an A statement to an I statement is invalid. We will see in the next chapter how this distinction affects inferences in other ways, but it is important to realize that an A statement by itself does not require that anything exist in order to be true. Saying that an A statement is true does not *mean* that its subject term exists.

Formally speaking, universal statements do not have existential import, while particular statements do have existential import. One cannot infer a statement that implies that something exists from one which does not, at least not validly. One is not precluded from adding a premise that something exists, but a good logician must realize that a premise with existential import must be added to a universal statement in order to validly derive a conclusion with existential import.

Basic Paraphrasing Into Standard Form

In Chapter 13 we will return to paraphrasing categorical statements much in greater detail, but in this opening chapter we should learn a few of the basics. People rarely speak or write using standard form categorical statements, so it is important to learn how to translate statements into standard form if one wants to apply what one learns to arguments people actually make. Here we will learn about statements with missing nouns and quantifiers, and non-standard verbs and quantifiers.

Missing nouns

While actual standard form may be rare in general discourse, sometimes people get very close by only leaving out a predicate term. When an adjective is used in the predicate of a sentence which modifies the subject of the sentence, the result is a predicate adjective.

Examples: Some Presidents are competent.
All Presidents are incompetent.

In the first example, the word "competent" modifies the subject term "Presidents." The word "competent is not a term, however, since it does not contain a plural noun. This problem is easy enough to fix, however, by adding a plural noun. The first example becomes "Some Presidents are incompetent leaders," and the second example becomes "All Presidents are incompetent executives." Usually it is best to add a larger term than the subject, so that the subject term is a subclass of the predicate, but the particular choice will depend on context.

Missing quantifiers and the indefinite article

Examples: Marsupials are mammals.
Insects are flying creatures.
A great white shark is a fish.
A woman is the CEO of Yahoo.

Often people will leave out a quantifier altogether. Such quantificational ambiguity leads to quite a bit of confusion and misunderstanding. Using standard form allows us to be much more clear. The problem is that in some cases, such statements are universal and in others they are particular. The same thing can be said about statements which begin with the indefinite article "a". Great care must be exercised to understand these statements and paraphrase them correctly.

The general principle to be used is that such statements should be turned into universal statements when the universal statement would be true, and particular statements when the particular statement would be true. The first example should be a universal statement, because it is true that "All marsupials are mammals." The second example, however, would be false as a universal; not all insects are flying creatures, such as . So, it should be rendered as "Some insects are flying creatures."

In the same way, one of the examples beginning with "a" should be treated as universal and the other as particular. All sharks are fish, so the third example should be paraphrased as "All great white sharks are fish." It is also clear that not every woman is the CEO of Yahoo. In this case, we should use "Some women are CEO's of Yahoo. Notice that we simply turned the singular subject and verb into their plural forms as well.

Non-standard verbs

Examples: No animals were harmed.
Some insects fly.

Often the verb used in a statement is a form of the infinitive "to be" which is not "are". Any such verb is still considered a copula, or linking verb, but the statement containing it would not be in standard form. Every such statement must be rewritten so that it does contain the verb "are". The first example includes a past tense verb. We should also make sure that a predicate term is included. The first example becomes "No animals are creatures who were harmed."

The second example doesn't include a copula at all, but an action verb. Somehow we need to add a copula, as well as a predicate term. In this case, we can use "Some insects are flying creatures" or "Some insects are creatures which fly."

Non-standard quantifiers

Examples: Any student who wants to pass better study.
A bunch of students are studying at the library.

Standard form only allows three quantifiers, but in English there are many others. So, any statement with a nonstandard quantifier must be paraphrased. Quantifiers such as "each", "every", and "any" are universal and will be replaced by "all", with any other adjustments necessary being made as well. "None" and "not any" can be replaced by "No." Our first example becomes "All students who want to pass are students who better study."

Remember that we are using the word "some" in a technical sense, and so any quantifier which indicates that at least one member of the subject is included in the predicate will use the quantifier "some." Some examples are "a couple", "a few", "several", "a number of" and "numerous". So, our second example can be written as "Some students are people who are studying at the library."

There are always two considerations when paraphrasing an ordinary language categorical statement into standard form. The first is that it actually must be in standard form, and the second is that the meaning of the original is retained in the paraphrase. As long as these criteria are met, the paraphrase will be successful.

Chapter Eight Exercises

Paraphrase each of the following statements using standard form categorical statements, then diagram each one using a Venn diagram. Make sure both the subject and the predicate terms are *terms*. Some of these exercises will require significant paraphrasing in order to fit standard categorical form. If you can, state whether the statement is true or false.

Basic Concept Exercises

1. Some diseases are not curable.
2. Every animal that has hair is a mammal.
3. No diamonds are rubies.
4. Some animals are vertebrates.
5. Some clowns are funny.

6. No clowns are scary.
7. All diamonds are hard.
8. All diamonds are white.
9. All categorical statements are true.
10. Some categorical statements have ambiguities.

Intermediate Exercises

11. Bats are mammals.
12. Dolphins are not mammals.
13. There are happy marriages.
14. Children should be seen and not heard.
15. Fast food restaurants serve burgers.
16. No one who teaches logic is unable to do proofs.
17. Every time I travel is a time I lose my luggage.
18. A few Presidents have worn beards.
19. Many Presidents have been left-handed.
20. Not a single American President has been an only child.

Challenging exercises

21. Each logic student must learn to do proofs if he wants to pass.
22. The Constitution forbids cruel and unusual punishment.
23. Only citizens are allowed to vote.
24. The only citizens who are not allowed to vote are felons.
25. We should remove all pollutants from our water.
26. If you're a fan of Justin Bieber, then you must be a pre-teen girl.
27. My nephews are fans of Justin Bieber.
28. My nephews are all adults.
29. It is false that every teacher is a professor.
30. It is not the case that no mammals are oceanic creatures.

In-Context Exercises

A. In the following dialog, the starred lines can be understood as basic categorical statements. How many of them can you rewrite in standard form?

Samantha: Hey David. How's it going?
David: All right. I've been really thinking about something, though.
Samantha: What's that?
David: I just can't seem to get an A on any of my logic tests.*
Samantha: Do you usually get A's on tests in your other classes?
David: That's just it. I've gotten an A on every test I've taken so far.*
Samantha: Sometimes a class is just harder than others.*
David: It looks like logic classes are the hardest of all.*
Samantha: Do you understand the textbook?
David: Well, I never bought the textbook.*
Samantha: You can't pass if you don't read the textbook!*
David: I know, I know, but I have read the book in the library.

Samantha: At least that's something. Do you do the homework?
David: Not all of it.*
Samantha: Maybe that's your problem.
David: Maybe. But it seems like I understand everything we go over in class.*
Samantha: Have you talked to your professor?
David: No, I haven't talked to any of my professors.*
Samantha: That's probably where you should start. When are his office hours?
David: She doesn't have any.*
Samantha: Really?
David: Yeah, but she did offer to meet outside of class.
Samantha: Why haven't you done that?
David: I don't know. No reason, I guess.
Samantha: Are you just going to wait until she asks you personally?
David: No. I suppose I probably should ask to meet her at some point.
Samantha: You should ask the very next time you see her.
David: I will.
Samantha: Good. In other matters, how's your love life?
David: Every girl I know asks me that.*
Samantha: Oh, yeah.
David: Yeah. And no one who asks me that question is ever interested in a relationship* with me. What does that tell you about my love life?

Logic Puzzle: Cosmology and Epistemology

Given these two true statements, answer the following questions.

1) Some cosmologists are philosophers.
2) All epistemologists are philosophers.

True or false: it necessarily follows that some cosmologists are epistemologists?

True or false: it is still possible that some cosmologists are epistemologists?

CHAPTER

9

Immediate Inferences and the Square of Opposition

In the previous chapter, we learned about individual categorical statements. Logic generally does not concern individual statements. It is important, however, to fully understand individual categorical statements, both to make sure we build a good foundation for continuing, but also for better communication. We can't really understand what someone is saying if we improperly interpret their categorical statements.

Immediate Inference
An argument with one premise which leads directly to its conclusion

When we begin to reason using categorical statements, then logic is required. An **immediate inference** is an argument which relies on a single premise. A single statement is given as the reason to believe another statement. As in all deductive inferences, the aim is for the conclusion to follow with maximal relevance, so that the argument is a valid argument. If so, then anyone who believes the premise would have an overwhelming reason to believe the conclusion as well.

It may seem like there is not much complexity to categorical immediate inferences, since there are only four standard forms for categorical statements. There can only be a limited number of inferences available for four statements (12, excluding blatantly circular arguments). If we add the possibility of false claims, the number of inferences jumps to 56. Once we add term complements in the next chapter, the number of possible immediate inferences expands enormously. For example, one might ask whether the claim "It is true that all S are P" is relevant to the claim "It is false that no non-P are non-S". To use a more commonplace example, does the fact that "All people who voted for Johnson are conservative" imply that "It is false that no liberals are people who did not vote for Johnson." (Answer: it would, as long as liberals exist, and "liberal" and "conservative" are term-complements.)

In this chapter, we will examine cases where the subject and predicate terms do not change, and then we will turn to more challenging cases in the following chapters.

Corresponding Statements

Corresponding Statements
Categorical Statements with the same Subject and Predicate terms

In order to begin to see what immediate inferences are valid, let's assume that a particular A statement is true. So, we assume that "All S are P" is true. Will it follow that the other **corresponding statements** (those with the same subject and predicate terms) are true or false? Let's first ask about the O statement.

If all S are P, will it be possible, not possible, or guaranteed that Some S are not P? Let's use a familiar example: All dogs are mammals. We know that all dogs are mammals, so it is not possible that some dogs are not mammals. If there were a dog which was not a mammal, then it would not be true that all dogs are mammals. Since it is true that all dogs are mammals, it must be false that some dogs are not mammals. It follows that, in a formal sense, if the A statement is true, then the O statement is false, or spelled out more completely, If *All S are P* is true, then it is false that *Some S are not P*, for any S and P (as long as S exists).

For the moment, we will keep things fairly simple. We know there are such things as dogs, so let's see what follows from the A statement in that case (we will soon see that this assumption has caused all sorts of trouble for the traditional approach). Considering that "All dogs are mammals", could it be that "No dogs are mammals"? Not given the fact that dogs exist. Consider the Venn diagram for the statement "All dogs are mammals", which is an A statement. In the diagram, seen in Figure 9.1, the left crescent area is shaded. If we were also to assert that No dogs are mammals, we would have to shade in the middle football area. In that case, as we see in Figure 9.2, there would be no room for dogs to exist!

Skill 9.1

Recognizing Corresponding Categorical Statements

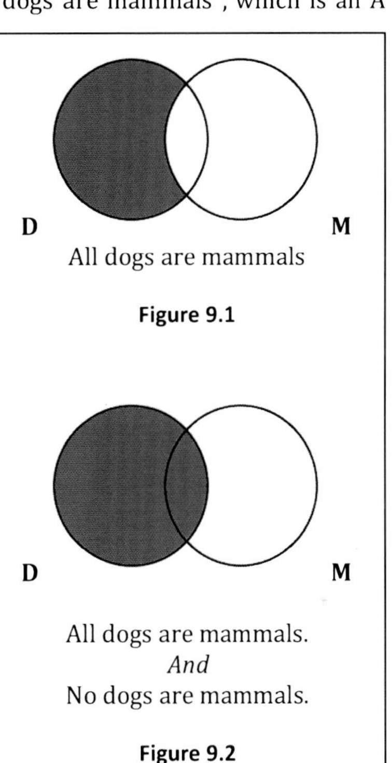

Figure 9.1

Figure 9.2

So, given that dogs exist, the fact that "All dogs are mammals" would show that it cannot be the case that "No dogs are mammals". If the A statement is true, then the E statement is false.

In a similar way, the truth of an A statement will guarantee the truth of the corresponding I statement. Again, assuming that dogs exist, then there must be a dog somewhere in the S circle. Since the left crescent is shaded and no dog could exist there, if we were going to place a dog on the Venn diagram, it would have to go in the middle football region. Finally, that would show that there is at least one dog which is a mammal, which is the same as saying "Some dogs are mammals." Remember that we are not saying "Only some dogs are mammals", but that there is in fact at least one dog which is a mammal.

Skill 9.2

Judging the Validity of Immediate Inferences Involving Corresponding Statements

So, the truth of the A statement (given that the subject term exists), will guarantee that the corresponding I statement is true and the corresponding E and O statements are false. The E statement works in a parallel way. The truth of the E statement (given that the subject term exists), will guarantee that the corresponding O statement is true and the corresponding A and I statements are false.

In this case, it is easy to see that the I statement must be false. If it is true that "No fish are mammals", then it cannot be that "Some fish are mammals." To establish that a true E statement guarantees a false A statement, we need only recall the previous figure showing both statements on the same Venn diagram. Given that the E statement is true, the A statement would close out the subject circle, which would not allow the S term to exist. If we are assuming that the subject term exists, then the A statement must therefore be false.

Furthermore, given that the football region is shaded for E statements, the only place the subject term could exist is in the left crescent region. Given that there is a member of the S class in the left crescent region, we would know that Some S are not P. Given that "No fish are mammals", we would be guaranteed that "Some fish are not mammals", i.e. there is at least one fish which is not a mammal (since we know that fish exist).

The I and O statements work a little differently, but also in a parallel fashion. Let's first look at the I statement. Say we know that an I statement is true: Some S are P. As an example, let's consider that "Some students are smart." It should be easy to see that it cannot also be true that "No students are smart." The fact that there is at least one smart student guarantees that it is false that "No students are smart." So, the truth of an I statement guarantees the falsity of the corresponding E statement.

Now, consider the corresponding A statement: "All students are smart." Will the fact that we know for sure that at least one student is smart guarantee that all students are smart? Not at all. It may not be the case that all students are smart, and yet, it could be true. We are not asserting that *only* some students are smart, but only that some students are smart. This statement is consistent with all students being smart or not. Remember the old sock drawer. The fact that I know that "Some of the socks in the drawer are black" will not guarantee that "All of the socks in the drawer are black", but they all could be.

What all this amounts to is that logic alone will not tell us anything here. Given only that "Some students are smart", it could be either true or false that "All students are smart." We call this being logically undetermined. If our only information is that an I statement is true, then the A statement is logically undetermined.

It would also be the case that the O statement is undetermined. Given only that "Some students are smart", it may be that "All students are smart", in which case it would be false that "Some students are not smart." But it could also be that "Some students are not smart." Logic alone cannot tell us which one is true (I prefer to think, based on my experience, that all students are smart in some fashion or to some degree).

So, the truth of an I statement *does* guarantee the falsity of its corresponding E statement, but the A and O statements would both be undetermined. In parallel fashion, the truth of an O statement guarantees the falsity of the A statement, and makes the E and I statement both undetermined.

To see why, first consider the example: "Some children are not spoiled." The corresponding A statement is that "All children are spoiled." If it is true that "Some children are not spoiled", then it must be false that "All children are spoiled." All we need to do to prove the A statement wrong is to find one child who is not spoiled, but if the O statement is true, then such a child necessarily exists.

Given only that "Some children are not spoiled", we cannot say for sure whether there are other children who are spoiled. Maybe there are and maybe there aren't. So, we cannot say for sure whether the statement "Some children are spoiled" is true or false, nor can we say whether the statement "No children are spoiled" is true or false. As before, the E and I statements would both be undetermined (In my view, however, there are at least some spoiled children, although we may disagree on the best way to "unspoil" them).

So far, we can summarize what we have learned in the following table:

Table 9.1

If	Then
A is true	O is false, E is false, I is true.
E is true	A is false, I is false, O is true.
I is true	E is false, A and O are undetermined.
O is true	A is false, E and I are undetermined.

Before we continue to examine what follows when each of these statements is false, let's take a quick look at how to use what we have learned. We can use this table to evaluate certain immediate inferences. In the argument, "All tigers are mammals, so it is false that no tigers are mammals", the premise is an A statement, and the conclusion asserts the falsity of the corresponding E statement. Our table confirms that given the truth of the A statement, we know that the E statement is false. So, given that the premise is true, we know that the conclusion is true, which is the definition of a valid argument. So, we can use the table to confirm that the immediate inference is valid.

This example is pretty basic, and hopefully the reader was able to determine the validity of the argument without any information learned in this chapter. When we shift over to unfamiliar situations or items, however, even the basic inferences can sometimes be difficult to accurately evaluate. It is also important to have the basics down before we start dealing with more difficult immediate inferences.

Keep in mind that if the conclusion is undetermined, then the argument is invalid. So the argument "Some particles are electrons, therefore some particles are not electrons" is invalid, even though both premise and conclusion are true. The truth of the I statement does not guarantee the truth of the O statement, and so the argument is invalid.

So, we know what follows if each statement is true, but what follows if we know that a statement is false. We'll start with an A statement. For example, it is false that "All primates are monkeys." Again assuming that primates exist, the only way for it to be false that "All primates are monkeys" is if there are some primates which are not monkeys. If there failed to be some primates which were not monkeys, then it would be true that all primates were monkeys. This tells us that the O statement, that "Some primates are not monkeys", would follow from the falsity of the A statement.

When it comes to the corresponding E and I statements, nothing can be said. Given the falsity of the A statement, the E and I statements are undetermined. Perhaps the following concrete examples will show why:

It is false that all mammals are dogs.	But...	It is false that no mammals are dogs.
It is false that all mammals are fish.	But...	It is true that no mammals are fish.

So the falsity of the A statement says nothing about the corresponding E statement. The E statement could still be true or false. Similarly, it says nothing about the corresponding I statement, as the parallel examples show:

It is false that all mammals are dogs.	But...	It is true that some mammals are dogs.
It is false that all mammals are fish.	But...	It is false that some mammals are fish.

The astute reader will realize that these are exactly the results we should expect. We already saw that when the O statement is true, the E and I statements are undetermined. Since the falsity of the A statement guarantees the truth of the O statement, it should follow that the E and I statements do not have a guaranteed truth value either.

We can examine the E statement in the same way. Consider the statement "It is false that no coins are nickels." This statement is true, and we know it to be true because we know that some coins are nickels. Given the existence of coins, the only way for the E statement to be false is for the I statement to be true.

Now we can apply what we know when the I statement is true. Just as before, that means that the A and O statements are undetermined. Generally one or the other will be true, but the fact that the I statement is true does not tell us whether it is the A statement or the O statement.

When we say that "it is false that Some metals are transparent", it follows that "No metals are transparent." The falsity of an I statement guarantees the truth of the E statement. To assert that it is false that there is an x in the middle football region of a Venn diagram is to say that the middle area is empty, which implies that "No S are P" for any terms we are using. So, saying that an I statement is false implies that the E statement is true.

Assuming again that metals (the S term in this example) do exist, if it is false that some metals are transparent, then it must follow that "Some metals are not transparent." The falsity of the I statement guarantees the truth of the O statement. Accordingly, since the O statement is true, we are guaranteed that the A statement is false. Since "Some metals are not transparent", it would follow that it is false that "All metals are transparent."

Putting it all together, the falsity of an I statement guarantees the truth of the corresponding E and O statements, as well as the falsity of the A statement. In a parallel fashion, the falsity of an O statement guarantees the truth of the corresponding A and I statements, as well as the falsity of the corresponding E statement, which any student who is willing to check should verify for himself. Remember finally that all of these inferences depend on the existence of the subject term.

The preceding section may have seemed a bit tedious. Typical students may have a difficult time following the thread of argument the entire time, and may well wonder how they could possibly retain all of the information contained therein. It is not as important that one followed ever step in the argument, although that it definitely helpful, as it is to be know what statements follow from what. Let's summarize in a table the information we have confirmed so far. We now have information about what follows when each statement is true as well as when it is false.

Table 9.2

If	Then
A is true	O is false, E is false, I is true.
A is false	O is true, E and I are undetermined.
E is true	A is false, I is false, O is true.
E is false	I is true, A and O are undetermined.
I is true	E is false, A and O are undetermined.
I is false	A is false, E is true, O is true.
O is true	A is false, E and I are undetermined.
O is false	A is true, E is false, I is true.

One could of course just remember the content from the table, but even that seems like a daunting task. Fortunately, there is an easy way to organize all of the information in the table in a clear graphical fashion.

The Square of Opposition

Skill 9.3

Using the Square of Opposition to Determine Validity

The easiest way to keep track of the logical relationships between corresponding statements is to remember the square of opposition, as shown below.

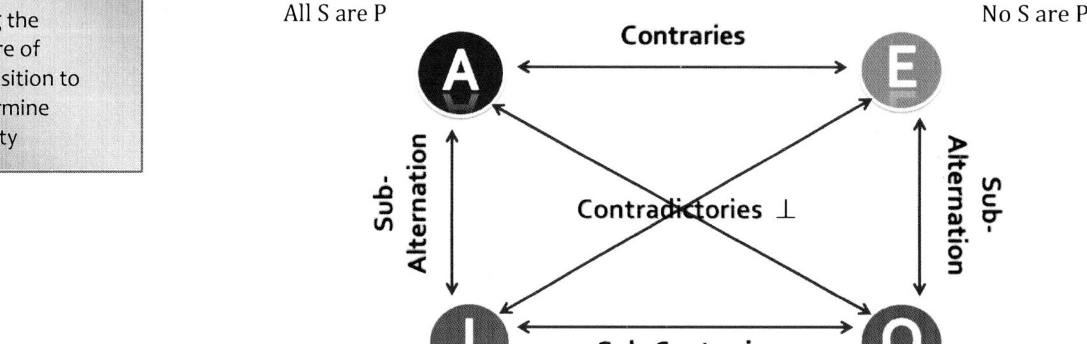

Every logical connection between corresponding statements is shown on this chart. Instead of memorizing the entire table, one can simply remember the square of opposition and the four relationships it displays.

The easiest relationship to remember is that of contradictories. Two statements are contradictory to each other if they always have the opposite truth value. When the truth of one statement guarantees the falsity of the other, while its falsity guarantees the truth of the other statement, the two statements are contradictories. If one is true the other is false, and if one is false the other is true. Another way of saying the same thing is that it is impossible for both statements to be true, but it is also impossible for both of them to be false.

As can be confirmed by checking the table, the relationship of contradictories holds between A and O statements, and it also holds between E and I statements. Once you have a truth value for an A statement, you know that the corresponding O statement will have the opposite truth value, and vice versa.

The next relationship we will examine is that of contraries. Two contrary statements have a kind of propositional conflict, but it is not that of contradictories. Two contrary statements cannot both be true, but they could both be false. Take animals to be the subject term and mammals to be the predicate term. We know that it is false that "All animals are mammals", but it is just as false that "No animals are mammals." Yet, as long as animals exist, it cannot be that both statements are true.

So, if one person utters an A statement, while another utters the corresponding E statement, since the statements are contraries we know that they can't both be right. At least one of them is mistaken, and perhaps both are. So, if I say that "All carbonaceous chondrite meteorites are objects older than 3 billion years", and you say that "No carbonaceous chondrite meteorites are objects older than 3 billion years" then at least one of us is wrong. If it turns out that some carbonaceous chondrite meteorites are older than 3 billion years and some are younger, then we're both wrong.

The sub-contrary relationship is similar to the contrary relationship, but instead of being impossible for both statements to be true, it is impossible for both statements to be false. An I statement and its corresponding O statement cannot both be false (assuming as we have been that the subject term exists). It is easy to see that they can both be true. It is true that some knives are sharp, and it is true that some knives are not sharp.

It may be a little harder to see why they can't both be false. Consider the statement "Some books are interesting". If that statement were false, then it could not be false that "Some books are not interesting". Otherwise no books could exist, and we are assuming, rightly, that they do. We could look at it another way. Assuming that books exist, we can pick one up. If it were false that some books are interesting, then the book we are examining cannot be interesting. But if that is so, then it must be true that some books are not interesting, in particular the one we are examining.

What this means is that if we know that one of the I or O statements is false, then we know that the other is true. Knowing that one of them is true, however, tells us nothing about the other. Keep in mind that it is much easier to verify that one of these particular statements is true, just by observing the existence of one object. To show that one of these statements is false, one would have to know something about every single object in the class, whether by observation, definition, or some other means.

Finally, we turn to the relationship of sub-alternation. This relationship is pictured along the sides of the square of opposition, both between A and I statements as well as E and O statements. As we have already seen, the truth of the A statement implies the truth of the I statement, and the truth of the E statement implies the truth of the O statement. We can picture this relationship as allowing "truth" to flow down the sides of the square of opposition. When the top statement is true, then so is the bottom statement.

We also saw that when the I statement is false, then so is the A statement, and when the O statement is false, then so is the E statement. We can picture this relationship as allowing "falsity" to flow upward along the sides of the square of opposition. If a statement on the bottom of the square is false, then the statement on the same side of the square on the top is also false.

It is not the case, importantly, that truth flows upward, or that falsity flows downward. The fact that an A or an E statement is false tells us nothing about the I or the O statement, respectively. We can remember this distinction easily if we recall that Socrates used to think of the truth as being solid and immoveable, whereas a false statement is flighty and capable of changing all the time. The "weightier" truth will be pulled down by its mass, but it cannot rise up from the bottom to the top, while the lighter false statement will rise from the bottom, but it cannot move from the top down.

If you can remember all of these connections, you will know all you need to know about the connections which hold between corresponding statements when we assume that their subject terms exist. Using the square, we can quickly assess the statements which follow when we are given the truth value of any other statement. Given that the A statement is true, we can assert the E statement is false based on contraries (which cannot both be true), the O statement is false (contradictories always have opposite truth values), and the I statement is true (truth flows downward).

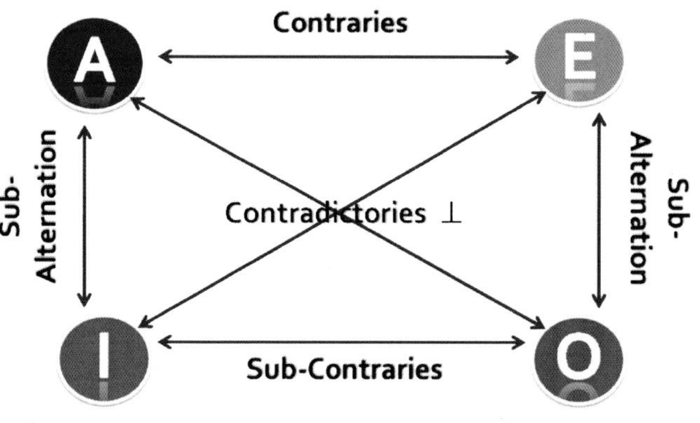

The Square of Opposition

Knowing that the A statement is false, however, only allows one to assert that the O statement is true. The E statement could still be true or false, and falsity does not flow downward to the I statement. Feel free to go over the other possibilities again using the square of opposition to guide you.

The Importance of Existence

The entire previous discussion depended upon the assumption that the subject term exists. When the subject in question does exist, then all of the relationships above work as described. Unfortunately, bad things start to happen when the subject in question does not exist.

Remember that the point of this discussion is determining whether a certain statement follows from another statement. The problem is that when the subject term does not exist, the relationships on the square of opposition do not work. In these cases, the truth of a statement used as a premise may not guarantee the truth or falsity of a conclusion in the same way as when the subject term does exist.

For example, consider the statement "All students who earned a 95 on the test received an A." If I uttered that statement to one of my classes, so that I was talking about a particular test, I would think that this statement would be true. My tests generally are based on a ten point scale, with an A going to any student who earns above ninety percent. So, it seems that the statement above would be true.

The problem, however, is that on the traditional standpoint we would have to conclude that some students who earned a 95 on the test received an A. It certainly is possible, however, that no student earned a 95. If that is the case, then even though the A statement is true, it would seem that the I statement can be false, specifically when the subject term does not exist.

This situation creates a real problem. Remember that a valid argument cannot have any exceptions. But it seems like an inference from an A statement to an I statement can have exceptions, and so is not valid. Apparently the square of opposition is not as universal as it was thought to be. The real problem is that this situation means that we can't say whether one statement follows from another unless we have information about whether certain terms exist.

Before we see the best way to deal with the problem, let's explore some of the other difficulties. Assume again that the A statement is true, but that no students earned a 95 on the test. Then consider the E statement: no students who earned a 95 on the test received an A. Since no such student exists it would appear that this statement is true. So, it seems as if A statements and E statements are not really contraries. In this situation, they are both true.

We have seen that subalternation fails, as well as the contrary relationship. It is easy to see that the sub-contrary relationship is doomed as well. Since no student earned a 95, the I statement and the O statement are both false. It is false that some students who earned a 95 received an A, but it is also false that some students who earned a 95 did not receive an A. So, I and O statements are not actually subcontraries.

Finally, we can examine the contradictory relationship. It would seem like in the case just mentioned the A statement and the O statement do have opposite truth values, but consider another situation. Let's say I accidentally assert the following statement: "All students who earned a 95 on the test received an F". Imagine that a student calls me on it, and says that the syllabus indicates that exams are graded on a standard ten-point scale. I think I would certainly say that I misspoke. My statement was false. It was not a true statement.

Consider the corresponding O statement, however, which is that "Some students who earned a 95 on the test are students who did not receive an F." As long as no student earned a 95, this statement would be false. So, in this situation, when the subject term does not exist, both the A statement and the O statement appear to be false, meaning that they are not strictly contradictories.

Most modern logicians, judging by the textbooks I have seen, handle the issue of contradictories by holding that all universal statements about non-existent objects are true, albeit vacuously, even when they assert contradictory properties. On this view, it is true that "All cats over 300 pounds are animals with four legs", and it is true that "All cats over 300 pounds are animals with only two legs." All such cats also have three legs, an infinite number of legs, and no legs. Your author personally finds this position difficult to accept, and prefers to hold that none of the relationships on the square of opposition hold for subjects which do not exist. Students who continue in studying logic should try to understand the issue well, so that they can form their own judgments on the matter.

So, what are we to do? We could just throw out the entire square of opposition, but it seems very useful when we are discussing existing subjects. As long as we are discussing objects which exist, the square does its job well. So, all we have to do is recognize that every inference that relies on the square of opposition potentially commits a **begging the question** fallacy.

Begging the Question
A fallacy which occurs when an argument relies on a missing premise which is actually false

We can understand what a begging the question fallacy is by considering the following example: "All cows with tails are herbivores, therefore all cows are herbivores." Many of my

Enthymeme
An argument with a missing premise, conclusion, or both

students intuitively decide that this is a valid argument, but technically speaking, it isn't. The truth of the premise, by itself, does not guarantee the truth of the conclusion. It just so happens that this argument is best considered an **enthymeme**: an incomplete argument. An enthymeme is an argument with a concealed premise, conclusion, or both. The argument above relies on the premise that "All cows have tails." Putting both premises together does result in a valid argument: "All cows with tails are herbivores, and all cows have tails, so all cows are herbivores."

We could immediately identify the original cow argument as invalid, but while true, that would obscure the fact that there is a simple premise upon which the argument relies. We should instead clarify that the argument is enthymematic, pull out the hidden premise, and then we are in better position to recognize the validity of the argument.

Consider this argument: "All gas giant planets with moons have rings, therefore, all gas giant planets have rings." When asked whether this is a valid argument, it would be technically correct to say that it is not. The most complete answer, however, is to add the missing premise which would make the argument valid, and then assess its soundness. The argument relies on the premise that "All gas giant planets have moons." Adding it results in a valid argument, and it is a true statement, so it should be added to the argument, resulting in a sound argument.

An argument commits a begging the question fallacy when it leaves out a dependent premise which is actually *false*. Here is an argument: "All politicians are lawyers, so all politicians tell lies." If someone were to point out that technically, this argument is invalid, we would rightly point out that should we add the obvious premise, that "All lawyers lie", then the argument would be valid. It is clearly a false premise, however (especially if we mean that all lawyers lie more than people do typically), and so we would also rightly assert that this argument commits a begging the question fallacy.

Existential Fallacy
A fallacy committed in an argument when it relies on the existence of a non-existent term

So, how should we deal with arguments which rely on the square of opposition? By recognizing them as enthymematic. Every argument based on the relationships within the square of opposition depends on an additional premise, namely that the subject term exists. If the subject term in fact does exist, then the argument is valid and as long as the categorical statement is true, the argument is sound. If the subject term does not exist, then the argument commits a begging the question fallacy. In these cases, the fallacy is also known specifically as an **existential fallacy**. Even in a case where there is uncertainty about the existence of the subject term, the concern that a potential fallacy is occurring is important to note.

One might wonder why it took scholars so long to recognize the deficiency in Aristotle's system, but considering the respect they had for Aristotle it may be seen as excusable, if that's the right word. People really thought that Aristotle's system could analyze any argument. Enormous effort was put into showing how his system could handle even arguments which didn't at first sight appear to work. Consider also that it is difficult to formulate the claim that a subject term exists using standard categorical terminology. We could use the very odd sounding "Some S are S", but it is difficult to step outside the box when all of the people teaching you something teach it the same way.

Technically the inferences we are looking at are not immediate inferences, since they rely on two premises instead of one, but since the existence claim is so often simply assumed, they will often appear to be immediate inferences.

Let's do a complete analysis of an argument relying on the square of opposition.

> It is false that all residents of California are surfers. Therefore, some residents of California are not surfers.

This argument relies on the relationship of contradictories. The premises assert that an A statement is false, and the conclusion asserts that the corresponding O statement is true. The relationship is used properly, so along with the claim that residents of California exist, the argument is valid. Does the argument commit an existential fallacy? No, because it is true that residents of California exist.

The following argument is invalid:

> It is false that all residents of California are surfers. Therefore, it is false that some residents of California are surfers.

This argument is invalid because it relies on the relationship of subalternation, but it does so improperly. Falsity does not flow downward, so regardless of the existence of California residents the argument is invalid. In addition, we can say that the argument commits the fallacy of **illicit subalternation**. This fallacy occurs whenever the subalternation relationship is used improperly. It should be noted that an argument which uses the contrary relationship improperly is said to commit the fallacy of **illicit contraries**, while using the subcontrary relationship improperly means one has committed the fallacy of **illicit subcontraries**.

Illicit Subalternation
A fallacy committed in an argument when the conclusion is obtained from the premise through subalternation in an improper fashion

Illicit Contraries
A fallacy committed in an argument when the conclusion is the contrary of the premise, but is drawn in an improper fashion

Illicit Subcontraries
A fallacy committed in an argument when the conclusion is the subcontrary of the premise, but is drawn in an improper fashion

Consider the next argument:

> It is false that some current students in Mr. Monge's logic class who already have Bachelor's degrees are students who are failing his class. Therefore, it is false that all current students in Mr. Monge's logic class who already have Bachelor's degrees are students who are failing his class.

This argument also relies on subalternation. It asserts that an I statement is false, and that therefore the corresponding A statement is false. This argument does rely on the relationship of subalternation in the correct way, and so, along with the claim that the subject term exists, the argument is valid. Unless the person analyzing this argument knows that there are students currently in my logic class who already have Bachelor's degrees, he cannot be sure that the missing premise is true. Accordingly, he should assert that the argument relies on the premise that there are current students in Mr. Monge's logic class with Bachelor's degrees, but it is unknown whether such students do in fact exist. So, we cannot be sure that it is appropriate to add the missing premise. The argument potentially commits an existential fallacy and so we cannot be sure that the argument is sound.

So far, we have only dealt with corresponding statements and claims that they are true or false. So, for any two terms, S and P, we could say eight possible things. We could say that All S are P, No S are P, Some S are P, or Some S are not P, and we could claim that each of these statements is false. So, in an immediate inference, both the premise and conclusion will be one of these eight statements.

In Table 9.3, we summarize every possible immediate inference which is possible using these eight statements. For ease of reference, each statement is presented using the capital letter associated with it, and two lower case letters representing the terms. So, "All S are P" will be written "Asp." "No S are P" is written "Esp," and so on. The premise is listed across the top, and the conclusion along the side. Obviously, if one were to say All S are P, therefore All S are P, the result would be a circular argument, and is marked in the table by "circ." Only those inferences which are valid are marked, so all boxes that are empty represent invalid inferences. Inferences relying on contradictories are marked as "valid" and are valid assuming either that all universal statements about non-existent subjects are true, or that the subject term exists. The boxes marked "val. (S)" indicate that the appropriate inference is valid when the assumption is made that S exists. In those cases where S does not exist in actuality, one should not add this assumed premise and the result is an existential fallacy.

Table 9.3

Conclusion \ Premise	Asp	Esp	Isp	Osp	Asp is false	Esp is false	Isp is false	Osp is false
Asp	circ.							valid
Esp		circ.					valid	
Isp	val. (S)		circ.			valid		val. (S)
Osp		val. (S)		circ.	valid		val. (S)	
Asp is false		val. (S)		valid	circ.		val. (S)	
Esp is false	val. (S)		valid			circ.		val. (S)
Isp is false		valid					circ.	
Osp is false	valid							circ.

"val. (S)" means the inference is valid if we add the premise that S exists.

Chapter Nine Exercises

Basic Concept Exercises

For each of the following statements, identify the letter and whether the statement is true or false, then provide each other statement on the square of opposition and state whether the truth value of the original statement is sufficient to know the truth value of the other statements. The first exercise has been completed as an example.

1. Some frogs are amphibians. True I statement:
   A: All frogs are amphibians, und.
   E: No frogs are amphibians, F.
   O: Some frogs are not amphibians, und.

   Note: One might know independently that all frogs are amphibians, but it doesn't follow solely from the fact that some frogs are amphibians.

2. Some dogs are not cats.
3. Some spiders are hairy.
4. Some spiders are scary.
5. All spiders are scary.
6. Some dogs are mammals.
7. Some students are smart.
8. No IBM's are virus-free machines.
9. Some apples are red.
10. All apples are green.

Intermediate Exercises

For each argument below, decide whether the argument is valid or invalid using the square of opposition. If the argument potentially begs the question, then say so, and state the premise which is being assumed.

11. All S are P
    ∴ No S are P

12. No S are P
    ∴ Some S are not P

13. All S are P
    ∴ Some S are not P

14. It is false that Some S are P
    ∴ No S are P

15. No M are N
    ∴ All M are N

16. It is false that All P are Q
    ∴ It is false that Some P are Q

17. Some N are M
    ∴ It is false that Some N are not M

18. It is false that Some D are L
    ∴ Some D are not L

19. It is false that All A are B
    ∴ No A are B

20. It is false that Some A are not R
    ∴ It is false that No A are R

Challenging exercises

Determine whether the following arguments are valid or invalid using the square of opposition. If the argument assumes a missing premise, state what it is, and make a judgment about whether the premise should be added. If so, the resulting argument is valid. If not, the argument begs the question and commits an existential fallacy. Make clear which of these possibilities you judge to be the case.

21. All primates are mammals.
    ∴ Some primates are not mammals.

22. Some pirates are not well-meaning merchants.
    ∴ No pirates are well-meaning merchants.

23. No fishermen are people who tell tall tales.
∴ It is false that Some fisherman are people who tell tall tales.

24. All apples are green.
∴ Some apples are green.

25. It is false that some apples are red.
∴ Some apples are not red.

26. It is false that All mammals are primates.
∴ Some mammals are primates.

27. It is false that Some pirates are not well-meaning merchants.
∴ It is false that No pirates are well-meaning merchants.

28. It is false that All roses are red.
∴ It is false that Some roses are red.

29. Some apples are red.
∴ Some apples are not red.

30. It is false that All nonagenarians are frail.
∴ No nonagenarians are frail.

In-Context Exercises

Decide, using the square of opposition, whether the second speaker in the following exchanges is accurately stating an implication from the statement of the first speaker.

A. **Erik:** It's not true that every piece of evidence for ghosts has been proven to be false.
Marguerite: So, some pieces of evidence for ghosts has been proven to be false.
B. **Angie:** Some professors will come down hard on you if you plagiarize.
Bernadette: So, some professors won't come down hard on students who plagiarize.
C. **Sue:** It's not the case that every unsound argument is invalid.
Axel: So, some unsound arguments are not invalid.
D. **Sue**: It's not the case that every unsound arguments is invalid.
Brick: So, No unsound arguments are invalid.
E. **Henry:** I've found that every sonatas is harmonious
Jasmine: So, there is not a single non-harmonious sonata.

Logic Puzzle: Professor Egnom's Favorite Number

This style of puzzle is a little different, but it should be manageable. Professor Egnom has some favorite numbers, including 18, 63, 72, 54, 27 and 90. But he really hates the number 35. What property do all of his favorite numbers share, that the number 35 does not?

CHAPTER

10

Immediate Inferences and Statement Operations

One should always keep in mind that the square of opposition fundamentally only involves arguments that have a single categorical premise, and a conclusion with a corresponding categorical statement. There is a little more complexity in that we can assert the truth or falsity of each statement, but there are really only four relationships which must be known. Our premise must assert the truth or falsity of only one of the standard form categorical statements, and the conclusion must assert the truth or falsity of the three remaining categorical statements. So, there are only eight possible premises, with six possible conclusions for each one, not counting the truth or falsity of the premise (From "All S are P" we could conclude "All S are P," but that would be blatantly circular. We could also conclude "It is false that All S are P," but that is obviously invalid). Once we put specific content into our argument, we can have an unlimited number of possible arguments, but so far there are a very limited number of forms for arguments.

Term Complement
A term which includes everything not included in a given term, often formed by using the prefix 'non-'

Before we continue, we should introduce the concept of a **term complement**. Every term has a term complement, which is the set of all things outside of the term. So, the term complement for felons is everything that is not a felon. The term complement for people who can come to my party is everyone and everything which cannot come to my party. Understanding term complements leads to another useful limitation. When discussing felons, it is probably not useful to include in the term complement anything but people, perhaps even adult people. I probably don't need to consider chairs, dogs, or computers. To account for this, we restrict our discussion to only adult people. This restricted discussion field is called a "universe of discourse", which means that we are not considering every possible thing in the universe, but only some limited aspect of it.

Skill 10.1
Performing and Recognizing Statement Operations

So, the term complement of "dogs" is "non-dogs," and term complement of "people" is "non-people." Once we add term complements and allow the predicate and subject terms to change position, a far greater number of forms become possible. With these additions in place, we can introduce the concept of a statement operation.

Statement Operations

Skill 10.2
Using Statement Operations to Evaluate Arguments

A statement operation is a way of altering a statement in a very specific way. The idea is the same as that in mathematics. Say the operation of adding 3 to a number. We can take this operation and apply it to any number we want. So if we take 4 and use the operation of adding 3 to it, we get out a new number, in this case 7. We can symbolize this operation in the common fashion: $4 + 3 = 7$. Whatever the metaphysical status of this equality, we can conceive of the relationship as an operation on the number 4, or any number. We can also conceive of this operation as a function, which maps certain numbers to others.

We will be introduced to only three statement operations: conversion, contraposition, and obversion. Each of the operations takes a certain statement, and turns it into another one, but always in the same fashion. Let's begin with conversion, the simplest operation.

Conversion

Conversion
A statement operation which exchanges the subject and predicate terms

Take this argument: "All neutron stars are spinning stars, therefore all spinning stars are neutron stars." The premise and conclusion are not corresponding statements: the subject term of the conclusion is not the subject term of the premise. Therefore, we cannot apply the square of opposition to this argument. Examining the argument carefully, however, reveals that the conclusion simply exchanges the subject and predicate terms of the premise. The premise is "All N are S", and the conclusion is "All S are N". The conclusion is simply the converse of the premise.

Conversion, as a statement operation, simply takes any categorical statement, and exchanges the subject and predicate terms. The statement which is created is called the converse of the original statement. Conversion does not alter the type of statement; an A statement remains and A statement; an I statement remains an I statement, etc. But the subject and predicate terms are exchanged.

Here is a table of conversion for each of the four types of statements, and the Venn diagram for each one.

Table 10.1

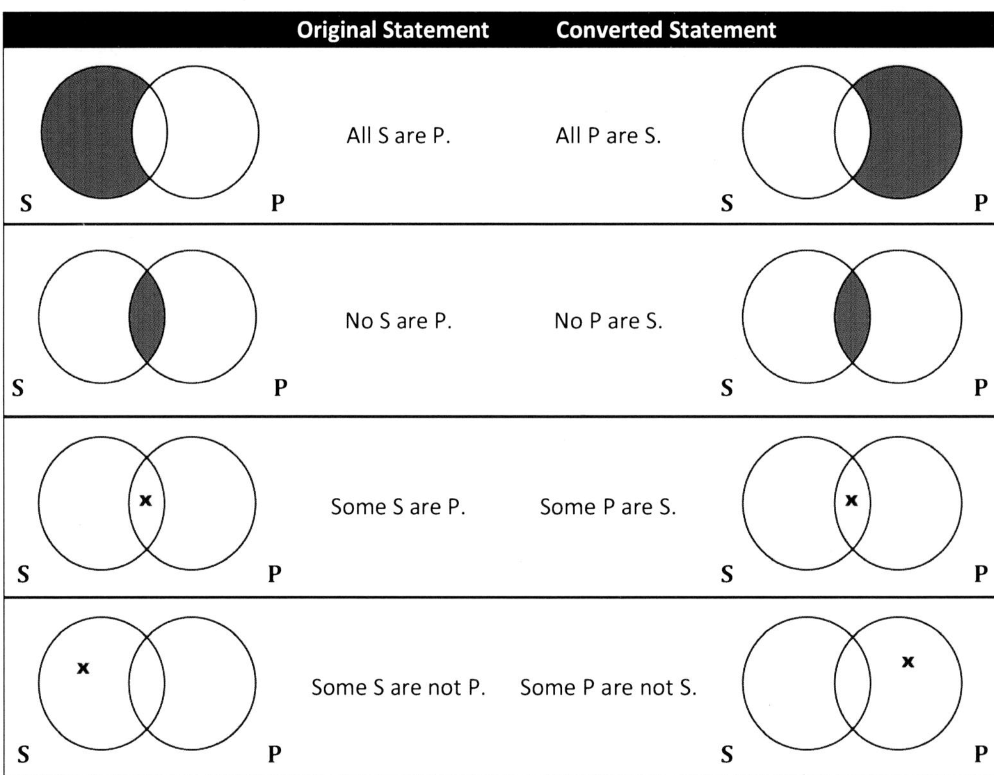

Original Statement	Converted Statement
All S are P.	All P are S.
No S are P.	No P are S.
Some S are P.	Some P are S.
Some S are not P.	Some P are not S.

The reader should notice that although the converted statement has the subject and predicate terms switched, the Venn diagrams for the converted statements still put the S circle on the left. This is essential in understanding which statements will retain their truth values though conversion.

Examining the Venn diagrams for the A statement, it is easy to see that the Venn diagram for the converse is not the same diagram as the one for the original statement. So, *A statements do not retain truth value through conversion*. The truth value of the converse of an A statement is not necessarily the same as the truth value of the original statement.

The E statement, however, is identical in both cases. The Venn diagram for the converse is the same as the Venn diagram for the original statement. They assert the same information about the world. Thus, if the original E statement is true, then so is the converted E statement. If the original statement is false, then so is its converse. E statements do retain truth value through conversion.

I statements work the same as E statements, as can be seen using Venn diagrams. In essence, the converse of an E or I statement flips the Venn diagram horizontally. Since both of them assert something about the middle section of their respective Venn diagrams, their converses both mean the same thing, and thus they both retain truth values.

O statements work like A statements. They both assert something about the left crescent region of their respective Venn diagrams, and so flipping them asserts something different. Neither A nor O statements mean the same thing as their converses, and so neither one retains their truth value through conversion. This does not guarantee that they have opposite truth values. They sometimes have the same truth value and sometimes they do not. There is no way to tell which situation holds unless we have additional information.

Note that when we take a converted statement and convert it again, we end up with the original statement. Technically, this means that conversion is its own inverse. What this means is that if conversion retains truth value, it retains it in both directions. If a statement retains truth value through conversion, then it is logically equivalent to its converse, in which case either both statements are true, or both statements are false. It is impossible for logically equivalent statements to have different truth values.

	Original Statement		Converted Statement	
A	All monkeys are mammals. (True)	A	All mammals are monkeys. (False)	Not Equivalent
E	No scientists are philosophers. (False)	E	No philosophers are scientists. (False)	Equivalent
I	Some dogs are brown animals. (True)	I	Some brown animals are dogs. (True)	Equivalent
O	Some coins are not nickels. (True)	O	Some nickels are not coins. (False)	Not Equivalent

Table 10.2

Table 10.2 presents an example for each statement type, and shows which statements are logically equivalent. An A or O statement is not logically equivalent to its converse, while an E or I statement is logically equivalent. So, in an argument, if the premise is an E or I statement, and the conclusion is just the converse of the premise, then the argument is valid, since the premise and conclusion must have the same truth value. If the premise is true, then the conclusion would have to be true. If, on the other hand, the premise is an A or O type statement, and the conclusion is the converse of the premise, the argument is invalid. The truth of the premise would not guarantee the truth of the conclusion. In this case, we would say the argument commits the fallacy of **illicit conversion**.

Illicit Conversion
A fallacy which occurs when the conclusion of an argument is derived from the premise through conversion of an A or O type statement

Obversion

Take this argument: "All neutron stars are spinning stars, therefore no neutron stars are non-spinning stars." Again, the premise and conclusion are not corresponding statements: the subject and predicate terms are not identical in both statements. Close examination, however, reveals that the subject term is the same in both cases, and the predicate term of the conclusion is simply the term complement of the predicate term of the premise. Lastly,

Obversion
A statement operation which replaces the predicate term with its term complement and changes the quality of the statement

the conclusion is an E statement, while the premise is an A statement. This argument relies on the operation called **Obversion**.

Although it may seem confusing at first, a little practice and concentration will help. The operation of obversion does two things. First, it takes a statement and changes its quality, but not quantity, which means it changes from affirmative to negative or vice versa, but it stays universal or particular. So, A statements go to E statements, and E statements become A statements; I statements become O statements, and O statements turn into I statements. Second, it changes the predicate term to its term complement. That's it.

When obversion is applied, the statement "All bats are nocturnal animals", becomes "No bats are diurnal animals", where diurnal animals (animals active during the day) is the term complement of nocturnal animals (keeping in mind a universe of discourse limited to animals). See the chart below to see how obversion affects all four standard form statements, along with their respective Venn diagrams.

Obversion	
A ⟷ E	
I ⟷ O	

Table 10.3

Original Statement	Obverted Statement
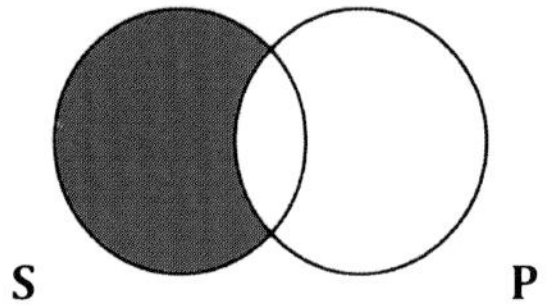 All S are P. (A)	No S are non-P. (E) 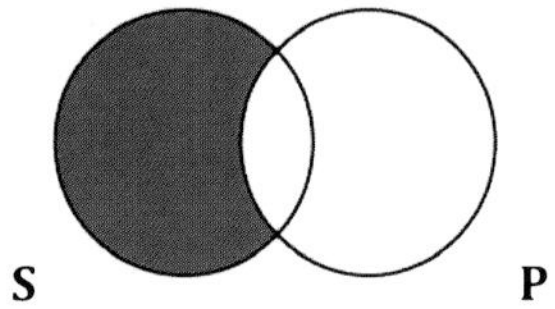
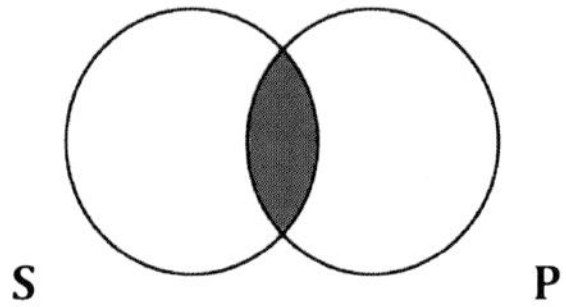 No S are P. (E)	All S are non-P. (A) 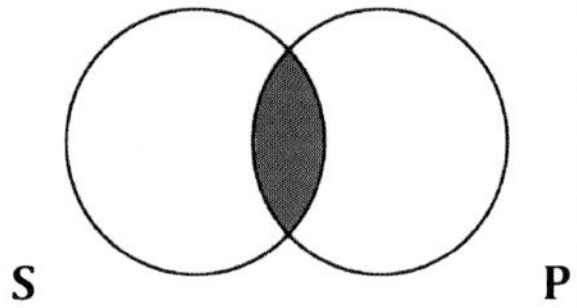
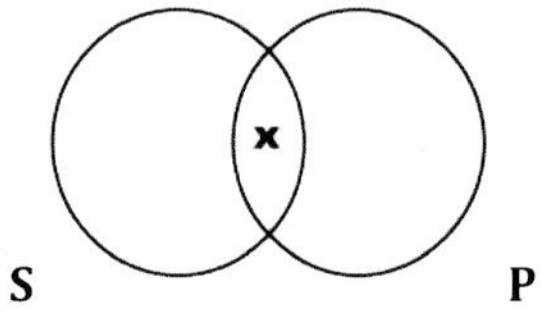 Some S are P. (I)	Some S are not non-P. (O) 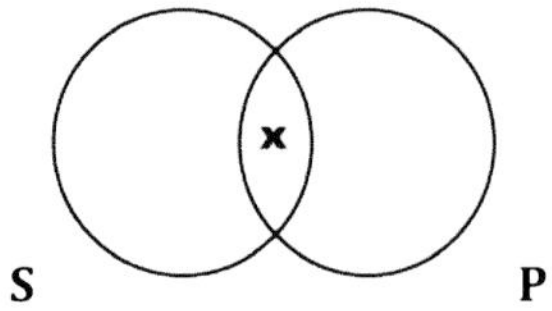
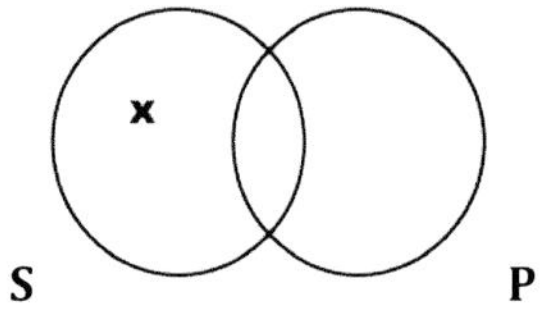 Some S are not P. (O)	Some S are non-P. (I) 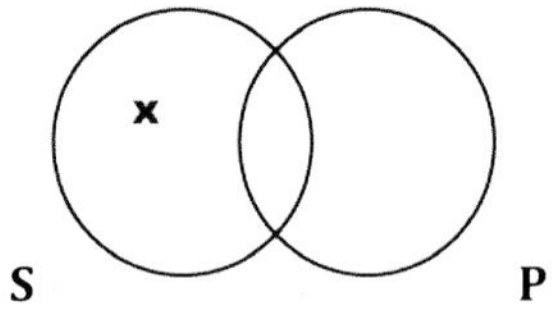

There are several things to note here. The first is that obversion is its own inverse. Take a statement, obvert it, then obvert the statement once more, and we will arrive at the original statement again. Obversion will either retain truth value in both directions, or not at all.

Second, we should note that the Venn diagram for each type of statement is exactly the same before and after obversion. Obversion always retains truth value! Any immediate inference where the conclusion is simply the obverse of the premise is a valid argument. The following argument is valid: "It is false that some coins are not nickels, therefore it is false that some coins are non-nickels."

The Venn diagrams are more difficult to understand, but most students are capable of doing so. The trick is to understand how term complements work on a Venn diagram. While the term refers to an area inside the circle on the Venn diagram, its term complement refers to any area outside of the same circle. To say that "No S are non-P", as it does in the table above, is to say that none of the members inside of the S circle are found outside of the P circle. Thus, we must shade the corresponding region, which is the area inside of the S circle but outside of the P circle. The other statements can be understood using the same approach.

The following table may also help in understanding how to construct Venn diagrams for the various obverted statements. It will also help to understand a type of notation for areas on the Venn diagram. To identify the area inside of S and inside of P, we use SP. The area outside of S, which is its term complement, is represented by S-bar, or $\overline{S}$. So, the area outside of S but inside of P is identified as $\overline{S}P$. The area outside of P, but inside of S is $S\overline{P}$. The area outside of both S and P is $\overline{SP}$.

Obverted Statement From Table 10.3	Standard Venn Diagram Using non-P	Standardized Venn Diagram Using P
On both diagrams to the right: 1 = $S\overline{P}$, 2 = SP, 3 = $\overline{S}P$, 4 = $\overline{SP}$	S, non-P (areas 2, 1, 4, 3)	S, P (areas 1, 2, 3, 4)
No S are non-P. (E)	S, non-P. Area 1 is shaded.	S, P. Area 1 is shaded.
All S are non-P. (A)	S, non-P. Area 2 is shaded.	S, P. Area 2 is shaded.
Some S are not non-P. (O)	S, non-P. Area 2 has an "x".	S, P. Area 2 has an "x".
Some S are non-P. (I)	S, non-P. Area 1 has an "x".	S, P. Area 1 has an "x".

Table 10.4

In Table 10.4, the first Venn diagram is drawn using the subject term and predicate term as they appear in the obverted statement (S and non-P), then same statement is drawn on a Venn diagram using S and P. The standardized diagrams are the same as they were shown in table 10.3, and again show that the obverted statement always means the same thing as the original statement. In Table 10.5, we will see an example of each type of statement before and after obversion. As noted earlier, every statement is logically equivalent to its obverse. There is no fallacy of illicit obversion, since obversion is always permitted.

Table 10.5

	Original Statement		Obverted Statement	
A	All monkeys are mammals. (True)	E	No monkeys are non-mammals. (True)	Equivalent
E	No scientists are philosophers. (False)	A	All scientists are non-philosophers. (False)	Equivalent
I	Some dogs are brown animals. (True)	O	Some dogs are not non-brown. (True)	Equivalent
O	Some coins are not nickels. (True)	I	Some coins are non-nickels. (True)	Equivalent

Contraposition

Contraposition
A statement operation which switches both the predicate and subject terms with each other, and then with their term complements

Contraposition is the most complicated of the operations we will examine. It changes the positions of both terms as well as replacing them with their term complements. Here is an example of an argument which relies on contraposition: "All dwarf planets are objects without atmospheres, therefore all objects with atmospheres are non-dwarf planets." As the reader can confirm with careful observation, contraposition takes a statement, exchanges the subject and predicate terms for each other, and then replaces each with its term complement. In symbolic form, we are taking "All S are P", and after applying contraposition, we obtain "All non-P are non-S."

As with both of the other statement operations before, contraposition is its own inverse. Contraposing a contraposed statement will yield the original statement. This means that if contraposition retains truth value for a statement, it will retain it in the opposite direction as well. Also, like conversion, contraposition does not change the statement type. If you contrapose an A statement, the result will be an A statement. The only operation which changes the statement type is obversion.

Table 10.6 displays contraposition for each type of statement, as well as the respective Venn diagram for each statement. Both Venn diagrams are constructed with the S circle on the left and the P circle on the right. As with obversion, it can be very challenging for the beginning student to construct a Venn diagram using S and P for a statement which involves non-S and non-P, but we will go through that construction in Table 10.7. For now, looking at the Venn diagrams will indicate which statement types retain truth value through contraposition.

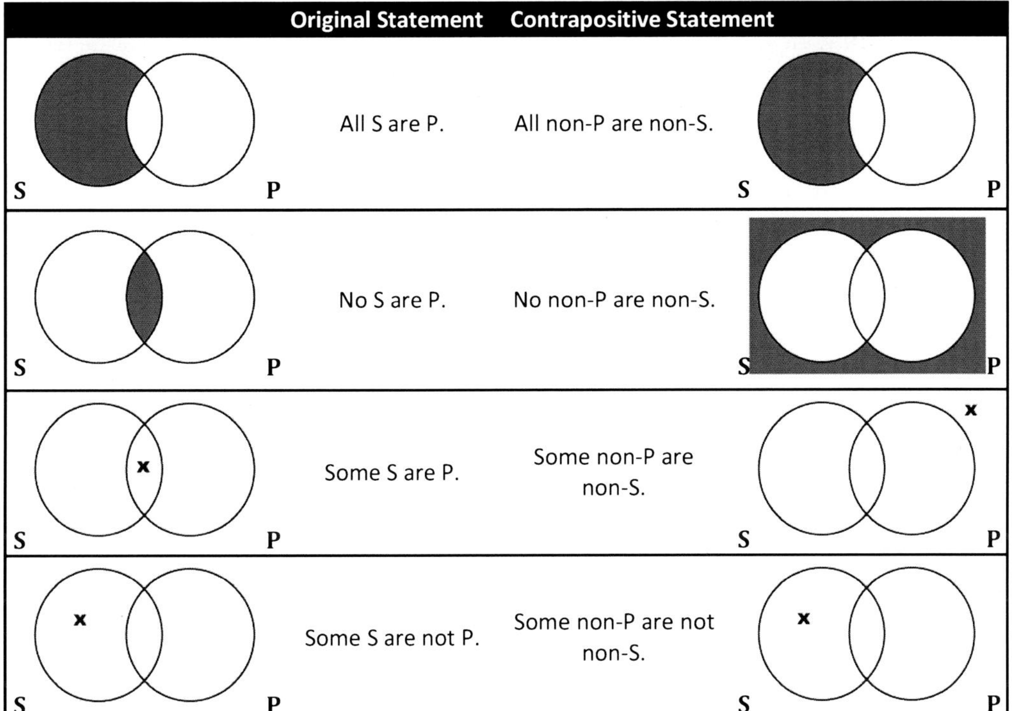

Original Statement	Contrapositive Statement
All S are P.	All non-P are non-S.
No S are P.	No non-P are non-S.
Some S are P.	Some non-P are non-S.
Some S are not P.	Some non-P are not non-S.

Table 10.6

As Table 10.6 indicates, the Venn diagram for the A statement and the O statement are identical to their respective contraposed statements, while those for the E and I statements are not. Contraposition retains truth value for both A and O statements, but not E and I statements.

Like obverted statements, contraposed statements involve term complements, which can be difficult to diagram. They are even more difficult, as they involve two term complements. It should help again to remember that if something is a P, then it is inside the P circle, whereas if it is in the term complement of P, or non-P, then it is outside the P circle. If it is outside of P, then it is inside of $\overline{P}$.

Table 10.7 is intended to help the student understand how the Venn diagrams for the contraposed statements in Table 10.6 were constructed. Pay careful attention attention to the first row. The standard Venn diagram uses non-S and non-P as the circles, where the standardized Venn diagram uses S and P. Each numbered area is mapped from the first diagram to the second. Each numbered area corresponds with the same numbered area on the other diagram. The standardized Venn diagrams were placed in the Table 10.6, so that each Venn diagram in that table used the same terms for each circle, which allows for a quick visual comparison.

Table 10.7

Contraposed Statement from Table 10.6	Standard Venn Diagram	Standardized Venn Diagram
On both diagrams to the right: $1 = S\overline{P}$, $2 = SP$, $3 = \overline{S}P$, $4 = \overline{SP}$	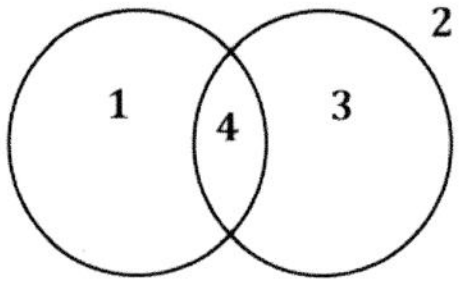 1, 2, 3, 4; non P, non S	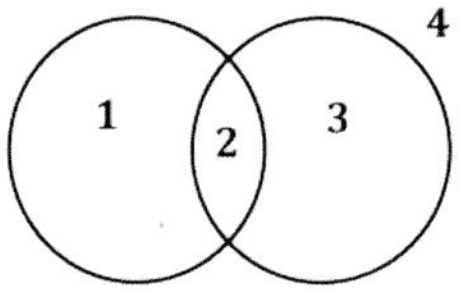 1, 2, 3, 4; S, P
All non-P are non-S.	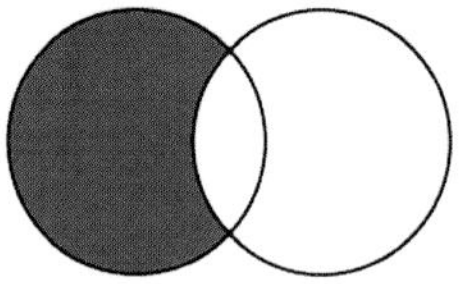 non P, non S. Area 1 is shaded.	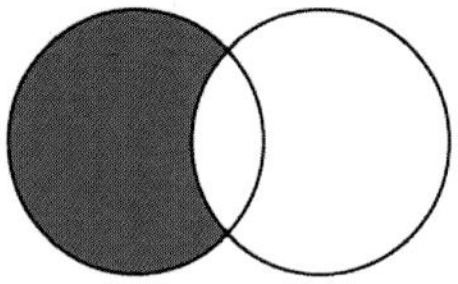 S, P. Area 1 is shaded.
No non-P are non-S.	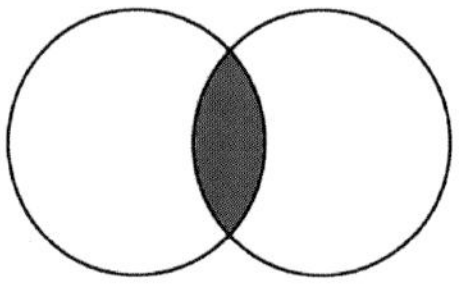 non P, non S. Area 4 is shaded.	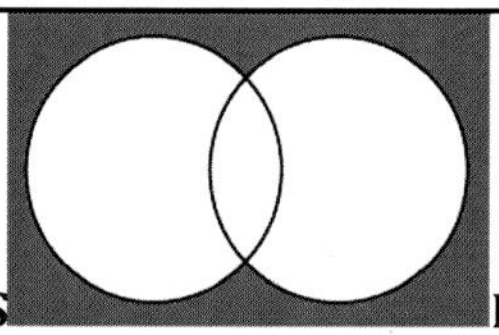 S, P. Area 4 is shaded.
Some non-P are non-S.	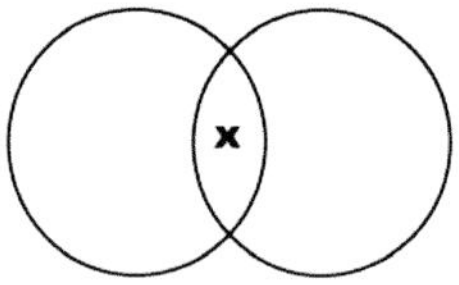 x; non P, non S. Area 4 has an "x".	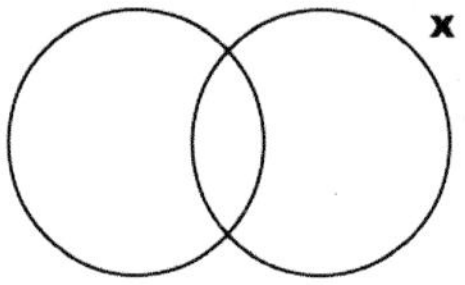 x; S, P. Area 4 has an "x".
Some non-P are not non-S.	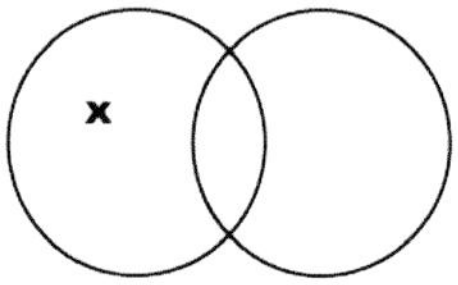 x; non P, non S. Area 1 has an "x".	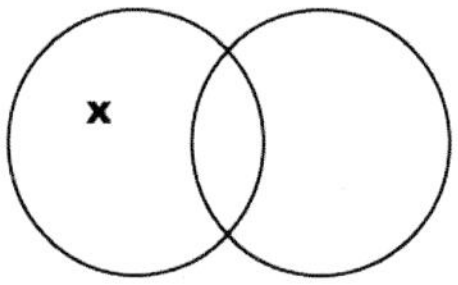 x; S, P. Area 1 has an "x".

As before, the beginning student need not completely understand Table 10.7, though it can't hurt. What is essential is that the student knows which statements retain truth value through contraposition. Tables 10.7 contains the proof that the Venn diagrams in Table 10.6 are correct, and Table 10.6 contains the proof that A and O statements retain truth value through contraposition, while E and I statement do not. These facts are shown in Table 10.8. An A statement is logically equivalent to its contrapositive statement, and the O statement is equivalent to its contrapositive statement. As the examples in the table show, even when an E statement is true, its contraposed statement can be false, but it can be true as well. An I statement might have the same truth value as its contraposed statement, but it might not as well.

	Original Statement		Contraposed Statement	
A	All monkeys are mammals. (True)	A	All non-mammals are non-monkeys. (True)	Equivalent
E	No fish are mammals. (True)	E	No non-mammals are non-fish. (False – birds)	Not Equivalent
I	Some fish are mammals. (False)	I	Some non-mammals are non-fish. (True – birds)	Not Equivalent
O	Some coins are not nickels. (True)	O	Some non-nickels are not non-coins. (True – quarters)	Equivalent

Table 10.8

The fallacy of illicit contraposition occurs in an argument when the conclusion is the contraposed premise and the premise is either an E statement or an I statement. If the premise (and conclusion) is an A or O statement, then the argument is valid.

Illicit Contraposition
A fallacy which occurs when the conclusion of an argument is derived from the premise through contraposition of an E or I type statement

Extended Proofs

Occasionally we will be confronted by an immediate inference which does not fit any of the relationships or operations we have outlined above. Getting from the premise to the conclusion cannot be accomplished by any of the relationships on the square of opposition, nor any of the statement operations. In that case, it is still possible to prove, in some cases, that the conclusion follows from the premise. We can do it by constructing a step by step proof.

Consider the following argument:

All fish are animals with gills.
∴ No animals without gills are non-fish.

Skill 10.3

Constructing Extended Proofs for Immediate Inferences

The premise and conclusion are not corresponding statements; the subject and predicate terms are not exactly the same. So, we cannot use any of the relationships on the square of opposition. Yet, no single operation will allow us to transform the premise into the conclusion. Is it possible, though, to use several operations, or relationships to get to the conclusion? If so, then the argument is still valid.

It is something of an art form to construct a proof, but it shouldn't be too daunting. The important thing is to take it step by step and not give up. Keep in mind three things:

1) We need the premise's terms transformed into the terms of the conclusion (are they the terms or the term complements?)
2) We need the terms in the correct positions
3) We need the statement to be the right letter statement.
4) We need the truth value of each statement labeled properly.

If we can determine a way to ensure all of these conditions are met, we will have done our job. First, let's rewrite the argument using letters. It may not be technically necessary, but it generally makes analysis much easier.

All F are G
∴ No non-G are non-F

When we examine the premise, we see that we start with F and G, but the conclusion uses non-G and non-F. Is there any operation which will transform both terms to their term complements? Yes, contraposition! Before we apply it, however, we must ensure that it is acceptable in this case. Does contraposition retain truth-value for A-type statements—Yes, so we can apply it. To keep track of our steps, we should set up a proof, as done below:

All F are G	
All non-G are non-F	contraposition
∴ No non-G are non-F	

The next thing to look at is whether the terms are in the correct positions, which a cursory examination reveals that they are. In fact, now the statements are corresponding statements, which means that they can be analyzed using the square of opposition. The second step in the proof (technically a subconclusion) is the contrary of the conclusion.

All F are G	
All non-G are non-F	contraposition
∴ No non-G are non-F	contraries (make sure to verify)

The next question is whether the truth of the second statement, which is an A-type statement, guarantees the truth of the conclusion, which in this case is the corresponding E-type statement. The answer is no. In fact, the truth of the A-type statement guarantees the falsity of the corresponding E-type statement. In this case, we can assert that the argument is invalid.

Be careful here, though. We are only entitled to assert that the argument is invalid because we found a path to show that the truth of the premise guaranteed the falsity of the conclusion. If we were unable to complete the proof, all we have is an incomplete proof which proves nothing. If we can construct a proof which shows that the conclusion must be true, then the argument is valid. If we construct a proof showing that the conclusion must be false (given that the premise is true), then the argument is invalid. Otherwise, we just can't say one way or the other.

Let's try it one more time on the following argument:

All spiders are animals with eight legs.
∴ Some eight legged animals are not non-spiders.

There is no one-step procedure to transform the premise to the conclusion, so we must consider creating a proof (you may want to verify for yourself). Again, it's a good idea to rewrite the argument:

All S are E
∴ Some E are not non-S

In this case we will need to turn the premise from an A statement to an O statement, and we need to turn S to its term complement. Plus, we need to change the positions of the terms. Okay, it may be a lot, but let's take it slowly. If we make a mistake, we can always start over from scratch. If we start by contraposing the premise, we will end up with non-E in our subject position when we need E, but it would allow us to have non-S in the predicate position. Before we contrapose the premise, then, we should obvert it. That will at least put the terms in the right positions. If you didn't follow that, I will lay it out below:

All S are E	
No S are non-E	Obversion
No E are non-S	Contrapostion (whoops!)
∴ Some E are not non-S	

Hopefully, enterprising students saw that something went wrong. Although we can obvert any statement we want, when we obvert an A statement, we obtain an E statement, and we cannot legitimately contrapose an E statement. We'll have to start again.

We know that we want to change the positions of the terms, but we can't use conversion on an A-type statement. We can, however, use it on an I statement. If the A statement is true, we know the I statement must be true by subalternation. So far, we have the following proof:

All S are E	
Some S are E	subalternation* (this step introduces possible question-begging)
_______	
∴ Some E are not non-S	

Now, we can do conversion, and at least get the terms in the right positions.

All S are E	
Some S are E	subalternation*
Some E are S	conversion
_______	
∴ Some E are not non-S	

Now, we need to consider whether it is possible to transform the third step into the conclusion using a single step. We need to go from an I statement to an O statement, and turn the predicate term into its term complement. Hopefully, each student can see that this is the exact definition of obversion, which allows us to complete the proof, showing the argument to be valid (given that S exists).

All S are E	
Some S are E	subalternation*
Some E are S	conversion
∴ Some E are not non-S	obversion

Every operation was used properly and every step is appropriate. This argument does rely on the assumption that S exists, since S is the subject term of the step which relied on subalternation, but it is true that spiders exist, thankfully (without spiders the fly population would overrun the planet). So, the argument including the assumption that S exists is valid.

Keep in mind that the method of proof we have been considering will only work for arguments that are maximally relevant, whether positively or negatively. For any argument which is invalid but not maximally relevant, no proof can be constructed, no matter how long one tries. Failure to complete a proof, however, does not establish that such a proof is impossible (See the Fallacy of Appeal to Ignorance in Chapter 25).

Using the Counterexample Method

Skill 10.4

Using the Counterexample Method to Prove an Argument is Invalid

While an argument can be proven to be valid by an extended proof, and an argument which is maximally relevant in the negative direction can be proven invalid, most invalid arguments cannot be proven invalid using a proof. There is another simple technique, however, which can prove any invalid argument to be invalid. It is called the Counterexample Method.

In any argument, if the premise can be true, while the conclusion is false, the argument must be invalid. The trick is to realize that the validity of an argument of the kind we are considering depends on the form of the argument, and not its content. Regardless of the terms in an argument, if a premise is an I statement, and the conclusion is the conversion of the premise, then the argument is valid. So, validity depends on the form of the argument alone.

So, the first step in the counterexample method is to identify the form of the argument by using letters in place of the terms. Here is an example:

All friends of mine are cool. Therefore, All non-friends of mine are uncool.

The argument becomes:

<u>All F are C</u>
∴ All non-F are non-C

The next step is to devise a substitution instance for the letters which makes the premise true and the conclusion false. This can be difficult, but with enough practice it can become second nature. Always keep in mind that we are trying to use examples where everyone will immediately agree that the premise is true and the conclusion false. Any controversy or doubt is problematic. Let's try making the premise "All dogs are mammals", so:

Substitution key: F = "dogs" and C = "mammals"

This will make the premise true, but we need to check the conclusion. It would be "All non-dogs are non-mammals." This is false. Just because something is not a dogs does not mean it is not a mammal. A cat is not a dog, but it is still a mammal. So, this substitution into the argument form makes the premise true and the conclusion false, which is just what was required to prove the argument to be invalid.

Let's try one more controversial example:

Some recent Republican Presidents are deficit raisers. Therefore, No deficit reducers are recent Democratic Presidents.

Here, the universe of discourse will be recent Presidents, and since we have recently only had Democratic and Republican Presidents, we can treat these as term complements. The form of the argument is:

<u>Some R are D</u>
∴ No non-D are non-R

In order to prove this argument is invalid to everyone's satisfaction, I need a substitution instance which makes the premise obviously true and the conclusion obviously false. Make sure that you choose simple example with which everyone will be familiar. Let's try "reptiles" for R. Then, I need to choose D so that the premise is true. Some reptiles are lizards. That's true. So, let's try "lizards" for D:

Substitution Key: R = "Reptiles" and D = "Lizards"

This example would make my premise true, but what about the conclusion? Is it true or false that No non-lizards are non-reptiles? The wording is challenging, but is there anything that is not a lizard that is not a reptile. Birds are neither lizards nor reptiles, which means the conclusion is false. Some non-lizards are non-reptiles, namely birds, which means the conclusion must be false. This substitution works as a counterexample to the claim that the argument is valid, and it proves that the argument is indeed invalid, as it could possibly have a true premise and a false conclusion.

If you had trouble with the conclusion, you might try to obvert it. Obversion always retains truth value, so it always means the same thing. To say that "No non-lizards are non-reptiles" is the exact same thing as saying that "All non-lizards are reptiles," which is more clearly false. There are lots of things that are not lizards that are not reptiles, including people, fish, monkeys, and many others.

Using Venn Diagrams

Skill 10.5

Using Venn Diagrams to Evaluate an Argument

We will present one final technique in this chapter to evaluate immediate inferences. This technique relies on being able to draw Venn Diagrams with great proficiency, even ones with term complements. In order to capture all of the inferential relationships on the square of opposition, we must also use circled x's.

First, let's try a Venn diagram with term complements. We'll diagram "All S are non-P," but we will do so on a Venn diagram of S and P. It is a universal statement, so we will be shading in a region, the trick is to figure out which one. The subject of the statement is S, which means that we will have to shade one of the regions of S. The statement says that "All S are non-P," which tells us that if there is something in S, it must be in non-P, or outside of P. If we have an S, it must be outside of P, or it can't be inside of P. So, we shade the area of S inside of P. We show this example in Figure 10.1. Notice that this diagram is the same as "No S are P," which is exactly as it should be, since the obverse of "All S are non-P" is "No S are P."

As can be seen in the diagram, we have also drawn two circled x's. These x's are required in order to correctly determine validity based on existential assumptions. Focus on the S circle. We have shaded in the middle football region, so if an S did exist, it would have to be found in the left crescent region. We haven't asserted that S exists, but if an argument assumes that S exists, we can see it by drawing in the circled x. Similarly, if P exists, then it would have to be in the right crescent region. Any time we shade a region, we can draw two circled x's on the diagram, on opposite sides of the shaded region.

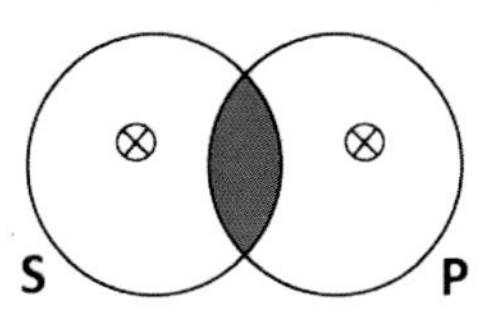

Figure 10.1

Here is another example: "No non-S are non-P." This diagram is little more challenging. Again, it is a universal statement, which means we must shade a region. The subject is non-S, so we will have to shade one of the regions *outside* of S. The statement says that there are no individuals within non-S that are also in non-P, so that area must be empty. We must shade the area outside of both circles. We can also draw two circled x's, one in each crescent region, depending on whether S exists or whether P exists. The complete diagram is shown in Figure 10.2.

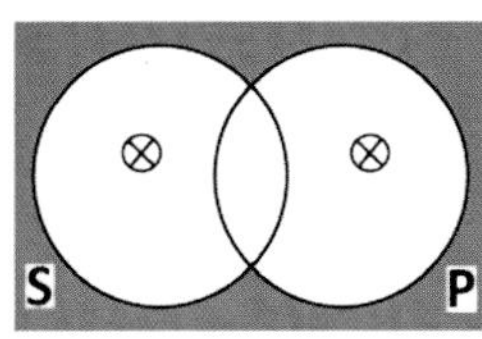

Figure 10.2

To determine whether an immediate inference is valid using Venn diagrams, we would need to draw the diagram for the premise, then draw the diagram for the conclusion. As long as everything included in the diagram for the conclusion is included in the diagram for the premise, the argument is valid. Keep in mind that a circled x on the premise diagram will support a regular x on the conclusion diagram.

Let's see an example. Let's use Venn diagrams to prove or disprove the validity of the following argument: "It is false that some non-S are P, therefore Some S are P." The first thing to realize is that in order to diagram a false statement, one simply diagrams the contradictory statement. So, to diagram "It is false that some non-S are P" we simply need to diagram "No non-S are P." This statement will require a shaded region, and it will have to be the region outside of S, but inside of P. The conclusion is the standard I statement. We will put both of them together in Figure 10.3.

The first Venn diagram, the one for the premise, has the region of P outside of S shaded, and so we drew in two circled x's. The one inside of S and P assumes that P exists, and the one outside of P and S assumes that non-S exists. The diagram for the conclusion has an x in the middle football region. The conclusion says nothing more than the premise, so the argument is valid, assuming that P exists.

1) It is false that some non-S are P

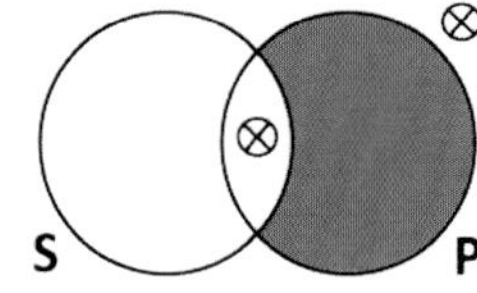

2) ∴ Some S are P

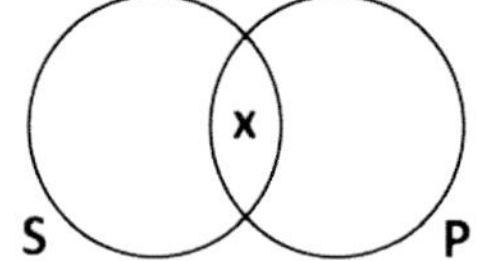

Figure 10.3

There are a great many more possible variations which are possible, but all the basics are covered here. One benefit of using Venn diagrams is that they can prove not only that an argument is valid, but that it is invalid as well.

Chapter Ten Exercises

Basic Concept Exercises

For each of the following statements, identify the statement operation, if any, which could be used to transform the statement on the left into the statement on the right. Then, state whether the new statement retains the truth value of the original.

1.	All S are P	No S are non-P
2.	Some A are non-B	Some non-B are A
3.	Some C are not non-M	Some non-M are not C
4.	No B are D	No non-D are non-B
5.	Some D are non-G	Some D are not G
6.	Some dogs are mammals.	Some non-mammals are non-dogs.
7.	All apples are green.	No apples are non-green.
8.	All snowflakes are unique.	All non-unique things are non-snowflakes.
9.	Some apples are not red.	Some non-red fruits are not non-apples.
10.	Some students are smart.	Some non-students are not smart.

Intermediate Exercises

For each argument below, decide whether the argument is valid or invalid by identifying the statement operation which transforms the premise into the conclusion. If no single operation will work (you cannot transform the premise into the conclusion in one step), then complete a proof to show the argument is valid (there are two valid arguments which will require two step proofs.

11. All S are P
∴ No S are non-P

12. No S are P
∴ No non-P are non-S

13. All S are non-P
∴ All non-P are S

14. All non-S are P
∴ All non-P are S

15. Some S are non-P
∴ Some non-P are S

16. All primates are mammals.
∴ No primates are non-mammals.

17. Some non-pirates are baseball players.
∴ Some baseball players are not pirates .

18. All fishermen are people who tell tall tales.
∴ No people who fail to tell tall tales are fishermen.

19. Some stars are not white dwarfs.
∴ Some white dwarfs are not stars.

20. It is false that some apples are red.
∴ It is false that some red fruits are apples.

Challenging exercises

Determine whether the following arguments are valid or invalid using the square of opposition *or* statement operations. If your decision cannot be completed in one step, construct a proof showing the argument to be valid or invalid. If possible, make a judgment as to whether the argument is sound.

21. Some valid arguments are not sound. Therefore, some sound arguments are not valid.
22. Everyone who is eligible to be president is older than 35. So, all people who are older than 35 are eligible to be president.

23. All sound arguments have true premises. So, all arguments with false premises are unsound.
24. It is false that some philosophers are not teachers, so it is false that no philosophers are teachers.
25. No person who earned an A on the test has to do homework, so every person who has to do his homework received a B or below.
26. No deductive arguments are valid. So no invalid arguments are non-deductive.
27. It is false that some numismatists are philatelists, so it is false that some philatelists are numismatists.
28. All immoral people are people who should not be politicians, which implies that all people who should be politicians are moral people.
29. Some children who do not listen to their parents are spoiled brats, so it is false that all spoiled brats are children who listen to their parents.
30. All teachers who give challenging tests are teachers who motivate their students. So, no teachers who do not motivate their students are teachers who give challenging tests.

In-Context Exercises

A. You have been given several purported proofs by your fellow students. They want to know whether their proofs are sufficient or deficient. If there are any problematic steps, identify them. If not, declare the proof to be sufficient.

1.		
	1) No S are P	
	2) Some S are not P	by sub-alternation*
	3) Some S are P	by sub-contraries*
	4) Some S are not non-P	by obversion
	5) ∴ F: All S are non-P	by contradictories*

2.		
	1) Some A are not B	
	2) F: All A are B	by contradictories*
	3) F: All non-B are non-A	by contraposition
	4) ∴ F: No non-B are A	by obversion

3.		
	1) F: Some non-S are P	
	2) No non-S are P	by contradictories*
	3) All non-S are non-P	by obversion
	4) All P are S	by contraposition
	5) ∴ All P are non-S	by contraries*

4.		
	1) All G are non-H	
	2) F: Some G are non-H	by contradictories*
	3) F: Some G are not H	by obversion
	4) ∴ Some G are H	by sub-contraries*

B. Prove the following arguments are valid by using extended proofs or Venn diagrams. Each one is valid.

1. 1) It is false that Some S are not P.
   2) ∴ It is false that No non-P are non-S.

2. 1) No non-S are P.
   2) ∴ It is false that All P are non-S.

3. 1) Some non-A are B.
   2) ∴ Some B are not A.

4. 1) It is false that All M are non-N.
   2) ∴ Some N are non-M.

5. 1) All non-R are non-P
   2) ∴ Some R are P

Logic Puzzle: Has Creationism Evolved?

The following speakers make the following statements. Can each of them be speaking truly? If not, determine the maximum number of speakers who could be speaking truly, and which ones they could be.

Professor Green: All modern mammals evolved from a single pair of reptiles.
Senator Braun: All modern humans evolved from Adam and Eve.
Governor White: Some modern mammals did not evolve from Adam and Eve.
Mr. Black: All modern birds evolved from a single pair of reptiles.

CHAPTER

11

The Circle of Opposition

Skill 11.1

Using the Circle of Opposition to Evaluate Immediate Inferences

We saw at the end of Chapter 9 that when we limit ourselves to corresponding statements, we could make a chart with every immediate inference on it. It only had eight rows and eight columns, for a total of 64 possibilities (including blatantly invalid and circular inferences). When we add the possibility of term complements and switching the position of the terms, there are many more possibilities. In fact, using the four categorical statements, two terms and their term complements, and saying both that a statement is true and that it is false, there are 64 possible statements which we can make.

So, in every immediate inference, once we know what the terms are, our premise must fit one of these patterns, as well as our conclusion. There are 64 possible conclusions for each of 64 possible premises, which gives us a total of 4096 possible immediate inferences! That would be quite a table to make, although it could be done. It would take a long time to complete, as well. For every inference we would have to prove one way or the other that it was valid, which we could do using the techniques from Chapter 10. Even if we had done so, however, the table would be quite large. We could perhaps squeeze it into several pages, but we might need a magnifying glass to read it.

What would be great is if there were a way to capture all of the information on the table in a format could fit on a single page. Fortunately, there is. I call it the Circle of Opposition. It basically expands upon the square of opposition, but it adds in term complements and switching terms.

The basic insight is that all 64 statements can be organized into only eight equivalence classes. There really are only eight possible things which can be said about two terms using categorical statements. Think about a Venn diagram for S and P. There is the space inside the S circle, but outside of the P circle: $S\overline{P}$. There is the area inside both circles: SP. There is the area inside of P but outside of S: $\overline{S}P$. Then there is the region outside of both S and P: $\overline{SP}$. For each of these regions, we can either say the region is empty, or that there is something in it. So, there are a total of only eight things we can say. It just so happens that for each of them, there are eight ways to say it.

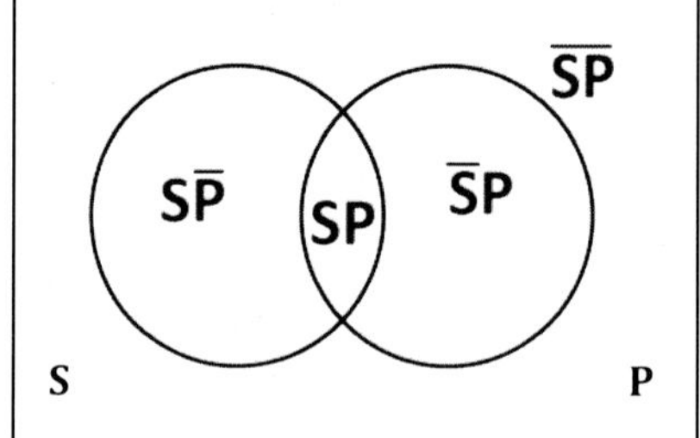

We'll use a short-hand way of writing our statements. We will use the capital letter of the statement, and lower case letters for each of the terms. So, All S are P, will be written Asp. We can also use bars for the term complement. So, No S are non-P will be written $Es\overline{p}$. So, how can we say that area $S\overline{P}$ is empty: Asp (All S are P). But we can also say it by $A\overline{ps}$, by $Es\overline{p}$, and by $E\overline{p}s$. We can also say it by claiming that particular statements are false. We could say that by F: Ops, by F: O$\overline{ps}$, by F:Is$\bar{p}$, and by F: I$\bar{p}$s. The same thing applies for each of the other seven possibilities. With this in mind, we can begin the understand the Circle of Opposition.

Around the Circle are the eight possible claims which can be made about the relationship between S and P. Within each annular sector (the eight sections of the outer ring) are the four ways to say each thing using true categorical statements. Every single valid immediate inference can be found on the circle, once one learns how it works.

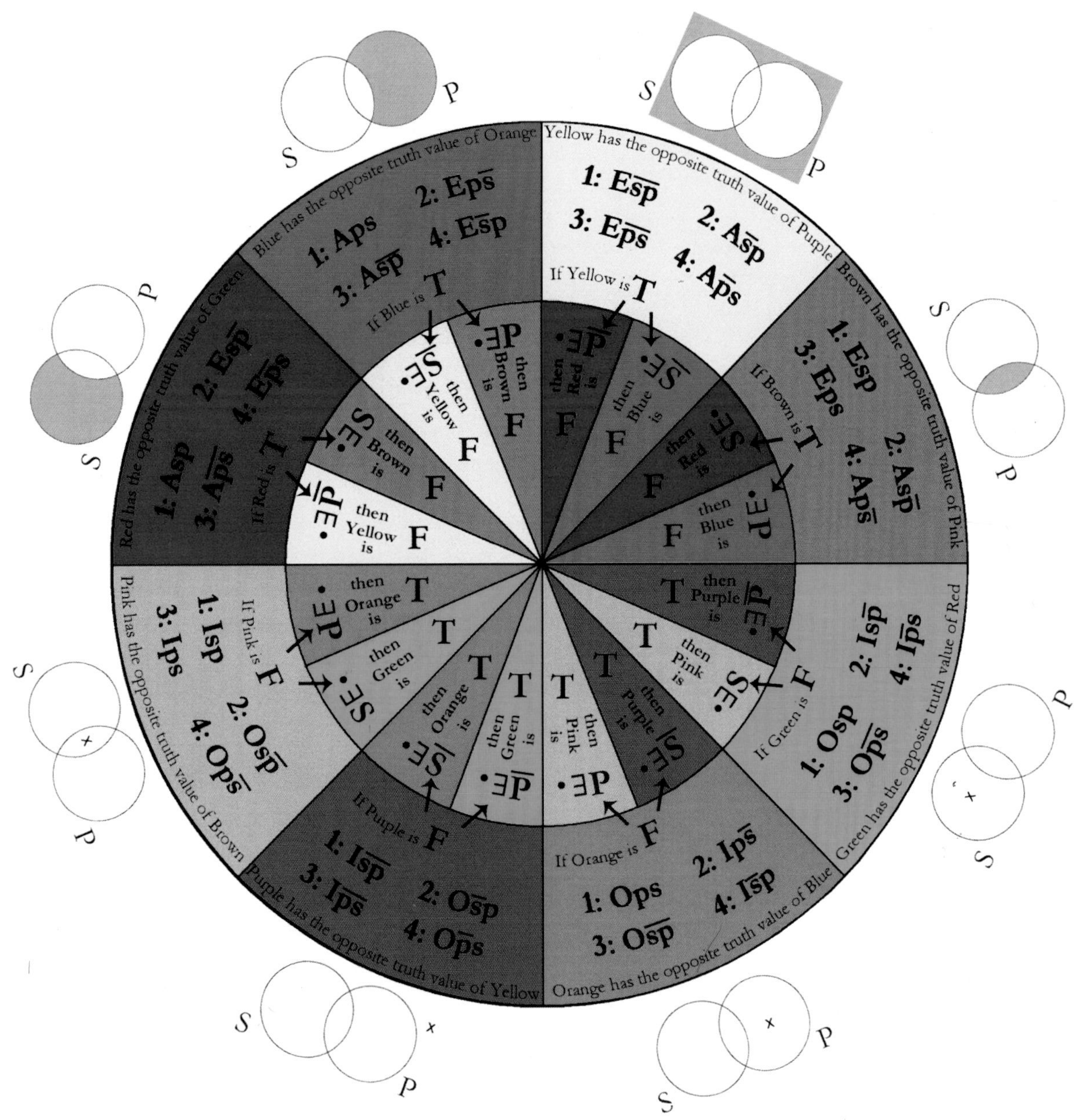

The Circle of Opposition

The first thing to see is that the four statements within each annular sector is logically equivalent. Red1 is equivalent to Red2 and all the other Red statements. So, if an argument has a premise which is red, and a conclusion which is red, then the argument is valid. The argument is valid regardless of the existence of any term.

Next is to understand that every Red statement is the contradictory of every Green statement. Given that we understand all universal statements about non-existent terms to be true, or that S exists, then every Red statement will have the opposite truth value of every Green statement. Every Blue statement will have the opposite truth value of every Orange statement. If any Yellow statement is false, then so is every other Yellow statement, and every Purple statement is true.

Finally, for True universal statements, or false particular statements, we can also follow the arrows to the inner circle sectors. The given existential condition is listed in the appropriate sector. For example, say we know that a Red statement is true. We follow the arrows, and we can see that if non-P exists, then all of the Yellow statements are false, and if S exists, then all of the Brown statements are false. Furthermore, we will also know that the Green statements are false (contradictories), which allows us to follow the arrows in the Green annular sector. So, if non-P exists, then all of the Purple statements are true. And, if S exists, then all of the Pink statements are true.

Just a note on the symbols being used. The dot is just a symbol which represents "and", and the upside down E is an existential quantifier, which is just a fancy way to say that something exists. So, putting everything together from the Red annular sector, the chart tells us everything we need: If Red is $T \bullet \exists \overline{P}$, then Yellow is F. All this says is If Red is true and non-P exists, then Yellow is false.

If a universal statement is false, or a particular statement is true, then all one can say is that the contradictory statements have the opposite truth value, again, as long as the all subject terms exist, or we understand every universal statement about non-existent entities to be true. This is a significant asymmetry, but it makes sense. If I know that all khakis are half-off, I have much more specific information than if I know that it is false, and when I heve more specific information, I can say more.

Let's see an example of how we can actually use the Circle of Opposition. Here is an example of an argument:

<u>All A are B</u>
∴ Some non-B are A

The first step is just to recognize the color of the premise and conclusion. In order to do so, we need to pick our key for S and P. It doesn't matter how we choose, as long as we are consistent across the premise and conclusion. Let's use S for A and P for B. So, our premise is All S are P, and our conclusion is Some non-P are S.

Looking at the Circle of Opposition, that makes our premise Asp, which is Red, and our conclusion is I$\overline{p}$s, which is Green. Knowing that a Red statement is true guarantees that the Green statement is false, so our argument is invalid.

Here is another example:
It is false that Some non-G are H
∴ Some non-H are non-G

In this case, we will use S for G and P for H. The premise is $I\bar{s}p$, which is Green, and the conclusion is $I\overline{ps}$, which is Purple. As shown on the Circle, if a Green statement is false, then the purple statement is true, as long as non-P exists, or in this case non-H.

It really is that simple. Every valid immediate inference can be found on the Circle of Opposition. If an immediate inference is not found on the Circle, then it is invalid.

Chapter Eleven Exercises

Basic Concept Exercises

For each of the following statements, identify its color on the Circle of Opposition.

1. All S are P
2. Some A are non-B
3. Some C are not non-M
4. No B are D
5. Some D are non-G
6. Some animals are non-mammals.
7. All apples are non-purple.
8. All non-animals are non-motile.
9. Some apples are not non-red.
10. Some video games are non-violent.

Intermediate Exercises

For each argument below, decide whether the argument is valid or invalid by using the Circle of Opposition. Identify the color of the premise and the conclusion, and state whether there are any existential assumptions.

11. All S are P
    ∴ No S are non-P

12. No S are P
    ∴ Some non-P are not S

13. All S are non-P
    ∴ Some non-P are non-S

14. It is false that Some non-S are P
    ∴ All non-P are S

15. Some S are non-P
    ∴ Some non-P are S

16. All primates are mammals.
    ∴ No primates are non-mammals.

17. Some non-pirates are baseball players.
    ∴ Some baseball players are not pirates .

18. All fishermen are people who tell tall tales.
    ∴ No people who fail to tell tall tales are fishermen.

19. Some stars are not white dwarfs.
    ∴ Some white dwarfs are not stars.

20. It is false that some apples are red.
    ∴ It is false that some red fruits are apples.

Challenging exercises

For each argument below, decide whether the argument is valid or invalid by using the Circle of Opposition. Identify the color of the premise and the conclusion, and state whether there are any existential assumptions.

21. Some valid arguments are not sound. Therefore, some sound arguments are invalid.
22. Everyone who is eligible to be president is older than 35. So, all people who are older than 35 are eligible to be president.
23. All sound arguments have true premises. So, all arguments with false premises are unsound.
24. It is false that some philosophers are not teachers, so it is false that no philosophers are teachers.
25. No person who earned an A on the test has to do homework, so every person who has to do his homework received a B or below.
26. No deductive arguments are valid. So no invalid arguments are non-deductive.
27. It is false that some numismatists are philatelists, so it is false that some philatelists are numismatists.
28. All immoral people are people who should not be politicians, which implies that all people who should be politicians are moral people.
29. Some children who do not listen to their parents are spoiled brats, so it is false that all spoiled brats are children who listen to their parents.
30. All teachers who give challenging tests are teachers who motivate their students. So, no teachers who do not motivate their students are teachers who give challenging tests.

In-Context Exercises

A. Decide, using the Circle of Opposition, whether the second speaker in the following exchanges is accurately stating an implication from the statement of the first speaker.

1. **Eric:** All activist judges deserve to be removed from office.
   Margaret: So, some non-activist judges deserve to remain in office.
2. **Angel:** No hemophiliacs are people who should take blood thinners.
   Bernard: So, It is false that some people who should not take blood thinners are hemophiliacs.
3. **Susan:** Every metallic element is found on the right of the periodic table.
   Madison: So, then it's not the case that some non-metallic elements are found on the right side of the periodic table.
4. **Marilyn**: Some phalaenopsis orchids do not require nitrogen-enriched fertilizer.
   Grant: So, all plants that require nitrogen-enriched fertilizer are not phalaenopsis orchids.
5. **Chase:** It is false that some justifiable homicides are cases where the accused deserves to be imprisoned.
   Bernie: So, all cases where the accused deserves to be imprisoned are unjustifiable homicides.

Logic Puzzle: Who's Going on the Expedition?

There are five scientists who are planning an expedition, each of which has the features below:

Anthony: a physicist, 35 years old, married, professor, U. S. citizen
Bella: a biologist, 37 years old, unmarried, forensic expert, Canadian
Cynthia: a chemist, 43 years old, married, pharmacologist, Peruvian
Daniel: an astronomer, 45 years old, married, observatory manager, Italian
Egbert: a sociologist, 56 years old, married, pollster, U.S. citizen

The number of scientists who will be selected for the expedition is undetermined, but it will be between two and four. Using the statements below, determine which scientists will be sent on the expedition.

1) It is false that all of the scientists who went on the expedition are married.
2) Some of the scientists chosen are not younger than 40.
3) None of the scientists who did not go are educators.
4) Not every scientist who went was a U.S. citizen.
5) All of the scientists chosen except one were male.
6) No scientist chosen was a non-natural scientist.

CHAPTER

12

Categorical Syllogisms

One of the most interesting features of categorical reasoning is that sometimes when two categorical statements are put together certain valid conclusions can be drawn which don't follow from the individual statements themselves. Sometimes the whole is greater than the parts.

As an example, consider the following arguments:

All birds have wings; therefore, all birds fly.
All animals with wings fly; therefore, all birds fly.

Neither of these arguments is valid, but the following argument is:

All birds are winged creatures, and all winged creatures fly; therefore, all birds fly.

In this argument, the truth of the premises would guarantee the truth of the conclusion (although one of the premises is false, which makes the argument valid, but unsound). It is important to note that the argument's validity does not depend on the content of the argument, but its form. The location of each of the terms and the logical structure are enough to guarantee that the argument is valid. Here is the logical form:

All B are W
All W are F
∴ All B are F

In this case, our key is as follows: B=birds, W=winged creatures, and F=flying creatures. But no matter what terms we use to replace our capital letters, the resulting argument will always be valid, though it may not be sound. Let's try it!

All logic professors know logic well.
All people who know logic well are rich.
∴ All logic professors are rich.

The conclusion is false (trust me), but so is the second premise. If both premises were true, then the conclusion would have to be true. As with all valid arguments, the falsity of the conclusion means that at least one premise must be false.

Aristotelian logic focuses strongly on the concept of the syllogism. The word syllogism has taken on several different meanings, but we will define a categorical syllogism as a deductive argument with two dependent premises which are both categorical statements. We will first learn how to rewrite categorical syllogisms so that they are in standard form, and then we will learn how to evaluate them using Venn diagrams.

Standard Form Categorical Syllogisms

One advance that Aristotle made when dealing with categorical syllogisms was that we should try to standardize them as much as possible. Once we take a jumbled mess and organize it, it is often easier to see connections and similarities which are otherwise obscured. In order for an argument to be in standard form, it must meet the following criteria:

Skill 12.1

Ensuring that a Categorical Syllogism is in Standard Form

1. The syllogism must be composed of three standard-form categorical statements.
2. The subject term of the conclusion must also occur once and only once in the second premise, and not in the first premise.
3. The predicate term of the conclusion must occur once and only once in the first premise, and not in the second premise.
4. The other term in the first premise must occur also in the second premise.

Once we have taken a categorical syllogism and ensured that it is written in standard form, we can analyze it. Traditionally, the predicate term of the conclusion is called the **major term**, and the first premise is called the **major premise**, while the subject term of the conclusion is called the **minor term**, and the second premise is called the **minor premise**. The term which occurs once in each of the premises is called the **middle term**. We will use these terms throughout the rest of the chapter.

Major Term
In a standard form categorical syllogism, the major term is the predicate term of the conclusion

It should be clear that every standard form categorical syllogism will have the following structure:

1. Quantifier <u>P or M</u> are/are not <u>M or P</u> major premise
2. Quantifier <u>S or M</u> are/are not <u>M or S</u> minor premise
3. Quantifier <u>S</u> are/are not <u>P</u> conclusion

Minor Term
In a standard form categorical syllogism, the minor term is the subject term of the conclusion

The following argument forms using categorical symbolism are in standard form:

All P are M	Some M are P	Some B are M	Some T are M
<u>No S are M</u>	<u>Some M are not S</u>	<u>All M are A</u>	<u>Some M are R</u>
No S are P	Some S are P	Some A are B	Some R are T

Middle Term
In a standard form categorical syllogism, the middle term is the one which appears once in each premise

Each of these arguments is in standard form, but it is important to know that it is standard practice to use either letters which have something to do with the original statements, or else S for the subject term (of the conclusion), P for the predicate term (of the conclusion), and M for the middle term.

Once we have the argument in standard form, we must identify two features of the argument. The first one is easy. The **mood** of the argument is simply a chain of three letters, which mark the type of each statement in order.

Mood
The mood of a standard form categorical syllogism is a series of three letters, which represent the letter type of the three statements in order

All P are M	Some M are P	Some B are M	Some T are M
<u>No S are M</u>	<u>Some M are not S</u>	<u>All M are A</u>	<u>Some M are R</u>
No S are P	Some S are P	Some A are B	Some R are T
Mood is AEE	Mood is IOI	Mood is IAI	Mood is III

To get the correct mood, it is essential that the argument is in standard form. If it is not, then the mood will generally be incorrect as well.

Figure
The figure of a standard form categorical syllogism is a number between 1 and 4 which signifies the placement of the terms in the premises

Once we know the mood of the syllogism, the only other thing we need to know about it is where the terms fit in. The conclusion always has its subject term and predicate term fixed, but the premises may be in one of only four different configurations. Once you have determined the mood and the **figure**, you will have everything you need in order to determine whether the argument is valid. The way to determine the figure is easy. If the middle term occurs in the subject position in the major premise, and the predicate position of the minor premise, then the syllogism is in figure 1. If it occurs in the predicate position of both premises, the syllogism is in the second figure. The third figure has the middle term in the subject position of both premises. Lastly, the fourth figure has the middle term in the predicate position of the major premise, and the subject position of the minor premise.

Skill 12.2

Finding the Mood and Figure of a Standard Form Categorical Syllogism

It may be easier to remember the figures by thinking of them as appearing on a traditional collar, as in Table 12.1.

Table 12.1

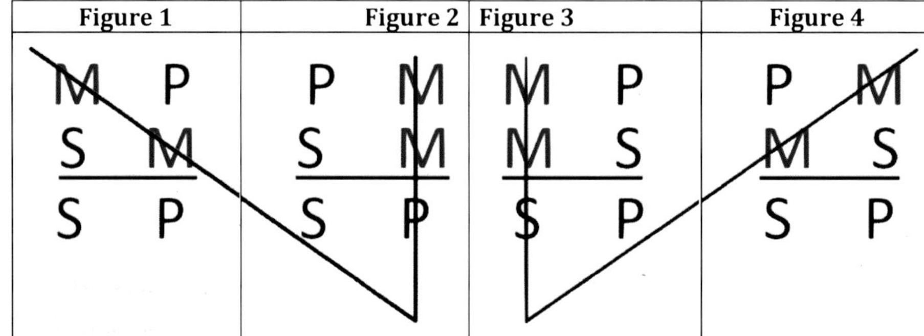

Be careful with the second and third figures. Notice that the middle terms are on the outside of their respective collars, while the other terms are within the collars. The first and fourth figures should be easier to remember.

As an example, let's look at the following argument:

Some houses are buildings made with brick.
Some buildings made of brick are objects susceptible to earthquake damage.
Therefore, some houses are objects susceptible to earthquake damage.

It may first help to rewrite the argument form by replacing the terms with capital letters, as done below:

Some H are B.
Some B are S.
∴ Some H are S.

Notice that H represents the subject term, and also that H appears in the first premise. So the argument is not in standard form. We will rewrite in again, ensuring that it is written in standard form, by reordering the first and second premise.

Some B are S.
Some H are B.
∴ Some H are S.

Now that the argument is represented in standard form, we can find the mood and figure. The mood is easily identified as III, and it is in figure 1 according to Table 10.1, and we will combine the two as III-1.

Now that we have identified the mood and figure it is a simple matter to determine the validity of the argument. All we need to do is consult a table constructed for the purpose. It may seem like cheating, but the whole point of ensuring the argument was in standard form was to make it easy to determine validity.

The reference table takes a little care, however, because the issue of existence affects categorical syllogisms as well. In Table 12.2, the first section lists argument moods which are unconditionally valid without adding any assumed existential premises. Notice that the moods are listed only under the figures for which they are valid. If a mood is listed under more than one figure, it means that the mood is valid in all figures under which it is listed. For each figure, any moods which are not listed are invalid for that figure.

Skill 12.3

Using a Table to Judge the Validity of Standard Form Categorical Syllogisms

Figure 1	Figure 2	Figure 3	Figure 4	
AAA-1 EAE-1 AII-1 EIO-1	AEE-2 EAE-2 AOO-2 EIO-2	AII-3 IAI-3 EIO-3 OAO-3	AEE-4 IAI-4 EIO-4	These moods are **unconditionally valid** under each respective figure.
AAI-1 EAO-1	AEO-2 EAO-2		AEO-4	These moods are **valid when an existential assumption is added**, namely that the *subject term exists*.
			AAI-4	These moods are **valid when an existential assumption is added**, namely that the *predicate term exists*.
		AAI-3 EAO-3	EAO-4	These moods are **valid when an existential assumption is added**, namely that the *middle term exists*.

Table 12.2

Remember that the syllogisms which require an existential assumption to be added potentially commit begging the question fallacies, and that this possibility should be disclosed and considered in any complete evaluation.

Using Venn Diagrams

Although it is useful to consult the table for valid syllogisms, it is unlikely that students will readily have the table available at all times. Furthermore, so far the only argument any student could make for the table is an argument based on authority. One of the most important reasons for studying any field is to get beyond simple arguments from authority, and understanding the reasoning behind the judgments made by those authorities. Only then will one be in a position to judge the reasoning for oneself instead of simply following the judgments of others. For these reasons, we will learn a technique by which we can actually establish the validity or invalidity of any syllogism. We will learn to draw Venn diagrams for categorical syllogisms.

Skill 12.4

Using Venn Diagrams to Judge the Validity of Categorical Syllogisms

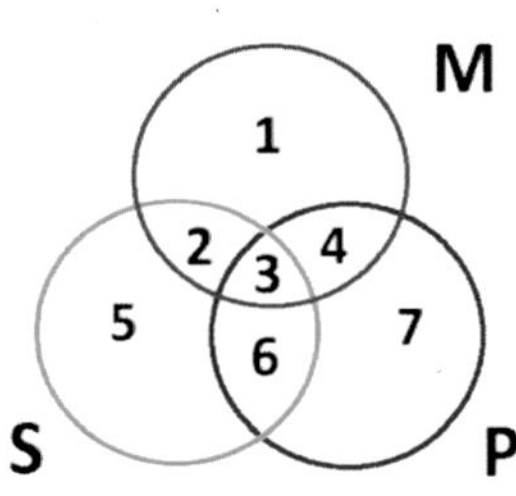

Once someone has gained proficiency in drawing syllogisms for two terms, it is only a little more challenging to draw them for three terms. Obviously, for three terms, we must draw three overlapping circles. To keep things orderly, we will always draw the Venn diagrams as in the diagram to the right, with the subject term on the bottom left, the predicate term on the bottom right, and the middle term on top, just as it is in a standard form categorical syllogism. We have also numbered every area on the Venn diagram, so that it is easier to refer to them.

For categorical syllogisms, we have two premises, so we must draw both of them on our Venn diagram. For the first example, we will draw the conclusion on a second Venn diagram, but this is only a temporary measure. Soon, you will be able to simply ask yourself whether the conclusion would be true given the Venn diagram of the premises.

We have already learned how to draw Venn diagrams for each categorical statement. There were only four different diagrams, corresponding to each of the four types of statements. The only thing to keep track of is which terms are being used. To illustrate a simple example, let's diagram an argument known since the middle ages as a Barbara syllogism. Here it is in standard form:

Example 12.1

All M are P
<u>All S are M</u>
∴ All S are P

First, we will draw the first premise on the diagram. All M are P is drawn just like we did for any A statement: the crescent area of M is shaded. On the diagram, it will look like Figure 12.1:

Figure 12.1

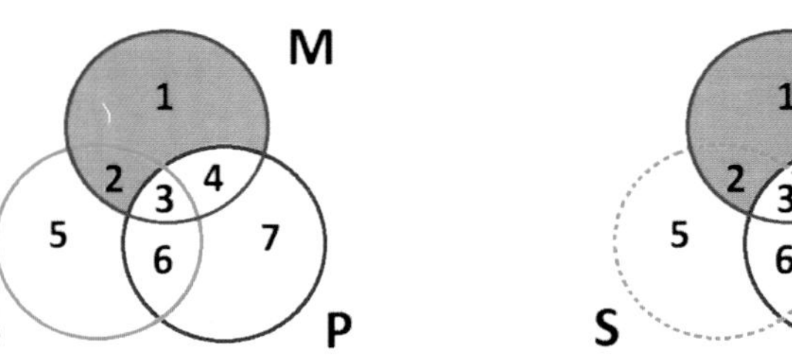

It may be helpful to only consider two circles at a time, as is shown in the diagram on the right in Figure 12.1. Since the premise only involves the terms M and P, we really only need to consider those two circles. We can safely ignore the presence of the S circle for the time being. The S circle doesn't move, but we needn't consider it when we are shading for the first premise in this case. In the same way, when we add the second premise to our diagram, which only includes the M and S terms, we can safely ignore the P circle.

Figure 12.2

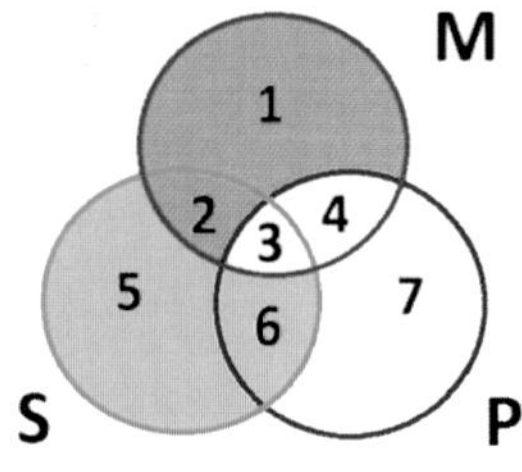

Let's do that now, adding the premise that All S are M. As shown in Figure 12.2, we will shade areas 5 and 6. Now that we have the premises both diagrammed, the last thing we need to do is draw a Venn diagram for the conclusion.

In Figure 12.3, the diagram on the left represents the premises of the syllogism; it is the same diagram as Figure 12.2. The diagram on the right represents the conclusion of the syllogism. It indicates what must be the case for the conclusion to be true.

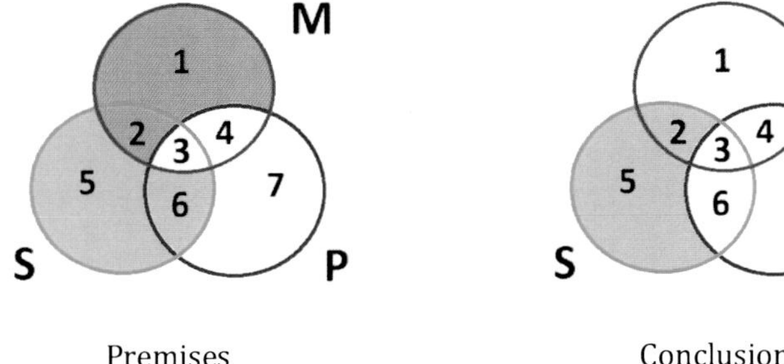

Figure 12.3

The color on the shading doesn't matter. What matters is whether every piece of information on the conclusion diagram is included on the premises diagram. In this case, in order for the conclusion to be true, areas 2 and 5 would have to be shaded. In the diagram of the premises, areas 2 and 5 are both shaded. So, the argument is proven to be valid. If the premises were true, then they would guarantee the conclusion to be true.

Remember that the conclusion diagram is actually unnecessary. All one needs to ask is what information would have to be present in the diagram of the premises in order to make the conclusion true. If it is present, then the argument is valid, and if it isn't, then the argument is not valid.

The Barbara syllogism form (AAA-1) is one of the simplest, and the one which is most intuitively obvious. Other syllogisms are more challenging. Let's examine an argument with both a universal and a particular statement.

Example 12.2

All M are P
Some S are M
∴Some S are P

The first thing to notice is that one premise will require shading, and the other one will require us to draw an "x". It should be clear that we cannot draw an "x" in a shaded region; the shading asserts that an area is empty, so it crowds out any particular individuals. For this reason, we will first diagram the universal statement, regardless of which premise it is.

After shading All M are P, our diagram is shown in Figure 12.4. The next thing we must do is diagram the particular premise "Some S are M" on the same diagram. The thing to notice is that in looking at only the S and M circles, diagramming this premise would direct us to put an "x" in the middle football region between the two, in the region composed of areas 2 and 3. Yet, area 2 is already shaded in, and so no "x" can be placed there. That means that we are required to put the "x" completely inside of area 3, as in Figure 12.5.

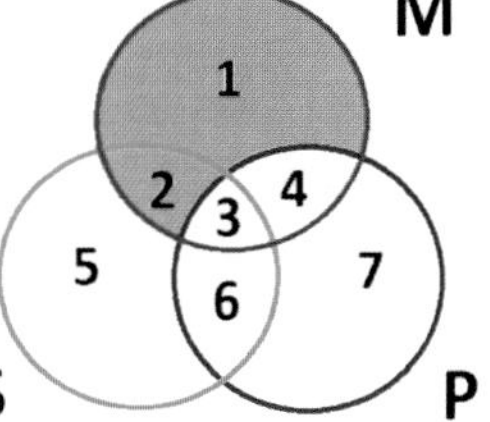

Figure 12.4

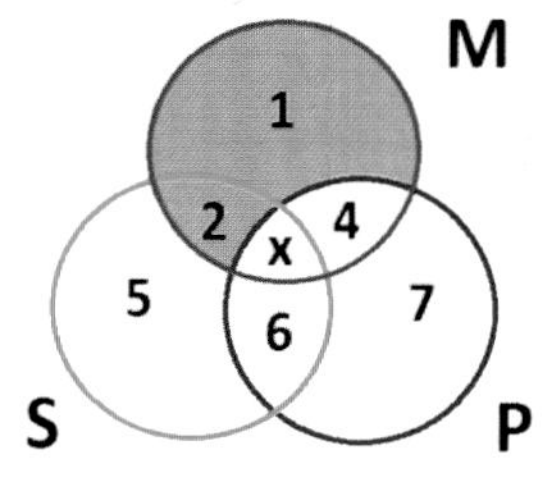

Figure 12.5

The only question remaining is whether the argument is valid. Here, instead of drawing the conclusion on a separate diagram, we will simply ask, what would be required for the conclusion to be true? In order for Some S are P to be true, we would need to have an "x" in the football region between S and P. On a three-circled Venn diagram, we would need to have an "x" somewhere in the region composed of areas 3 and 6. It wouldn't matter where or how many; all we need is at least one "x" anywhere in that football shaped region.

Upon inspection, it is clear that we do have an "x" in the necessary area, and so the argument is valid. There is no "x" in area 6, but that is not what is required; all we need is an "x" anywhere within the region including 3 and 6. So, example 12.2 is valid.

So, far, we have seen examples of arguments with two universal premises, and arguments with one universal premise and one particular premise. When we have two particular premises, however, there is an additional difficulty to address. Let's explore that issue by actually examining such an argument.

Example 12.3

Some A are B.
<u>Some B are C.</u>
∴Some A are C.

The question, as always, is whether any argument having this form is valid. Let's see by drawing it on a Venn diagram. Let's focus on the first premise: Some A are B. Don't get distracted by the new letters. It is easy to see that there must be an "x" placed somewhere within the football region between A and B. Unfortunately, the football region is divided between 2 and 3. So, where should the "x" go. We cannot just place it in area 2. Doing so would indicate that we knew the individual in question (which is definitely in both A and B) is *outside* of C. We cannot place it in area 3, since that would indicate that it was necessarily *inside* of C, and we don't know that it is. What we would need is a way to indicate that the individual is definitely in area 2 or 3, but we don't know whether it is in area 2 or area 3, or both. The answer is simply to draw the "x" on the line between area 2 and 3. We do so in figure 12.6.

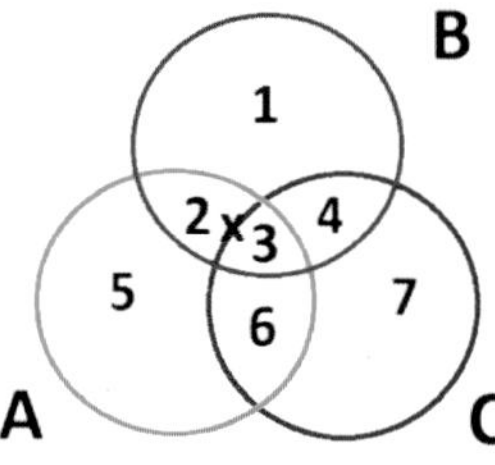

Figure 12.6

The "x" on the line indicates that there is an individual, and we know it is both an A and a B, but we don't know whether it is a C. The next step is to diagram the second premise. The second premise asserts that there is at least one B which is a C, but we don't know whether it is in A or outside of A. As we did before, we need to place an "x" in the football region between B and C, but it has to be placed on the line of the A circle. We add this information to the Venn diagram in Figure 12.7.

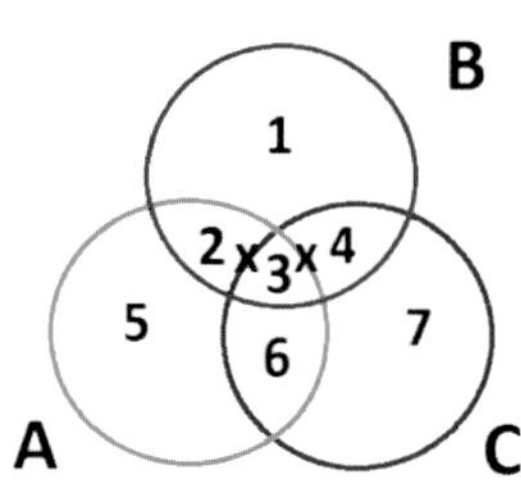

Figure 12.7

All that remains is for us to analyze the Venn diagram, to see whether it would guarantee that the conclusion is true. The conclusion was that Some A are C. In order for it to be true that some A are C, we would need to find an "x" inside the football region between A and C. In this case, we would need to find the "x" somewhere in the 3 or 6 areas. Although one might look at the above diagram and think that two halves of an "x" makes for a whole"x", that is not how it works. The question is whether the truth of the premises guarantees the truth of the conclusion. The premises only say that there is an "x" somewhere in areas 2 and 3, and an "x" somewhere in areas 3 and 4. The fact is that these premises are consistent with an "x" being in area 2 and an "x" being in area 4. This scenario would make both premises true, and yet the conclusion could still be false. Since the truth of the premises does not guarantee the truth of the premises, the argument is invalid.

The last thing to note is that the mood and figure of the argument is not III-4. The premises are not in the right order to be in standard form. Were we to rearrange the premises the argument would be III-1, but it is not necessary to rearrange the premises in order use Venn diagrams. Just remember to diagram universal premises first, wherever they occur. When using the reference table, however, failing to ensure that the argument's premises are in the right order can be disastrous.

Every time we have two particular premises, there will be two "x's" on two different lines. It is also possible that there is an "x" on a line when there is one universal premise and one particular premise. The following comprehension check example has this scenario. See if you can draw the "x" on the right line.

Comprehension Check Exercise

1) Some P are M
2) All S are M
3) ∴ Some S are P.

The answer is in the box on the next page.

Venn Diagrams Involving Potential Question-Begging

So far we have learned how to draw Venn diagrams which will establish the validity or invalidity of all of the syllogisms which do not involve potential question-begging. Now we will learn how to draw those. The central insight required is that if a term exists, then there must be an "x" somewhere in the term's circle. We may not know where it belongs, but it must be somewhere. We also know that an "x" cannot be placed in a shaded region, so the more shaded regions in a circle, the fewer the areas where the "x" can be placed. Finally, if three of the four areas of any circle are shaded, and the term exists, then we know that the "x" would have to go in the last open region. We indicate that the existence of the term was not directly asserted, but rather assumed, by using a circled "x" instead of a regular one. We used the same technique for Venn diagrams involving only two terms, and we are just expanding its use to those with three terms.

Let's see an argument where this technique is required.

All B are A
No B are C
∴Some A are not C

Example 12.4

First, we draw a Venn diagram for both of the premises, which we do in Figure 12.8.

Figure 12.8

As we can see in Figure 12.8, areas 1, 3 and 4 are shaded. Before we continue, we should ensure that we understand why this argument is strictly invalid. The conclusion asserts that there is an "x" somewhere in the region bounded by areas 2 and 5. But the premises could be true, without there being an "x" in areas 2 or 5, as the Venn diagram shows. Thus, the argument is strictly speaking invalid.

The argument can be seen as an enthymeme, however, with a missing existential premise, and the Venn diagram above can show us how. Let's concentrate on the middle term, B. It is divided into four areas: 1, 2, 3, and 4. The only one which is left open is 2, which means that were B to exist, it would have to be placed in area 2. Since the existence of this object is an assumption, we draw it as a circled "x", as we do in Figure 12.9.

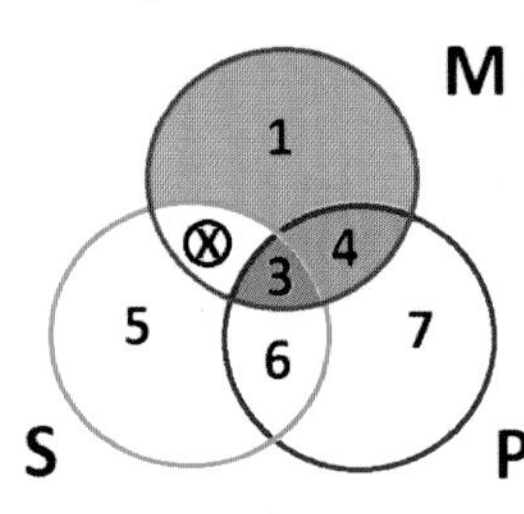

Figure 12.9

We now see that the conditions for the truth of the conclusion are satisfied: there is an "x" somewhere in the region bounded by areas 2 and 5 (a circled "x" is just as good as a normal "x"). What this means is that this argument, along with a premise which states that the middle term exists, would be valid. If it is true that the middle term exists, then we will rightly say that the potential question-begging fallacy was avoided, but if we not know for sure, we need to indicate that there is a potential fallacy present. We can do so by asserting that the argument is conditionally valid, on the condition that the middle term exists.

We will always know what condition is required by seeing which term had three areas shaded, and a circled "x" in the fourth region which made the conclusion true. In this case it was the middle term, B, but there are other arguments where the other terms are involved. Since the circled "x" will be placed within the fourth remaining area of a specific term's circle, that term is the one whose existence will be required.

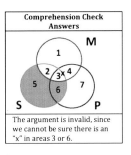

Comprehension Check Answers

The argument is invalid, since we cannot be sure there is an "x" in areas 3 or 6.

Reducing the number of terms

Skill 12.5

Using Statement Operations to Reduce the Number of Terms in a Categorical Syllogism

It is unlikely that you will come across an argument which is already in standard form. People simply don't talk or write that way, not even logicians. You have already learned a little about how to paraphrase from ordinary English into categorical standard form. Now we need to learn one other way to transform ordinary language arguments into standard form ones. Consider the following argument:

> It is unjust for the majority to force a minority to obey it, but in every democracy, the minority is forced to obey the majority. It follows that no democracy is just.

We want to know whether this argument is valid or not. The first step is to rewrite it using standard form categorical statements, making sure that we identify the conclusion correctly. We also need to be careful about selecting terms that retain the meaning of the statements, but also work in multiple statements. Here is one way to do so:

All institutions where the minority is forced to obey the majority are unjust institutions.
All democracies are institutions where the minority is forced to obey the majority.

∴ No democracies are just institutions.

It might be easy to think the argument must be invalid because the conclusion is obviously false, but remember that a valid argument can have a false conclusion, as long as the premises are not all true. We can be sure about its validity by using the techniques we have learned. Let's continue by using letters to represent the terms, as shown here:

All F are U
All D are F
∴ No D are J

Unfortunately, this argument is still not in standard form. The predicate term, represented by J, does not appear in either of the premises. Recognizing that unjust institutions and just institutions are term complements, however, provides us the key we need to solve the problem. Instead of U, we can use non-J, and we are left with the following:

All F are non-J
All D are F
∴ No D are J

We are making progress, but J and non-J are still not the same term; they are term complements. So, we can't use the techniques we have learned so far (technically, even at this point we could draw Venn diagrams to determine validity, but the average student may find it too difficult at this point). If only there were a way to transform one statement so that it replaced a term with its term complement. Indeed, there is, and we learned about it earlier: statement operations.

Both obversion and contraposition will allow us to replace a term with its term complement. Obversion will change the predicate term of a statement, and contraposition will change both terms. Examining our first premise, it should be clear that the one to use is obversion. Applying obversion will allow us to replace the non-J with J, its term complement. Remember that we also have to change the quality of the statement, but not its quantity. We should also ensure that applying the operation will retain truth value. This technique will not work unless the operation results in a logically equivalent statement. Obversion retains truth value for all statements, so we can use it for any statement. Using it here yields the following:

No F are J
All D are F
∴ No D are J

At last, we have our terms in place. The last thing we need to check before testing for validity is that the terms are still in the right place. The minor premise, which includes the subject term, is listed second, and the major premise is listed first. We are ready. At this point we can draw Venn diagrams, or use the mood and figure. The argument is an EAE-1, which is unconditionally valid.

We should note two things: it doesn't matter which statements are chosen upon which to operate, and it is not required to eliminate every "non-" term, only that we reduce the number of terms down to three. Instead of the way we proceeded above we could have performed obversion on the conclusion; the result is shown below.

All F are non-J		All F are non-J
All D are F		All D are F
∴ No D are J	through Obversion →	∴ All D are non-J

The resulting argument is an AAA-1 syllogism, which is also valid unconditionally. The predicate term here is non-J, or unjust institutions, but as long as the same exact term occurs in the major premise, which it does, then there is no problem.

CHAPTER TWELVE EXERCISES

After ensuring that the argument is in standard form, identify its mood and figure. Then draw a Venn diagram to determine whether the argument is valid or invalid.

Basic Concept Exercises

1. All M are P
   No S are M
   ∴ All S are P

2. All M are P
   All S are M
   ∴ All S are P

3. Some P are M
   No S are M
   ∴ Some S are not P

4. No P are M
   Some S are not M
   ∴ Some S are not P

5. All S are M
   No P are M
   ∴ No S are P

6. Some M are not P
   Some S are M
   ∴ Some S are not P

7. All Mare P
   No M are S
   ∴ No S are P

8. Some M are not P
   All M are S
   ∴ Some S are not P

9. No P are M
   Some M are S
   ∴ Some S are not P

10. All P are M
    Some M are S
    ∴ Some S are P

Intermediate Exercises

11. Some diseases are not curable illnesses, and no curable illnesses are things to be worried about. Thus, some diseases are not things to be worried about.
12. Every animal that has hair is a mammal. Dolphins are mammals. Therefore, dolphins have hair.
13. No prime numbers are divisible by seven. Some numbers which are divisible by seven are divisible by four. So, no prime numbers are divisible by four.
14. All numbers divisible by 8 are divisible by 4. No prime numbers are divisible by 8. So, no prime numbers are divisible by 4.
15. All repeating decimals can be written as fractions. Some repeating decimals are rational numbers. Therefore, some rational numbers can be written as fractions.
16. All cases of strangulation are cases where the victim's eyes exhibit petechiae. No cases where the suspect is accused are cases where the victim's eyes exhibit petechiae. So, no cases where the suspect is accused are cases of strangulation.

17. Some even numbers are divisible by both 7 and 5. No numbers divisible by both 7 and 5 are prime numbers. So, no prime numbers are even.
18. All numbers divisible by 4 are divisible by 2, and there are no prime numbers which are divisible by four. That must mean that there are no prime numbers which are divisible by two.
19. All numbers divisible by 4 are numbers divisible by 2. Some numbers divisible by 4 are numbers divisible by 3, so some numbers divisible by 2 are also divisible by 3.
20. None of the exercises in this chapter are too difficult for an enterprising student to successfully tackle, but some of the exercises in this chapter are very challenging, which shows that some very challenging exercises are not exercises which are too difficult for an enterprising student to successfully tackle.

Challenging exercises

In the following categorical arguments, either a premise or a conclusion is missing. Decide whether there is a statement which can be added which will make the argument valid, and either provide the valid argument in standard form, or state that there is none.

21. Every marsupial is a mammal, and every mammal is a warm-blooded creature.
22. No warm-blooded animals are reptiles, but some warm-blooded animals are lizards.
23. There is not a single teacher who is a millionaire, so no philosophers are millionaires.
24. No person who is not in a position of power or authority can be guilty of racism, so no member of a minority is a racist.
25. All human activities are governed by mechanistic laws, and no activities governed by mechanistic laws are actions governed by free will.
26. All Cepheid variable stars have the same absolute magnitude, but not every star with the same absolute magnitude has the same apparent magnitude.
27. All people who have dyslexia sometimes misread sentences and reverse letters or words, and John sometimes misreads sentences and reverses letters or words.
28. It can't be the case that all impressions of feet that are the size of sasquatch feet are fake, but all cases of non-faked sasquatch footprints must have been made by actual sasquatches.
29. Footprint impressions attributed to Bigfoot exhibit a mid-tarsal break, but no human foot has a mid-tarsal break.
30. My boss said: "Don't put out any jeans which are larger than 14 on the sales floor." Well that means that I won't be putting any of the jeans we have out on the sales floor.

In-Context Exercises

A. Find any argument that relies on categorical reasoning in the following dialog. Rewrite the argument in symbolic form, and decide whether the argument is valid or invalid.

Howard: Did you hear? They finally discovered extraterrestrial life!

Michelle: I heard something about some new creature they found that some people are saying is extraterrestrial. But I haven't heard why they think they're extraterrestrial.

Howard: All terrestrial life has DNA with four different base pairs, but the creatures they found, they call them fire hydras because they're like hydras but they're found in lava, the fire hydras have five different base pairs.

Michelle: Wait a minute, that doesn't seem to prove anything to me. Let's assume that the fire hydras are terrestrial. All your evidence shows is that some terrestrial life has DNA with five different base pairs.

Howard: That doesn't make any sense. What are you trying to say?

Michelle: I'm just saying that maybe the fire hydra is a terrestrial creature.

Howard: I can't believe that you would disagree with all of the scientists. You must be extremely arrogant.

Michelle: Well, that may be, but I just wanted to know what the reasons are that the scientists have. If you can't explain those reasons, I don't think I should just accept whatever you, or they, say.

Howard: Well, how about this? If the fire hydra were terrestrial, it would have had to evolve from some other creature on Earth. But there is no other creature from which it could have evolved.

Michelle: I see your logic, but I'm afraid you may be begging the question. How do you know that there is no other creature from which it evolved?

Howard: What about this. If the fire hydra evolved, it would have evolved from the water hydra, right?

Michelle: Let's say that's true.

Howard: All cases of evolution from diverse species involve intermediate species. The case of the fire hydra does not involve intermediate species between it and the water hydra. There are no such intermediate species.

Michelle: You say that, but how do we really know. Couldn't the intermediate species have existed long ago, but have now gone extinct? Besides, I think your entire argument relies on a bad assumption. You seem to think that all terrestrial creatures evolved from the same microbial life forms billions of years ago, so that accepting that fire hydras are terrestrial means that all fire hydras evolved from the same microbial life forms billions of years ago. Perhaps fire hydras are a new terrestrial life form, which arose from microbes only short while ago. If life was created once, why couldn't it be created again?

Howard: There's no use even reasoning with you, if you'll just accept anything. I'm outta here!

B. For each of the following triads of terms, draw a complete Venn diagram

a. Sound arguments / Valid arguments / Arguments with all true premises
b. Sound arguments / Invalid arguments / Arguments with false premises
c. Turtles / Amphibians / Vertebrates
d. Stars / Our Sun / Galaxies
e. Deductive arguments / Valid arguments / Unsound arguments

f. Odd numbers / Even numbers / Prime numbers
g. Dogs / Mammals / Fish
h. Humans / Lawyers / Doctors
i. Inductive arguments / Valid arguments / Arguments with all true premises
j. Prime numbers / Numbers divisible by 3 / Numbers divisible by 7
k. Fish / Dolphins / Mammals
l. People who annoy you / People whom you love / Your family members
m. Tomatoes / Fruits / Vegetables

Logic Puzzle: Monists, Scientists, Philosophers, and Evidentialists, Oh My!

Suppose the following three statements are true:

All monists are philosophers.
All scientists are evidentialists.
Some philosophers are scientists.

Which of the following statements also must be true?

1. All scientists are philosophers.
2. All evidentialists are monists.
3. Some evidentialists are philosophers.
4. Some scientists are monists.
5. Some monists are evidentialists.

CHAPTER

13

Challenging Categorical Paraphrases

Paraphrasing into standard form

Skill 13.1

Standardizing Categorical Statements

In general, when dealing with categorical arguments, it is best to rewrite them in as simple a form as possible. Then we can be sure that we are dealing with the proper statement and its corresponding Venn diagram. It can take a great deal of skill to take a categorical statement in English and rewrite it in standard form, but if we are to eliminate all debate and conclusively prove to everyone involved in a debate whether an argument is valid, we will need to eliminate all ambiguity and possibility of misunderstanding. For this reason we will always attempt to paraphrase a categorical statement by putting it into standard form. A categorical statement is in standard form when it begins with one of the three quantifiers ("All", "Some", or "No"), has the subject term (or a letter to represent the subject term), the copula ("are" or "are not"), and the predicate term (or a letter to represent it). The only time the copula "are not" is used is in O statements. So, the statement "All mathematicians are not people who love poetry" is not in standard form, but there is way to rewrite it in standard form. Ask your professor if you can't figure out what it is.

Often it is helpful to first determine whether the correct statement is universal or particular. Is it about all of the members of a group, or only some? Then determine whether it is affirmative or negative. Lastly, figure out the best way to write each of the terms. If it sounds simple, it often is, but there are many cases where it will not be so easy.

Let's look at some statements in ordinary English, and see how we can restate them to fit in standard form. Some of these examples are fairly basic and don't really cause any confusion, but we will still rewrite them in standard form to provide uniformity and to more easily allow statement operations, which we will see in the next chapter. Other cases are more serious; they are often misunderstood and people can be misled by them. We will start with the simpler examples.

Missing nouns

Examples: All musicians are talented.
No animals are completely immobile.

People usually don't speak or write in standard form categorical statements, but sometimes they are pretty close. Remember that for our purposes, we require each term to contain a plural noun. The word "talented" does not contain a plural noun, nor does the phrase "completely immobile". In these cases, we need to add an appropriate plural noun. We can simply take the subject term and use it, and rewrite the example as "All musicians are talented musicians." It may sound odd, and in English it is redundant, but logicians are not as worried about these things as others are. They care most about clarity and precision, and uniformity as much as it can support clarity and precision.

A term roughly synonymous to the subject term will work as well. One can also choose a broader term, if it works. Musicians are a sub-category of artists, so it would be appropriate to add the term "artists" to obtain "All musicians are talented artists." The second example could become "No animals are completely immobile creatures." Note that one would not want to use a sub-category of the subject term. For example, while it may be true that all musicians are talented, it would not be true that all musicians are talented drummers.

If this seems like needless fuss to you, consider that we will want to be able to operate on statements by moving terms around. So, we will take "All musicians are talented people" and convert it to "All talented people are musicians." When every term includes a plural noun, we can do so easily. The string of words "All talented are musicians" isn't even a sentence, much less a statement.

Missing quantifiers and articles

Examples: Snakes are poisonous.
Mammals are vertebrates.
A killer whale is a mammal.
A boy in my class likes me.

Many times people will assert categorical statements without specifically offering any quantifier. Usually the statement in these cases is an affirmative statement, so the only question is whether the statement is universal or particular. We can resolve this ambiguity by using the principle of charity: Use whichever statement is more likely to be true. For the first example, it is not true that all snakes are poisonous, so it would be inappropriate to paraphrase the first example as a universal statement. The statement "Some snakes are poisonous" is a much better paraphrase.

For the second example, it is actually true that all mammals are vertebrates, so this statement should be recognized as a universal statement. It should be paraphrased as "All mammals are vertebrates."

The third and fourth examples demonstrate that paraphrasing is not a rote mechanistic process. Ingenuity and understanding is often required to obtain a proper paraphrase. Although the third example uses the article "a", it should be clear that it is referring to all killer whales. So, it should be phrased as "all killer whales are mammals." The fourth example also uses the article "a", but in a different sense. Here, the article is used to refer to a particular individual in the class, and not to all of them. As such, the statement should be rephrased as an I statement: "Some boys in my class are people who like me."

Non-standard verbs

Examples: Some person is over eight feet tall.
No people will be at the movies.
All people breathe.

Often the verb used in a statement is a form of the infinitive "to be" which is not "are". Any such verb is still considered a copula, or linking verb, but the statement containing it would not be in standard form. Every such statement must be rewritten so that it does contain the verb "are". In some cases, you can reword a singular statement so that it is plural. We can rewrite the first statement as "Some people are individuals who are over eight feet tall." Note that we also had to add the word "individuals" to put the argument into standard form.

The second example includes a future tense verb. It might be acceptable to drop the future tense if it plays no role in the logic of the argument in which the statement is found, but a more precise approach is to add another group term, such as "individuals". The second example is rendered "No people are individuals who will be at the movies."

The third example doesn't include a copula at all, but an action verb. We also must add a group term in order to properly paraphrase these statements. The new statement must begin with "all people are..." and end with a group term. The statement "All people are creatures who breathe" would work, as would "All people are individuals who breathe." One could even use "All people are breathers" if one doesn't object to its awkwardness.

Non-standard quantifiers

Examples: Every item in the store is on sale.
A few gorillas have escaped.

Standard form is very limiting in terms of quantifiers. Only three are allowed, but English has many different ways to quantify statements. The standard is always the same here, if the quantifier implies universality, then use a universal quantifier, whether positive or negative. Words like "each", "every", and "any" will be replaced by "all", with any other adjustments necessary being made as well. A negative universal can be signified by words such as "none" and "not any". So our first example becomes "All items in the store are sale items."

There are numerous ways to express a particular quantifier as well. The thing to consider here is that we are using the word "some" in a technical sense in order to make it more amenable to deductive analysis. So, any statement which asserts that at least one individual thing exists can be expressed as a particular categorical statement. In some cases, a bit of meaning may be lost, but as long as the logic only depends on the existence of at least one thing, the paraphrase will work. The near synonyms "a couple" and "a few" are easily replaced by "some", as well as expressions like "several", "a number of" and "numerous". So, our second example can be written as "some gorillas are escaped animals."

When we start to get to quantifiers which imply even larger percentages of the whole, we could use the word "some", but even more meaning will be lost. For quantifiers such as "many", "most", or "the majority" it is better to treat the arguments they are found in as inductive, and analyze them using a more complicated inductive analysis involving probability, but we will leave that for a later chapter.

A special case: Few people have climbed Mt. Everest.

While the non-standard quantifier "a few" can easily be replaced by "some", the word "few" by itself has an added meaning. As in the example, when we say that "few people have climbed Mt. Everest", we are saying not only that there are some people who have climbed Mt. Everest, but that there are some who have not. Accordingly, this statement should be translated using two standard form categorical statements: "Some people are individuals who have climbed Mt. Everest, and some people are not individuals who have climbed Mt. Everest". The expression "almost all..." should be interpreted in the same way.

One thing to consider here is that categorical logic was built up around the syllogism, following Aristotle. Strictly defined, a syllogism can only have two premises. So, some of the techniques logicians have devised to evaluate syllogisms will not work if there are more than two premises. So when paraphrasing such statements for these techniques, you must select either of the two simple statements; choose either the I statement or the O statement. The rule is that, following the principle of charity, you should use whichever statement would make the argument in which it is found to be a valid argument. For the Venn diagram technique you will be learning in this text, it is perfectly acceptable to use three premises.

Exceptional Statements

Examples: Everyone except felons has a right to vote.
All children except emancipated minors must obey their parents.
No one but my friends can come to my party.

These exceptional cases, which involve exceptions to universal statements, raise several issues. The first issue is that these statements generally assert two of the basic categorical statements. Understanding these two statements requires us to understand term complements well. Consider the first example "Everyone except felons has a right to vote." This statement is asserting both that all people besides felons have a right to vote, and also that no felons have the right to vote. We limit our discussion to only adult people, and our two terms are "felons" and "people with a right to vote". Within the universe of discourse, the term complement for "felons" is just "non-felons". Putting everything together, we see that the proper paraphrase for the first example is "All non-felons are people who have the right to vote, and no felons are people who have the right to vote. Note that the first part of the compound statement is false, non-citizens do not have the right to vote.

It is instructive to see what a Venn diagram for this example is. When we add term complements, the diagrams can become a bit more complex. We will use the letter "F" to stand for "felons" and "V" for people who have the right to vote. So, we will need to diagram the statement "all non-F are V, and no F are V."

It is easy to diagram "No F are V" using what we have already learned, as shown in Figure 8.11. What is harder to is symbolize "All non-F are V." We could switch our Venn diagram to include non-F and V, but then we would have to reconsider "No F are V", and we would face the same problem. So, we will face the problem head on.

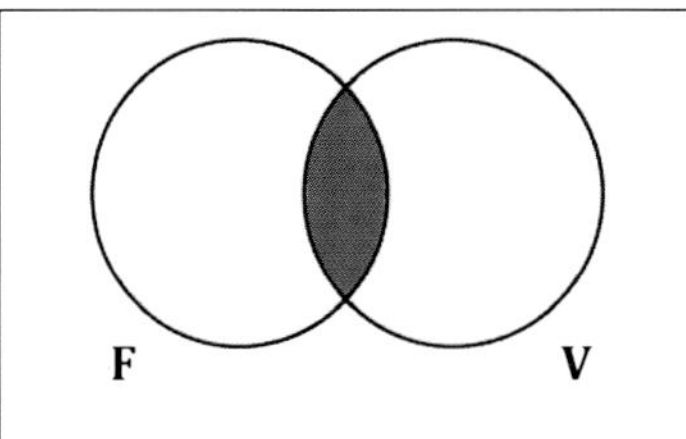

Figure 8.11
Universe of Discourse = Adults

When we say that all non-F are V, we are saying that anything which is outside of F, which includes everything outside of the F circle, is necessarily inside of the V circle. There is nothing outside the F circle unless it is inside of the V circle. In other words, the area which is outside of both circles is empty. In English, every non-felon has a right to vote, so every non-felon is inside of the V circle. Remember that we show that an area is empty by shading it. So to complete our diagram, we must shade the area outside of both circles, as is done in Figure 8.12.

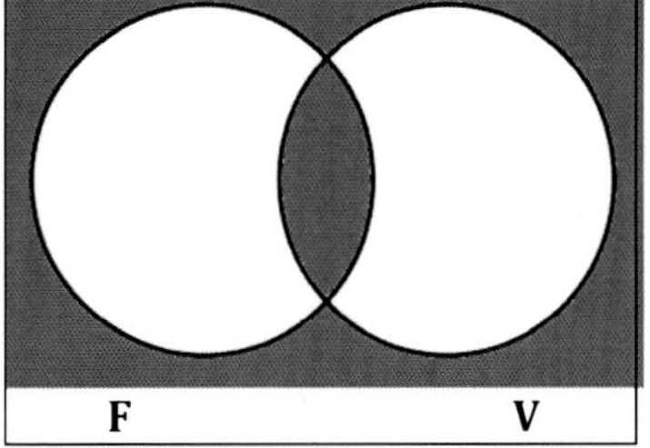

Figure 8.12
Universe of Discourse = Adults

The second example involving emancipated minors works the same way as the first example. It breaks down into the same basic statements, only the group terms and universe of discourse are different. The statement itself gives a strong hint to the proper universe of discourse. It discusses children, some of whom are emancipated minors, and some of whom must obey their parents. It is natural, then, to use "children" as our universe of discourse. The first term is emancipated minors, and the second term is people who must obey their parents, and the statement becomes "all non-emancipated minors are children who must obey their parents, and no emancipated minors are children who must obey their parents." Using E to represent emancipated minors, and O to represent children who must obey their parents, we obtain the diagram in Figure 8.13.

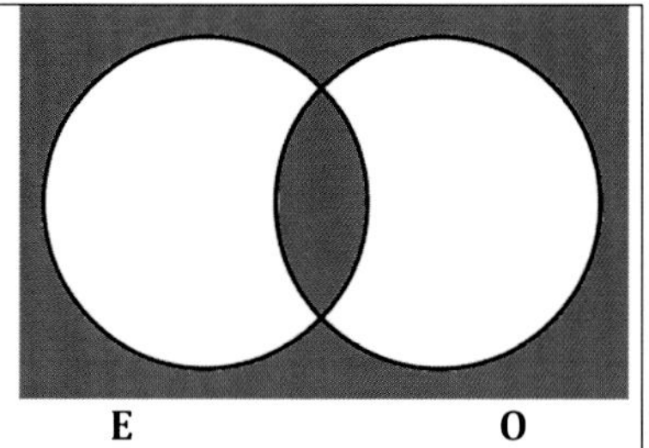

Figure 8.13
Universe of Discourse = Children

The third example is a bit different, as it includes an execption to a negative universal. We will restrict our universe of discourse to people, and we will use F for "my friends" and P for "people who can come to my party". The statement itself is then paraphrased into "All my friends are people who can come to my party, and no people who are not my friends are people who can come to my party," or "All F are P, and no non-F are P." The first part of that statement is easy to diagram, since it is a standard A statement. The second part includes a term complement, so it will be a little more difficult.

To say that "no non-F are P" is to say that nothing outside of F is inside of P. So, the area outside of f but inside of p is empty and must be shaded. Accordingly we end up with the diagram as in Figure 8.14.

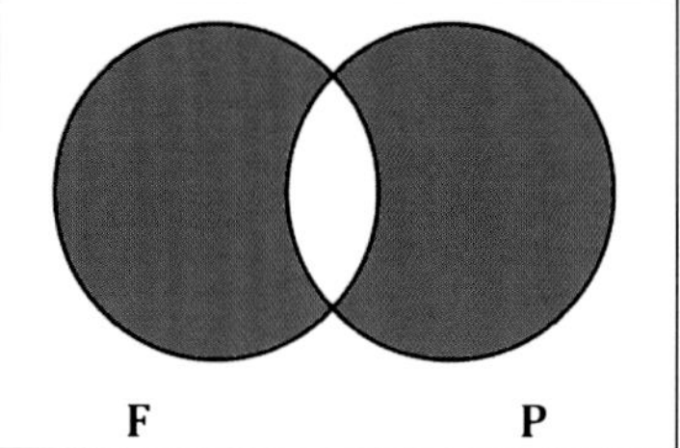

Figure 8.14
Universe of Discourse = People

As we saw in the previous chapter, in standard form categorical syllogisms only two premises are considered at a time. If you have any reason to reduce your premises to only two, you should always follow the principle of charity and use the simple statement which will make the argument in question valid.

Only

Examples: Only women can have babies.
Gorillas eat only bananas.
The only mammals which can fly are bats.

The word "only" is a versatile word. Depending on where it is placed in a sentence it can give the sentence a variety of meanings. We will only address a few cases, and it will be incumbent upon the reader to extend these guidelines to other cases. As a general rule, the word "only" occurs in universal statements, and the predicate term of the statement immediately follows the word "only". Students quite often get this one wrong, so make sure you follow carefully.

Consider the first example. It is definitely true that only women can have babies, but it is also false that all women can have babies. So, it would be a mistake to paraphrase the first statement as "all women are people who are capable of having babies." Consider, though, that if a person is capable of having a baby, then that person is definitely a woman. So, the proper way to paraphrase the first example is "all people who are capable of having babies are women."

The second example asserts that gorillas only eat bananas, which is false, but we want to know how it should be paraphrased. What the statement is saying is that if a gorilla does something with a banana, it is going to eat it. So, we can change this statement to "All instances of gorillas doing something with a banana are instances of gorillas eating a banana." Logicians are well aware that this sentence is hard to get a handle on. It is long and awkward, and would probably earn you a bad score in an English paper. But it is precise and can be used in standard categorical logic, for which reason they will prefer it.

The statement "Gorillas only eat bananas" is often interpreted the same as "gorillas eat only bananas," but they technically don't have the same meaning. Consider that gorillas could do all sorts of things with bananas; they could throw them, barter with them, smoke them, or numerous other things. The statement that "gorillas only eat bananas" states that of all the things that gorillas could do with bananas, they only eat them. This statement is consistent with the fact that gorillas could eat other foods as well, which they do, unlike the statement "gorillas eat only bananas", which rules out any other food. If we wanted to paraphrase "gorillas eat only bananas," we can write "All foods that gorillas eat are bananas."

Finally, when we use the phrase "the only" things are usually reversed. The term that immediately follows this phrase is the subject term. The third example, "The only mammals which can fly are bats," becomes "All mammals which can fly are bats." It doesn't matter where in the sentence the phrase occurs. For example, we can assert the same piece of information as follows: "Bats are the only mammals which can fly."

Singular Statements

Examples: Socrates was a man.
I love Paris in the springtime.

Technically, "Socrates" is not a group term, and so cannot be used in categorical reasoning. However, such singular statements are often used in arguments. If categorical logic could not apply to such statements, it would be severely limited. In one sense, it would be perfectly fine to leave categorical logic limited in this fashion. Modern logic captures these sorts of statements much more intuitively and smoothly. Logicians would not recommend using categorical logic to handle such statements, but instead to use modern propositional or predicate logic. Traditional logicians did not have the benefit of modern logic, so it was incumbent upon them to either admit that their logic was very limited, or devise a technique to incorporate such statements into categorical logic, which they did. In any case, these techniques work, and may be useful in some cases, especially for students who have not yet learned propositional or predicate logic.

The trick is to take an individual thing and treat it as a group term. We can do this to the term "Socrates" by treating it as "people identical to Socrates." Then the only question is whether the statement is a universal or a particular statement. When we say that Socrates was a man, we are definitely asserting that all the things which are identical to Socrates (of which there is only one) were men. So, a universal statement seems appropriate. But we are also asserting that Socrates did exist, so our statement would seem to have existential import, and thus a universal statement alone would not be appropriate. But we could use a particular statement. The solution is to use both. To assert that "Socrates was a man" is to assert both that "All things identical to Socrates are men, and Some things identical to Socrates are men."

The second example is a little more challenging. It involves a singular statement and a transitive verb. Yet it is easily captured in the statement "All people identical to me are people who love Paris in the Spring, and some people identical to me are people who love Paris in the Spring." As before, it sounds awkward, but it allows us to evaluate any argument containing the statement using standard techniques. As with exceptional statements, in a categorical syllogism, often only one of the statements can be used. Applying the principle of charity, again, simply use whichever statement would make the argument in question valid.

Conditional Statements

Examples: If your cell phone rings in class, then you will have to leave for the day.
If an animal has rabies, then you should not play with it.

Conditional statements are usually a sign that one should apply modern logical analysis. Modern logic arguably is built up around the conditional. Nevertheless, in some cases, conditional statements can be easily captured using traditional logic, generally when the antecedent (the "if" part) relates to the same subject as the consequent (the "then" part). In both of the examples, this condition holds. Conditional statements are paraphrased using universal statements, and they are affirmative or negative depending on whether the conditional involves an affirmative or negative expression.

The first example may involve a "negative" experience, but it is phrased in an affirmative way, so when we paraphrase it we use an A type statement: "All students who have their cell phones ring in class are students who will have to leave for the day." The second example includes a negative statement, so we use a negative universal statement. It becomes "No animals with rabies are animals with which you should play."

Here is another conditional statement: "If Sasha is going to Bill's 18th birthday party, then Marisela is not." In this case the subject of the antecedent and consequent are different, so it would be unwise to use categorical logic in this case. We will see how to handle statements such as these in chapter 14.

Times and Places

Examples: Always eat your vegetables.
He never brushes his teeth in the morning.

Some statements which are not amenable to straightforward paraphrasing can still be captured using categorical logic if we allow our subject to range not over specific entities, but over times, places or cases. Adverbs like "always" and "never" or adverbial phrases are often indicators that this approach will work best. It would not work to translate the first example as "All vegetables are things which you should eat." You should not eat every single vegetable in the world. But we could use the statement "All cases where you are served vegetables are cases when you should eat the vegetables which you are served." This statement is clearly an A statement of the form All S are P.

Notwithstanding the grossness of the second example, it can be stated in terms of times. "He never brushes his teeth in the morning" becomes "No times that he brushes his teeth are times which are in the morning". Astute students will recognize that it is still possible to state this example in an affirmative sense by using a term-complement, by saying that "All times that he brushes his teeth are times which are *not* in the morning." Let's hope that even though the example as stated does not have existential import, he at least brushes his teeth at least once a day.

Final Suggestions

Examples: *All* prisoners are not violent.
All mammals are not cold-blooded.

As always, the context of a statement is very important. We have learned that the statement "All mammals are not cold-blooded" should be rewritten as "No mammals are cold-blooded." This is a true statement and is unlikely to be uttered in an ambiguous way. The first example, however, may well be uttered in an ambiguous way. Imagine a context where people are discussing prisoners, and one person expresses the view that every prisoner is violent. The other person may utter the first example, putting stress on the word "all". They almost certainly would not mean that "no prisoners are violent", as that would be absurd. Instead, this statement should be interpreted as "not all prisoners are violent", which would become "Some prisoners are not violent."

Do not consider the rules you have learned here to be completely mechanistic procedures. Once we have statements in standard form, then it is possible to be much more mechanistic, but taking ordinary language and rewriting it into standard form is quite often more of an art than a science. Always consider the intent of the person asserting a statement, and use your best judgment in paraphrasing to capture what the person means to say.

Chapter Thirteen Exercises

Basic Concept Exercises

Paraphrase each of the following statements using standard form categorical statements. Make sure both the subject and the predicate terms are *terms*.

1. There are no such things as stars without planets.
2. The only citizens who are not allowed to vote are felons.
3. The middle ages were brutal.
4. It is false that Hillary Clinton will be the next President.
5. The death penalty is unconstitutional.
6. Glass is immune to most acids.
7. Lightning can be found anywhere on the globe, as long as there's a thunderstorm present.
8. I hate gardening.
9. Don't drink and drive.
10. We should remove all pollutants from our water.

Intermediate Exercises

For the following exercises, rewrite the argument using standard form categorical statements, then use any method to determine whether they are valid. Each one is a categorical syllogism.

11. The death penalty is cruel and unusual punishment, and all cruel and unusual punishments are unconstitutional, so the death penalty is unconstitutional.

12. A society which allows slavery is unjust. Our society does not allow slavery, so our society is just.
13. Universal healthcare is fundamentally unjust because every system which forces people who live healthy lives to help pay for the healthcare expenses of those who live unhealthy lifestyles is unjust, and that is exactly what universal healthcare does.
14. If an argument is sound, then it must be valid, but all valid arguments are deductive, which seems to show that all deductive arguments are sound.
15. Every number over 100 must be a composite number, since only composite numbers can be divided by more than two numbers, yet every number over 100 can be divided by more than two numbers.
16. All (solar) planets orbit the Sun, are spherical, and have cleared out their orbital paths, and while Pluto orbits the Sun and is spherical, it has not cleared its orbital path. Thus, Pluto is not a planet.
17. None but employees are allowed into the meeting. Since I am an employee, I am allowed into the meeting.
18. If you're wise, then you won't make any mistakes. There is no teacher who hasn't made a mistake. So, no teacher is wise.
19. If you believe in conspiracy theories, then you are paranoid. Could a paranoid person be credible? It's just not true that any conspiracy theorists are credible.
20. A person involved in a sex scandal proves that they don't have any self-control. Only people with self-control should ever be elected into office, so no person involved in a sex scandal should ever be elected.

Challenging exercises

For the following exercises, rewrite the argument using standard form categorical statements, then use any method to determine whether they are valid. These examples may be immediate inferences, categorical syllogisms or enthymemes.

21. Any argument that is sound is necessarily valid. That makes every unsound argument invalid.
22. If you do the right thing, it will make you happy, which shows that if you do something and it makes you unhappy, then it is not moral.
23. There were no waves at the beach today, and Johnny only goes to the beach when there're waves.
24. Not all dinosaurs were sauropods, but dinosaurs were all cold-blooded. So, there must have existed some cold-blooded non-sauropods.
25. Whenever a woman gets married, she should take the last name of her husband. But no true feminist would take the last no of her husband, so no true feminist should get married.
26. I know that there are hadrons that are baryons, since there are protons that are hadrons.
27. If you apologize to me expecting that I have to forgive you, then your apology is insincere. Yet, every apology is made with the expectation of forgiveness.
28. Whenever you leave chicken unrefrigerated for more than eight hours, there is a strong chance that it will become contaminated. Would you want to eat contaminated chicken?
29. The classroom policy in la-la land is that "every person who either earned an A on every quiz or earned a B or above on every test does not have to take the

final", but the teacher insisted that every person who received an A on every quiz must take the final. It looks to me like every person who received a B or above on every test earned below on A on at least one quiz.

30. "Count no man happy till he dies, free of pain at last."

Last line of Sophocles' *Oedipus Rex*

In-Context Exercises

A. In the following argument, rewrite any categorical statements in standard form.

The fair-use doctrine is completely misunderstood. One can use someone else's words without violating their copyright protection. Not all cases where someone copies another author's words are infringements on their rights. If the copying does not result in the loss to the copyright owner of the ability to profit from owing the copyright, then no violation has occurred. That's why a teacher can use pretty much any small piece of writing in a classroom as an example without paying the copyright owner. Of course, should the teacher not reveal the source of the material, one could still consider it a case of plagiarism.

Logic Puzzle: What's a Hagfish?

You have five speakers, who make the following comments:

1. Prof. Ringling says: All Hagfish are Chordates.
2. Prof. Howser says: Some Chordates are not Vertebrates.
3. Dr. Hugh says: All Chordates are Vertebrates.
4. Mrs. Coolidge says: Some Chordates are Hagfish.
5. Mr. Manfield says: If something is a Hagfish, then it's not a Vertebrate.

Given that one and only one of the speakers is mistaken, determine using logic alone which one it would have to be.

Logic and Metaphysics

Metaphysics is one of the major areas of study of philosophy, and can be defined as the study of existence. As the name implies, though, it is not only the study of what exists physically, but in any way whatsoever. Whereas physics studies material objects that exist "physically" and the interactions between those objects (traditionally by appealing to "forces"), metaphysics studies anything which exists, or even existence itself. Although one might consider physics to be a branch of metaphysics, they are generally considered today two separate areas of study.

It may be difficult for modern students to wrap their heads around metaphysics, especially in a materialistic culture. That is not to say that America is materialistic in the usual sense of the word (although it is), but to say that American culture generally eschews the abstract and tends to focus more on the practical. "Seeing is believing" is an expression that captures this sort of view. We Americans generally have been taught to conceive of the universe as a material, physical place, and those who don't still seem to place the non-physical in another realm entirely.

This is a philosophical predilection, and it is not one shared by all cultures, nor even all Americans. As the proverbial fish has a hard time seeing the water around him, Americans sometimes have a hard time understanding how existence could be conceived as anything other than physical, except maybe the afterlife and the deity. These would certainly be considered metaphysical issues, but they are not the only ones.

Consider numbers. Do numbers exist? We seem to think that they do, and yet they don't seem to have any physical existence. What about "justice"? Is it a physical thing which can be measured and scientifically analyzed? Or does it not exist at all? Ideas in general seem to be difficult to classify as physical entities, although many philosophers and scientists are trying to show that they are. What about forces? Does gravity exist? In one sense, of course it does. Anyone who has ever dropped anything can confirm that it does, and yet, in what sense does it exist? Is it an object? Is it a property of objects? Where does it exist? Specifically, does it exist in an area even when no objects are present, or does it 'pop' into existence when they appear? Is it an illusion, resulting from a misunderstanding of space-time, or is it the result of an exchange of particles on a sub-atomic level?

I hope one can see that metaphysics concerns itself with some important issues, regardless of one's views on spiritual entities. Spiritual entities can of course be studied with an eye toward metaphysics, but so can a great many other areas, including "scientific" ones. In this brief section, we cannot cover much, but perhaps we can introduce a metaphysical issue which may be at the heart of the switch from syllogistic logic to more modern forms. It is the issue of groups.

Is a group a thing? Let's choose a group, say turtles. Do "turtles" exist? Schooled from a modern perspective, most of us will simply say "yes" without really understanding the question. Of course, turtles exist. I saw a turtle just the other day. And I've seen other turtles in the past. So, of course turtles exist. This answer really just avoids the question. Of course individual turtles exist, but when we discuss "turtles" as a group, does the term have any metaphysical status above and beyond simply a collection of individuals. Is the sum, as the saying goes, greater than the parts?

We in America and the western world tend to think not. We have mostly followed the analytic tradition arising out of England in the modern era, which tended to reject any kind of ontological status for groups. We think of the individual as having primary existence, and any group being simply a function to target a collection of individuals. The name is no more than a place holder. We think that the individual truly exists, and groups only secondarily or dependently have existence, if at all. Historically, and throughout much of the world today, especially in more eastern traditions, the individual was not considered metaphysically primary.

In the Confucian worldview, for example, no individual is thought to exist apart from the relationships to which he belongs. In some sense, the groups are the primary metaphysical entities, and the individuals are merely expressions of those groups. For a Confucian, what happens to society as a whole is far more important than what happens to any one individual in society.

Plato, too, regarded the individual as secondary to the group, although in a complicated fashion. He seemed to think that group membership was explained by appeal to the "form" of an object, an archetypical entity. He argued that there was a "form" of alligator, which is like the perfect example of an alligator, although not existing in our physical world, nevertheless having real existence. All alligators were alligators because they participated in the universal form of alligators. This metaphysical issue became known as the problem of universals, and arguably continues to this day.

As early as the Renaissance, the view that groups had a real existence apart from the individuals which composed them began to be criticized in the West. This metaphysical understanding, the primary reality of the individual, had implications in all areas of life. It influenced views of marriage, political realities, and religion. Political Liberalism can be understood as rejecting the idea that the society is fundamental, and instead the individual is. This emphasis on the individual eventually had its effect on logic.

Aristotelian logic, with its emphasis on groups, or terms, and the relationships between such groups, makes perfect sense within a worldview which takes groups to be primary. When the culture shifted to an individualistic perspective, many of the flaws of syllogistic logic became more apparent. What was needed was a logic which had its roots in and focused on the individual. The shift to truth-functional logic under such logicians as George Boole and others began this transformation of logic, but it found its culmination in the predicate logic of Gottlob Frege.

In truth functional logic, the fundamental item is the simple statement, which can be conceived of as saying a single thing about a single thing. We will be turning to truth functional logic next. Although modern logicians use a version of predicate logic, it is still based upon truth functional connections. Predicate logic takes individuals as truly primary, along with properties which can be asserted of those individuals. In this introductory textbook, we will only briefly cover predicate logic.

So, are individuals primary or groups? That is an important question, one which has no simple answer. It involves one's assumptions about the world in ways which are not amenable to scientific analysis or measurement. I do think it is important, however, for modern students to realize that they are often indoctrinated into one metaphysical doctrine without even being exposed to any alternative viewpoints. Unfortunately, this produces people who cannot even conceive of looking at the world in ways other than they have been taught.

Fortunately, however, even Plato could use and appreciate predicate logic. Predicate logic may have been derived because of the societal drive toward the individual, but it does not depend upon it.

CHAPTER

14

Truth-Functional Propositional Logic

As powerful as categorical reasoning is, there are still some arguments which it cannot handle. A difficult example which traces back at least to De Morgan is the following:

<u>All horses are animals</u>
∴ All heads of horses are heads of animals.

This argument looks intuitively valid, yet it is not clear how that validity could be captured by syllogistic logic. Syllogistic logic also seems incapable of handling disjunctive arguments, such as the following:

All numbers are either odd or even.
Four is a number.
<u>Four is not odd.</u>
∴ Four is even.

Perhaps a solution could be found to get around these limitations, but if so, it would probably look very odd, like the solution for dealing with individuals. If you recall, the premise "Four is a number" must be turned into "All things identical to four are numbers, and some things identical to four are numbers." No one wants to deal with something more complicated than this.

Fortunately, modern logicians over the last three hundred years abandoned syllogistic logic. Perhaps abandoned is too strong a word. It is still taught, and it works fine in many cases. In any case, Venn diagrams are still incredibly useful, and having the ability to draw them and understand them is still indispensable in many areas of logic, probability and math. But when confronted with the limitations of syllogistic logic, modern logicians instead looked back to an entirely different sort of logic, the logic of the stoics, which is now called **propositional logic**.

Propositional Logic
The logic which deals with statements as wholes

Propositional logic, by itself, is probably less useful than syllogistic logic, but predicate logic builds upon propositional logic, and goes beyond both of them. The argument above can be captured in quantificational predicate logic, but these techniques are fairly challenging for beginning students. One shouldn't get to predicate logic, however, until one has some proficiency in propositional logic. We will aim do so in the next few chapters.

The first thing to learn is actually that you must unlearn something, though not in the sense of forgetting it entirely. In categorical logic, the basic subject matter concerned terms. These terms were replaced by letters in order to more clearly see the underlying logic of arguments. So, most students will immediately see a capital letter and understand it as a term. The first thing to learn about propositional logic is that *letters do not represent terms; they represent statements.*

Students who do not quickly recognize this difference will suffer in their ability to understand what is going on. Again, the subject matter of propositional logic is statements: capital letters represent statements, which are always formed in complete sentences. This is what makes it *propositional* logic, as opposed to syllogistic logic.

So, the basic component of an argument is considered to be a statement, and statements are represented by letters. Yet, the premises of an argument cannot always be simply a letter. For example, consider an argument based on the one above:

Four is either even or odd
Four is not odd.
∴ Four is even.

Again, the argument is intuitively valid, but if we were to capture each premise with a single capital letter, the argument would just consist of a string of letters, as shown here:

E
N
∴ V

This way of symbolizing obscures the validity of the argument. If we are going to use symbolism to clarify the validity, something else must be done. The problem here is that the argument relies on a few logically important words, which cannot be hidden in the content of the capital letters. The words "or" and "not" in this argument are critically important in understanding the validity of the argument, and so cannot be hidden, but must be visible. They constitute the formal structure of the argument and cannot be subsumed within letters. Let's rewrite the argument while leaving the logical connectives intact, as we do here:

E or O	E represents "Four is Even"
Not O	O represents "Four is Odd"
∴ E	

Here, E stands for "Four is even", and O stands for "Four is odd". Now, it is much easier to see the validity in the form of the argument itself. These logical connectives form the heart of propositional logic. Traditionally, logicians prefer to use symbols to represent these logical connectives, but we could use words just as easily. It shouldn't be too difficult to learn five new symbols, and it makes our symbolic forms more concise.

At this point we can be more precise. More specifically, each capital letter will represent a **simple statement**. A simple statement is one which has a single subject and a single predicate. It will say one thing about one thing. If we say something about more than one thing, then we must use more than one capital letter. If we say more than one thing about one subject, then we must use a separate capital letter for each thing that we say.

Simple Statement
A statement which includes one subject and one predicate

So, to say that "The Earth is round", we can use a single letter, perhaps E. In this case, a capital E is a good choice because it will call to mind the subject matter of the statement, but technically any letter may be chosen. Now, if we were to say that "The Earth is round and blue", we would need to use two letters. In this case, it would be odd to choose E, so we should probably go with "R and B" to stand for "The Earth is round and the Earth is blue."

A statement which includes both simple statements (capital letters) and symbolic connectives is called a compound statement. We will use a lower case letter to represent a **statement variable**, which could turn out to be a compound statement or a simple one.

Statement Variable
A lower case letter which can represent simple or compound statements

Before we continue, we should take some time here to understand what makes propositional logic a kind of truth-functional logic. A function is a type of relation which pairs things together. It takes an object from one set of things, and matches it to an object in another set. The first set, from which the first object is taken, is called the domain, and the set of objects to which that object is matched is called the range. Any relation is also a device for matching objects in this way, but there is something special about a function. In a function, each member of the domain has an exclusive member to which it is matched. In a non-functional relation, some members of the domain are matched to more than one member of the range.

For example, if we were to take people, and match them to things that they like, the resulting relation would not be a function. Most people like more than one thing. We would still end up with a map, so to speak, from the members of the domain, in this case people, to members of the range, which could include anything. This relation, however, would not match each member of the domain to a single member of the range, so it would not be a function.

If we were to map every person, however, to their biological mother, then we would have a function. Every member of the domain, which would still include all people, would be matched to a single woman, a mother from the range of the function. It would be the case that more than one person in the domain could be matched to the same mother, as would be the case for all siblings, but no person would have more than one biological mother (at least for now).

If we take the three holidays Christmas, Halloween, and Independence Day, and map them to the months in which they occur, the result is a function, as shown in Table 14.1. But taking months, and mapping them to holidays would not result in a function, since each month has more than one holiday. Furthermore, adding Easter to the list would not result in a function, since Easer sometimes occurs in March and sometimes in April, as shown in Table 14.2.

Table 14.1
A function

Holidays (Domain)	Months (Range)
Christmas →	December
Halloween →	October
Independence Day →	July

Table 14.2
A non-functional relation

Holidays (Domain)	Months (Range)
Christmas →	December
Halloween →	October
Independence Day →	July
Easter →	March
↘	April

The point of these examples is to understand that some logical connectives work like functions. They will connect two statements in such a way that the resulting truth value can always be determined. The result is perfectly predictable. Consider a logical connective to be like a junction box with inputs and outputs. In a function, the result is always the same, given the same inputs. In the following box, the connective is an "and" and it is connecting X and Y. What makes this connective a function is that whatever the truth values of X and Y, the truth value of the statement "X and Y" is always dependent on the truth values of X and Y. No other information is needed nor is relevant. In this case, when X and Y are both individually true, then the statement "X and Y" is necessarily a true statement.

Contrast this situation with a junction box which is not truth-functional, say "John believes X and Y". It should be clear that the truth value of this statement does not depend on the truth value of X and Y by themselves.

In this example, the truth of the component statements does not guarantee the truth of the outcome. Given that X is true and Y is true, it could still be the case that "John believes 'X and Y'" is either true or false. These types of connectives are not truth-functional, they don't map the truth values of the simple statements reliably. In this introductory textbook, we will only be dealing with connectives which will work in a functional manner.

To put it perhaps more clearly, a connective which always has the same output given the same input is a functional connective, and we will learn five of them in the pages that follow, namely Negation, Conjunction, Disjunction, Material Implication, and Material Equivalence.

Skill 14.1

Translating Statements into Symbolic Form

Negation

The simplest connective is negation. Technically speaking, a negation is an operation, since it does not connect two statements, but only operates on a single one. It is general practice, however, to speak of connectives loosely, so that it includes the operation of negation as well. One way to operate on a statement to make it a negation is to preface the statement with "It is false that..." So, were I to negate the statement "Jupiter is the largest planet", I could write "It is false that Jupiter is the largest planet". It should be clear that negation is necessarily part of the logical structure of an argument. Imagine if we were to use a letter for the one statement, and a completely unrelated letter for its negation, say J for "Jupiter is the largest planet", and K for "It is false that Jupiter is the largest planet, We would be completely unable to see that there is a strong logical connection between these two statements. For this reason, we need to treat a negation as a logical operation, and not as an unrelated statement.

Negation	~ tilde
Alternate symbols	–, ¬, N
English phrases which are negations	not It is false that It is not the case that Term complements "Un-" antonyms
Well-formed formulas (wffs)	~A ~A • B ~(A ∨ B) ~~~D ~(p) where p stands for any statement
Non-wffs	M~ M~N

Table 14.3

The symbol we will use for a negation is the tilde, and it will always precede the statement which it is negating. So, it is permissible to write ~M to negate M, but never M~. The tilde can never go between two statements by itself, either, not being strictly a connective.

So, a negation will always be in the form of ~p, where p represents any statement, and may be called the negated statement. It is important to understand this point, especially in understanding **well-formed formulas**. Not every string of letters and symbols will have a meaning. This string of letters and symbols "A~B", for example, does not have any

Well-Formed Formulas (wffs) A well-formed formula is a properly structured symbolized statement

meaning in the system we are learning. The tilde only operates on a single statement, and so it cannot be used to connect two statements, at least not by itself.

Accordingly, one way to judge whether a tilde is being used in a "grammatical" way, at least one in accord with the rules for symbolizing, is to ask whether the tilde immediately precedes a well-formed formula. We will return to this point when we have learned another symbol.

The tilde may also be used when dealing with antonyms or term complements. Whereas I might use D to represent "Alphie is a dog", to express "Alphie is a non-dog" I would use ~D, since "Alphie is a non-dog" is equivalent to "It is false that Alphie is a dog" or "Alphie is not a dog." Remember, we don't use letters such as D to stand for terms, but for entire statements.

Skill 14.2

Recognizing Well-Formed Formulas

Keep in mind that the negation is a truth-functional operator, so the only thing required to determine whether a negation is true, is the truth value of its negated statement. No matter what statement with which we are dealing, the negation of that statement will result in a statement with an opposite truth value. Let us say "Today is Monday," symbolized as M. For some readers of this textbook, this statement will be true, and for others it will be false. It is also the case that the statement "It is not Monday" will be false for all and only those people for whom "Today is Monday" was true. We can show all of this on a basic table, which will capture all of the possibilities.

p	~p
T	F
F	T

Today is Monday	Today is not Monday
If this statement is True	Then this one is False
If this statement is False	Then this one is True

Any statement for which p stands will be either true or false. The cases where ~p are true are exactly those cases where p is false, and ~p is false exactly in those cases where p is true. Every compound statement has a truth value, just as every simple statement does. The point about truth functional logic is that we can determine the truth values of compound statements in all cases by simply referring to the truth values of their component statements. Negation is a very simple case, but conjunction is not much more difficult.

Conjunction

Everyone has learned about conjunctions in the sense of English, but in logic the term has a slightly narrower meaning. Generally, words or phrases which connect two statements are logical conjunctions, but the exception is the word "or" and any word that functions as "or" does. A conjunction in logic is a connective which connects two statements in such a way as to assert that both of the two statements are true. So, any conjunction in English which does this should be translated into symbolic form using a dot, the symbol for logical conjunction.

The word "and" is clearly a logical conjunction. When I say "I ate a sandwich and fries," I clearly mean that it is true that I ate a sandwich and it is also true that I ate fries. If we were to rewrite this statement in symbolic form, we would appropriately use a dot here to get 'S • F.' Most conjunctions in English work the same way, such as "in addition", "also", and "furthermore".

Conjunction	• dot
Alternate symbols	&, ∧, K (in Polish notation)
English words or phrases which are conjunctions	And In addition Also Furthermore, But, However,
Well-formed formulas (wffs)	~A • B ~(A • B) (A • B) • C F • ~ R
Non-wffs	G • M • N • O F ~• R

Table 14.4

It is a little odd, however, to think of some conjunctions as simply saying this and nothing more. For example, if I were to ask whether the words "and" and "but" meant the same thing, I dare say no competent English speaker would say that they do. Yet, we are saying that they should both be translated using the same symbol. The reason is that the word "but" does exactly what we said was required for a conjunction: it connects two statements in such a way that it indicates that both statements are true.

So, to say that "I didn't finish my homework, and I'm going to the party" asserts that it is true that "I did not finish my homework" and it is true that "I am going to the party." Now consider the statement "I didn't finish my homework, but I'm going to the party." It clearly also asserts that it is true that "I didn't finish my homework" and also true that "I'm going to the party." So, both are appropriately translated using a logical conjunction.

One might wonder why, then, we have two different words. First, because we like to do that in English. Even when one word will work for something, we like to have many words for the sake of variety, and perhaps to allow shading of meaning. It is not too often that two different words have exactly the same connotation. Secondly, because the word "but" does mean something more that the word "and", but it is subtle and rarely relevant in any actual case. The word "but" seems to indicate an emphasis or a warning to the reader. We will say "A, but B" in a situation where it is normal, or to be expected, that whenever A is true, B is false. The word "but" is used to clarify that the situation is not as one might expect it to be. In a situation where one would normally expect that if one didn't finish one's homework, one would not go to the party, we would say "I didn't finish my homework, *but* I'm going to the party," to show that the typical situation is not the actual situation. Since the speaker of this sentence is clearly asserting that both simple statements are true ("I didn't finish my homework", and "I'm going to the party"), then it is appropriate to use a conjunction to translate this statement.

This additional expectation of an unusual situation is rarely relied upon in an argumentative context, but if it were, it would be necessary to capture that additional expectation. Generally, however, the word "but" can be translated with a conjunction alone. Similar things can be said with regard to the words "although" and "however".

It is important to understand the well-formed formulas in Table 14.4, as we will see the same patterns over and over. Every conjunction connects two statements, and so every dot should have a statement to its left and a statement to its right. If this is not the case, then the formula in question is not well-formed. We also will require that the statement be unambiguous, so that parentheses are required in order to clarify which connective is the controlling one. A string of three letters interspersed with two dots, will not be considered well-formed. We need to enclose one pair in parentheses. So, 'S • T • U' is not a wff (a standard abbreviation for well-formed formula), but '(S • T) • U' and 'S • (T • U)' both are. In both cases, the dot outside the parentheses is the controlling one (called the main operator—see Chapter 15).

Notice that it is possible to have the dot next to the tilde, but only when the tilde follows the dot. Consider the statement 'S • ~ T.' The tilde applies to the T, and the dot has a statement to its left 'S' and a statement to its right '~T.' On the other hand consider the formula 'S ~ • T.' This is not a well-formed formula, and so it doesn't represent a statement. There is a statement the right of the dot 'T,' but to its left we only have 'S~,' which is not a statement. It may be necessary to negate a conjunction, but we do not do so by putting the tilde in front of the dot, but by placing the conjunction in parentheses and then placing a tilde in front of it, like this: '~(S • T).'

One other important issue involving the tilde is that it will always be considered to have the minimum possible scope. This means that if it is in front of a simple statement, it will be considered to apply only to that simple statement. So, '~S • T' is also a statement, but it means '(~S) • T', and not '~(S • T).' The first statement '~S • T' is a conjunction of a negation '~S' and a simple statement 'T,' and the second '~(S • T)' is a negation of a conjunction composed of the simple statements 'S' and 'T.'

As we already stated, a conjunction in logic is a way to connect two statements in such a way that we are asserting that both statements are true. This rule determines the basic truth table for any conjunction. No matter what statements are being conjoined, if you know the truth values of the component statements, then you can determine the truth value of the conjunction. In essence, a conjunction is true only in case both of its conjuncts are true. If either conjunct, or both conjuncts are false, then the conjunction is false.

Since a conjunction is composed of two statements, we have more than just two possibilities to consider. Using 'p • q' to stand for any conjunction, we know that p can be true or false, and that q can be true or false. That means there are a total of four possible combinations of truth values for p and q, as is shown in the following truth table.

Table 14.5

p	q	p • q
T	T	T
T	F	F
F	T	F
F	F	F

We can capture the exact same information in a single column by placing the truth values of each simple statement directly under its representative letter. The following table contains the same information as the previous one.

Table 14.6

p • q
T T T
T F F
F F T
F F F

It may be difficult to see now, but it will be much easier to understand and evaluate more complicated truth tables if we can write in all truth values directly under each letter and symbol. Notice that the truth values under p in Table 14.6 are exactly the ones in the same order as under p in Table 14.5, and the same can be said for q respectively. Keep in mind that the truth table is based on a very simple idea, and it just looks like it's getting complicated. We all know what the word "and" means. When I say "A and B" I just mean that A is true and that B is true. So, my compound statement "A and B" is true only in those cases where both A and B are both true, and it is false otherwise. The truth table indicates exactly that.

Disjunction

There is a very simple English conjunction which we left out of our previous discussion, the word 'or'. The reason for this is simple: in logic 'or' is not a conjunction. When we use the word 'or' we are not asserting that both of the statements connected by the 'or' are true, we mean that at least one of them is. When I say "Today is either Monday or Tuesday", I am not asserting both that it is Monday and that it is Tuesday, but that it is one of the two and not any other. We use a wedge to symbolize this logical connection, which will look like this: 'M ∨ T.' The symbol is suggestive of the Latin word for 'or' which is 'vel'.

Disjunction	∨ wedge
Alternate symbols	A (in Polish notation)
English words or phrases which are disjunctions	Or Either...or Unless
Well-formed formulas (wffs)	~A ∨ B ~(A ∨ B) (A ∨ B) • C F ∨ ~ R
Non-wffs	∨ G M ∨ N • O F ~∨ R F •∨ R

Table 14.7

There are not too many other ways to say 'or' in English, but the word 'unless' functions the same way. There are other ways to translate the word unless', which we will explore later, but for now, it is easiest to simply substitute the wedge for the word 'unless'. So, when we say "unless you eat your vegetables, you won't be eating dessert", we can write 'V ∨ ~D.'

There is something very important to note here. The disjunction we have learned, which is represented by the wedge, is an inclusive disjunction. All that means is that the compound statement is still considered true if both disjuncts are true. When I say "I will get gas on Friday or Saturday", I probably don't mean it is impossible that I will do both. Having told you that I will get gas on Friday or Saturday, let's say I get gas on Friday, but I only have enough cash to get a gallon, so I return on Saturday to fill up the tank. I don't think that we would say I told you an untruth. But if I waited until Sunday to get any gas at all, then my statement would indeed have been untruthful.

A disjunction which instead meant that one and only one of the disjuncts is true is an exclusive 'or' and cannot be represented by the wedge alone. When a parent says to a child "You can have an X-box or a PS-3 for your birthday", they almost certainly mean that the child can have one or the other, but not both. The method for translating such a statement will be left for one of the chapter exercises.

The inclusive 'or', as we have said, asserts that at least one of its disjuncts is true, and perhaps both of them. So, the only time the disjunction is false is when both disjuncts are false. We can display this in a basic truth table like we did before. As we did with conjunction, we can create our truth table either with reference columns out to the left, or without, as shown below (quick test: was that an inclusive or an exclusive "or"?). (Another quick test: Was the "or" in the parenthetical question an inclusive or an exclusive "or"?)

p	q	p ∨ q
T	T	T
T	F	T
F	T	T
F	F	F

p ∨ q
T T T
T T F
F T T
F F F

Table 14.8

As can be seen in the tables above, a disjunctive statement is true in every case where one disjunct or more is true. The only time it is false is when both disjuncts are false.

Material Implication

Material Implication	⊃ horseshoe
Alternate symbols	→ ,C (in Polish notation)
English words or phrases which are conditionals, or material implications	If Only if Given that Provided that Sufficient condition Necessary condition Implies Universal Categoricals
Well-formed formulas (wffs)	~A ⊃ B ~(A ⊃ B) (A ⊃ B) • C F ⊃ ~ R
Non-wffs	⊃ G M ∨ N ⊃ O F ~⊃ R F •∨ R

Table 14.9

We learned long ago about conditional statements. A conditional statement is often expressed using the words "if" and "then", but there are numerous others ways to express it. No matter how it is expressed in English, we will translate it the same way, using a "horseshoe".

The horseshoe works a little bit differently than the wedge or the dot. We sometimes talk about the left or right disjunct, but both conjunction and disjunction are commutative: they can be written forward or backward without changing meaning. So, 'A ∨ B' and 'B ∨ A' both mean the same thing. The conditional really matters which way it is written; 'A ⊃ B' is not the same as 'B ⊃ A.' For this reason, the component statements in a conditional statement have special names.

Antecedent
The statement in a conditional which comes before the horseshoe

Consequent
The statement in a conditional which comes after the horseshoe

The statement that comes before the horseshoe is called the **antecedent**, and the statement that comes after the horseshoe is the **consequent**. So, in the compound statement 'A ⊃ (D ∨ B),' the simple statement 'A' is the antecedent, and the compound statement 'D ∨ B' is the consequent. Make sure you learn these words; we will be constantly using them.

There are an incredible number of ordinary English phrases which are most naturally translated using the horseshoe. The most basic is the conditional 'if' statement, which precedes the antecedent of the conditional. The statement "If I study hard, then I will pass" will be translated 'S ⊃ P'. A few other ways to articulate a conditional statement are presented below. They are divided into phrases which introduce, or precede, the antecedent statement, and those that precede the consequent statement. Since the direction of the implication matters, it is important to ensure that the antecedent and consequent are placed accordingly.

Here are some phrases which introduce the antecedent, regardless where they come in a statement:

If ___antecedent___
Provided that ___antecedent___
Given that ___antecedent___
On condition that ___antecedent___
All ___antecedent___ are P

No __antecedent______ are P (Note: in this case the consequent P will be negated.)
C is a necessary condition for __antecedent_______ (Note: here C will be the consequent.)

So, the expression "Provided that I finish Math, I will earn my degree" is translated as 'M ⊃ D'. The sentence "All mosquitos are disease infested insects" is translated as 'M ⊃ D' (Remember, though, that every letter must stand for a complete simple statement. In this case, M stands for something like "a thing is a mosquito" and the D stands for "a (that) thing is a disease infested insect.")

The following phrases introduce the consequent, regardless where they come in a statement:

Only if ______consequent______
Implies that __consequent______
All S are ______consequent______
No S are ______consequent______ (Note: in this case the consequent will be negated.)
A is a sufficient condition for __consequent______ (Note: here A will be the antecedent.)

The last phrase may take more explaining. For claims of necessary or sufficient conditions, one must be very careful how one writes the conditional. In the case of sufficient conditions whatever phrase replaces the "consequent" in the sentence above will appear as the consequent of a conditional statement. So, to say that "being a monkey is a sufficient condition for being a primate," we write M ⊃ P, where M stands for "a creature is a monkey" and P stands for "a (that) creature is a primate."

Another way to remember the placement of the statements when given a necessary or sufficient condition is the SUN rule. Notice that the U looks like a horseshoe turned on the side. Remember, given that S is a sufficient condition for y, the S will be the antecedent of the conditional. On the other hand, given that N is a necessary condition for y, the N will occur as the consequent of the conditional. That's how we get S U N. "Breathing oxygen is a necessary condition for mammalian life" is translated L ⊃ O (and is true), whereas "breathing oxygen is a sufficient condition for mammalian life" is translated O ⊃ L (which is false—we also need food, water, etc.).

Keep in mind that any time someone is indicating that one statement is true on the condition that another statement is true, the horseshoe is the appropriate symbol to use. We can use this information to figure out the basic truth table for the horseshoe. Here it is:

p	q	p ⊃ q
T	T	T
T	F	F
F	T	T
F	F	T

p ⊃ q
T T T
T F F
F T T
F T F

Table 14.9

This table may take a bit more explaining than those for the first three symbols. Let's consider an actual conditional statement. Let's say there is a possible curve on an exam, and your friend makes the claim that "if you earn an 80% on the exam, then you will receive an A." In this case we will use E = p = "you earn an 80% on the exam" and A = q = "You receive an A for the exam. Perhaps he is engaging in wishful thinking, but you're not sure. In the case that you earn an 80%, and you actually receive an A, you would certainly accept that what your friend has said is true. This situation corresponds to the first line of the basic truth table, where both antecedent and consequent are true, and the conditional is true.

The second line of the truth table corresponds to the situation where E is true, you receive an 80%, but you do not receive an A, the consequent is false. In this case, you would certainly think that your friend had misspoken. For this reason, the conditional is considered false on the second line of the truth table, where the antecedent is true but the consequent is false.

Consider the bottom two rows of the truth table, where the antecedent is false. In these cases, you have not earned an 80%. Perhaps you earned something higher, perhaps lower, but definitely not an 80%. Either way, would either scenario convince you that what your friend had said was false? It would seem not. After all, he did not say anything about what would happen if you didn't get an 80%. If you receive an 81%, and also an A, it would not show that your friend's statement was false.

The bottom line is that the material conditional is considered true whenever the antecedent is false. Although this convention does not match perfectly with what we think and expect when dealing with conditional statements, it will generally do a passable job. The technical term for a conditional statement with a false antecedent is a counterfactual conditional, and the logical apparatus proposed for dealing with them will come in time for the student who continues to study logic.

The following example may also help some students in understanding the material conditional. Let's suppose I say that "I promise that I will buy you ice cream if you get an A on your paper." If you get the A and I buy you ice cream, then I have kept my promise. If you earned the A, but I didn't buy you ice cream, then I would have clearly broken my promise. Now, if you don't get the A and I don't buy you ice cream, I also have not broken my promise. It may be harder to see, but if you don't get the A, but I still buy you ice cream, then I still haven't broken my promise. Perhaps I say that you worked very hard, and that your hard work should be rewarded. After all, I didn't promise that if you didn't get an A, I wouldn't buy you an ice cream. The statement 'A ⊃ I' is not the same as the statement '~A ⊃ ~I'. The only time it is clear that I have broken my promise is when you get the A, but I don't buy you ice cream.

For now, just remember that when dealing with the material conditional, use the truth table outlined above. There is inherent in its use a basic presumption that the conditional is true unless proven false, but perhaps that is in accord with a basic principle of charity. The material conditional also does not require there to be any actual connection between the antecedent and the consequent, as it seems to in ordinary English. The statement that "If the moon is round, then Earth is the third planet from the Sun" is considered true as a material conditional. Both the antecedent and the consequent are true statements, so the material conditional is considered true. For the beginning student, this shouldn't cause too much trouble.

For the material conditional, to say that A implies B says no more than it is not the case that A is true while B is false. It doesn't say anything about what must be the case, or what will always be the case. It only applies to the current matter of fact, and not to any definitional claims or claims of necessary connections or relevance between statements. In a sense, we can think of the material conditional as the least amount of information possible for a conditional. A conditional statement in English no doubt does mean more than the material conditional, but it includes the information included in the material conditional. The student who continues in logic will have plenty of opportunity to study ways to try to capture the full meaning of the conditional in English.

Material Equivalence

We could easily do without the last symbol in our toolbox, but it will serve to make certain translations much simpler. The triple bar will represent the concept of material equivalence. We can consider material equivalence to be an assertion that two statements have, at the present time, the same truth value. If both statements involved in the material equivalence have the same truth value, then the material equivalence is true. If the two statements have opposite truth values, then the equivalence is false.

Material Equivalence	≡ triple bar
Alternate symbols	↔ ,E (in Polish notation)
English words or phrases which are material equivalences	If *and* only if Sufficient & necessary condition Just in case definitions
Well-formed formulas (wffs)	~A ≡ B ~(A ≡ B) (A ≡ B) • C F ≡ ~ R
Non-wffs	≡ G M ∨ N ≡ O F ~≡ R F •≡ R

Table 14.10

The thing about material equivalence is that for the beginning student it is easily confused with implication. Part of the problem is that the language is similar. We will use the words "if" and "only if" in both. The careful student, however, will notice that the equivalence requires both phrases in the same sentence.

For example, consider the statement "This solution is an acid *if and only if* the litmus paper dipped in it turns red," which we can write A ≡ R. Notice that the statement uses the phrase "if and only if", which is sometimes abbreviated "iff". If it were the case that we said "This solution is an acid *if* the litmus paper dipped in it turns red," we would have written A ⊃ R. If we had said "This solution is an acid *only if* the litmus paper dipped in it turns red," we would have written R ⊃ A. So, when we say "R if and only if A", we are in effect saying both A ⊃ R and R ⊃ A. In essence, material equivalence is material implication in both directions.

It should be easy to construct the basic truth table, but we will show it here anyway:

p	q	p ≡ q
T	T	T
T	F	F
F	T	F
F	F	T

p ≡ q
T T T
T F F
F F T
F T F

Table 14.11

The one note of caution we should mention concerns the last line of the truth table. Notice that even though both sides of the equivalence are false, the equivalence is still true. That is because material equivalence doesn't assert anything about the actual truth of the statements, only that they have the same truth value. When both statements are false, they do have the same truth value, which makes the equivalence true.

Chapter Fourteen Exercises

Rewrite each of the following statements in truth-functional symbolic form.

Basic Concept Exercises

1. California is a state.
2. It is false that the United States is at war.
3. If we go on Space Mountain, then we can't see the Jedi Training show.
4. Neither you nor your brother are allowed to go to the movies.
5. I can't take a picture if I don't have a camera.
6. I'll get either an A or a B.
7. Austen can count in both English and Spanish.
8. Unless you study, you will not pass.
9. If the chargers win, they'll be the champs.
10. Anthony is making a funny face.

Intermediate Exercises

11. If the chargers win the semi-finals, they will be the champs, unless they have to play against Green Bay.
12. We can go to Disneyland either Tuesday or Thursday, but not both.
13. Our solar system has eight planets, and either two or three dwarf planets.
14. Water is a necessary condition for life to exist.
15. Improving one's skill at translating statements is difficult, and one will only gain proficiency if one practices regularly.
16. It is necessary to release the mechanism before opening the cockpit door.
17. Being a decent shooter is a sufficient condition for making our team, but not for starting.
18. Mr. Monge is incredibly devious, and many of his challenging exercises are almost impossible to figure out, but not the next one.
19. I will have a peanut butter and jelly sandwich.
20. If garlic is a cure for cancer, then eating garlic is sufficient condition for not getting cancer.

Challenging exercises

These examples can be especially challenging. For group terms, use a conditional. For example, for "All dolphins are mammals," use 'D ⊃ M', where 'D' stands for "a creature is a dolphin, and 'M' stands for "a (that) creature is a mammal."

21. If all dolphins are mammals, then they must have hair and give birth to live babies.
22. BMW manufactures cars and motorcycles, while Mercedes Benz manufactures cars.
23. Rainy days and Mondays always bring me down.
24. No good deed goes unpunished.
25. Ferraris are very fast.
26. Always wear your seatbelt.

27. BMW manufactures cars and motorcycles, while Mercedes Benz manufactures only cars.
28. If all black widow spiders are poisonous, and some poisonous animals are nocturnal, then some black widow spiders are nocturnal.
29. The Big Bang could not have occurred unless there was a force present, and a material substance upon which the force could act, unless our universe does not follow Newtonian mechanics and something can come from nothing.
30. The first amendment protects freedom of religion, but it doesn't mandate freedom from religion, nor does it proclaim that a student cannot make a public speech if that speech contains religious material.

In-Context Exercises

Take the following arguments and capture the premises and conclusions in symbolic form using the key provided.

A. If a number were an idea, then arithmetic would be psychology. But arithmetic is no more psychology than, say, astronomy is. Astronomy is concerned, not with ideas of the planets, but with the planets themselves, and by the same token the objects of arithmetic are not ideas either.

Gottlob Frege, *The Foundations of Arithmetic*, 1893, §27.

Key: I = "Numbers are ideas."
A = "Arithmetic is psychology."

B. If all black widow spiders are poisonous, and some poisonous animals are nocturnal, then some black widow spiders are nocturnal. But, no black widow spiders are nocturnal, so either not all black widow spiders are poisonous, or some poisonous animals are not nocturnal.

Key: B = "A creature is a black widow spider."
A = "A (that) creature is poisonous."
N = "A (that) creature is nocturnal."

C. If I do not have income, then I deserve food stamps. I won $2,000,000 in the lottery last month, but I have the money in my mattress, and I didn't earn any interest, so (this month) I have no income. That shows that (this month) I deserve food stamps.

Key: I = "I have income."
D = "I deserve food stamps."
N = "I earned interest."
M = "I have my money in my mattress."

D. If the number two were an idea [in the sense of a psychological phenomenon], then it would have straight away to be private to me only. Another man's idea is, ex vi termini, another idea. We should then have it might be many millions of twos on our hands. ...

Gottlob Frege, *The Foundations of Arithmetic*, 1893, §27.

Key: I = "The number two is an idea."
P = "The number two in my head is private to me."
M = "There are millions of twos (one for each person)."

Note that the conclusion is implied, as is one of the premises.

E. Yet, in spite of all this [even if there were millions of twos], it would still be doubtful whether there existed infinitely many numbers, as we ordinarily suppose. 10^{10}, perhaps, might be only an empty symbol, and there might exist no idea at all, in any being whatever, to answer to the name.
Gottlob Frege, *The Foundations of Arithmetic*, 1893, §27.

Key: I = "Numbers are ideas."
M = "There are numbers which do not exist."
F = "There are a finite number of numbers."

Note that the conclusion is implied, as is one of the premises.

Logic Puzzle: The Zoo

You are trying to create a zoo, and have a large enclosure which you wish to stock with animals. Unfortunately, some animals eat other animals and so would you cannot put them in the enclosure together. Given the following relationships, determine the maximum number of animals you can put in the enclosure, and which ones.

1. Animal A eats animal B.
2. Animal A eats animal C.
3. Animal C eats animal D.
4. Animal B eats animal D.
5. Animal E eats animal A.

CHAPTER

15

Compound Statements and Truth Values

Now that you have learned about the five truth-functional connectives, we can introduce some more complicated issues. You have been introduced to the notion of a well-formed formula, but we should say a bit more about the concept. In ordinary English, it can be difficult, if not impossible, to assign truth values to incomplete or ungrammatical sentences. The same thing applies to symbolized statements. It doesn't make sense to ascribe a truth value to a formula which is not well-formed.

In a well-formed formula, every letter and every symbol carries a truth value, but there is one symbol in every well-formed formula of special importance. It is often called the **main operator** (whether it's an operator or actually a connective), and it carries or holds the truth value of the entire statement. It is a very simple concept, but one upon which much else depends.

Main Operator
The operator or connective which has scope over an entire symbolic statement

One way of defining the main operator is to say that it is the operator which has the largest scope in the statement. The scope of an operator is that part of the statement to which the symbol applies. Let's look at a few examples in symbolized form.

$A \supset (B \vee C)$

Skill 15.1
Identifying the Main Operator of a Statement

In this statement, the horseshoe has scope over the entire statement. It is the controlling operator, which is the one which carries the truth value for the whole statement. The wedge only has scope over the B and the C, which does not exhaust the material in the statement. The antecedent for the horseshoe is A, and the consequent is $(B \vee C)$, and nothing else remains in the statement. So, the horseshoe is the main operator, and at root, the statement is a conditional statement (one whose consequent happens to be a disjunction).

$[(W \equiv R) \vee {\sim}(G \bullet H)] \vee {\sim}W$

This example may look complicated at first, but once you know what you're doing, it will seem like child's play. The scope of the triple bar is the W and the R, which doesn't exhaust the statement, so it can't be the main operator. The first wedge has scope over a large part of the statement, but still only part of it: the part within the square brackets. The second wedge, however, does have scope over the entire statement. The left disjunct is $[(W \equiv R) \vee {\sim}(G \bullet H)]$, and the right disjunct is ${\sim}W$. So, at root the statement is a disjunction and the main operator is the second wedge.

Now that we have learned how to identify the main operator of the statement, we will turn to identifying when a formula is well-formed. Every capital letter is a well-formed formula. In this text, we will take the strict view that only single capital letters are well-formed. So, A and B are well-formed formulas, but AB is not. Should we have reason to do so, we can also use subscripted numbers to distinguish different simple statements, so A, A_1, and A_2 are all also well-formed formulas, and they will represent different simple statements.

We will define other well-formed formulas in a recursive fashion. If p and q are both well-formed formulas, then so are the following:

~p
p ∨ q
p ⊃ q
p • q
p ≡ q

So, consider a formula: S ⊃ (P • ~T). Since T is a well-formed formula, then so is ~T. Since P and ~T are well-formed formulas, then so is P • ~T. Since S and P • ~T are well-formed formulas, then so is S ⊃ (P • ~T). Since it is a well-formed formula, we should be able to specify the main operator, which is the horseshoe.

We should say something about parentheses. Different people can use different standards, but your author prefers at this stage to use parentheses, and not any kind of order of operations. So, any formula which has more than one connective must use parentheses to disambiguate the statement. The tilde, technically an operator, is an exception. We will interpret the tilde to have the smallest scope possible, so that ~A ∨ B is still a well-formed formula. Here, the tilde will have scope only over the A. If we want to negate the entire disjunction, and not just the A, then we need to put the disjunction in parentheses, like so: ~(A ∨ B).

For other statements, we use parentheses around the connectives with smaller scope, as in this example: (R • P) ≡ (R ⊃ S). This statement is an equivalence between a conjunction and a conditional. We might instead have grouped the statement as follows: [(R • P) ≡ R] ⊃ S. In this case the statement is at root a conditional statement, with an equivalence as the antecedent. The equivalence is between a conjunction of R and P and the statement R. If for any reason we had even more levels of grouping, we can use the braces, as in the following statement: {[(A ⊃ B) ∨ ~C] • B} ∨ ~B.

Given all this, a simple way to check to whether a statement is well-formed is to ensure that each connective has the correct number of well-formed formulas around it. For the tilde, just ensure that is has scope over a simple statement, or else it is outside of parentheses which enclose a well-formed formula. For each other connective, ensure that there is a well-formed formula on its left, and another well-formed formula on its right. You'll get the hang of it if you apply yourself.

Here's an interesting test. Is the formula ~~M well-formed or not? Most of my students have the intuition that it is not, but let's apply the test. M is a well-formed formula, so, by our rules, so is ~M. But since ~M is a well-formed formula, we can also negate it. So, ~~M is a well-formed formula. Logically speaking, the negation of a negation is the same as an assertion. So, ~~M is the same as M, but that just makes it more clear that it is a well-formed formula. It is clear and unambiguous, and we can easily determine its truth value, given the truth value of M. Yes, it may be redundant, and that is why your English professors will criticize double negations. The logician's main concern, however, is the truth of statements and what follows from them, so they don't have the same problem with double negations.

Determining the Truth Value of Complex Statements

Let's put what we have learned to the test. What we want to be able to do is determine the truth value of compound statement. Since every statement can be true or false, every compound statement will have a truth value. If we can represent the compound statement using truth functional connectives, then we can determine the truth value of the statement with nothing other than the truth values of the component simple statements. So, if I know the truth values of A, B, C, D, and E, then I can determine the truth value of the statement

(D ⊃ A) ∨ {~A ⊃ [(B • C) ≡ (E ⊃ ~B)]}

It may not be pretty or easy, but the truth value of the compound statement will be a function of the truth values of the component simple statements. Let's start off with a statement which is a little easier, though, how about:

Skill 15.2

Determining the Truth Value of Compound Statements

A ≡ (B ∨ ~C)

This equivalence won't be too challenging, and we can build from there. The first thing to notice is that we cannot immediately determine the truth value of the main operator. To do that we must look to the triple bar's left, and to its right, and we don't know the truth value of either. If we knew the original English statement, we could make a judgment about the truth values of the simple statemetns, but for simplicity's sake we will be given the truth value of the component statements: A, B, and C are all true. Now we know that the left side of the equivalence (A) is true, but we still don't know the truth value of the disjunction. In general, in determining the truth value of a compound statement, we must start on the connective with the least scope, which in this case will be the tilde.

It is helpful, though, if we can see what we are doing. So, here is the statement again, but this time with truth values written underneath:

```
A ≡ (B ∨ ~C)
T    T     T
```

We have already determined that we should start with the tilde, since it has least scope. To determine the truth value of the tilde, you must know the truth value of the statement which is being negated, and the tilde will have the opposite truth value. If I say it is not raining when it is raining, then I am not saying what is true. In the case above, it is easy; the negated statement is just C. Since C is true, then the tilde is false, and we can write that in.

```
A ≡ (B ∨ ~C)
T    T    FT
```

The connective with the next smallest scope is the wedge, so we next turn to it. As always, the value of the wedge is determined by examining its left disjunct and its right disjunct. To the left of the wedge is B, which is true, and the right of the wedge is ~C. We just determined that ~C is false. So, the value of the wedge when it has one true disjunct and one false disjunct is true, according to our basic tables and common sense, so we can write that in.

```
A ≡ (B ∨ ~C)
T    T T FT
```

We have colored the left disjunct red and the right disjunct blue. Notice that we only color the truth value of the tilde blue, because it carries the truth value for the entire statement ~C. In general we need not use colors; I only include them here for the sake of learning. Every student is more than welcome to use different colors if it helps. The last thing to figure out is the truth value of the triple bar, which is the main operator. Again, we will color the statement to the left of the equivalence in red, and the statement to its right in blue.

```
A ≡ (B ∨ ~C)
T     T T FT
```

Again, notice that we only shade the truth value of the wedge in blue, since it carries the truth value for the entire statement in parentheses. So, we examine the basic truth table for the triple bar, and we see that when both sides of the triple bar are true, then the triple bar is true, so we can complete our work by filling that in.

```
A ≡ (B ∨ ~C)
T (T) T T FT
```

You will notice that the truth value for the main operator, which is the truth value for the entire statement, is circled to indicate its importance for the statement. So, to determine the truth value of a compound statement, the first thing to do is to plug in the truth values for each of the component simple statements. Then, starting with the symbols which have the smallest scope, either look at the negated statement if you are dealing with a tilde, or look at the statement to the left and the right of the symbol in question. Using your common sense about what the symbols represent, or using the basic truth tables, determine the truth value for each symbol. Finally, once you have found the truth value of the main operator, you are done.

Let's look at one more example. We will use the standard that A, B, and C are all true, whereas X, Y, and Z are all false.

Step One	Step Two	Step Three
(C • ~X) ⊃ ~(A ≡ ~Y)	(C • ~X) ⊃ ~(A ≡ ~Y)	(C • ~X) ⊃ ~(A ≡ ~Y)
T F T F	T TF T TF	T T TF T T TF

In step one, we just write in the truth values for each simple statement. In step two, we see that we can determine the truth value of the two negated statements (shown in green). In step three, we can see that the dot and triple bar come next. Each one has a statement to its left (in red) and a statement to its right (in blue). The dot is true when both conjuncts are true, and the equivalence is true whenever its component statements have the same truth value, which they do.

Here a word might be in order. The symbol with the next smallest scope is the remaining tilde. Notice that we do not just distribute the tilde through the statement like you could in math. We must first determine the truth value of the negated statement, which in this case is 'A ≡ ~Y,' and whose truth value is true. The tilde simply flips it to the opposite truth value. The tilde will make a true statement false, and a false statement true.

Step Four	Step Five
(C • ~X) ⊃ ~(A ≡ ~Y)	(C • ~X) ⊃ ~(A ≡ ~Y)
T T TF F T T TF	T T TF (F) T T TF

Finally, we color the left side of the horseshoe, its antecedent, in red, and its consequent in blue. The only time the horseshoe is false is when the antecedent is true and the consequent is false, as we have in this case, and we fill in the final truth value as appropriate. So, given that A and C are true, and X and Y are false, then we know the compound statement above would be a false statement.

At this point every student should be able to determine the truth value of a compound statement when given the truth values of all the component statements. There are times, however, when one can determine the truth value of a compound statement even when one is given the truth values of only some of the component statements. It is left to the student to determine these times in the Challenging Exercises.

Chapter Fifteen Exercises

Determine the truth values of the following statements. For symbolic forms, assume that A, B, and C are true, and X, Y, and Z are false. If the statement is in English, first symbolize the statements, then use your own knowledge to determine its truth value, if possible.

Basic Concept Exercises

1. (A ∨ B) • ~X
2. A ⊃ (B ∨ ~C)
3. Y ≡ (~B ⊃ ~X)
4. (A • B) ⊃ ~(X ∨ Z)
5. ~Z ⊃ [~A ⊃ ~(C ∨ ~B)]
6. (~A ∨ B) ⊃ (A ⊃ B)
7. [(X ∨ Y) ∨ Z] ⊃ ~[(A • B) ≡ ~C]
8. A ⊃ ~{B ⊃ [(C ∨ X) ≡ (~A • Z)]}
9. (~A ≡ X) ⊃ [(B • C) ⊃ ~(~Z ∨ Y)]
10. Z • ({A ⊃ [B ⊃ ~(X ∨ Y)]} • (~X ⊃ Y))

Intermediate Exercises

11. World War I occurred before the Korean War and the Vietnam War, after the Civil War.
12. Neil Armstrong was the first man on the moon if and only if John Glenn was the first man to orbit the Earth.
13. Columbus was the first non-American to set foot in America, unless either the Vikings or the Chinese voyaged to America before 1492.
14. Aristotle and Plato were philosophers, and Newton and Galileo were not, unless all physicists are philosophers.
15. If the Fifth Amendment protects people from self-incrimination, then it must be that the Fourth Amendment or the Eighth Amendment guarantees the right to a speedy trial.
16. Both penicillin and tetracycline are antibiotics, and if penicillin is derived from mold, tetracycline is derived from bacteria.
17. If computers could be made to think like human beings, then they would have rights, and we would have to allow them to vote and give them freedom of speech.
18. If you do the right thing, it will make you happy, but if you do the wrong thing, you will be unhappy.

19. The Windows Registry file must have certain file associations for windows to run executable files, and your computer is not running executable files.
20. If you believe that Nietzsche was a genius and had the right philosophy, and he held that Christianity was a slave religion, then how can you possibly be a Christian?

Challenging exercises

In the following exercises, we have added P, Q, and R. We will treat these statements as having an undetermined truth value. Consider whether the truth value of the following compound statement can still be determined. If so, write the in the truth value of the statement. If not, place a question mark under the main operator.

21. A • (R ∨ P)
22. X • (R ∨ P)
23. B ∨ (~R ⊃ ~P)
24. Y ∨ (~R ⊃ ~P)
25. C ⊃ (R ≡ P)
26. Z ⊃ (R ≡ P)
27. (A • B) ≡ (R • P)
28. R ⊃ (A • B)
29. R ⊃ ~(A • B)
30. P ∨ ~P

In-Context Exercises

Use what you learned in the challenging exercises to determine the truth or falsity of the following statements. If you don't know the truth of one of the simple statements, and can't easily find out whether it is true, you should consider it to be undetermined.

A. Either Mr. Monge owns a goldfish, or Barack Obama is the President.
B. If Pluto is a planet, then Ceres and Eris are both planets.
C. It is both the case that Mr. Monge lives in a house, and that he is over ten feet tall.
D. If love is just an emotion, and an emotion only exists when it is felt, then love only exists when it is felt, and no one loves anyone all the time.
E. The fact that either the National debt is over sixteen trillion dollars or the National deficit is over one and a half trillion dollars, would indicate that our leaders are fiscally incompetent and deserve to be removed from office.

Logic Puzzle: On the Farm

There are three farmers, Rob, Ernie, and Casey, who are trying to coordinate their crops. Each one will plant either fruits or vegetables. Given the following statements, determine what crop each will plant.

1. At least one of them will plant vegetables.
2. If Rob plants vegetables, then at least one of the others will not.
3. If Ernie plants vegetables, then at least one of the others will not.
4. If Casey plants vegetables, then at least one of the others will not.
5. Rob and Ernie will both plant vegetables if and only if Casey does.
6. If Ernie or Casey plants vegetables, then so will Rob.

CHAPTER

16

Statement Classification and Comparison

Logical Truth and Self-Contradiction

Skill 16.1

Using Truth Tables to Classify Statements

In the previous chapter, we learned how to determine the truth value of a compound statement by using the truth values of the component statements and the basic meanings of the connectives. In the exercises, we also learned that sometimes we can determine the truth value of a compound statement when we have only partial information, when we know the truth value of only some of the component statements. In this chapter, we will learn about some peculiar statements, which have the feature that you need not know any of the component statements' truth values in order to determine the truth value of the entire compound statement.

Let's first look at an example. Consider the statement: $(P \vee Q) \bullet \sim(\sim P \supset Q)$. Given that we don't know the truth values of P or Q, is there any way to determine the truth value of the entire compound statement. Really think about it. It may seem daunting, but you might alight on the idea yourself.

If you have really thought about it, good for you. Regardless whether you solved it or not, I think that the struggle itself will help expand your mind and make connections you might not otherwise have made. In any case, the solution is rather simple and elegant. Since there are only a limited number of truth values for P and Q, there are only a limited number of possibilities which must be considered. The solution is to put those possibilities on a truth table, and see what happens.

Let's say that again. We know that P is either true or false, and we know that Q is either true or false. What we need to know is how many possible combinations of truth values are there. No matter what, either P and Q are both true, or P and Q are both false, or one is true and the other is false. There are no other possibilities, given that P and Q are both true or false. So, all we need to do is to consider each and every one of those possibilities. We will organize them in a table so that we can quickly analyze the results.

In our truth table, we will start by placing reference columns along the left side. This will allow us to quickly see what is asserted on each line of the truth table, and help keep track of what is going on. Since we have only two unique simple statements, we will have two reference columns.

P	Q	

That's basic enough. Now we just need to determine the possibilities. One possibility is that both statements are true, and we will consider that possibility first. In order to keep a certain pattern about which we will soon learn more, we will next consider the possibility that P is true while Q is false. Then we will have P false while Q is true, and finally, the possibility that both are false. Now our truth table will look like this:

P	Q	
T	T	
T	F	
F	T	
F	F	

No matter what, we will find ourselves on one of these lines of the truth table. In a sense, each line of the truth table represents a possible way which the universe might be, and the table captures all of the possibilities. There's no way for a possibility to slip through the cracks. We are considering every possible universe on our truth table, which is why it is so powerful. Our universe is going to be one of the lines of the truth table, but without knowing what statements P and Q represent, we can't say which one it is.

The next thing we do is put the statement into the truth table and begin calculating the truth values. We do this just like we did in the previous chapter, but instead of being given the truth values independently, we just read them off of our reference columns. You can determine the truth value of the compound statement if I told you that P and Q were both true, right? That's all you are doing on the first line of the table. After completing it, your table will look like this:

P	Q	(P ∨ Q) • ~(~P ⊃ Q)
T	T	T T T F F FT T T
T	F	
F	T	
F	F	

All you do next is complete every line of the truth table. Again, you do so by plugging in the truth values from the reference columns for each line of the truth table. As we go along, you will learn your own sort of style for doing so, whether it is to complete each line one at a time, or perhaps completing the truth values of a symbol on every line of the truth table, and then turning to another symbol. You will also learn various shortcuts and other techniques. But all that will come in time. For now, we will examine how the table will look when it is finished.

P	Q	(P ∨ Q)	•	~(~P ⊃ Q)
T	T	T T T	F	F FT T T
T	F	T T F	F	F FT T F
F	T	F T T	F	F TF T T
F	F	F F F	F	T TF F F

You will notice that a box is drawn around the main operator and the truth values all the way down the truth table to distinguish it and note its importance. You should also note that the truth value is false on every single line of the truth table. This is a very intriguing result. It tells us that the compound statement above is false, no matter what truth values P and Q have. This also means that it doesn't even matter what statements P and Q represent; choose any two statements you want, and the compound statement above will turn out false.

What this also means is that the falsity of the statement is due to its form or structure alone, and does not depend on the truth values of the component parts. The term "logically false" is sometimes used for statements of this kind, but the more common term is "**self-contradiction**". A statement is self-contradictory when it is false in every possible universe.

If someone utters a self-contradictory compound statement, we can be sure that they are confused or don't have any clue about what they are speaking.

Self-Contradiction
A statement which cannot possibly be true

As we have seen, some statements are false by virtue of their form alone. It is also the case that some statements are true by virtue of their form alone. Although these statements are sometimes called 'logically true', the more common term is '**tautology**'. A tautology, or tautologous statement, is one which is true by logic alone. A tautology is guaranteed to be true in every possible universe. As before, we can identify tautologies by placing them on truth tables. A tautology will be true on every line of its truth table.

Tautology
A statement which cannot possibly be false

The truth values of tautologies and self-contradictions do not depend on their component simple statements. For most statements, however, their truth values do depend on their component simple statements. For this reason, they are often called '**contingent statements**.' Contingent statements can be recognized by the fact that on a truth table they will have some lines that are true, and some lines that are false ('some' in the logical sense of 'at least one').

Contingent Statement
A statement which can be both true and false

Let's consider another example: 'D ⊃ [~(D • E) ∨ ~(E • G)].' Now, things are getting interesting. The careful reader will note that this statement has an added complexity: in it there are three unique simple statements instead of only two. There is no need to get flustered, though, since the basic idea is the same. We need to ensure that we consider all of the possible combinations of truth values on a truth table. In this case, however, there are more than four possibilities.

Let's see if we can figure it out. There are four combinations of truth values for D and E alone. But we also have to consider G. We need to consider those four combinations for cases where G is true, but we will have four more possibilities for when G is false. So, in total we would have eight possible combinations of truth values.

In general, every time we add a simple statement to our compound statement, we need to double the number of lines on our truth table. So, if you had 4 simple statements, you would need 2 x 2 x 2 x 2 (or 2^4) = 16 lines on your truth table. If you had 7 simple statements, you would need 2 x 2 x 2 x 2 x 2 x 2 x 2 (or 2^7) = 128 lines on your truth table. Let's hope that never happens!

Number of simple statements	Number of lines on truth table
1	$2^1 = 2$
2	$2^2 = 4$
3	$2^3 = 8$
4	$2^4 = 16$
5	$2^5 = 32$
6	$2^6 = 64$
8	$2^8 = 256$
10	$2^{10} = 1024$

Table 16.1

Table 16.1 indicates how many lines would be required on a truth table given the number of simple statements in the compound statement. Now that you know how many lines you need, you need to know what pattern of truth values to use so that you will ensure that all possible combinations of truth values appear in your truth table. For the first simple statement, always make half true and half false. So, if you had a total of sixteen lines on your truth table, the first simple statement will have eight true lines, followed by eight false lines. For each statement after the first, divide the number of true lines in half, ensuring that you continue to the last line of the truth table. That means, in this case, to write four lines true, four lines false, then four true lines and finally four false lines. Then, start with two true lines, two false lines, two true lines, etc. If you have done it correctly, the last column will be the final simple statement, and it will alternate T, F, T, F... all the way to the bottom.

If you having a difficult time visualizing it, Table 16.2 should help. If the truth table has only one simple statement, then the truth table will look like the portion of the table below bordered in yellow. A truth table with two simple statements will look like the portion of the table here bordered in red. The green border encloses the region of the truth table which will need to be constructed for three simple statements. Finally, in the case that there are four simple statements, you would construct the entire table here. Each reader should ensure that they understand how the pattern here can be extended to even larger numbers of simple statements.

	S	T	U	V	
1	T	T	T	T	
2	T	T	T	F	
3	T	T	F	T	
4	T	T	F	F	
5	T	F	T	T	
6	T	F	T	F	
7	T	F	F	T	
8	T	F	F	F	
9	F	T	T	T	
10	F	T	T	F	
11	F	T	F	T	
12	F	T	F	F	
13	F	F	T	T	
14	F	F	T	F	
15	F	F	F	T	
16	F	F	F	F	

Table 16.2

You should now know how to classify any single statement, no matter how complex, as tautologous, self-contradictory, or contingent. Construct the proper truth table, and then analyze it correctly. Next, we will see other ways to use truth tables.

Propositional Agreement and Conflict

Skill 16.2

Using Truth Tables to Compare Statements

In categorical logic, we learned that some statements "agree" with other statements in the sense that they always have the same truth value. We called this type of agreement logical equivalence. We also learned that some statements do not agree, they conflict in some way. Contradictories, contraries and subcontraries had this characteristic. It shouldn't be a surprise that the same issue arises in truth-functional logic as well. In propositional logic, when we are comparing two statements, there are generally four possible categories. We still have logically equivalent and contradictory, but we include consistent and inconsistent.

Logically Equivalent
Two statements are logically equivalent when they always have the same truth value

Two statements are **logically equivalent** if and only if they *necessarily* have the same truth value. They don't just happen to have the same truth value in the world as it is, in which case they are materially equivalent. No matter what the universe looked like, logically equivalent statements would still have the same truth value as each other. If one of the statements is true, then so is the other, and if either one is false, then they are both false.

Another way to say the same thing is to say that two statements are logically equivalent iff they are materially equivalent for every possible state of the universe. So, if '~(A ∨ B)' and '~A ∨ ~B' were logically equivalent, then the material equivalence between them should be a tautology. Let's see whether this is so in the truth table below.

A	B	~(A ∨ B)	≡	(~A ∨ ~B)
T	T	F T	T	F F F
T	F	F T	F	F T T
F	T	F T	F	T T F
F	F	T F	T	T T T

These two statements are not materially equivalent on every line of the truth table, so we know that they are not logically equivalent. It is possible that they have different truth values.

Two statements are **contradictories** if it is not possible for them to have the same truth value. Logic alone guarantees that if one of them is true, then the other is false, and if one is false, the other is true. In this case the material equivalence between them would always be false, since they never have the same truth value.

Contradictories
Two statements are contradictories when they always have opposite truth values

Let's consider these two statements: '~(A ⊃ B)' and '~A ∨ B.' To determine whether they are contradictory to each other, we put their equivalence on a truth table and see whether it is a self-contradiction. We do so here:

A	B	~(A ⊃ B)	≡	(~A ∨ B)
T	T	F T	F	F T T
T	F	T F	F	F F F
F	T	F T	F	T T T
F	F	F T	F	T T F

The equivalence is a self-contradiction, so our two statements are contradictory to each other. It is not possible for both of them to be true at the same time.

There are two other possibilities which we need to consider, but the problem is that using an equivalence between the two statements will not distinguish between them. Instead of using an equivalence, then, we can just put the two statements on the same truth table, and simply ask the right kinds of questions. In fact, we never need to create the equivalence, since we can ask the right questions to determine whether the statements are logically equivalent or contradictory as well.

After creating the truth table with both statements on it (as we do below), the first thing we will ask is "do the statements always have the same truth value?" If so, then the statements are logically equivalent. Then ask "do the statements always have opposite truth values?" If so, then they are contradictories. Let's use this technique to compare the two earlier statements (the one's which were not logically equivalent) again. This time we will just put the two statements on the same truth table. Then we simply compare the truth values on each line. Make sure you always compare the truth values of the main operators (in this case they are in bold). They are not always the same (lines 2 and 3), so they are not logically equivalent. They are also not always the opposite (lines 1 and 4), so they are not contradictory.

A	B	~(A ∨ B)	~A ∨ ~B
T	T	**F** T	F **F** F
T	F	**F** T	F **T** T
F	T	**F** T	T **T** F
F	F	**T** F	T **T** T

Consistent
Two (or more) statements are consistent when it is possible for them to both (all) be true

We still need to determine if they are **consistent** or inconsistent. Fortunately, the assertion that a statement is consistent and the statement that it is inconsistent are contradictories. So, all we need to do is test whether it is consistent, and that will tell us whether it is inconsistent. What it means for two statements to be consistent is that it is possible for both statements to be true at the same time. The bare possibility is all that is required. It can be highly unlikely, but if the statements are consistent, then there is some arrangement of the universe where both statements are true.

Hopefully, the astute reader has already tried to figure out what this would mean in terms of the truth table. Remember that the truth table considers all possible logically distinct states of the universe, so if there is something that is logically possible, it will necessarily end up on the truth table somewhere. So, in order for two statements to be consistent, there must be at least one line of the truth table where the statements are both true. So, in the truth table above, is there any line where both statements are true? Yes, line four. So, these two statements are consistent.

Inconsistent
Two statements are inconsistent when it is not possible for them both to be true

If the two statements are not consistent, then they are **inconsistent**. Nothing more needs to be done. If, on the truth table in question, there is no line where the statements are both true, then the statements are inconsistent.

An important point needs to be mentioned here. As a quick quiz, what else can be said about every pair of contradictory statements? Would they have to be consistent or inconsistent, or could they be either one? Careful reflection here should convince you that every pair of contradictory statements is also inconsistent. It should also be easy to see that most every pair of logically equivalent statements is also consistent (there is only one exception. Can you think of it?). However, in every case, you should assert the stronger piece of information. If two statements are both logically equivalent and consistent, it is generally fine to merely assert that they are logically equivalent. Similarly, for contradictory statements (which are also inconsistent), it is generally expected that you will assert that they are contradictories. Usually you will only identify two statements as inconsistent when they are *not* contradictory.

One last thing. We have only talked about pair-wise comparisons. So far, we have only discussed comparing two statements at a time. The issue of consistency and inconsistency often, however, applies to groups of statements. So, we could ask whether five statements are all consistent. If we put all five of them on a truth table and we find at least one line where they are all true, then they are consistent as a set. If not, they are said to be an inconsistent set. This method is often used in mathematical or scientific theories to determine whether the theory is consistent, which is considered an important feature of any theory.

Let's see one last example. Let's compare' and 'B • ~A'.

A	B	(A ⊃ B) ≡ (B ⊃ A)	B • ~A'
T	T	T **T** T	T **F** FT
T	F	F **F** T	T **F** FT
F	T	T **F** F	F **T** TF
F	F	T **T** T	F **F** TF

The statements do not have the same truth value on every line, so they are not logically equivalent. They also do not have the opposite truth value on every line, so they are not contradictory. Yet, there is no line where both statements are true, which proves that the statements are inconsistent, and we are done.

Chapter Sixteen Exercises

For exercises with a single statement, classify the statement as tautologous, self-contradictory, or contingent. For those exercises with two statements (separated by a single slash), classify the pair of statements as logically equivalent, contradictory, consistent, or inconsistent. Use these instructions for all of the exercises.

Basic Concept Exercises

1. P ⊃ ~P
2. ~P ⊃ P
3. P ∨ ~P
4. P • ~P
5. A ⊃ (B ⊃ A)
6. ~A ⊃ (A ⊃ B)
7. ~(S ∨ T) / ~S ∨ ~T
8. ~(S • T) / ~S • ~T
9. ~(S ∨ T) / ~S • ~T
10. P ⊃ R / ~P ∨ R

Intermediate Exercises

11. (S • ~R) • (S ⊃ R)
12. (G ⊃ H) ∨ (~G ⊃ H)
13. (P ≡ Q) ⊃ (~Q ∨ P)
14. [(A • B) ∨ C] • [(~A ∨ ~B) • ~C]
15. [(A • B) ∨ C] ∨ [(A ∨ B) • C]
16. (M ⊃ N) ⊃ O / M ⊃ (N ⊃ O)
17. A • B / (B ⊃ A) ≡ ~(~B ∨ A)
18. P ≡ Q / (P • Q) ∨ (~P • ~Q)
19. P ⊃ (Q ⊃ R) / (P • Q) ⊃ R
20. (A ⊃ C) • (B ⊃ C) / (A ∨ B) ⊃ C

Challenging exercises

21. D ⊃ (E ≡ F) / (D • E) ⊃ (D • F)
22. D ⊃ (E ≡ F) / (~D ∨ E) ∨ (~D ∨ ~F)
23. (R • S) ∨ V / (R ∨ V) • (S ∨ V)
24. (R ∨ S) • V / (~R • ~S) ∨ ~V
25. [A ⊃ (G ≡ H)] ⊃ [(A • G) ⊃ H]
26. ~D ⊃ {[(E ∨ F) ∨ (~E ∨ ~ F)] ⊃ D}
27. {[(M ⊃ N) • (M ⊃ O)] • ~(N ∨ O)} • M
28. {[(A ⊃ ~B) • (C ⊃ ~D)] • (B ∨ D)} • (A • C)
29. (A ⊃ B) ∨ (C ⊃ D) / (A • ~B) • (C • ~D)
30. (A • B) ∨ (C • D) / [(A ∨ C) • (B ∨ C)] • [(A ∨ D) • (B ∨ D)]

In-Context Exercises

A. You are attending a conference on global warming, and the speakers make the following statements:

Professor Simpson says: Global warming will continue if and only if the Sun continues its sunspot cycle and carbon dioxide increases in the atmosphere.
Professor Broflavsky says that: Carbon dioxide will increase in the atmosphere provided that mankind continues to burn oil.
Professor Brown says the following: Global warming will not continue unless mankind continues to burn oil.
Doctor Stewart says this: If the sunspot cycle continues then Global warming will continue, even if mankind ceases to burn oil.
Mr. Hommeourscochon says this: If carbon dioxide increases in the atmosphere, then Global warming will continue.

Can all of these speakers be speaking the truth (Are the statements consistent)? If so, what could we say about Global warming, the sunspot cycle, carbon dioxide in the atmosphere, and whether mankind continues to burn oil.

Logic Puzzle: Only the Guilty Lie

You have four suspects to a crime, and one or more may be guilty. Determine who is guilty, assuming that the guilty party will lie and everyone else will say the truth.

Annie says "Barry is guilty."
Barry says "Charlene is guilty."
Charlene says "Annie or Barry is guilty."
Devin says "Barry or Charlene is guilty."

CHAPTER

17

Truth Tables and Validity

Skill 17.1

Using Truth Tables to Determine Validity

One of the original goals of formalizing logic was to determine whether arguments were valid. Questions of consistency and equivalence and the relationships between statements are related and important, but what we really want to know is whether a given argument is valid. This is the culmination, in an important sense, of everything we have covered so far.

One might expect, then, that this would be a very difficult chapter. Fortunately, it isn't. Everything we need has already been covered; we just have to learn how to put it all together.

Before we get there, let's do some review. A valid argument is one wherein the truth of its premises guarantees the truth of its conclusion. An invalid argument is one where it is possible for the premises to be true while the conclusion is false. A deductive argument is either valid or it is not, there is no in-between.

Now, imagine that we were going to place an argument on a truth table. There may be more than one premise, but that's fine; we just need to make sure that all the premises and conclusion are represented on the table. At this stage, let's not even consider any specific argument. Let's assume we have an argument with only two unique simple statements, and two premises. To put this argument on the truth table, we would need to set up our table as in the example below:

?	?	Premise 1	Premise 2	Conclusion
T	T			
T	F			
F	T			
F	F			

One should notice that there is a slight difference in this truth table. Notice that there is a double line separating the reference columns from the premises, and another double line separating the premises from the conclusion. Use this technique to show that we are analyzing the statements as an argument, and not just any group of statements.

Now we have to ask, if the argument were *invalid*, what would necessarily be the case?

Remember that in an invalid argument, it must be possible to have all true premises and a false conclusion. Remember also that the truth table envisions all logical possibilities. So, if an argument were invalid, then there would necessarily be a line on the truth table where the premises are all true and the conclusion is false. If there were no such line, then it would not be possible to have all true premises and a false conclusion, and that would show that the argument in question is valid.

So, to put all this together, if we construct a truth table for an argument and we find that there is a line (at least one) where the premises are all true, but the conclusion is false, then we know that the argument is invalid. If we do not find such a line, then we know the argument is valid. That's it.

It really is that easy. Let's see an example. Consider the argument here:

A ⊃ ~B
B ⊃ ~A
∴ A ≡ ~B

Let's construct a truth table and fill it in. You should be quite proficient at it by now, but there's always room to improve. Hopefully, you are also learning some short-cuts. Here it is:

A	B	A ⊃ ~B	B ⊃ ~A	A ≡ ~B
T	T	F	F	F
T	F	T	T	T
F	T	T	T	T
F	F	T	T	F

* this line proves that the argument is invalid.

Simple inspection reveals that the possible truth value combination on line four would result in all true premises and a false conclusion. This line proves that the argument is invalid.

As long as an argument is able to be symbolized using truth-functional logic, it can be put on a truth table, and we can determine its validity. Truth tables are said to be decisive: they will definitely show whether an argument is valid or invalid in a finite number of steps.

We should say something here about a feature of material logic which some consider to be problematic, at least if one wishes to use this logic for ordinary language. The view of logic we have been discussing is said to be explosive. It holds that from inconsistent premises, everything follows. Using a truth table, let's see why the techniques we have learned provide for an explosive logic. Consider the following argument, which has inconsistent premises.

A	B	C	A ≡ B	~A • B	C
T	T	T	T	F	T
T	T	F	T	F	F
T	F	T	F	F	T
T	F	F	F	F	F
F	T	T	F	T	T
F	T	F	F	T	F
F	F	T	T	F	T
F	F	F	T	F	F

A quick inspection reveals that there is no way to have all true premises and a false conclusion, *because there is no way to have all true premises*. The premises are inconsistent, so there is no way for them to all be true. This feature of the logic we are learning is often captured in the expression "from a contradiction, everything follows."

Explosive Logic
Any logic in which from a contradiction, anything follows

Notice that the conclusion, C, was not even contained in the premises, but it is still considered to follow. This result, however, is similar to the idea that a material conditional can be true even though the antecedent and consequent have nothing to do with each other.

Perhaps we can take comfort in the fact that a true contradiction is impossible. So, the world is safe from an **explosive logic**. Unfortunately, one might think that a belief system might contain inconsistencies. Our logic, then, would entitle a person with an inconsistent belief system to believe anything. To rectify this problem, some logicians have created non-explosive logics, or **paraconsistent logics**. This topic is far beyond the scope of what we will consider here. Hopefully, it may have whetted your appetite to learn more in the future.

Paraconsistent Logic
Any logic in which a contradiction does not imply everything

Another feature of the logic we are learning is that it also holds that any premises can lead validly to a tautology. If a conclusion is necessarily true, then any premises whatsoever will have the feature that it will be impossible to make all the premises true while making the conclusion false. So, a tautology follows from any premises. This result, while having the similar feature that the content of the conclusion may be completely unrelated to the premises, doesn't seem quite the same challenge as the issue of explosiveness. After all, if the conclusion is necessarily true, then any premises whatsoever will guarantee that the conclusion is true.

Chapter Seventeen Exercises

Use truth tables to determine whether the following arguments are valid. For each argument, the premises are separated by single slashes, and the conclusion is preceded by a double slash.

Basic Concept Exercises

1. P ⊃ ~P // ~P
2. ~P ⊃ P // P
3. A ∨ B // A • B
4. A • B // A ∨ B
5. A ∨ B // B ∨ A
6. M ⊃ N // N ⊃ M
7. R ≡ P // ~(R • ~P)
8. ~(R • ~P) // R ≡ P
9. A ⊃ B / A // B
10. A ⊃ B / ~B // ~A

Intermediate Exercises

11. G ⊃ ~M / ~M ⊃ G // G ≡ M
12. L ≡ ~P / ~P ⊃ ~L // ~L
13. G ⊃ (M ∨ D) / G ∨ (M • D) // M ∨ D
14. D ∨ (E • F) / ~E // D
15. G ⊃ ~(F • D) / G ∨ F // D
16. G ⊃ ~(F • D) / G • F // D
17. M ⊃ ~(N ⊃ O) / N ∨ O // M ⊃ ~O
18. R ∨ [P ∨ (Q • ~R)] / P ⊃ R // ~R ⊃ ~Q
19. (~A ∨ B) ≡ (X • ~Y) / ~B ∨ ~X / Y // ~A
20. L ≡ (B ∨ ~R) / Q ⊃ ~B / R ⊃ (~L • ~Q) // (B • Q) ⊃ (L • R)

Challenging exercises

21. Some diseases are not curable illnesses, and no curable diseases are things to be worried about. Thus, some diseases are things to be worried about.

22. Every animal that has hair is a mammal. Dolphins are mammals. Therefore, dolphins have hair.
23. Barack Obama will be reelected only if he successfully addresses the economy. Since President Obama will not successfully address the economy, he will not be reelected.
24. The Windows Registry file must have certain file associations for windows to run executable files, and your computer is not running executable files, so your registry is probably corrupted.
25. If you do the right thing, it will make you happy, which shows that if you do something and it makes you unhappy, then it is not moral.
26. The Constitution forbids the establishment of religion, and to include the words "under God" in the Pledge of Allegiance is an establishment of religion, which shows that the Pledge of Allegiance is unconstitutional.
27. Nothing should be illegal if there is no criminal intent present, and in smoking marijuana there is no criminal intent.
28. It seems that when an argument involves facts, it is deductive, but when it involves opinions, it is inductive. Since this argument I am making right now involves opinions, it must be inductive.
29. Murder is wrong. Any time you kill someone, that's murder. Capital punishment means killing someone, so it's wrong.
30. The state gets all of its rights from individuals. Individuals don't have the right to kill someone, so the state can't have that right either.

In-Context Exercises

A. A racist is someone who thinks that white people should be treated differently than black people. Anyone who supports race-based affirmative action thinks that white people should be treated differently than black people. Therefore, anyone who supports affirmative action is a racist.

B. If mankind were the cause of global warming, then how can you explain the fact that Mars and the other planets are also going through a warming phase.

C. If you send your children to American public schools, then they will be indoctrinated into American values and ideals. So, if you don't want your children indoctrinated in American values and ideals, then you don't want to send them to American public schools.

D. In order for us to have free will, then it must be the case that the future is unknowable. This is because if anyone can know the future, then our choices would not be free, but instead would be caused. If God has omniscience, then he knows everything, and nothing, including the future is unknowable. Therefore, if we have free will, then God is not omniscient.

E. If Casey Anthony killed her daughter, then she is guilty of murder and she deserves the death penalty, unless there was no premeditation, in which case she deserves life in prison. If Casey Anthony's mother searched for "Chloroform" on the computer, then Casey Anthony didn't, in which case, there was no premeditation. So, if Casey Anthony's mother searched for "Chloroform" on the computer, then Casey Anthony deserves life in prison.

Logic Puzzle: Peter, Paul and Mary

There are three suspects for a crime: Peter, Paul, and Mary. You have reason to believe that only one suspect is telling the whole truth. Take each of their statements below, and determine who is telling the truth and who is guilty. Keep in mind that saying that someone is lying is the same as asserting the negation of what he is saying.

Peter: Mary is guilty and Paul is lying.
Paul: Peter and Mary are both guilty.
Mary: I am guilty, but I didn't act alone.

CHAPTER

18

Indirect Truth Tables

Skill 18.1

Using Indirect Truth Tables to Determine Validity

Hopefully, while learning about truth tables you have found a few shortcuts along the way. Logicians often like to let students learn them on their own. We like to push students to use their own ingenuity. This next section deals with a shortcut so powerful, but not obvious, that every logician should have it in his or her toolbox. We call them indirect truth tables.

Consider the following argument. Go ahead, if you like, and construct a truth table for it.

1) $F \equiv (\sim D \supset H)$
2) $\sim H \supset (G \vee I)$
3) $\underline{\sim I \vee [(J \vee K) \supset (L \equiv \sim F)]}$
4) $\therefore K \supset \sim H$

There are eight simple statements. So, we would need two to the eighth power, or 256 lines on our truth table. Wow. That's a lot. Even with the shortcuts you may have picked up, that would still take a while. Besides that, there is so much potential for error. One little mistake, and all that work would be for naught. What a waste it would be to do all that work and get the wrong answer. Perhaps we can use our brains and figure out a way to determine the validity of the argument without all that work.

The argument will be either valid or it will be invalid. If it is valid, all we know is that a certain kind of line does not exist. It is much harder to show that something does not exist than to show that it does, so perhaps we should consider the case where the argument is invalid. If it were invalid, there should be a line somewhere on the truth table where all the premises are true and the conclusion is false. All we need to do to show the argument is invalid is to find that line of the truth table.

We are going to assume that such a line exists, and we will try to determine the truth value assignment for that line. If such a line did exist, we would know one thing about it: it would have all true premises and a false conclusion.

	Steps for completing an indirect truth table.
1.	Assume the argument is invalid.
2.	Mark the table accordingly (true premises, false conclusion).
3.	Continue filling in truth values, but only when forced to do so.
4.	If you complete a truth value assignment without any contradiction, then the argument is invalid.
5.	If you get a contradiction on every line, then the argument is valid

In direct truth tables, on every line we compute the truth values for the premises and conclusion by using the truth value assignment for that line. In indirect truth tables, we will go backwards: we will try to find a truth value assignment based on the truth values of the premises and conclusion. Let's see what we mean with a simpler example than the one above.

M	R	B	$\underline{(M \supset B) \bullet (R \supset B)}$	$M \vee R$	B

This argument isn't too bad. It would only require eight lines. But still, if we could figure it out in one line, we could save a lot of time. As we said, the first thing to do is to assume that the argument is invalid. Remember that we are not just assuming that it is invalid and going on with our lives. We will use our assumption to run a test. The test will tell us whether our assumption was good or bad. The next thing to do is to assign truth values appropriate to our assumption. So, we will mark the premises as true, and the conclusion as false.

M	R	B	(M ⊃ B) • (R ⊃ B)	M ∨ R	B
			T	T	F

The next thing to do is to try to complete the truth value assignment, while assigning truth values throughout to simple statements and connectives. The trick, though, is to only assign them when forced to do so. We are trying to complete our truth value assignment without running into a contradiction. So, if assigning True to a symbol or statement would result in a contradiction, then you should assign False. If assigning False would result in a contradiction, then assign True. If assigning either True or False would result in a contradiction, then we would know that our assumption was mistaken, and the argument is valid. We will see that again soon enough.

Based upon what we have already done, we know that B must be false. So, we can assign false to B throughout the truth table, as we do below.

M	R	B	(M ⊃ B) • (R ⊃ B)	M ∨ R	B
		F	F T F	T	F

No problems so far. The next step can be a little obscure, but it is essential to understand it in order to complete an indirect truth table. Consider the dot in the first premise. The only way to construct a line to show that the argument is invalid is to make the dot true. Remember the basic truth table for the dot, however, and you will know that there is only one way to make the dot true: both sides must be true. So, assigning False to either of the conjuncts would result in a contradiction, but assigning True would not. So, we will assign True to both conjuncts.

M	R	B	(M ⊃ B) • (R ⊃ B)	M ∨ R	B
		F	TF T TF	T	F

Now we know that if we are to construct a line to show the argument to be invalid, both conjuncts of the first premise would have to be true, AND that both of their consequents would have to be false. Reflect now on the basic truth table for the horseshoe. Is it possible to have a true conditional with a true antecedent and a false consequent? No; if the antecedent were true and the consequent were false, then the conditional would be false. For this reason, we know that both antecedents must be false. So, both Mand R must be false. Make sure you understand why. This step is essential in completing indirect truth tables. Let's fill in most of the remaining truth table.

M	R	B	(M ⊃ B) • (R ⊃ B)	M ∨ R	B
F	F	F	F TF T F T F	T	F

So, does the truth value assignment here, M=F, R=F, B=F, prove that the argument is invalid? Not quite yet. We need to make sure that we can complete the truth value assignment throughout the table, and we haven't looked at the second premise. We need to ensure that we are not forced into assigning contradictory truth values anywhere. We have been forced into assigning both M and R as false. It should be easy to see that if we complete the second premise with both disjuncts being false, that would make the second premise false. What this means is that if we assume that the argument is invalid, then we are forced into accepting that the second premise is both true and false. Since that can't be the case, we can only conclude that our assumption is wrong. Since we assumed that the argument was invalid, we can now say that the argument is not invalid, which means it is valid.

Technically, as long as you see the contradiction in your head, you will know that the argument is valid, but if you want your work to count as proof to someone else, you need to do more. Let's see how we can do so.

M	R	B	(M ⊃ B) • (R ⊃ B)	M ∨ R	B
F	F	F	F T F T F T F	F T/F F	F
				⊥	

Reductio Ad Absurdum
An argument pattern that rejects a claim because it leads to a contradiction

In this case, I have marked the contradiction as occurring on the main operator of the second premise. It would have been possible to mark it elsewhere, depending on what order I decided to determine the truth values. In general, it does not matter where the contradiction occurs, as long as a contradiction does indeed occur. We mark the contradiction with the symbol for contradiction, ⊥ (You may be more familiar with it when it is used as a symbol for perpendicular).

Always remember that you cannot just create a contradiction anywhere you want. To do so would be too easy and wouldn't show anything. You can't decide that a symbol or letter just has a truth value which happens to lead you into a contradiction. You have to be forced into it.

We should say something more about the reasoning involved in our decision. It takes the form of a common pattern of reasoning called a ***reductio ad absurdum***. In English, it is sometimes called reducing to an absurdity. The basic idea is that we make an assumption, and then derive conclusions from that assumption. If we ever run into a contradiction, then we know our assumption was mistaken. We can show the reasoning graphically, using what is called a proof line. We list any assumptions at the top, preceding a hash mark. We draw our conclusions below the hash mark, we can see below.

1. | The argument is invalid. (assumed)
2. | A line can be constructed with all true premises and a false conclusion.
3. | M ∨ R is true. (since it is a premise)
4. | M ∨ R is false. (since M and R would be false)
5. | ⊥

∴ The argument is *not in*valid (or *is* valid).

Notice that the conclusion we have drawn does not occur on the proof line itself. Once we get a contradiction, we can discharge the assumption, and we negate it, but our conclusion is real. It is not just an assumption, as it is proven to be the case by the *reductio ad absurdum* argument.

So, we have proven that the argument in the indirect truth table above is valid. It is impossible to construct a line where the premises are all true and the conclusion is false; trying to do so forces us into a contradiction. Let's consider another argument.

G	N	M	G ⊃ N	N ⊃ M	~G • M	G ∨ N
			T	T	T	F

We are free to start anywhere we can. The first premise is a conditional, and there are three basic ways to make a conditional true. We could start here, but that would require three lines, and we haven't seen how to do that yet. There is, however, only one way to make the third premise true. The dot is true only when both conjuncts are true, so let's fill in that information, and mark the values of G and M throughout the table.

G	N	M	G ⊃ N	N ⊃ M	~G • M	G ∨ N
F		T	F T	T T	TF T T	F F

It turns out that the only thing left to do is determine the truth value of N, and ensure that there are no contradictions. Let's look at the first premise. The antecedent is false, which means that the conditional will be true regardless of the truth value of N. So, we are not forced into making N either true or false, and we should move on. The second premise is similar. Whether N is true or false, the conditional will be true, since the consequent is true. So, again, we should look elsewhere.

The conclusion is a disjunction which is false, and the only way to make a disjunction false is for both disjuncts to be false. So, this tells us that N must be false. All we need to do now is complete the truth value for N and ensure that there are no contradictions.

G	N	M	G ⊃ N	N ⊃ M	~G • M	G ∨ N
F	F	T	F T F	F T T	TF T T	F F F

There are no contradictions, and we were able to get a complete truth value assignment. So, we know that the argument is invalid. We didn't get a contradiction, but that by itself is not what proves that the argument is invalid. What proves the argument invalid is the truth value assignment in the table: G =F, N = F, and M = T. This truth value assignment will give us all true premises and a false conclusion, and so it is proof that the argument is invalid.

If you would like to confirm our results, all you need to do is construct a direct truth table. If you were to do so, you would see that the line corresponding with the truth value assignment (which will be the seventh line) will prove the argument to be invalid.

Unfortunately, it will not always be the case that we are forced into placing any truth values. In these cases, we can still construct an indirect truth table, but we may have to build more than one line. All we need to do is to choose a symbol with which to begin, and then determine how many lines would be required. Table 18.1 will tell us how many lines will be required for any symbol. It shows how many ways on the basic truth table a given symbol can be true as well as how many ways it can be false.

	True	False
One way	~ •	~ ∨ ⊃
Two ways	≡	≡
Three ways	∨ ⊃	•

Table 18.1

What we want is a symbol which can be true (for a premise) or false (for a conclusion) in only one way, but if we don't have that, we can look for a triple bar (which will require two lines), or else we'll be stuck with a symbol which will have three ways of assigning truth values, and so three lines on the truth table. Let's take a look at an argument which cannot be completed in one line.

A	T	P	R	A ⊃ (T ∨ P)	R ⊃ (~T ∨ ~P)	P ⊃ ~T	A ≡ ~R
				T	T	T	F

All of the premises are horseshoes, so there are three ways that they could each be true. The conclusion, however, is a triple bar, which is false in only two ways. Since we might save some time starting there, let's do so. We can immediately list the two lines, using the two ways that the triple bar can be false, which are T ≡ F, and F ≡ T.

A	T	P	R	A ⊃ (T ∨ P)	~R ⊃ (~T ∨ ~P)	P ⊃ ~T	A ≡ ~R
				T	T	T	T F F
				T	T	T	F F T

Just like before, we can continue filling in truth values, but only when forced to do so. We might get a contradiction on one line, but if so, we must continue on to the other line. One must always get a contradiction on every possible line before one can declare the argument we are analyzing on the table to be valid. As long as we find one line which can be completed without contradiction, with a complete truth value assignment, then we know the argument is invalid, and we have the proof to show it. So, let's start filling in values.

A	T	P	R	A ⊃ (T ∨ P)	~R ⊃ ~(T ∨ P)	P ⊃ ~T	A ≡ ~R
T			T	T T	FT T	T	T F FT
F			F	F T	TF T	T	F F TF

We have filled in all of the values for A and R. The next step is to realize that a conditional which is true, with a true antecedent, must have a true consequent. Let's fill that in and then see where we are.

A	T	P	R	A ⊃ (T ∨ P)	~R ⊃ ~(T ∨ P)	P ⊃ ~T	A ≡ ~R
T			T	T T T	FT T	T	T F FT
F			F	F T	TF T T F	T	F F TF

On the first line, we are stuck. There are three ways for the wedge to be true. In the second premise, we could split the first line on the truth table in two, and consider each case where the consequent is true and also when it is false. But that is messy. Before we try that, we should at least look at the second line. If we get completely stuck on the second line, we can split the first line up, or we could even start all over using the third premise, and considering the three possible ways to make that conditional true.

Fortunately for us, we can still make progress. The second line would require the wedge in the second premise to be false, and it can only be false if both disjuncts are false. Let's make T and P false, and then fill in these values throughout the table.

A	T	P	R	A ⊃ (T ∨ P)	~R ⊃ ~(T ∨ P)	P ⊃ ~T	A ≡ ~R
T			T	T T T	FT T	T	T F FT
F	F	F	F	F T F F F	TF T T F F F	F T TF	F F TF

So, on the second line of the table, we are able to complete our truth value assignment without contradiction, so the argument is invalid. The fact that we didn't get a contradiction on the first line is irrelevant; it wouldn't have mattered either way. We know that given that all of our simple statements are false, the premises of the argument would be true and the conclusion false, so the argument is invalid, or in other words, the truth of the premises does not guarantee the truth of the conclusion.

Let's try one more example:

C	P	R	C • [~R ∨ (C ⊃ P)]	(P ⊃ ~C) ∨ (R ⊃ ~P)	P ⊃ ~R	~P • ~R
			T T T T	FT T	T	F

The dot in the first premise does require us to make both sides true, and we can write in that information, as we have done here. But we cannot complete the truth table in one line: even when we fill in true on both sides, we are unable to make any additional progress beyond that shown in the table above. Verify for yourself; on the first line of the truth table above, there is no other place where we are required to put in a truth value. We don't just want to put in any value somewhere. If we do so, we may get a contradiction without being forced into doing so, which will not show that the argument is valid. Technically, one could still prove the argument to be invalid if we don't get a contradiction, since any truth value assignment which makes the premises true and conclusion false is a proof that the argument is invalid, but we are trying to avoid just guessing and getting lucky.

So, instead, we will choose a different symbol. We could use the wedge in the second premise, but that looks a bit challenging. We are left with either the horseshoe in the third premise or the dot in the conclusion. The horseshoe has three ways to make it true, and the dot has three ways to make it false. We would generally want to choose a statement whose component simple statements are used most often throughout the argument, but here there is no difference on that measure. Let's choose the conclusion. We need to fill in the three ways the dot can be false, one on each line of the truth table. Notice that we still know that C needs to be true, so we can fill that in on every line as well. At this point, we have the following information:

C	P	R	C • [~R ∨ (C ⊃ P)]	(P ⊃ ~C) ∨ (R ⊃ ~P)	P ⊃ ~R	~P • ~R
			T T T T	FT T	T	T F F
			T T T T	FT T	T	F F T
			T T T T	FT T	T	F F F

We are now given all the information we need to complete the truth table. We have the truth values for every simple statement, and need only complete each statement to see if there is a contradiction on every line. The completed indirect truth table will look something like the following:

C	P	R	C • [~R ∨ (C ⊃ P)]	(P ⊃ ~C) ∨ (R ⊃ ~P)	P ⊃ ~R	~P • ~R
T	F	T	T T FT T/F T F F	F T FT T T T TF	F T FT	TF F FT
T	T	F	T T TF T T T T	T F FT T F T FT	T T TF	FT F TF
T	T	T	T T T T	T F FT T	T T T/F F	FT F FT

There are contradictions on the first and third lines. We got our contradictions in the first and third premise, respectively, but it is certainly possible to get contradictions in other locations on those lines. The second line, however, is completed without any contradictions, so it shows that the argument is invalid. The premises can be true at the same time the conclusion is false.

Chapter Eighteen Exercises

Use Indirect Truth tables to determine the validity of the following arguments.

Basic Concept Exercises

1. R ≡ P // ~(R • ~P)
2. ~(R • ~P) // R ≡ P
3. A ⊃ B / A // B
4. A ⊃ B / ~B // ~A
5. P ⊃ Q // ~Q ⊃ ~P
6. G ⊃ ~M / ~M ⊃ G // G ≡ M
7. L ≡ ~P / ~P ⊃ ~L // ~L
8. G ⊃ (M ∨ D) / G ∨ (M • D) // M ∨ D
9. D ∨ (E • F) / ~E // D
10. G ⊃ ~(F • D) / G • F // D

Intermediate Exercises

11. M ⊃ ~(N ⊃ O) / N ∨ O // M ⊃ ~O
12. R ∨ [P ∨ (Q • ~R)] / P ⊃ R // ~R ⊃ ~Q
13. (~A ∨ B) ≡ (X • ~Y) / ~B ∨ ~X / Y // ~A
14. L ≡ (B ∨ ~R) / Q ⊃ ~B / R ⊃ (~L • ~Q) // (B • Q) ⊃ (L • R)
15. F ⊃ G / G ⊃ H / H ⊃ I / I ⊃ J / J ⊃ K / K ⊃ L // F ∨ ~L
16. F ⊃ G / G ⊃ H / H ⊃ I / I ⊃ J / J ⊃ K / K ⊃ L // F • ~L
17. Q ⊃ (P • R) / S ⊃ (P • T) / U ⊃ (R ⊃ ~T) // S ⊃ (U ⊃ ~Q)
18. ~(E • F) / (A ⊃ C) ⊃ (B ⊃ E) / G ⊃ F // (G • B) ⊃ (A • ~C)
19. G ⊃ ~(F • D) / G ∨ F // D
20. L ⊃ M / M ⊃ L // L ≡ M

Challenging exercises

21. ~W ⊃ ~V / ~V ⊃ ~W / W ∨ V // W • V
22. L ∨ (M • N) / M ⊃ W / W ⊃ ~N / ~P ⊃ ~L // L • P
23. A ⊃ ~B / B ⊃ ~C / C ⊃ ~D // ~(A ⊃ D)
24. (B ∨ N) • (C ∨ O) / B ⊃ C / N ⊃ O // (B • C) ∨ (N • O)
25. A ∨ (B • C) / G ⊃ ~B / D ⊃ ~C // A • (G ∨ D)
26. R ⊃ Q / Q ∨ P / W ⊃ P / R ≡ W / (P • Q) ⊃ (S • T) / ~(S • T) // ~(R ∨ W)
27. (B ⊃ N) • (C ⊃ O) / B ∨ C / N ∨ O / ~C ⊃ ~O /~B ⊃ ~N // (B • C) ∨ (N • O)
28. If the expansion of the universe is accelerating, then either gravity works differently than we thought, or there is some kind of anti-gravitational force in the universe. If black holes are able to rip apart the fabric of space-time, then gravity works differently than we thought. If there is an anti-gravitational force in the universe, then gravity works differently than we thought. It follows that if black holes are able to rip apart the fabric of space-time, and the expansion of the universe is accelerating, then there is no anti-gravitational force in the universe.
29. If anyone can know the future, then our choices would not be free, but instead would be caused. If God has omniscience, then he knows everything, and

nothing, including the future is unknowable. Therefore, if we have free will, then God is not omniscient.

30. If Casey Anthony killed her daughter, then she is guilty of murder and she deserves the death penalty, unless there was no premeditation, in which case she deserves life in prison. If Casey Anthony's mother searched for "Chloroform" on the computer, then Casey Anthony didn't, in which case, there was no premeditation. Of course, if there was no premeditation, then Casey Anthony does not deserve the death penalty. So, if Casey Anthony's mother searched for "Chloroform" on the computer, then Casey Anthony deserves life in prison.

In-Context Exercises

A. Evaluate the following argument. First, translate it into standard form, then use an indirect truth table to determine its validity. Although it is possible without doing so, you might use subscripts to denote the time of a class, so T_9 can stand for I take Trigonometry at 9:00. Provide a key for your letters. There are a few hidden assumptions, such as that one cannot take two classes at the same time. One can capture this fact using the formula $\sim(C_{12} \bullet E_{12})$ for any two courses which are offered at the same time.

> If I want to finish college this semester, then I need to fulfill my humanities and math requirements. I can only take either College Algebra or Trigonometry to fulfill my math requirement. To fulfill my humanities requirement I can only take Philosophy or English 150. The only time Trigonometry is available is at 9:00, and College Algebra is only listed at 12:00. There is an English 150 class at 12:00, and there is only one Philosophy class, which is at 9:00. The English 150 class at 12:00 is taught by Professor Nestor, whom I hate with a passion. So, if I want to finish college this semester without taking Professor Nestor, I have to take the Philosophy course at 9:00 and the College Algebra course at 12:00.

Logic Puzzle: A Little Rascals Homage

There is going to be a big dance tonight, and you are wondering who is going to be there. The five people below make a statement about attendance. Is it possible that they are all correct? If so, what would it say about who is attending the dance?

Alfalfa: If I go, then Buckwheat is going with me, and I better not see Mrs. Crabtree.
Buckwheat: I'm not going if either Mrs. Crabtree or Spanky isn't going to be there.
Mrs. Crabtree: If either Darla or I is going, then so is Spanky.
Darla: I'm going, but if and only if Buckwheat isn't.
Spanky: If either Alfalfa or Darla is going, then I'm not.

CHAPTER

19

A Few Common Argument Forms

Skill 19.1

Recognizing Common Argument Forms to Determine Validity

Whether or not the average student will ever use truth tables again in their lives (there's a good chance they won't), it is still instructive to see them in order to understand a little about how arguments work, and how they can be proven to be valid. But still, they are of little practical value to most students. There are a few basic argument patterns, however, which are very useful to know. Few real world arguments which are based on truth functional logic involve very complex statements. Most of them involve very simple steps. If one can remember a few argument forms, and can gain some skill at recognizing them in ordinary language, one can actually apply the knowledge capable of being gleaned from truth tables without having to construct them.

Valid Forms

Let's first examine some valid argument patterns. If you can recognize that an argument fits one of these patterns, then you can declare the argument to be valid. You should be careful about being too sure at this point, however, since at this point you still may need to improve your recognition skills.

Modus Ponens and examples

Form	First Example	Second Example
$p \supset q$	$(A \vee B) \supset (D \bullet G)$	$\sim D$
p	$A \vee B$	$\sim D \supset \sim(R \vee S)$
$\therefore\ q$	$\therefore\ D \bullet G$	$\therefore\ \sim(R \vee S)$

Modus ponens is one of the most basic argument forms. Notice that in the form example, lower case letters are used. Lower case letters represent statement variables. They stand for any simple or compound statement. This is very important, and will help understand the other examples. Notice that the antecedent of the conditional premise is colored red. The other premise (whether it comes first or second in the argument) is just the antecedent itself. It is the full antecedent, not part, and nothing more is added. The conclusion, colored blue in this case, is simply the consequent of the conditional premise.

Hopefully, it is intuitively obvious that it is a valid form, but one is always welcome to construct a truth table to prove it. As one can see from the examples, an argument can still be a *modus ponens* argument even when it is very complex. The antecedent and consequent of the conditional premise can themselves be compound statements. The trick is recognizing that one premise is exactly the same as the antecedent in the other, whatever it is, and the conclusion is just the consequent of the conditional premise. Negations are just a special case of this general rule, but they also have another issue, which will be made clear in the next example. Notice now that the antecedent and consequent of the conditional premise can themselves be negations. As long as those negations are maintained in the other premise and the conclusion, respectively, then the argument form is still *modus ponens*. Notice also that the order of the premises doesn't matter at all. The conditional premise can be listed first or second.

Modus Tollens and examples

Form	First Example	Second Example
p ⊃ q	(A ∨ B) ⊃ (D • G)	~D ⊃ ~(R ∨ S)
~q	~(D • G)	R ∨ S (essentially ~~(R ∨ S))
∴ ~p	∴ ~(A ∨ B)	∴ D (essentially ~~D)

Modus tollens is another very common argument form. Look carefully to see how it differs from *modus ponens*. In this argument form, one denies the consequent of the conditional premise, and then one concludes that the antecedent is false as well. Let's say we accept that if Johnny has the flu, then he would have an elevated temperature. But Johnny didn't have an elevated temperature. If both premises were true, then it would definitely follow that Johnny did not have the flu. Now, if someone said, maybe he has a flu, but doesn't have an elevated temperature, they would be denying the first premise, which said that if he had the flu, then he would have an elevated temperature. The only way to consistently hold that the conclusion is false is to hold that one of the premises is false.

One could also put the argument form on a truth table, and confirm for oneself that it is valid. In fact, it may be instructive to put the middle example above on an indirect truth table. The enterprising reader should see this as a challenge.

As before, keep your eye on the colored statements. In this case, there is still a conditional premise, but the other premise negates the consequent, which is why the tilde is not colored. It is a part of the form itself, and not the matter of the argument. Whatever the consequent is, the entire consequent must be negated in order for the argument to fit *modus tollens*. The entire antecedent must be negated in the premise, as it is in all of the examples above.

Some students may be confused by the last example above. There is no tilde on the premise or conclusion, while there is a tilde on each antecedent and consequent. It doesn't look like modus tollens, but looks can be deceiving, as they are in this case. Since the antecedent is ~D, we would expect it to be negated in the conclusion, but it actually is. The statement D is logically equivalent to ~~D. So, we can consider the conclusion to be the negation of the antecedent. This usage is a little loose, but shouldn't cause any confusion.

Disjunctive Syllogism and examples

Form	First Example	Second Example
p ∨ q	(A ∨ B) ∨ (D • G)	~D ∨ ~(R ∨ S)
~p	~(A ∨ B)	D [essentially ~~D]
∴ q	∴ (D • G)	∴ ~(R ∨ S)

Where *modus ponens* and *modus tollens* involve a conditional premise, a disjunctive syllogism involves a disjunctive statement. Make sure you look carefully at the examples. In this case, we assert that one of two options must be correct, and then deny that one of them is true. We are thus entitled to assert the truth of the other disjunct. This argument form is sometimes called reasoning by elimination, especially when it involves more than two possible alternatives, and all but one of the alternatives is ruled out.

An inference which takes the exact form of disjunctive syllogism is always valid, but you must make sure it takes the exact form. There must be a disjunction as one premise, and the second premise must negate one of the disjuncts. We are therefore entitled to assert that the other disjunct is true. If I know that either A is true or B is true, but I find out that A is actually false, then it would follow that B is true. Be especially careful when the disjuncts involve negations, as in the second example above. In these cases, the second premise may be affirmative, but it is still negating one of the disjuncts. Remember that negating a negation results in an affirmation.

Although any argument which fits the form of disjunctive syllogism is valid, keep in mind that such an argument might have a false premise. If the disjunctive statement is false, then the argument commits the fallacy of false dilemma (see Chapter 25), and the conclusion is not necessarily true.

Pure Hypothetical Syllogism and examples

Form	First Example	Second Example
$p \supset q$	$(A \vee B) \supset (D \bullet G)$	$\sim D \supset \sim(R \vee S)$
$q \supset r$	$(D \bullet G) \supset S$	$\sim(R \vee S) \supset D$
$\therefore\ p \supset r$	$\therefore\ (A \vee B) \supset S$	$\therefore\ \sim D \supset D$

As we saw earlier, *modus ponens* and *modus tollens* both involve a conditional premise, but they also involved a second premise which might be any type of statement. As far as the form of *modus ponens* and *modus tollens* are concerned, the second premise can be anything, *as long as it matches the consequent of the conditional premise*. In a pure hypothetical syllogism, on the other hand, all of the statements in the argument are conditional statements.

Notice carefully how the premises in the pure hypothetical syllogism fit together. The consequent of one conditional must be the exact same as the antecedent of the other. They fit together like the links in a chain. In a sense, pure hypothetical syllogism allows us to remove the link, and connect the ends of the chain together directly.

As for all arguments, the order of the premises in a pure hypothetical syllogism does not matter. It is easier to identify this argument form when the consequent of the first premise matches the antecedent of the second premise, but always check to see whether the alternative is the case. Also, make sure that the conditional statement in the conclusion is in the correct order. In the first example above, the conditional $(A \vee B) \supset S$ does follow from the premises, but the conditional $S \supset (A \vee B)$ does not.

Also notice that the second example involves a very odd conclusion: $\sim D \supset D$. This conclusion may look bizarre, but it does follow from the given premises. As one can test on a simple truth table, or perhaps one can grasp intuitively, the conclusion $\sim D \supset D$ would also imply that D is true.

Constructive Dilemma and an example

Form	Example
$(p \supset q) \bullet (r \supset s)$	$[(A \vee B) \supset D] \bullet (P \supset \sim G)$
$p \vee r$	$(A \vee B) \vee P$
$\therefore\ q \vee s$	$\therefore\ D \vee \sim G$

Constructive Dilemma is another valid argument form. It doesn't allow us to assert that anything is definitely true, but only that a certain disjunctive statement (a dilemma) is true (except in the case of simple dilemmas discussed below). An argument only fits the pattern for constructive dilemma when it fits the pattern above exactly. It must include a conjunction of conditional statements (or at least have two conditional premises which could be conjoined). It must also include a disjunctive premise, the disjuncts of which occur as the antecedents of the two conditional statements, and the conclusion must be a disjunction, whose two disjuncts occur as the consequents of the two conditionals. That may sound like a mouthful, but with a little practice, you will be able to judge whether an argument fits this pattern more intuitively.

The constructive dilemma is a well-respected argument form with a long history. One of the most famous is from ancient Greece, related in a work by A. Cornelius Gellius.[5] A wealthy young man, Euathlus, wants to become a lawyer. He learns rhetoric from a famous sophist, Protogoras. They both agree that Euathlus will pay half of a hefty fee up-front, and the remaining half after he wins his first case. After his training, Euathlus tries to evade paying by not taking any cases.

Protagoras sues Euathlus for payment, and argues thusly:

If Euathlus loses the case, then he must pay me (by the judgment of the court).
If Euathlus wins, then he must pay me (by the conditions of the contract).
He will either win or lose the case.
Therefore, either way, he must pay me.

The student should note that this is a particular kind of constructive dilemma, one called simple, in which the conclusion is a single statement, because the consequent of both conditionals is the same thing. If one feels sorry for Euathlus because of this dilemma, fear not. He evaded paying the fee because the jury was confounded by his counterdilemma:

If I win the case, then I need not pay Protagoras (by the judgment of the court).
If I lose the case, then I still need not pay him (by the conditions of the contract).
I will either win or lose the case.
Therefore, either way, I need not pay Protagoras.

Now one might feel badly for the jury. Both constructive dilemmas seem to be sound, but they have conflicting conclusions. The juries found themselves in a rational dilemma, where they seem to have good reason to believe two conflicting claims. Such a situation is often called a paradox, and the student of logic will at some point have to deal with quite a few paradoxes.

Destructive Dilemma and an example

Form	Example
$(p \supset q) \bullet (r \supset s)$	$[(A \vee B) \supset D] \bullet (P \supset \sim G)$
$\underline{\sim q \vee \sim s}$	$\underline{\sim D \vee G}$
$\therefore \sim p \vee \sim r$	$\therefore \sim(A \vee B) \vee \sim P$

Destructive Dilemma is the final valid argument form about which we will learn. It starts off as does the constructive dilemma, with a conjunction of conditionals. The next premise,

[5] Attic Nights (Noctes Atticae), by A. Cornelius Gellius. Book 5, published in Vol. I of the Loeb Classical Library edition, in 1927, (revised 1946), translated by J. C. Rolfe. Found online at http://penelope.uchicago.edu/Thayer/E/Roman/Texts/Gellius/5*.html, accessed May 25, 2011.

however, and the conclusion are different. Here, the premise is a disjunction, but this time it is the negations of the consequents of the two conditional statements. The conclusion is also a disjunction, but the two disjuncts are the negations of the antecedents of the conditionals (if the antecedents are the same, there can be a simple statement as the conclusion).

In looking at the constructive conditional, one can consider it as a modus ponens argument distributed across a disjunction. The destructive dilemma can be seen as a modus tollens argument distributed across a disjunction.

There are of course many other basic argument patterns which are valid, but it is impossible to memorize all of them. This list is a helpful one, which captures a great many of the arguments you will come across. Keep in mind that any argument which doesn't fit these patterns can still be evaluated using truth tables.

Invalid Forms

Skill 19.2

Recognizing Common Formal Fallacies to Determine an Argument to Be Invalid

It is perhaps even more important that students learn some invalid argument patterns. After all, if one doesn't recognize an invalid argument, one might be manipulated by it (or the person making it). Like Illicit Contraposition and the earlier fallacies, the fallacies listed here are formal fallacies. They fail to establish their conclusions because of their structure or form. We can diagnose these fallacies by examining the form of the argument alone.

Denying the Antecedent Fallacy and examples

$p \supset q$	$(A \vee B) \supset (D \bullet G)$	$\sim D \supset \sim(R \vee S)$
$\underline{\sim p}$	$\underline{\sim(A \vee B)}$	$\underline{D}$
$\therefore \sim q$	$\therefore \sim(D \bullet G)$	$\therefore R \vee S$

Formal Fallacy
A specific pattern of mistaken reasoning arising from the structure or form of an argument

Unfortunately, many students often have a difficult time realizing that an argument commits the formal fallacy of denying the antecedent. First, we should note how this fallacy gets its name, which should help in learning to identify it. Notice that the second premise doesn't assert the same thing as the antecedent of the conditional premise. Instead, it asserts its *opposite*, or it *denies* it. So, instead of asserting the antecedent (as in modus ponens), this argument form denies the antecedent.

Let's confirm that this argument form is invalid. Recall that an invalid argument is one where the truth of the premises does not guarantee the truth of the conclusion. Accordingly, to show that the argument form is invalid, we need to devise a counterexample, where the premises are true and the conclusion is false. Here's one:

If I sprain my ankle severely, then I should go to the hospital.
<u>I didn't sprain my ankle.</u>
So, I shouldn't go to the hospital.

It shouldn't be too hard to devise scenarios where I should still go to the hospital even if I haven't sprained my ankle: I was just shot, I was in a serious car accident, I'm having a baby (I really would need to go to the hospital if that were true!). The truth of the given premises just does not guarantee the truth of the conclusion, so the argument is invalid. The conclusion might still be true, but we don't have a guarantee that it is.

As with all of these argument forms, be very careful when it comes to negations. Just because the second non-conditional premise[6] contains a negation doesn't mean the argument commits a denying the antecedent fallacy. It must be that the second premise denies the antecedent of the conditional statement, or in other words contradicts the antecedent.

Affirming the Consequent Fallacy and examples

$p \supset q$	$(A \vee B) \supset (D \bullet G)$	$\sim D \supset \sim(R \vee S)$
$\underline{q}$	$\underline{D \bullet G}$	$\underline{\sim(R \vee S)}$
$\therefore p$	$\therefore A \vee B$	$\therefore \sim D$

Another common formal fallacy is Affirming the Consequent. Although the fallacy can be easy for most people to detect in familiar situations, it can be very misleading in uncommon ones.

Let's say that a student who earns 71% will pass a test, and we know that a particular student has passed. We certainly wouldn't know that the student earned a 71%. There are many other possibilities, between 71% and 100%.

> If a student earns a 71%, they will pass.
> <u>A student passed.</u>
> So, that student earned a 71%.

This argument is invalid, because it affirms the consequent. Here is a similar argument, though: everyone who earns 70% or above will pass, Johnny passed the class, therefore Johnny earned a 70% or above. Most students who are familiar with the standard ten point scale might see this argument as valid. How is it different than the first argument, and does it also affirm the consequent?

The issue is the conditional. The fact that every student who earns a 70% or above will pass, by itself, would not allow us to conclude that a student who passed did earn a 70% or above. By itself, it is consistent with the possibility that everyone who earns a 60% or above would also pass. The reason the argument seems valid is because on a standard ten point scale, there is an equivalence, or biconditional, and not just a single conditional. On a standard ten point scale, one will pass *if and only if* one earns a 70% or above, which would be translated with a triple bar. This example illustrates the problem with thinking that we can apply everything we have learned in a purely mechanical way. When we say that a student who earns 70% or more will pass, we are defining passing, and the result is an equivalence The argument pattern shown below using the equivalence is valid.

$p \equiv q$
$\underline{q}$
$\therefore p$

---

[6] Technically, the second premise could be a conditional statement, but only if the other premise is a nested conditional, e.g. if one premise is '$\sim(A \supset B) \supset C$,' the other could be '$A \supset B$', and the argument would have two conditional premises and still be denying the antecedent.

Logicians will generally try to speak unambiguously, but other people quite often will use a single conditional when they intend the biconditional. Unfortunately, you must carefully and conscientiously consider a person's argument if you want to go a good job evaluating it. Formal methods are not a substitute for thought, but only a supplement.

Presidential Fallacy and examples

p ⊃ q	(A ∨ B) ⊃ (D • G)	p ⊃ q	D ⊃ (R ∨ S)
p ⊃ r	(A ∨ B) ⊃ F	r ⊃ q	W ⊃ (R ∨ S)
∴ q ⊃ r	∴ (D • G) ⊃ F	∴ p ⊃ r	∴ D ⊃ W
or			
∴ r ⊃ q			

Consider the following argument: All American presidents (so far) have been men, and all American presidents (so far) have been over thirty five years old. Therefore, all men are over thirty five years old. Obviously, this argument is invalid. It would be equally invalid if we concluded that all people who are over thirty five years old are men.

I include under the Presidential fallacy the similar argument form where two conditional statements have the same consequents. To argue that dogs are humans because all dogs are mammals and all humans are mammals is to commit the presidential fallacy.

I call this mistake in reasoning the presidential fallacy for a very simple reason. The material conditional is not commutative. It doesn't mean the same thing when it is backwards. For example, 'p ⊃ q' is not the same as 'q ⊃ p.' This distinguishes it from the dot, wedge, and triple bar, which are all commutative. They are like addition and multiplication, which are also commutative: 2 + 3 = 3 + 2, and 5 × 6 = 6 × 5. 'A • B' means the same thing as 'B • A,' and 'C ∨ D' amounts the same thing as 'D ∨ C.'

Subtraction and division are not commutative: 7 - 4 does not equal 4 - 7. Four divided by two equals two (4 ÷ 2 = 2), but two divided by four is one half (2 ÷ 4 = ½). In a similar vein, 'p ⊃ q' does not mean the same thing as 'q ⊃ p.' They cannot be interchanged with each other.

Looking closely at the form for the presidential fallacy, one can see that were we to commute one of the premises, we would have a valid pure hypothetical syllogism. Unfortunately, as we just pointed out, one cannot commute a conditional statement. So the argument form here is formally invalid; it involves an improper commutation. When one realizes that American Presidents have too often been involved with commuting the sentences of political cronies, one will see another reason I call this invalid argument form the Presidential fallacy.

Chapter Nineteen Exercises

Determine whether each of the following arguments is valid by identifying its form. If it doesn't fit any particular pattern, then use a truth table of either variety.

Basic Concept Exercises

1. A / A ⊃ B // B
2. B ∨ C / ~B // C
3. P ⊃ R / R ⊃ S // P ⊃ S
4. A ⊃ R / ~R // ~A
5. R ⊃ S / ~R // ~S

6. (P ⊃ G) • (D ⊃ H) / P ∨ D // G ∨ H
7. M ⊃ N / M ⊃ P // N ⊃ P
8. (Q ⊃ L) • (Q ⊃ D) / ~L ∨ ~D // ~Q
9. (A • C) ⊃ B / B // A • C
10. K ∨ P / K // ~P

Intermediate Exercises

11. (R ≡ S) ∨ ~L / L // R ≡ S
12. ~F ⊃ E / F // ~E
13. (D ⊃ P) ⊃ W / ~W // ~(D ⊃ P)
14. (R ∨ V) • (S ∨ V) / R ∨ S // V
15. J ⊃ ~(K ∨ P) / ~J // K ∨ P
16. (W • Z) ⊃ (S ∨ P) / ~(L ≡ D) ⊃ (W • Z) // ~(L ≡ D) ⊃ (S ∨ P)
17. B ⊃ (A ∨ C) / D ⊃ (A ∨ C) // B ⊃ D
18. [(I • J) ∨ B] ⊃ Q / (I • J) ∨ B //Q
19. (H ⊃ Q) • (S ⊃ D) / ~Q ∨ ~D // ~H ∨ ~S
20. ~(A ≡ B) ⊃ ~(G ≡ L) / ~(G ≡ L) // ~(A ≡ B)

Challenging exercises

21. Every animal that has hair is a mammal. Dolphins are mammals. Therefore, dolphins have hair.
22. President Obama will be reelected only if he successfully addresses the economy. President Obama will successfully address the economy. Therefore, President Obama will be reelected.
23. The Constitution forbids the establishment of religion, and to include the words "under God" in the Pledge of Allegiance is an establishment of religion, which shows that the Pledge of Allegiance is unconstitutional.
24. If someone doesn't support African American month, then he is a racist. Therefore, one must either support African American month, or be a racist.
25. All sets which can be put into a one-to-one correspondence with the natural numbers are countable sets. All sets which are identical to the set of real numbers are countable sets. Therefore, all sets which are identical to the real numbers are countable sets.
26. If I want to enjoy the pie I am going to make I need to add sugar to it, and if I am truly concerned for my health I will not add sugar. Since I must either add sugar or not, then either I am truly concerned for my health, or else I will enjoy the pie I am going to make.
27. The Windows Registry file must have certain file associations for windows to run executable files, and your computer is not running executable files, so your registry is probably corrupted.
28. A Liberal is someone who holds that individuals should make more of their own decisions than the state, but people who support universal healthcare want the state to make more decisions than the individual. So, supporters of universal healthcare cannot be liberal.
29. Congress has not voted to increase the debt limit for the United States. If the debt limit is not raised, then the United States will not be able to borrow any more money, since we are already at the limit. So, as of now the United States cannot legally borrow any money.

30. The government doesn't have the right to stop people from doing what they want to do, and people want to gamble their money. If our state doesn't allow some kind of gambling, then people will spend that money in other states, improving those state's economies and hurting our own. Besides, we can use the money raised to support our schools.

In-Context Exercises

Take the following arguments and decide whether each is valid by deciding what logical form it has. The first one is from the Euthydemus.

A. **Socrates:** Why, because I was stupid and made a mistake. And yet, perhaps, I was right after all in saying that words have a sense;-what do you say, wise man? If I was not in error, even you will not refute me, and all your wisdom will be non-plussed; but if I did fall into error, then again you are wrong in saying that there is no error,-and this remark was made by you not quite a year ago. I am inclined to think, however, Dionysodorus and Euthydemus, that this argument lies where it was and is not very likely to advance: even your skill in the subtleties of logic, which is really amazing, has not found out the way of throwing another and not falling yourself, now any more than of old.

B. If I see an opportunity to create otherwise nonexistent opportunities for moral urgency by burning an infant or two, then I should *not* do so. But if it is good to maximize moral urgency, then I should do so. Therefore, it is not good to maximize moral urgency. Plainly we do not believe that it is a good thing to maximize moral urgency. The fact that we approve of modern medical care and applaud medical advances is proof enough of this. –B .C. Johnson, "Why Doesn't God Intervene?"

C. Stan Smith: "You've got to spend money to make money."
Fran Smith: "But, you didn't make any money."
Stan Smith: "Then, by that logic, I didn't spend any [money]." ("American Dad"- "Red October Sky")

D. Fran Smith: "Stan, I'm your wife. If something's wrong, I want to help you."
Stan Smith: "Oh, so by that logic, if something is right, you'll want to hinder me. Great, Francine. Real quality wife-ing." ("American Dad" – "Of Ice and Men")

Logic Puzzle: The Marathon

Four of my friends are competing in a marathon. Each one is wearing a number and a color. Using the clues below, determine the number and color of each one, and in what order they finished.

1) Helga did not wear blue.
2) Frank did not wear green or red.
3) The one who wore number 24 wore either red or green.
4) The person who wore white came in just after the one who wore blue.
5) My friends were: the one who wore blue, Abel, the one who wore the number 47, and the one who finished third.
6) Martha wore the number 32.
7) The one who wore the number 16 wore the color blue.
8) The one who wore green came in third.

CHAPTER

20

Natural Deduction: Rules of Inference

Skill 20.1

Constructing Natural Deduction Proofs Using Rules of Inference

There are many other proof techniques, but in this introductory textbook we will learn only one more. It is called natural deduction, partly because it was thought to follow normal patterns of human reasoning better than former axiomatic methods. It does have one serious limitation compared to truth tables: it can only prove an argument to be valid. That can be a crippling drawback, but truth tables cannot always be extended to advanced logics, whereas natural deduction can be. For this reason, it is still considered essential for a modern logician or any field which relies on deductive logic, such as mathematics.

Although there are several main versions of natural deduction, the basic idea of each of them is that we give ourselves a limited amount of rules, ones which are very well-founded, and using only those rules, we try to derive a conclusion from the given premises. If we can derive the conclusion, then the argument is valid. If we cannot, then we just don't know whether it is because the argument is invalid, or we just haven't figured out how to do so. This uncertainty is the reason why we cannot declare that an argument is invalid simply because we have failed to prove that it is valid using a natural deduction proof (to do so would be to commit the fallacy of appeal to ignorance—see Chapter 25).

Fortunately, you already know some of the rules for the system we will learn here. You learned them in the previous chapter. The first five rules we will use are simply *modus ponens*, *modus tollens*, disjunctive syllogism, pure hypothetical syllogism, and constructive dilemma. The rules are exactly as we learned them before, although to simplify things, we will use abbreviations for each of them. As a reminder, we repeat these rules below, along with the abbreviation for each.

MP	MT	DS	HS	CD
$p \supset q$ $\underline{p}$ $\therefore q$	$p \supset q$ $\underline{\sim q}$ $\therefore p$	$p \vee q$ $\underline{\sim p}$ $\therefore q$	$p \supset q$ $\underline{q \supset r}$ $\therefore p \supset r$	$(p \supset q) \bullet (r \supset s)$ $\underline{p \vee r}$ $\therefore q \vee s$
Modus Ponens	Modus Tollens	Disjunctive Syllogism	(Pure) Hypothetical Syllogism	Constructive Dilemma

Constructing a Proof

Knowing the rules is only half the battle. We still need to see how to construct a proof. Again, there are several styles of proof construction around, but we will learn one which seems to your author to be the simplest and most clear. Keep in mind that his judgment may be influenced by the way he was taught to do proofs himself.

We will begin with a straightforward argument, and then go through the steps of constructing a proof. It may seem daunting at first, but with practice you will get the hang of it. Here is an argument:

1) $R \supset (M \vee N)$
2) R
3) $\underline{\sim M}$
4) $\therefore N$

This argument is valid, but one might not always know this ahead of time. I say this because knowing that it is valid will guarantee that we will be able to complete a proof. The first thing to do is create a proof line. Then we will number the premises and not the conclusion, although we will write the conclusion next to the last premise as a reminder toward our aim. Then we will put a hash mark under the premises, which signifies that everything above the hash mark is an assumption. So far, our proof should look like it does below.

1)	$R \supset (M \vee N)$	
2)	R	
3)	$\sim M$	// N
	N	(It can help to write the conclusion at the bottom, but don't give it a number yet)

The next step is to realize that we are trying to convert our premises into the conclusion by using our rules. Looking at the first two premises, we realize that we can apply *modus ponens* to derive '$M \vee N$'. We will write this formula as the next line in our proof, making sure to indicate what rule and what lines were being used to derive this line. After doing so, here is what our proof will look like:

1)	$R \supset (M \vee N)$	
2)	R	
3)	$\sim M$	// N
4)	$M \vee N$	1, 2, MP
	N	

Hopefully each reader can see where we are going next. If not, keep practicing and your brain will start to make the necessary connections. We have derived '$M \vee N$' and we already had $\sim M$ as a premise. If we use these lines, and the rule of disjunctive syllogism, we can derive the exact conclusion we need! The completed proof is shown below:

1)	$R \supset (M \vee N)$	
2)	R	
3)	$\sim M$	// N
4)	$M \vee N$	1, 2, MP
	N	4, 3, DS

Notice that in the completed proof there are a few essential properties. Each line below the hash mark has a justification, which includes a rule and the numbers of those lines upon which the rule was used. Each justification is used properly. The conclusion of the argument is the last line of the proof. Finally, no justification can use a line number greater than the line it justifies. One can only use lines which are already justified in order to justify a line, otherwise we fall prey to circular reasoning (See Chapter 25). Thus, the derivation we have constructed is a proof that the argument contained within it is valid.

This was a fairly simple argument with a straightforward proof. Not every argument will be this easy to prove. Some proofs can be very difficult and require real ingenuity to solve, but everyone can improve their skills through practice and application. Let's see another proof using just the rules we have already seen. Consider the argument:

1) G ∨ (L ⊃ N)
2) D ⊃ (N ⊃ G)
3) ~G
4) D
5) ∴ ~L

This argument is a little more complicated, but it shouldn't be beyond the beginning student's abilities, at least not to follow the proof. First, we create the proof line:

1)	G ∨ (L ⊃ N)	
2)	D ⊃ (N ⊃ G)	
3)	~G	
4)	D	// ~L
5)		
	~L	

Next, we try to devise a pathway to the conclusion. There is more information to work with here. One strategy we can use is simply to see what we could possibly derive given what we have. Notice that we are given both a disjunction involving G and the negation of G. These premises set up a disjunctive syllogism, so we should use it. Notice also that we are given a conditional with D as the antecedent, and a premise asserting D, which sets up *modus ponens*. We apply both steps, and see where we are at below:

1)	G ∨ (L ⊃ N)	
2)	D ⊃ (N ⊃ G)	
3)	~G	
4)	D	// ~L
5)	L ⊃ N	1, 3, DS
6)	N ⊃ G	2, 4, MP
	~L	

We now have two new conditionals which are available to use. We could try to find a way to use them individually, but if one looks closely, one will see that we can use a hypothetical syllogism to derive 'L ⊃ G'. Let's apply that step to our proof:

1)	$G \vee (L \supset N)$	
2)	$D \supset (N \supset G)$	
3)	$\sim G$	
4)	D	// ~L
5)	$L \supset N$	1, 3, DS
6)	$N \supset G$	2, 4, MP
7)	$L \supset G$	5, 6, HS
	$\sim L$	

We still need to get to our conclusion, but looking at line seven and the conclusion, it should be clear that we could apply *modus tollens* to derive the conclusion, but only if we had a negation of the consequent. Fortunately, we have ~G as one of our premises, and we complete the proof as follows:

1)	$G \vee (L \supset N)$	
2)	$D \supset (N \supset G)$	
3)	$\sim G$	
4)	D	// ~L
5)	$L \supset N$	1, 3, DS
6)	$N \supset G$	2, 4, MP
7)	$L \supset G$	5, 6, HS
8)	$\sim L$	7, 3, MT

The proof is complete, and we have shown that the argument is valid. Before we turn to the exercises, we will add a few more rules.

MP	**MT**	**DS**	**HS**	**CD**
$p \supset q$ $\underline{p}$ $\therefore q$ *Modus Ponens*	$p \supset q$ $\underline{\sim q}$ $\therefore p$ *Modus Tollens*	$p \vee q$ $\underline{\sim p}$ $\therefore q$ Disjunctive Syllogism	$p \supset q$ $\underline{q \supset r}$ $\therefore p \supset r$ (Pure) Hypothetical Syllogism	$(p \supset q) \bullet (r \supset s)$ $\underline{p \vee r}$ $\therefore q \vee s$ Constructive Dilemma
Conj	**Simp**	**Add**		
p $\underline{q}$ $\therefore p \bullet q$ Conjunction	$\underline{p \bullet q}$ $\therefore p$ Simplification	$\underline{p}$ $\therefore p \vee q$ Addition		

These additional rules are also rules of implication. We will see the contrast with rules of replacement in the next chapter, but for now keep in mind that rules of implication only work in one direction, and can only be applied to entire lines in the derivation. Conjunction and Simplification should be intuitively obvious. Addition may seem a little strange, but a little thought should convince the reader that it is at least a valid inference. If I know that my brother is forty, then it follows that either my brother is forty or my brother is fifty. In this case, the conclusion may convey less information than the premise, but for that very reason the argument is valid.

Let's see one more argument which requires at least one of these additional rules. I will simply write it on a proof line, but the argument should be clear within it:

```
1) | (B ⊃ C) • (B ⊃ D)
2) | (N ∨ E) ⊃ B
3) | N
4) | ~D                 // C • B
   |_
5) |
   |
   | C • B
```

Sometimes figuring out where to start is half the battle. Looking at the conclusion, we know that we are going to want to derive both D and B, and we can see that premise 1 contains both D and B, and premise 2 contains B. In order to get D from the first premise, though, it looks like we would need to have B, so let's concentrate on the second premise. We could derive B if we had 'N ∨ E', but we only have N. Here is where a new rule comes into play. The Rule of Addition states that whenever we have a statement, we can create a disjunction by adding any other statement we would like. Again, it seems odd because we are losing information, but it is a valid step. So, we can add E to N to get the antecedent in the second premise, and then use that to derive B. Let's see where we are at now:

```
1) | (B ⊃ C) • (L ⊃ D)
2) | (N ∨ E) ⊃ B
3) | N
4) | ~C                 // D • B
   |_
5) | N ∨ E              3, Add
6) | B                  2, 5, MP
   |
   | D • B
```

Now, that we have B, how can we use it? The first premise could be used in a constructive dilemma, but only if we had 'B ∨ L.' Since we have B, we can simply add L. Once we do that, we can apply the constructive dilemma to obtain 'C ∨ D.'

```
1) | (B ⊃ C) • (L ⊃ D)
2) | (N ∨ E) ⊃ B
3) | N
4) | ~C                 // D • B
   |_
5) | N ∨ E              3, Add
6) | B                  2, 5, MP
7) | B ∨ L              6, Add
8) | C ∨ D              1, 7, CD
   |
   | D • B
```

The next step is to derive D, and once we have line 8, it should be clear that we could derive D using disjunctive syllogism, as long as we had a negation of C, which we do, on line 4. Once we obtain D, we can conjoin it with B to derive the conclusion. The final proof is shown below:

1)	$(B \supset C) \bullet (L \supset D)$	
2)	$(N \vee E) \supset B$	
3)	N	
4)	$\sim C$	$// D \bullet B$
5)	$N \vee E$	3, Add
6)	B	2, 5, MP
7)	$B \vee L$	6, Add
8)	$C \vee D$	1, 7, CD
9)	D	8, 4, DS
10)	$D \bullet B$	9, 6, Conj

Chapter Twenty Exercises

For each of the following proofs, fill in the missing piece of information.

Basic Concept Exercises

1.

1)	A	
2)	$A \supset B$ $// B$	
3)	B	2, 1, ______

2.

1)	$A \vee C$	
2)	$\sim A$ $// C$	
3)	C	1, 2, ______

3.

1)	$(R \supset W) \bullet (B \supset T)$	
2)	$R \vee B$	$// R \supset W$
3)	$R \supset W$	____, ____

4.

1)	$A \bullet (B \supset T)$	
2)	$B \supset T$ $// A$	
3)	A	____, ____

5.

1)	$E \supset (A \supset B)$	
2)	________	$// \sim E$
3)	$\sim E$	1, 2, MT

6.

1)	$B \supset G$	
2)	$B \bullet D$	$// (B \bullet D) \vee G$
3)	$(B \bullet D) \vee G$	____, ____

7.

1)	$A \supset (B \equiv E)$	
2)	________	$// (B \equiv E)$
3)	$(B \equiv E)$	1, 2, ______

8.

1)	$(D \supset L) \bullet (N \supset P)$	
2)	________	$// L \vee P$
3)	$L \vee P$	1, 2, ______

9.

1)	$B \supset R$	
2)	B	
3)	$R \supset D$ $// B \bullet (R \supset D)$	
4)	$B \bullet (R \supset D)$	____, ____

10.

1)	$A \supset (W \supset R)$	
2)	$A \vee (R \vee W)$	
3)	$\sim(W \supset R)$	$// \sim A$
4)	$\sim A$	____, ____

Intermediate Exercises

Construct a natural deduction proof for each of the following valid arguments:

11. (R ≡ S) ⊃ L / ~L // ~(R ≡ S)
12. ~F ⊃ ~E / ~F // ~E
13. (D ⊃ P) ∨ W / ~(D ⊃ P) // W
14. (R ⊃ V) • (S ⊃ V) / R ∨ S // [(R ⊃ V) • (S ⊃ V)] • (R ∨ S)
15. J ⊃ (K ∨ P) / J / ~K // P
16. (H • ~G) ⊃ (S ∨ P) / H / ~R / G ⊃ R // S ∨ P
17. B ⊃ (A ∨ C) / (A ∨ C) ⊃ D / ~D // ~B
18. (I • J) ∨ (B ⊃ Q) / ~(I • J) / B // Q
19. (H ⊃ Q) • (S ⊃ D) / H ∨ S / ~Q // ~D
20. A ⊃ (G ≡ L) / (L ≡ M) ⊃ A / ~(G ≡ L) // ~(L ≡ M)

Challenging exercises

21. (L ⊃ M) / (M ⊃ G) / ~G // ~L
22. (A ⊃ C) / (~C ⊃ ~D) / A ∨ ~C // C ∨ ~D
23. (D ∨ W) ⊃ P) / [D ∨ (A ≡ L)] ⊃ R / D // P • R
24. B ⊃ (E ∨ D) / (E ∨ D) ⊃ (B ⊃ G)] / ~(B ⊃ G)] // ~B
25. O ⊃ (M ∨ N) / ~M ⊃ (O • G) / ~M // N
26. [R ⊃ (S ∨ T)] / [R ⊃ (M ⊃ G)] / (A ∨ C) ∨ R / ~(S ∨ T) / ~(A ∨ C) // M ⊃ G
27. ~D (~R ⊃ G) / (D ⊃ B) ∨ (R ⊃ D) / ~(D ⊃ B) // G
28. (A • ~N) ⊃ G / ~M ⊃ A / N ⊃ M / ~M // G
29. L ⊃ (W ⊃ G) / (D ∨ B) ⊃ R / R ⊃ V / L / (D ∨ B) ∨ W // V ∨ G
30. (E ⊃ D) • (W ⊃ A) / [~D • (W ≡ M)] ⊃ (E ∨ W) / ~D • ~J / D ∨ (W ≡ M) // A ∨ K

In-Context Exercises

Take each of the following monologues involving a reasoning process, and convert it to a natural deduction proof, then decide whether the proof is complete or incomplete. If you think the argument is valid, but the proof is incomplete, see if you can complete the proof on your own.

A. I have heard that every proton in every atom has a positive electric charge, but that has to be wrong. If every proton in every atom had a positive electric charge, then every proton in every atom would shoot apart from each other at incredible speed. For the universe to exist in a stable state, then it cannot be the case the every proton in every atom shoots apart from each other at incredible speeds. But the universe does exist in a stable state, which shows that it is not the case that every atom is in essence exploding, but that just shows that not every proton in every atom can have a positive electric charge.

B. I am trying to figure out what number the variable *a* represents. I know it is an integer, and that it must be either even or odd. I also know that it must be either prime or composite. It also must be the case that if *a* is odd and composite, then it cannot equal the number 2. I have been told that the number is not prime. I also have been told that it is not even. Since it is not prime, I can assert that it must be composite. Since it is not even, then it must be odd. So, I know that *a* cannot equal

2, since it is both odd and composite. Great, I've ruled out one possibility; only an infinite number of other possibilities to consider.

Logic Puzzle: Professor Egnom's Politically Correct Vote

Your author always votes based on the ideological commitments and character of the candidates, but Professor Egnom has a very different strategy. He always splits his vote among political parties, men and women, religion and ethnicities. When there is an election for President, Senate, and the House of Representatives, he always aims to have one Republican, one Democrat, and one Independent or third party candidate. He prefers to vote Republican or Democrat for President. He also would prefer to vote for at least one woman, and no more than one candidate from any ethnicity, and he doesn't care if that makes him a racist. He also prefers to have no more than two Christian candidates. He has narrowed down the acceptable candidates to those listed below. Is it possible that Professor Egnom can have all of his preferences satisfied? If so, will that determine for whom he will vote?

President:	Marco Rubio (male, Hispanic, Republican, Christian)
	Hillary Clinton (female, Caucasian, Democrat, Christian)
Senator:	Emily Kim(female, Asian, Libertarian, Buddhist)
	Eddie Jones (male, African-American, Republican, no religion)
	Sammy Edwards (male, Caucasian, Democrat, Atheist)
	Eva Lopez (female, Hispanic, Independent, Christian)
Representative:	Harris Feinman (male, Caucasian, Independent, Jewish)
	Violet Jeffers (female, African-American, Libertarian, Christian)
	Thomas Le (male, Asian, Republican, Christian)
	Eduardo Gomez (male, Hispanic, Democrat, Mormon)

Chapter

21

Natural Deduction: Rules of Replacement

Skill 21.1

Constructing Natural Deduction Proofs using Rules of Replacement

With only the Rules of Implication there are many proofs which can be completed, but there would be some valid arguments for which proofs could not be completed. Such a system would be incomplete. In this chapter, we will add ten new rules of a different type than we learned in the last chapter. These rules are the Rules of Replacement. Where the Rules of Implication were single conditionals, the Rules of Replacement are bi-conditionals, or equivalences. Using these rules and the subordinate proof techniques in Chapter 22, we will have a complete system.

The basic intuition behind the Rules of Replacement is that since two logically equivalent statements necessarily have the same truth value, replacing one for another in a proof, or elsewhere, will not result in a change in any of the relevant truth values. So, it is always permissible to replace one statement with one which is logically equivalent to it. We select a limited number of rules, however, so as to keep the system manageable.

The Rules of Replacement

Here are the ten Rules of Replacement we will use (the four dot symbol represents logical equivalence):

Com	**DM**	**Assoc**
$(p \lor q) :: (q \lor p)$ $(p \bullet q) :: (q \bullet p)$ Commutativity	$\sim(p \lor q) :: (\sim p \bullet \sim q)$ $\sim(p \bullet q) :: (\sim p \lor \sim q)$ De Morgan's Rule	$[(p \lor q) \lor r] :: [p \lor (q \lor r)]$ $[(p \bullet q) \bullet r] :: [p \bullet (q \bullet r)]$ Associativity
DN $p :: \sim\sim p$ Double Negation	**Exp** $[(p \bullet q) \supset r] :: [p \supset (q \supset r)]$ Exportation	**Impl** $(p \supset q) :: (\sim p \lor q)$ Material Implication
Taut $p :: (p \lor p)$ $p :: (p \bullet p)$ Tautology	**Equiv** $(p \equiv q) :: [(p \supset q) \bullet (q \supset p)]$ $(p \equiv q) :: [(p \bullet q) \lor (\sim p \bullet \sim q]$ Material Equivalence	**Trans** $(p \supset q) :: (\sim q \supset \sim p)$ Transposition
	Dist $[p \lor (q \bullet r)] :: [(p \lor q) \bullet (p \lor r)]$ $[p \bullet (q \lor r)] :: [(p \bullet q) \lor (p \bullet r)]$ Distribution	

There are two important differences between the Rules of Replacement and the Rules of Implication. The Rules of Replacement are bi-directional, so one can replace a statement on the left, anywhere one finds it, with one on the right, *or vice versa*. The second difference is that the Rules of Replacement can be used *within* a statement. They need not be used only on an entire line of a proof. For example, look at the rule for commutativity. Should we find a statement such as 'A ⊃ (C ∨ B)', for example, we can apply commutativity to the statement within the parentheses to obtain 'A ⊃ (B ∨ C)', whereas we could not directly apply disjunctive syllogism to the disjunction within the parentheses. To apply disjunctive syllogism we would first have to disengage the disjunction, perhaps through *modus ponens*.

Proofs using all eighteen rules can be significantly more complicated, but they can also simplify many proofs, and they can prove the validity of even more arguments. Let's see an example of a proof which will require at least one of the Rules of Replacement.

1)	A ⊃ (~B ⊃ ~F)		
2)	F ⊃ (B ⊃ E)		
3)	A		
4)	F	// E	
5)			

As you can see, we have already placed it on a proof line. As before, it is often a good idea to start working with what you have, just to see what you can derive quickly. Just make sure you are using a pencil. It is easy to see that we can apply modus ponens twice, so let's apply this observation to the proof.

1)	A ⊃ (~B ⊃ ~F)		
2)	F ⊃ (B ⊃ E)		
3)	A		
4)	F	// E	
5)	~B ⊃ ~F		1, 3, MP
6)	B ⊃ E		2, 4, MP
7)			

Now it may be harder to see what must be done. The first thing to notice is that the conclusion 'E' appears as the consequent of a conditional. So, if we had 'B', the antecedent of that conditional, then we could get the conclusion through *modus ponens*. Yet, we don't have 'B', at least not yet. There is a '~B' in line 5, but it occurs as the antecedent. Fortunately, the more familiar you are with the rules, the easier you will start to make connections. For now, consider the possible rules of replacement. Any time you see a conditional with both sides negated, you should immediately be reminded of transposition (although keep in mind that it can be used on conditionals all the time, whether they have two, one, or no negated sides). If we applied transposition to line 5, we would have 'F ⊃ B'. Now, again, we could obtain 'B' if we had 'F', but we do have 'F' on line 4. So, putting all of that together, we obtain the following proof.

1)	A ⊃ (~B ⊃ ~F)		
2)	F ⊃ (B ⊃ E)		
3)	A		
4)	F	// E	
5)	~B ⊃ ~F		1, 3, MP
6)	B ⊃ E		2, 4, MP
7)	F ⊃ B		5, Trans
8)	B		7, 4, MP
9)	E		6, 8, MP

We can check to make sure it is a completed proof by ensuring that each line after the hash has a justification, that it is correctly applied, that the conclusion is the last line of the proof, and that every justification uses line numbers prior to the line it is justifying. Everything checks out, so this is a completed proof.

When constructing a proof, one will often run into roadblocks. Sometimes, one will just get stuck and not see what else to do. One strategy to help is to try to work backwards. We started to do so in the last proof, but only quickly in the discussion. Here, we will show that it can be done on paper as well. Consider this argument:

1)	M ⊃ ~(U ∨ V)		
2)	[P ∨ (N • I)] ⊃ M		
3)	P • N	// ~U • ~V	
4)			
	~U • ~V		

We will work this argument entirely backwards. That is usually not a good idea, but hopefully it will allow the student to see how the technique works, so that he or she can apply it when needed. Often the best approach involves both the top-down strategy and the bottom up strategy.

The first thing we see is that our conclusion is a conjunction of negations. This should immediately incline us toward De Morgan's Rule. De Morgan's Rule basically says that when one has a negated conjunction or disjunction, one can distribute the tilde through it, *as long as one changes it* from a disjunction to a conjunction or vice versa. The statement we would need to get the conclusion through De Morgan's Rule would be ~(U ∨ V), but we can see it occurring in the first premise, as the consequent of a conditional. Let's write this on the proof line, and then continue.

1)	M ⊃ ~(U ∨ V)		
2)	[P ∨ (N • I)] ⊃ M		
3)	P • N	// ~U • ~V	
4)			
x	~(U ∨ V)		
	~U • ~V		x, DM

Notice that we provisionally give the line in question a variable, and then use it in the justification for the conclusion. If we could just get to line x, then we would have the completed proof. So, we must ask, what would we need to derive line x? Looking at the first premise, it should become clear: we would need 'M'. If we had 'M', we could use *modus ponens* to derive ~(U ∨ V). So, let's write that in on our proof line.

1)	M ⊃ ~(U ∨ V)	
2)	[P ∨ (N • I)] ⊃ M	
3)	P • N	// ~U • ~V
4)		
y	M	
x	~(U ∨ V)	1, y, MP
	~U • ~V	x, DM

Notice that I can just add space if necessary. Students will want to ensure that they leave plenty of room when they are using this technique. So, what would be required in order to derive 'M'? Looking at the second premise, we could get 'M' using *modus ponens*, as long as we could derive the antecedent. Let's write in the required statement, and see where we are.

1)	M ⊃ ~(U ∨ V)	
2)	[P ∨ (N • I)] ⊃ M	
3)	P • N	// ~U • ~V
4)		
z	P ∨ (N • I)	
y	M	2, z, MP
x	~(U ∨ V)	1, y, MP
	~U • ~V	x, DM

There is a very simple way to complete the proof at this point, but if you don't see it, then you'll have to follow my lead. Looking at line z, I see that I have a disjunction with one of the disjuncts being a conjunction. That arrangement should call to mind distribution. The rule is a little complicated, but if we are careful we can figure it out. If I know that either P is true or N and I are both true, then I know that both P and N are true, or else both P and I are true. I will write it in on the proof and we will see where we are.

1)	M ⊃ ~(U ∨ V)	
2)	[P ∨ (N • I)] ⊃ M	
3)	P • N	// ~U • ~V
4)		
w	(P • N) ∨ (P • I)	
z	P ∨ (N • I)	w, Dist
y	M	2, z, MP
x	~(U ∨ V)	1, y, MP
	~U • ~V	x, DM

If we could get line w, then we could use the rule of distribution on it to obtain line z, and all the way down to the conclusion. We now have to try to find a way to derive w. We haven't used premise 3 yet, so it is a likely candidate to use, and hopefully it is clear that we could use Addition. Remember that we can always add anything we need as a disjunction if we already have a disjunct as a line (we may also need to use commutativity). So, actually, line 4 is line w. All that remains is to renumber the lines and complete the justifications, as we do below.

1) M ⊃ ~(U ∨ V)
2) [P ∨ (N • I)] ⊃ M
3) P • N // ~U • ~V

4)w (P • N) ∨ (P • I) 3, Add
5)z P ∨ (N • I) 4, Dist
6)y M 2, 5, MP
7)x ~(U ∨ V) 1, 6, MP
8) ~U • ~V 7, DM

Check for yourself, and you will see that the proof is complete. If you were wondering, we also could have used simplification to obtain 'P', and then we could have simply added 'N • I', and the rest of the proof would remain the same. As in learning any skill, the best way to learn is by practice, and below you will find plenty of exercises upon which to practice.

CHAPTER TWENTY-ONE EXERCISES

For each of the following proofs, fill in the missing piece of information.

Basic Concept Exercises

1.
1) ~A ∨ B
2) A ⊃ B 1, ____

2.
1) (A ∨ C) ⊃ B
2) (C ∨ A) ⊃ B 1, ____

3.
1) (C ⊃ B) • (B ⊃ C)
2) (C ∨ B) • (~C ∨ ~B)
3) C ≡ B ____, ____

4.
1) ~(F • C)
2) F ⊃ C
3) ~F ∨ C ____, ____

5.
1) E ⊃ (A ⊃ B)
2) ________ 1, Exp

6.
1) ____________
2) G ∨ (C • E) 1, Dist

7.
1) A ⊃ ~(B ∨ E)
2) (~B • ~E) ⊃ A
3) A ⊃ (~B • ~E) ____, ____

8.
1) (D ⊃ L) • (N ∨ N)
2) (D • L) ⊃ (D • N)
3) (D ⊃ L) • N ____, ____

9.
1) M ⊃ (N ⊃ O)
2) (M • N) ⊃ O
3) M ∨ (N ⊃ O)
4) M ⊃ (N ⊃ O) ____, ____

10.
1) S ⊃ (R ⊃ P)
2) ~[(S ∨ R) • P]
3) (S ∨ R) ⊃ P
4) ~(S ∨ R) ∨ P ____, ____

Intermediate Exercises

Construct a natural deduction proof for each of the following valid arguments:

11. $(B \equiv D) \supset M$ // $\sim(B \equiv D) \vee M$
12. $\sim F \supset \sim E$ // $E \supset F$
13. $\sim F \supset \sim E$ // $F \vee \sim E$
14. $(M \supset P) \vee R$ / $\sim(\sim M \vee P)$ // R
15. $C \supset G$ / $(C \vee D) \bullet (D \supset M)$ // $M \vee G$
16. $G \supset (R \vee V)$ / $(V \vee R) \supset E$ // $\sim E \supset \sim G$
17. $(L \bullet K) \vee (L \bullet I)$ / $L \supset M$ // M
18. $(P \supset Q)$ / $\sim P \supset \sim Q$ // $P \equiv Q$
19. $R \supset (L \supset P)$ / $\sim R \supset \sim M$ // $M \supset (\sim L \vee P)$
20. $(K \bullet J) \vee (K \bullet Q)$ / $(J \bullet K) \supset \sim(A \vee C)$ / $\sim Q$ // $\sim A$

Challenging exercises

21. $(P \bullet M) \vee (L \bullet N)$ / $\sim P$ // L
22. $(A \bullet B) \vee (C \bullet D)$ / $\sim D$ // B
23. $(R \supset S) \bullet (B \supset \sim D)$ / $D \vee \sim S$ // $\sim R \vee \sim B$
24. $A \supset (F \bullet P)$ / $(P \vee F) \supset A$ / $A \vee \sim A$ // $P \equiv F$
25. $K \supset (L \supset P)$ // $L \supset (\sim K \vee P)$
26. $\sim A \supset (G \supset \sim P)$ // $P \supset (G \supset A)$
27. $M \vee C$ / $M \supset C$ // C
28. $(E \supset S) \bullet (L \supset N)$ / $E \supset L$ // $E \supset (S \bullet N)$
29. $E \supset (S \bullet N)$ // $E \supset (S \supset N)$
30. $L \supset (M \bullet V)$ / $\sim L \supset \sim(M \vee P)$ // $(L \bullet M) \vee (\sim L \bullet \sim M)$

In-Context Exercises

Take each of the following valid arguments, convert it into symbolic form, and then construct a natural deduction proof to show that it is valid. If you disagree with the conclusion, see if you can figure out which premise is false (or premises).

A. If we have freedom of speech, then we have the right to say things that are offensive, and if we don't have freedom of speech, then we live in a dictatorial society. Yet, if sexual harassment laws prohibit us from saying sexually demeaning things to women, then we do not have the right to say things that are offensive. As I understand it, sexual harassment laws do prohibit us from saying sexually demeaning things to women. It looks to me like we don't have freedom of speech and we live in a dictatorial society.

B. I have been following the George Zimmerman trial, and it seems pretty clear to me that if he was not acting in self-defense, then he is not guilty of manslaughter, but second degree homicide. Yet, if self-defense is as much a justification against manslaughter as it is against second degree homicide. In other words, if acting in self-defense means that one does not commit second degree murder, then acting in self-defense means one does not commit manslaughter. You told me that you didn't think it was second degree homicide, and therefore you must agree that it is not manslaughter either.

Logic Puzzle: The ExPLEx

You can't complete your work on the extrasolar planetary near light-speed explorer (The ExPLEx) until Dr. Loki gives you the results of his calculations on the duration of the trip. He refuses to tell you directly, but does give you the following information. Use the fact that the number corresponding to the duration of the trip is either even or odd (and not both), and the information Dr. Loki provided to determine the length of the trip. Then figure out why you decided to hire someone named "Dr. Loki" in the first place. (In case you have forgotten, or were never taught, every natural number is prime or can be broken down into prime factors. 11 is prime, while 28 is not. So, 28 can be broken down into the prime factors 2 and 7, with 2 being used twice in its prime factorization: $2 \times 2 \times 7=28$)

1) There are no more than 2 unique prime factors, although some of them may be used twice (but no more).
2) The duration, in astronomical time units, is even if and only if it is divisible by 2 ($E \equiv D_2$).
3) If the duration is divisible by 3, then it is not divisible by 2.
4) If the duration is not divisible by 3, then it is odd.
5) If the duration is odd, then it is divisible by 9 (i.e. 3×3).
6) The duration is either divisible by 25, or it is not divisible by 9.

CHAPTER

22

Natural Deduction: Subordinate Proofs

Skill 22.1

Constructing Natural Deduction Proofs using Subordinate Proof Lines

Although the eighteen rules we have learned are powerful, they still often require proofs that seem anything but natural. To some degree, this result is to be expected. We often reason competently but quickly, jumping a bit more than would make our logic clear to an outsider. Natural deduction, like any proof technique, is intended to be absolutely conclusive, so that no one, not even someone adamantly opposed to one's position, can disagree with the reasoning employed. So, every little step no matter how trivial is included. Another way to think about it is that the steps do not require any ingenuity whatsoever, in following them, that is, though unfortunately not in devising them. Even a simple computer could be programmed to follow them.

Fortunately, subordinate proof lines allow us to complete our system, and to often construct proofs which are far more natural-seeming, while still meeting the rigorous demands of a formal system. In this chapter, we will learn how to complete both a conditional proof and an indirect proof.

Conditional Proof

The basic idea behind a conditional proof is that when we assume something is true, and then derive anything based upon that assumption, we cannot assert that what we derive *is* true, but we can assert that it follows from the assumption which we made. That may be hard to follow, but it will make more sense when you see it in action. First, let's see the form of every conditional proof.

x)	p	ACP ("Assumed for Conditional Proof")
y)	q	justification
	$p \supset q$	x-y, CP

There are many things to notice here. The first is that the subordinate proof line is nested within the original proof line. There is also another hash mark on the subordinate proof line, right below the assumption, in this case represented by 'p'. We can assume literally any statement we would like. Generally, we will have in mind a conditional statement we will need to prove, which will tell us what assumption we should make. We also give our assumption a line number 'x', so that we can refer to it in our justifications. Every line below 'p' will need a justification from a line which comes before it.

At any point on the subordinate proof, we can "discharge" our assumption, which means we will end our subordinate proof and go back to the original proof line. As can be seen above, 'y' is the last line on the subordinate proof. When we return to the original proof line, we must discharge the assumption by writing a conditional statement, with the assumption as the antecedent, and the statement on the subordinate proof line as the consequent of the conditional. For our justification, we will write 'x-y, CP'. The 'x' and 'y' are the line numbers which begin and end the conditional proof, and we put a hyphen between them to show that it includes all the lines between. 'CP' stands for 'conditional proof'.

That's it. It may seem like a lot, but when you get the hang of it, it will seem much simpler. Let's show how conditional proof can be used with an actual example. We will construct a proof for the following argument:

```
1)  | M ⊃ (U • V)
2)  | V ⊃ (N • I)       // M ⊃ I
    |—
3)  |
    |
    | M ⊃ I
```

The conclusion is a conditional statement. That is a very good sign that one ought to try conditional proof. Let's set up the subordinate proof line:

```
1)  | M ⊃ (U • V)
2)  | V ⊃ (N • I)       // M ⊃ I
    |—
3)  |  | M              ACP
    |  |—
x   |  |
    | M ⊃ I             3-x, CP
```

Although we don't have a number yet for the conditional proof, we can assign 'x' to the last line of the subordinate line, and write in as much of the justification for the conclusion as we can. Now that we have assumed 'M', we can use it in our derivation, and it should be clear that we can use it with the first premise to obtain 'U • V'. Let's write that in.

```
1)  | M ⊃ (U • V)
2)  | V ⊃ (N • I)       // M ⊃ I
    |—
3)  |  | M              ACP
    |  |—
4)  |  | U • V          1, 3, MP
x   |  |
    | M ⊃ I             3-x, CP
```

As you can see, we can apply the rules just as we did before. Now, it should become fairly clear how to proceed. We need to obtain 'V', which can use to obtain 'N • I', from which we can obtain 'I'. Let's fill in the rest of the proof.

```
1)  | M ⊃ (U • V)
2)  | V ⊃ (N • I)      // M ⊃ I
    |--
3)  |  | M             ACP
    |  |--
4)  |  | U • V         1, 3, MP
5)  |  | V • U         4, Com
6)  |  | V             5, Simp
7)  |  | N • I         2, 6, MP
8)  |  | I • N         7, Com
9)  |  | I             8, Simp
10) | M ⊃ I            3-9, CP
```

Notice that we have filled in the justification for the conclusion, and that this proof satisfies all the conditions required of a proof. Every line has a justification, and the justification is correctly used. No line is justified by a line which comes after it. The conclusion is the last line of the proof. Notice in particular that the subordinate proof line is correctly discharged: the conditional statement immediately after it uses the assumption of the conditional proof as the antecedent, and the last statement on the subordinate proof line as the consequent. Thus, the proof is complete, and the argument is valid.

Students will often worry about what assumption should be made, but in general this shouldn't be a problem. One shouldn't engage in conditional proof unless one is trying to derive a conditional statement, but if you know what conditional statement you need to derive, then just assume the antecedent of that conditional statement. We will continue with one more example.

```
1)  | (A ∨ D) ⊃ (U ⊃ B)
2)  | N ⊃ U              // (A • N) ⊃ B
    |--
3)  |
    |
    | (A • N) ⊃ B
```

This argument is a little more complicated, but if we proceed step by step, we should be able to conquer it. The first thing to notice is that the conclusion is a conditional statement, which means it might be a good idea to derive it using conditional proof. The antecedent of the conditional is 'A • N', so we should assume this conjunction. Let's set up the conditional proof:

```
1)  | (A ∨ D) ⊃ (U ⊃ B)
2)  | N ⊃ U              // (A • N) ⊃ B
    |--
3)  |  | A • N                  ACP
    |  |--
4)  |  |
    |  |
x   |  |
    | (A • N) ⊃ B    3-x, CP
```

Now that we have the conjunction, we could use Simplification to obtain the conjuncts. Once we obtain 'A' we could use it and modus ponens on the first premise, but first we need to use Addition to obtain 'A ∨ D'. These steps are added to the proof below.

```
1)  | (A ∨ D) ⊃ (U ⊃ B)
2)  | N ⊃ U              // (A • N) ⊃ B
    |---
3)  |  | A • N               ACP
    |  |---
4)  |  | A                   3, Simp
5)  |  | N • A               3, Com
6)  |  | N                   5, Simp
7)  |  | A ∨ D               4, Add
    |  |
x   |  |
    | (A • N) ⊃ B       3-x, CP
```

We are still working on the subordinate proof line, and we are trying to derive 'B'. If we use the first statement, we could obtain 'U ⊃ B' and then use the second premise in a hypothetical syllogism. These steps are added below.

```
1)  | (A ∨ D) ⊃ (U ⊃ B)
2)  | N ⊃ U              // (A • N) ⊃ B
    |---
3)  |  | A • N               ACP
    |  |---
4)  |  | A                   3, Simp
5)  |  | N • A               3, Com
6)  |  | N                   5, Simp
7)  |  | A ∨ D               4, Add
8)  |  | U ⊃ B               1, 7, MP
9)  |  | N ⊃ B               2, 8, HS
    |  |
x   |  |
    | (A • N) ⊃ B       3-x, CP
```

Finally, we can use 'N' and 'N ⊃ B' to derive 'B', which is exactly what we need the complete the subordinate proof line and the entire proof itself. Here is the entire proof:

```
1)  | (A ∨ D) ⊃ (U ⊃ B)
2)  | N ⊃ U              // (A • N) ⊃ B
    |---
3)  |  | A • N               ACP
    |  |---
4)  |  | A                   3, Simp
5)  |  | N • A               3, Com
6)  |  | N                   5, Simp
7)  |  | A ∨ D               4, Add
8)  |  | U ⊃ B               1, 7, MP
9)  |  | N ⊃ B               2, 8, HS
10) |  | B                   9, 6, MP
11) | (A • N) ⊃ B            3-10, CP
```

If you are trying to construct a proof, and you just can't make further progress, it is okay to put it aside for a while. In fact, if you can't make progress after five or ten minutes, it's a good idea to set it aside and come back to it later. Sometimes a little time away from the problem helps us see things from a different angle.

Indirect Proof

We have already essentially seen the basic idea behind indirect proof, when we saw *reductio ad absurdum*. As with a *reductio ad absurdum*, we make an assumption, and if we derive a contradiction, we reject the assumption that we made. So, every Indirect Proof follows the form presented here:

```
   |
   |—
x) | | p          AIP ("Assumed for Indirect Proof")
   | |—
   | |
y) | | q • ~q            justification
   |~p            x-y, IP
```

As with Conditional Proof, we begin a subordinate proof line with an assumption. The proof line continues until the assumption is discharged, only in this case, the last line of the subordinate proof must be a straightforward contradiction. It must be a statement of the form 'q • ~q', although 'q' can represent any statement. The assumption is discharged in this case, however, by negating the assumption. As with Conditional Proof, there are no restrictions on what assumptions can be made, and one will be guided by the conclusion, or whatever line one is aiming to derive.

The justification is analogous to Conditional Proof as well. The first line and last line of the subordinate proof are listed, separated by a hyphen, and 'IP' is used to indicate 'Indirect Proof'. Keep in mind that a proof cannot end on a subordinate proof line, but must end on the main proof line. We can use Indirect Proof any time we would like, but it can only be used to derive a negation. If we assume a negated statement, however, we will derive a double negation, and we can use to Rule of Double Negation to eliminate both of them, and end up with a non-negated statement.

As always, it will greatly facilitate one's understanding to follow along on an actual argument, so let's construct a proof for the following argument.

```
1) | W ⊃ (P ⊃ G)
2) | ~G ∨ ~W        // ~(W • P)
   |—
3) |
   |
   |~(W • P)
```

When we see that the conclusion is a negation, we should immediately consider deriving it through Indirect Proof. In this case, the negation is of a conjunction, but that makes no difference. The first step, then, is to set up our subordinate proof line.

1)	W ⊃ (P ⊃ G)	
2)	~G ∨ ~W	// ~(W • P)
3)	W • P	AIP
4)		
x		
	~(W • P)	3-x, IP

We assume 'W • P' simply because that is the negated statement we need. We will be trying to derive a contradiction. It is not necessary to see which one, but in the above argument we have available 'W' (once we simplify the assumption), and we see that '~W' appears as a consequent of a conditional. It looks like a good candidate. Let's pull out the 'W', 'P', and then use 'W' with the first premise.

1)	W ⊃ (P ⊃ G)	
2)	~G ∨ ~W	// ~(W • P)
3)	W • P	AIP
4)	W	3, Simp
5)	P • W	3, Com
6)	P	5, Simp
7)	P ⊃ G	1, 4, MP
x		
	~(W • P)	3-x, IP

At this point, the path should begin to be clear. We can obtain 'G' which we will use to obtain '~W', and then the last step is to conjoin 'W' and '~W'. The completed proof is shown below.

1)	W ⊃ (P ⊃ G)	
2)	~G ∨ ~W	// ~(W • P)
3)	W • P	AIP
4)	W	3, Simp
5)	P • W	3, Com
6)	P	5, Simp
7)	P ⊃ G	1, 4, MP
8)	G	7, 6, MP
9)	~~G	8 DN
10)	~W	2, 10, DS
11)	W • ~W	4, 10, Conj
12)	~(W • P)	3-11, IP

The proof is complete, and establishes that the argument within it is valid. In this case the conclusion itself was a negation, but in the next example it isn't. Yet, we can still use an Indirect Proof. This proof will be more involved than the previous examples, but hopefully the reader will see that with a systematic approach and determination, any proof can be completed.

1)	B • (~E ∨ ~F)	
2)	D ⊃ (B • C)	
3)	C ⊃ (E ∨ F)	// ~D ∨ ~(E ≡ F)
	~D ∨ ~(E ≡ F)	

Since the conclusion is not a negation, we cannot use Indirect Proof to derive the conclusion directly. Working from the bottom up, however, we could transform the conclusion into either a conditional (through Material Implication) or a negation (through De Morgan's Rule). Or we could try to derive the conclusion directly. Since we could still use some practice with Indirect Proof, let's turn it into a negation, and then set up the Indirect Proof. We do so below.

1)	B ⊃ (~E ∨ ~F)	
2)	D ⊃ (B • C)	
3)	C ⊃ (E ∨ F)	// ~D ∨ ~(E ≡ F)
4)	D • (E ≡ F)	AIP
x		
y	~[D • (E ≡ F)]	5-x, ÎP
	~D ∨ ~(E ≡ F)	y, DM

At this stage some things should be begin to become clear. The assumption we made is a conjunction, so it can be simplified, and once we obtain 'D' we can use it with the second premise to obtain 'B' and 'C' (after Simplification). We may not know quite where we are heading, other than a contradiction, but sometimes it helps to pull out at much information as we can. After doing so, our proof will look like it does below.

1)	B ⊃ (~E ∨ ~F)	
2)	D ⊃ (B • C)	
3)	C ⊃ (E ∨ F)	// ~D ∨ ~(E ≡ F)
4)	D • (E ≡ F)	AIP
5)		
6)	D	4, Simp
7)	B • C	2, 4, MP
8)	(E ≡ F) • D	4, Com
9)	(E ≡ F)	8, Simp
10)	B	7, Simp
11)	C • B	7, Com
12)	C	11, Simp
x		
y	~[D • (E ≡ F)]	5-x, IP
	~D ∨ ~(E ≡ F)	y, DM

It should be clear that we can use 'B' and 'C' to obtain 'E ∨ F' and '~E ∨ ~F', and we should do so next. At that point, however, it is easy to get stuck. How are we supposed to turn all of this into a contradiction? One thing to think about is whether you have used a piece of information fully. We have used 'D' and modus ponens, but what about the other conjunct 'E ≡ F'? So far, we have only Simplified it out of the conjunction. Since it is an equivalence, we can always apply the Rule of Material Equivalence. We could use either form, though, so which one to use? Since we will have 'E ∨ F' and '~E ∨ ~F', perhaps we can try the form which uses conjunctions, and then try to see whether De Morgan's can be used in some way to get our contradiction. If it works, great. If not, then we'll go back and try something else. I will only focus on this part of the proof below.

9)	(E ≡ F)	8, Simp
10)	B	7, Simp
11)	C • B	7, Com
12)	C	11, Simp
13)	E ∨ F	3, 12, MP
14)	~E ∨ ~F	1, 10, MP
15)	(E • F) ∨ (~E • ~F)	9, Equiv
x		
y	~[D • (E ≡ F)]	5-x, IP

If we look closely at line 14, we see that we have a disjunction of negated statements. That situation immediately calls to mind De Morgan's Rules, and applying it would give us '~(E • F)'. Yet, that is a negation of one of the disjuncts in line 15. So, it would allow us to assert the other disjunct, which is '~E • ~F'. Hopefully, the reader sees that this formula also recalls De Morgan's Rule. Applying it, we would obtain '~(E ∨ F)', which contradicts line 13. All that remains is to conjoin these contradictory statements and our proof is complete.

1)	B ⊃ (~E ∨ ~F)	
2)	D ⊃ (B • C)	
3)	C ⊃ (E ∨ F)	// ~D ∨ ~(E ≡ F)
4)	D • (E ≡ F)	AIP
5)		
6)	D	4, Simp
7)	B • C	2, 4, MP
8)	(E ≡ F) • D	4, Com
9)	(E ≡ F)	8, Simp
10)	B	7, Simp
11)	C • B	7, Com
12)	C	11, Simp
13)	E ∨ F	3, 12, MP
14)	~E ∨ ~F	1, 10, MP
15)	(E • F) ∨ (~E • ~F)	9, Equiv
16)	~(E • F)	14, DM
17)	~E • ~F	15, 16, DS
18)	~(E ∨ F)	17, DM
19)	(E ∨ F) • ~(E ∨ F)	13, 18 Conj
20)	~[D • (E ≡ F)]	5-19, IP
21)	~D ∨ ~(E ≡ F)	20, DM

Notice that in this case the contradiction involved a disjunction, but that is perfectly fine. A contradiction is a contradiction, no matter how complex. Before we turn you over to the exercises, let's try one more example. This one involved nested subordinate proof lines. Yes. That's right. We can put one subordinate proof line inside another one. Let's see how it can be done.

```
1)  | ~[M • (P • R)]
2)  | (~R • P) ⊃ M          // (M • P) ≡ ~R
    |—
3)  |
    |
    | (M • P) ≡ ~R
```

As before, this conclusion is neither a negation, nor a conditional, but it is a bi-conditional, which means it can be converted into a conjunction of conditionals using the Rule of Material Equivalence. Then we will simply need to prove each conditional statement individually. One of them can be established simply using Commutativity on the second premise. We will use a Conditional Proof to try to establish the other one. One we set it up, our proof should appear as it does here:

```
1)  | ~[M • (P • R)]
2)  | ~R ⊃ (P • M)          // (M • P) ≡ ~R
    |—
3)  |  | M • P                             ACP
    |  |—
    |  |
w   |  | ~R
x   | (M • P) ⊃ ~R                         3-w, CP
y   | ~R ⊃ (M • P)                         2, Com
z   | [(M • P) ⊃ ~R] • [~R ⊃ (M • P)]      x, y, Conj
    | (M • P) ≡ ~R                         z, Equiv
```

The important thing to note is that within the first Conditional Proof, we are trying to establish a negation. Any time we are trying to establish a negation, we can use Indirect Proof. Let's set it up.

```
1)  | ~[M • (P • R)]
2)  | ~R ⊃ (P • M)          // (M • P) ≡ ~R
    |—
3)  |  | M • P                             ACP
    |  |—
4)  |  |  | R                                     AIP
    |  |  |—
    |  |  |
v   |  |  |
w   |  | ~R                                4-v, IP
x   | (M • P) ⊃ ~R                         3-w, CP
y   | ~R ⊃ (M • P)                         2, Com
z   | [(M • P) ⊃ ~R] • [~R ⊃ (M • P)]      x, y, Conj
    | (M • P) ≡ ~R                         z, Equiv
```

Now, in order to complete the proof, all we have to find is a contradiction. The first premise says that it is not the case that 'M', 'P' and 'R' are all true, so if we can conjoin them, that will give us our contradiction. We will need to use Associativity to ensure that the statements align properly. The completed proof is shown below.

```
1)  | ~[M • (P • R)]
2)  | ~R ⊃ (P • M)              // (M • P) ≡ ~R
    |--
3)  | | M • P                             ACP
    | |--
4)  | | | R                                      AIP
    | | |--
5)  | | | (M • P) • R                     3, 4, Conj
6)  | | | M • (P • R)                     5, Assoc
7)  | | | [M • (P • R)] • ~[M • (P • R)]  6, 1, Conj
8)  | | ~R                                4-7, IP
9)  | (M • P) ⊃ ~R                        3-8, CP
10) | ~R ⊃ (M • P)                        2, Com
11) | [(M • P) ⊃ ~R] • [~R ⊃ (M • P)]     9, 10, Conj
12) | (M • P) ≡ ~R                        11, Equiv
```

As one can check for oneself, this proof is complete, and the argument within it is valid. As you have seen, nesting subordinate proofs requires the same kind of process and justification as a single subordinate proof. There are no additional issues or concerns. If one is deriving statements on a conditional proof, and one is aiming at deriving a negation, one can begin an Indirect Proof. If one was deriving statements on an indirect Proof, and one required a conditional statement to establish the contradiction, then one could open up a Conditional Proof.

Chapter Twenty-Two Exercises

For each of the following proofs or partial proofs, fill in the missing piece of information.

Basic Concept Exercises

1.
```
1) | A ∨ B
   |--
2) | | ~A            ______
   | |--
3) | | B             1, 2, DS
4) | ~A ⊃ B          2-3, ______
```

2.
```
1) | ~A ∨ ~B
   |--
2) | | A • B                 ____
   | |--
3) | | ~(A • B)              1 DM
4) | | (A • B) • ~(A • B)    __, __
5) | ~(A • B)                __, __
```

3.
```
6) | | ~(A ∨ B)      2, DM
7) | | R             1, 3, MP
8) | ~A ⊃ R          4-8, __
```

4.
```
6) | | ~(A ∨ B)      2, DM
7) | | R • ~R        1, 3, MP
8) | ~(A ⊃ R)        4-8, __
```

5.

3)	________	ACP
	…	
8)	R	
9)	$(\sim A \bullet B) \supset R$	3-8, CP

6.

3)	________	AIP
	…	
8)	$L \bullet \sim L$	
9)	$\sim[(A \bullet B) \supset R]$	3-8, IP

7.

3)	________	ACP
	…	
8)	________	
9)	$(W \supset R) \supset V$	3-8, CP

8.

4)	$\sim A$	AIP
	…	
7)	$O \bullet \sim O$	2, 5, Conj
8)	________	4-7, IP

9.

1)	$A \supset B$	
2)	$\sim(A \bullet B)$	
3)	A	____
4)	B	1,3, MP
5)	$A \bullet B$	3,4, Conj
6)	________	___, ____
7)	________	___, ____

10.

1)	$A \supset B$	
2)	$(B \vee D) \supset C$	
3)	A	____
4)	B	1,3, MP
5)	$B \vee D$	4, Add
6)	________	___, ____
7)	________	___, ____

Intermediate Exercises

Construct a natural deduction proof using either Conditional or Indirect Proof for each of the following valid arguments:

11. $A \supset M$ / $B \supset M$ // $(A \bullet B) \supset M$
12. $\sim R \supset \sim P$ // $P \supset R$
13. $L \supset \sim G$ // $\sim(L \bullet G)$
14. $H \supset (P \supset R)$ / $\sim R$ // $\sim(H \bullet P)$
15. $H \supset \sim E$ / $G \supset E$ // $H \supset \sim G$
16. $(A \supset G)$ / $\sim A \supset \sim G$ // $A \equiv G$
17. $D \supset (P \bullet V)$ / $(V \vee W) \supset A$ // $\sim A \supset \sim D$
18. $R \supset (L \supset P)$ / $\sim R \supset \sim M$ // $M \supset (\sim L \vee P)$
19. $(J \supset H) \bullet (K \supset L)$ / $J \vee K$ / $(H \vee L) \supset E$ // E
20. $(A \supset F) \bullet (L \supset B)$ / D / $(F \vee B) \supset \sim D$ // $\sim(A \vee L)$

Challenging exercises

Construct a natural deduction proof for each of the following valid arguments:

21. $(A \vee B) \supset (N \bullet M)$ / $(M \vee B) \supset (G \bullet \sim A)$ // $\sim A$
22. $E \supset (S \bullet N)$ // $E \supset (S \supset N)$
23. $D \supset (E \supset L)$ / $L \supset \sim L$ // $\sim D \vee \sim E$
24. $(A \bullet B) \vee (C \vee D)$ / $\sim D$ / $C \supset (\sim D \supset B)$ // B
25. $G \supset [(H \bullet P) \supset \sim G]$ / $(H \bullet G) \supset P$ // $H \supset \sim G$
26. $(N \vee S) \supset L$ / $(O \vee S) \supset D$ / $N \vee O$ // $L \vee D$

27. $P \vee K$ / $(P \bullet {\sim}K) \supset (S \bullet G)$ // $K \vee S$
28. $C \equiv {\sim}(B \bullet K)$ / $K \supset B$ // $C \equiv {\sim}K$
29. $D \supset (S \supset N)$ / $D \supset S$ / $G \supset (N \vee D)$ // ${\sim}G \vee N$
30. B // $(P \supset L) \vee ({\sim}P \supset M)$

In-Context Exercises

Take each of the following valid arguments, convert it into symbolic form, and then construct a natural deduction proof to show that it is valid. If you disagree with the conclusion, see if you can figure out which premise is false (or premises).

A. Iron in the mantle of the earth is moving toward the earth's center. If no other factors modify the earth's moment of inertia, this will decrease the earth's moment of inertia. It the moment of inertia of a rotating body decreases, if its speed is not otherwise affected, its speed of rotation increases. If the speed of the earth's rotation increases, days get shorter. In fact, days are getting longer, not shorter; the earth is not speeding up, but slowing down. Thus, either the earth's moment of inertia is being changed by factors other than the sinking of iron, or its speed is being affected by factors other than its change in moment of inertia. (Harold C. Urey, "The Origin of the Earth," *Scientific American)*

B. Me (to the woman who became my wife): Hey, if today is Tuesday, then will you marry me?
The woman who would become my wife: No!
Me: So, you're saying that it is false that if today is Tuesday, then you will marry me.
My wife: That is absolutely false!
Me: Great. But today is not Tuesday.
My wife: Yeah. So?
Me: Then you are saying that you will marry me.
My wife: That's ridiculous.
Me: Really. You are saying that it is false that if it is Tuesday, then you will marry me. But today isn't Tuesday. It logically follows that you will marry me.
My wife: Wow. I can't be illogical. I guess we'll have to get hitched.

...And some people say that symbolic logic isn't practical.

Logic Puzzle: Who's the Eldest Sibling?

There is a family of four children, Martha, Maggie, Manny, and Mike. Based upon the following statements, determine who the eldest is. Consider that the youngest child always lies, and everyone else tells the truth.

Martha: I am the eldest, and Manny is the youngest.
Maggie: Manny is neither the youngest nor the eldest.
Manny: Either Maggie is the youngest, or Mike is not the eldest.
Mike: I am not the eldest.

Logical Paradox

We have been working so far under the assumption that every statement has one of two truth values. In many cases, this assumption works out fine. Take the statement "Today is Thursday." At any given time, this statement either is true or false. So is the statement "The President of the United States is Barack Obama." This principle, which we can symbolize as '$p \vee \sim p$' for any p, is generally called the Law of Excluded Middle. The idea is that there is no 'middle ground' between the alternative truth values. This Law is one of the Three Classical Laws of Thought often attributed to Aristotle. The other two are the Law of Identity and the Law of Non-Contradiction.

The Law of Identity simply holds that things are identical to themselves and to nothing else. If one thing were identical to something else, then it couldn't be something else, but in fact there would only be one thing. The Law of Non-Contradiction holds that one thing cannot be both *p* and not *p*, at least not at the same time in the same respect. We can symbolize it as $\sim(p \bullet \sim p)$.

Classical Logic, including truth-functional logic, abides by these three laws. Each of them has an almost inescapably strong intuitive claim to truth. Of course, a person can be standing in one second, and not standing the next. But he can't be standing and not standing at the same time. In a more complicated example, a person can be a father to one person, but not a father to another. In some sense the person is both a father and not a father, but this is why Aristotle adds the proviso about being "in the same respect." One cannot be the biological father of a person and not be the biological father of that same person.

We know all too well that someone can be a father, but not really be a father, but again, when we say something like this, we use the word "father" in two different senses. In one sense we mean legally, either biologically or adoptive, and in the other we mean that we expect a father to do certain things for his children, and if he fails to do them, we might say that he isn't a real father, but we mean that he isn't acting the way we think fathers should.

These differences in meaning are why logicians are always careful about their language. It is why they try to symbolize carefully, and use the same letter to represent the same statement, no matter how it is worded, but different letters to represent different statements, even when they superficially seem the same. Sure, ambiguous or vague statements can have multiple truth values, but that is why we try to disambiguate and clarify as much as we can before we do any logical analysis.

However, there is a wrinkle or two, even in principles which seem so intuitively obvious, at least to those of us raised in the Western tradition which followed Aristotle. The problem has many names and forms, but it is often called the paradox of the liar.

A paradox is a situation or thing which seems to have contradictory features, although sometimes the word just indicates that an idea is contrary to the conventional wisdom. An oxymoron, like a "wise fool" is a compact version of a paradox (By the way, the word "sophomore" just means a "wise fool"). The paradox of the liar is a statement which seems to be both true and false. It has led to all kind of speculation and consternation over the centuries. Here is the statement: "This statement is false."

That was it. That one seemingly innocuous statement has caused logicians to go mad. The statement seems clear and unambiguous, and it doesn't seem to have more than one respect to it, so what is its truth value? Assuming that the statement is true, then what it asserts must be correct. Yet, if what it asserts is correct, then it is false, since that is what it asserts. So, if it is true, then it is false.

Now that wouldn't be so bad. We could just say that it is a self-contradictory statement. But the real problem is this. Let's assume that the statement is not true, or that it is false. If it is false, then what it asserts must be false, or wrong. But it asserts that it is false, and if that is wrong, then it must be true. So, if the statement is true, it must be false, and if it is false, then it must be true!

The Liar's Paradox seems to count against the Law of Non-Contradiction, and according to Classical logic, if one contradiction is true, then all others can be derived, which amounts to triviality: everything would be true and everything would also be false. There must be something going wrong here.

There are many approaches to this paradox, but none of them is satisfying even to a large plurality of scholars. The first is to accept that some contradictions are true. This position is often called Dialetheism, from the Greek root *di-*, or "two," and *aletheia*, or "truth." Dialetheists generally save themselves from triviality by rejecting Classical logic. They will use a paraconsistent logic which is not explosive, or which does not allow all contradictions to follow from one contradiction.

This approach may have some practical value. Consider a trial, where together the witnesses make inconsistent or even contradictory statements. According to a Classical logician, one should decide to accept or reject witness testimony in a way which avoids contradiction. Otherwise, everyone, including the judge, is both guilty and not guilty. Yet, if one's logic is not explosive, perhaps one could incorporate even inconsistent statements and still reason from them effectively.

In any case, this solution is not satisfying to many scholars. Another approach is to reject the Law of Excluded Middle. Perhaps sentences such as this really are neither true nor false, but some value in between. Perhaps we need a multi-valued logic, which three categories instead of two.

After all, there are many statements which might be said to have a feature such as this. Is my father bald? Yes. No one would disagree. Am I bald? No. I have a full head of hair (Thanks, mom). Yet, my brother seems to be somewhere in between. Sometimes we say there is a fine line between being bald and not being bald, but it seems pretty broad to me. The same thing can be said for many predicates, such as rich. There are clearly some people who are rich, and clearly some people who are not. But there also seem to be a whole lot of people who are difficult to classify.

The standard way to deal with such cases is to just make our definitions more precise. Once we have precise definitions, we can say with more certainty whether someone is short or tall, for example. But perhaps this is really just avoiding reality instead of confronting it head on. What if we just allow that some statements are true, some are false, and some, such as the Liar's Paradox, are neither.

This approach certainly has had some practical benefit. The logic of belief seems clearly to be multi-valued. I can believe a statement is true, or I can believe it is false, or I can have neither belief. Moral reasoning also seems to have multiple values. An action can be morally obligatory, impermissible, or permissible. So, a logic which allows three values might apply to all reality.

Unfortunately, this approach hasn't resolved the issue. There are other ways to handle belief and logic, but more importantly, there are ways to reformulate the Liar's Paradox so that it applies to multi-valued logics as well. So, regardless of what good has come out of this approach, it doesn't solve the underlying issue.

There are other approaches as well, such as outlawing self-referring statements, but the debate still continues. Edison said that necessity was the mother of invention, and if so, the need to resolve this paradox will probably lead to many more creative attempts at a solution. Perhaps one of the readers of this textbook will devise one of them.

CHAPTER

23

Analyzing Inductive Arguments

We have seen a great deal about how to handle deductive arguments (though we have only scratched the surface), but we haven't learned much about inductive arguments. Way back in Chapter 7 we learned about the basic terminology for inductive argument evaluation: inductive arguments are weak or strong, cogent or uncogent, and even compelling or uncompelling, but we haven't had much of a chance to apply what we have learned. You may want to review that chapter a little before you continue.

In this chapter we will explore a few of the most common types of inductive arguments. We will also learn a little about how to evaluate them, and we will learn in particular how to criticize them. Some students find that they are much better at dealing with inductive arguments than deductive ones. Whether this is true or not for each reader, it is the case that inductive reasoning does not have the same either/or nature that deductive reasoning has. Inductive reasoning generally involves shades of gray. Don't be mistaken, however. We will still require a rigorous approach. There may in some sense not be one precise answer as there is when it comes to deductive validity, but there are right and wrong answers, and we will require each other to defend our judgments with strong reasoning.

Analogies

Skill 23.1

Recognizing, Analyzing, and Evaluating Analogies

Arguments by analogy are very frequently used. From ethics, to law, to science, and in daily life, people use analogies to justify their positions, as well as to convince others. Proficiency in understanding and evaluating analogies will be very helpful in whatever field one chooses to enter.

The first order of business is to understand what an analogy is. Very simply, an analogy is a comparison between two things. We generally don't mean any comparison, though, but one which is or can be used to ground further connections. For example, when Forrest Gump says "Life is like a box of chocolates—You never know what you're going to get," it seems unlikely that this simile is going to be used to ground any other conclusions. We won't be concluding that life will therefore have other things in common with boxes of chocolates. He is just pointing out one interesting similarity between the two things. We will call these illustrative analogies, and contrast them with argumentative analogies.

An illustrative analogy is merely intended to make a point, or to illustrate a concept. It helps us to understand an issue or idea, but it doesn't establish a further point. Argumentative analogies, on the other hand, are intended to ground conclusions. Here is an example of an argumentative analogy:

> My Intro to Philosophy class was very challenging, and I took it with Professor Russell. I'll bet that the Logic class he is teaching will be very challenging, too.

In this case, we are not just fleshing out an idea; we are actually asserting that one thing is true on the basis of the comparison or similarity. We are making an argument. The structure of this argument is as follows:

1) My Intro to Philosophy class was challenging.
2) The professor for my Logic class is the same as my Intro to Philosophy class.
3) ∴ My Logic class will be challenging as well.

As with any argumentative analogy, this one relies on the fact that two things share certain properties, and that they therefore share another property. In this case, the two analogs, or things being compared, are the two classes. The claim that the two classes are similar depends on the idea that the two classes are taught by the same professor. The additional property is the property of being challenging. We can identify the Intro to Philosophy class as the **primary analog**, as we know that it has the property in question. It is asserted in one of the premises. The **secondary analog** is the Logic class. We don't know for a fact that it has the property in question, but we are asserting that it does in our conclusion.

Primary Analog
Of the two things compared in an analogy, the one which is known to have the property in question

So, we can restate any analogy in the following way:

Secondary Analog
Of the two things compared in an analogy, the one which is concluded to have the property in question

1) The primary analog has a certain property p.
2) The primary analog is similar to the secondary analog.
3) ∴ The secondary analog has property p.

Remember that an argument by analogy is an inductive argument. No matter how strong the analogy, it cannot guarantee that the conclusion is true. There is always another piece of information which can be added to the premises which will undermine the argument, namely that the secondary analog does not have the property in question. So, all we can ask of an argumentative analogy is that it makes the conclusion likely to be true.

Figure 23.1 displays a visual representation of an argument by analogy.

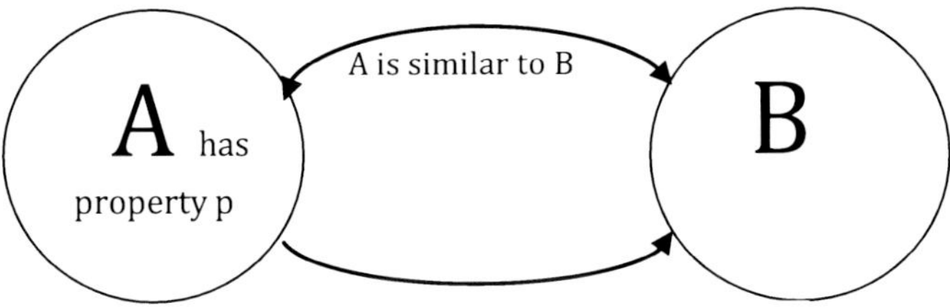

Figure 23.1

We can also think of the analogs as classes or groups. We may be comparing doctors and lawyers, for example, and not only individuals. In an analogy, however, the individuals or group which constitutes the primary analog is a different group than the secondary analog. This distinguishes them from generalizations, which we will cover later in this chapter.

Evaluating Analogies

Just like other inductive arguments, argumentative analogies can be strong or weak. In this section we will learn a few techniques to help us determine how strong or weak an analogy is. There are no absolute standards which will mathematically determine the answer, but the following guidelines will at least give us some basis for making a determination.

1. The more relevant similarities between analogs, the stronger the argument.
2. The more relevant disanalogies, the weaker the argument (usually).
3. Having more primary analogs strengthens the argument.
4. Increasing the diversity of primary analogs strengthens the argument.
5. The strength of the conclusion is affected by how specifically it is stated.

Each of these criteria is fairly straightforward, but let's see how each one works in an actual argument. Consider the following argument:

My car is white and gets 25 miles to the gallon. Here is a new car I am thinking of buying. It is also white, so I bet it will get 25 miles to the gallon.

In this case the primary analog is the original car, the secondary analog is the new car, and the property in question is getting 25 miles to the gallon. We are only offered two similarities: they are both cars, and they are both white. This analogy is horrible. The similarities given do not seem relevant at all to the property in question. It should be common knowledge that cars can get wildly different mileage ratings, from single digits for large trucks to over 50 for some hybrid vehicles. And being white seems to have nothing whatsoever to do with how good a car's mileage is.

If we could say that the new vehicle and the old vehicle are both regular engine sedans, that would be a relevant similarity, but still by itself could not make this argument strong. The conclusion is much too specific. The more similarities between the analogs we could add, the stronger the argument would be. The fact that the cars have the same number of cylinders, the same engine size, and other similarities will make the argument even stronger.

Of course, the more differences we know between the analogs, the weaker the argument would generally be. It is a matter of practicality that most people who make arguments by analogy are not going to offer up differences between the analogs. It would be nice if they did, but the job of finding differences is usually up to the person evaluating the argument.

Disanalogy
A difference between the primary and secondary analogs

In general, a **disanalogy**, or difference between analogs counts against the strength of the argument. So, if you got 25 mpg in your Ford, and the new car were a Toyota, it would tend to weaken the argument. Just as it is with similarities, some differences are more relevant to the given property in question than others. A difference in car color, for example, seems completely irrelevant to the mileage.

There are some exceptions to this rule, however, generally in cases where additional information is available. Consider the case where my conclusion is that the new car will get greater than 25 miles per gallon. My current car gets over 25 miles per gallon, but it was a truck, while the new car is a compact. It is generally true that trucks get worse gas mileage than compact cars, so in this case, even though there is a significant disanalogy, it actually tends to strengthen the argument. This rule can be very challenging. Unless one is confident that the difference in question makes it more likely that the conclusion has the property in question, it is safer to make the judgment that the difference weakens the argument.

We have only been dealing with cases where there is a single primary analog, but consider a case where we have more than one primary analog. The more primary analogs, the stronger the argument will be. Let's say we had ten cars, each of which got better than 25 miles per gallon. In that case, it would greatly strengthen the conclusion that the new car will get better than 25 miles per gallon. A single primary analog can be sufficient to ground a strong argument, but it can always be strengthened by having more analogs.

In those cases where we have multiple primary analogs, and there is some uncertainty about the secondary analog, it is always better to have diversity among the primary analogs. Knowing that the new vehicle is a truck would mean that we probably would want the primary analogs to all be trucks. If we don't know whether the new vehicle is a truck, or a sedan, or a coupe, or a race car, then the more diversity among the primary analogs, the stronger the argument. The idea is that regardless what the new vehicle turns out to be, the more diversity among the primary analogs, the more likely that the secondary analog matches at least one of the primary analogs.

Finally, we should consider the specificity of the conclusion. The more specific the conclusion, the weaker the argument. Let's consider a specific case by filling in some details. Your current vehicle is a four-door sedan with six cylinders, and it gets 25 miles to the gallon. The new vehicle is a four-door sedan with six cylinders. We conclude that the new vehicle will get exactly 25 miles to the gallon. I'm afraid I would tend to think of this argument as fairly weak. There are so many other factors which can affect mileage, that these similarities are insufficient to establish such a specific conclusion.

If we made our conclusion less specific, however, and said that the new car will get somewhere around 25 miles to the gallon, say between 20 and 30, then the new argument is much stronger. We could make it even stronger by making the conclusion even more vague, but at the cost of making it less useful. In general, what we are looking for in a strong argument is that the similarities provided are sufficient to substantiate the specificity of the conclusion. The more the similarities, the more specific we can make the conclusion.

Weak Analogy
A fallacy which occurs whenever an analogy fails to support its conclusion

Relying on a **weak analogy** is considered fallacious reasoning. We will soon learn about many other fallacies, but for now it is enough to say that fallacious reasoning is mistaken reasoning. It means that there is a flaw in the reasoning process somewhere. Anytime an argument relies on an analogy where the information given is insufficient to ground the conclusion, the argument commits the fallacy of weak analogy.

Conflation
Treating two dissimilar ideas or issues as if they were the same

Conflation is related to analogical reasoning. To conflate two ideas or issues is to treat them as the same when they really should be treated differently. As when one criticizes an analogy, when one argues that someone is conflating two ideas, one should be prepared to point out the relevant difference between the two ideas.

Inductive Generalizations

Skill 23.2

Recognizing, Analyzing, and Evaluating Inductive Generalizations

People make generalizations all the time. A generalization is simply a statement about a class. In logic, we are not interested in statements alone, however, but in the process of reasoning by which one justifies a generalization. One such process is called an inductive generalization. In this process, a sample is taken from an entire class or group, and when it is found that the members of the sample have a certain property, it is concluded that the entire class has the same property.

Generalizing in this way is very natural and is recognized as a perfectly acceptable form of reasoning, when it is done well, and it is recognized as fallacious when it is done poorly. Before we look at how to evaluate generalizations, we need to see more clearly the structure of a generalization.

In every generalization, there is a sample, which is a part of a group, about which we have gathered some information. We then conclude that some property of the sample holds for the entire group. We can display the relationship visually in Figure 23.2.

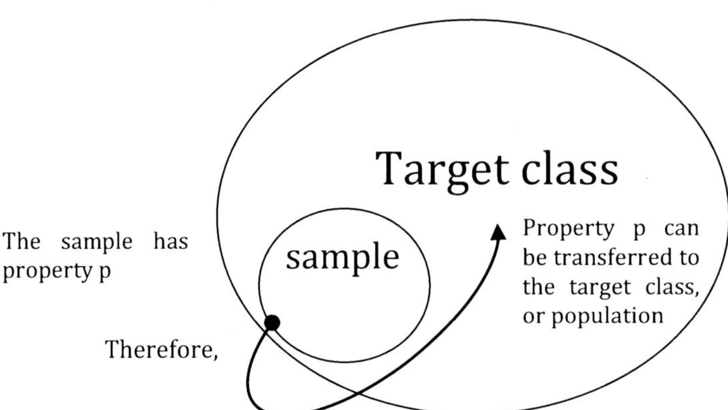
Target class
sample
The sample has property p
Therefore,
Property p can be transferred to the target class, or population

Figure 23.2

Inductive Generalization
An argument which draws a conclusion about a group based on a sample of that group

One major distinction between an **inductive generalization** and an analogy is that an analogy compares two different things, whereas in a generalization, the sample is a part of the target class. There are a great number of similarities between the two forms of reasoning, though. In fact, for every analogy, there is an implied target class. We leave it to readers to develop this comparison more fully, should they have the interest.

One interesting thing about generalizations is that the property in question is often a statistical one. Often all we know about the sample is that a certain percentage of the members of the sample have a certain property, and on that basis it is concluded that the same percentage applies to the members of the target class.

Electoral polls are an example of this type of generalization. We want to know whether a certain proposition will pass. We ask a certain number of voters, and 61% of them say they will vote in favor of the proposition, and we conclude that the proposition will pass. This is a perfect example of a generalization. Can you identify the sample and the target class on your own?

The sample is the voters we actually asked. They constitute the sample. The target population is a little harder to ascertain, but it consists of all the people who will actually vote on the day of the election. Pollsters generally only poll registered voters, because otherwise their sample, which includes people who can't vote, will not be included within the target population, which consists only of voters. The generalized conclusion is that around 61% of actual voters will vote in favor of the proposition, which allows us to draw the further conclusion that the proposition will pass.

Evaluating Generalizations

Generalizing well is perhaps one of the most important processes of reasoning. We generalize about most everything, all the time. We conclude that because we know one person in a group, we know something about other members of that group. Of course, we sometimes do so far too quickly without thinking. Hopefully, in this section we will learn how to slow down a bit and make generalizations on the basis of good reasoning. Here are the criteria we will use in order to evaluate generalizations.

1. The larger the sample, the stronger the argument.
2. The more representative the sample, the stronger the argument.
3. The strength of the conclusion is affected by how specifically it is stated.

Everyone will recognize that from the basis of a single individual, we cannot draw conclusions about any group to which that individual belongs. Everyone can also be surprised by how quickly one does exactly the thing we all recognize is improper. This aspect of human psychology is more properly explored in a psychology textbook, or a piece on naturalized epistemology. Here we are engaged in practical, normative epistemology, and here we recognize that even the most hesitant judgment about any group must be based on more than one member of the group. In fact, even fairly loose generalizations generally require many more than one member in the sample.

Sample size is the first criterion to consider. There are advanced formulas which can tell us what sample size we will need in order to achieve 95% confidence that our population matches our sample with an error margin of plus or minus 5%. That sort of analysis is far more than most people need in their ordinary lives (and more than they would ever have the time or inclination to use). Should any reader hope to go into sociology or many other fields, he or she might want to learn much more, which one can do in a statistics class or perhaps a course on probability theory. For our purposes, we do need to point out the basic principle involved: the larger the sample size, the stronger the argument will be.

Let's say we are conducting a poll for the next Presidential election. We find out that a poll says that 95% of people say they will vote for the Libertarian candidate. Is that a good reason to think that around 95% of voters will vote for the Libertarian candidate? If the poll only included 20 people, then we easily recognize that our sample is insufficient to ground our conclusion. We would need a much larger sample size. Any argument which rests upon a sample which is too small is said to commit the fallacy of **hasty generalization**.

Hasty Generalization
A fallacy which occurs whenever the sample in an inductive generalization is too small to support the conclusion

Suppose we increase our sample. To what would we need to increase our sample to ensure that our argument is strong? The answer is that it depends, and involves probabilities and error margins, and the idea that there is no clear numerical strength to which we can reach. Even a hundred people in the sample would make for a technically strong argument, in the sense of the conclusion being over 50% true. We generally expect a much higher level of strength, however, before we start acting on an argument. In the case, of a political poll, where our population is in the hundreds of millions, the answer might surprise you. We only need around twelve hundred to fifteen hundred people in our sample to ground a solidly strong conclusion.

We could always add more and make the argument stronger, but a sample of around this size will make for a very strong argument. Doubling the sample size at this point only strengthens the argument a small percentage, and the larger we get, the smaller the payoff.

The sample size, however, is not the only thing to consider. Let's say we did survey 2,133 people, and 75% of them said that they would vote for the Libertarian candidate, and we conclude that around 75% of all voters will vote for the Libertarian candidate. This argument can't be said to commit a hasty generalization, but it could still suffer from a fatal flaw. We might have asked only Reason magazine employees. Reason magazine is a libertarian organization, so the problem here is not that the sample is too small, but that it is not representative of the whole population of voters. We have oversampled employees from Reason magazine, and there is no reason to think that voters generally will vote in the same fashion as these employees will.

Any argument where the sample is not representative of the target population is said to commit the fallacy of **biased generalization**, also called skewed sample. We can also say that a certain group has been oversampled or undersampled. What we want is a representative sample. The best way to achieve this is a random sample, but it is notoriously difficult to get a truly random sample. Pollsters often rely on advanced mathematical formulas to take their actual results and adjust them as if their sample were representative. Such a practice can be controversial, but it does recognize that our attempts to achieve random results don't always accomplish their aim.

Biased Generalization
A fallacy which occurs whenever the sample in an inductive generalization does not represent the target population well

One confusion for many students is the idea that objectivity requires equal measures on both sides. Perhaps the word "bias" is being equivocated here (See "equivocation" in Chapter 25). We don't mean any kind of prejudice or subjectivity, but only biased in terms of unrepresentative. For example, if we wanted to know how many students were in support of the fascist practice of banning smoking on campus (will this terminology skew the results?), how many smokers should we put in our sample? We all know that it cannot be either 100% or 0% of our sample, but if you thought 50/50 smokers versus non-smokers, your results could be just as bad. We are only looking for a representative sample, so we want the percentage of smokers in our sample to equal the percentage of smokers among the student body. Without that information, our results will be seriously undermined. Plus, keep in mind that just because a majority of students thinks we should do something doesn't mean that we should do it.

One last thing to consider is the specificity of the conclusion: the more specific the conclusion, the weaker the argument. Our conclusion could be very specific, with a specific percentage. In order to rely on such a conclusion, though, we would need an outrageously large sample which was impeccably representative. With an ordinary sample size, as discussed earlier, we can support a conclusion within a few percentage points. As we increase the range on the conclusion, the stronger the argument will be, given the same sample. I can make a strong argument with almost any sample, as long as I increase the vagueness of my conclusion. For example, most any sample will support the conclusion that on election day, between 0% and 95% of voters will vote for George Washington.

Causal Arguments

Skill 23.3

Recognizing, Analyzing, and Evaluating Causal Arguments

What do we mean when we say that smoking causes cancer? Apparently, we do not mean that everyone who smokes will immediately get cancer, but we can't even mean that they will necessarily get cancer eventually. Many people smoke at some point in their lives and never get cancer. We must mean something, though, right?

Although the philosophical analysis of causes and their metaphysical status may be complex, we do have some sense of what we mean by causation. The problem is that it is not very clear. When we say that A causes B, we seem to mean something along the lines of "were A not to occur, then B wouldn't occur." This simplification, while appropriate for the beginner in logic, will not completely work. For example, we say that smoking causes cancer, but it is not the case that if one doesn't smoke, then he won't get cancer.

Any student who would like to study experimental sciences should learn a lot more about the reasoning behind judgments of causation, but here we will outline just a few ideas, and learn a few fallacies associated with causal reasoning. First, we will look at two basic ways people use to justify causal claims.

Causal Argument
An argument which concludes that one thing is the cause of another, or which uses a cause to ground a conclusion

We often say that one thing causes another. Sometimes we mean that one particular event caused one other particular event. Aristotle long ago identified four "causes" but only one of them resembles the way the term is used today. The problem with particular events is that they can't be duplicated, or replicated, as scientists are wont to say.

Instead, we focus on types of events. We can certainly replicate a type of event: we can have a single mouse ingest a certain new food additive, and then we can have other mice ingest the same type of food additive. Obviously, each mouse can't ingest the exact same additive, but we can try to ensure that the additive is as nearly the same as every other, perhaps by taking samples from the same batch.

Now, if one mouse dies, can we say that it was the additive that caused the mouse's death? In general, no. After all, that mouse might have died no matter what. We should have tried to use only healthy mice in our experiments, but it is always possible that one mouse would die regardless of the additive. What we need to do is compare the number of mice who would die in general to the number of mice who died as a result of the food additive.

Let's say that out of 1000 mice, typically one mouse dies a week. We give the mice a food additive, and in one week three mice die. Is this good evidence that the food additive caused the deaths? Probably not. As always, scientists will use the laws of statistics to calculate the probabilities involved, but this amount would not make it likely that the food additive was the cause. If one mouse on average dies a week, then there is still a good chance that three will happen to die in one week.

If three continue to die every week, that would make for a stronger argument, but still not very strong. We are looking for a difference which is recognized as statistically significant. Since this is inductive reasoning, we are not looking for an absolute guarantee, but only an argument we can recognize as strong. The more mice that die in any week, the stronger the argument that the food additive was the cause. Certainly over ten mice dying would be judged sufficient to conclude that the additive was the cause.

Keep in mind, however, that we can never know with the kind of certainty which is characteristic of deductively valid arguments. After all, it is always possible that ten mice just happened to die all at once, completely apart from the additive. Or there was a sickness which spread, or many other possibilities. The point is that we can never achieve maximal relevance with causal arguments. All we can get is the probability that the conclusion is true, based upon the truth of the premises.

Evaluating Causal Arguments

Learning to evaluate causal arguments would require much more than one section of one chapter, but we can offer the students a quick checklist of related fallacies. This approach will not make one skilled in doing experimental science, but it will give the student some protection from the kind of simplistic mistakes which are often made with causal reasoning. We will learn that some typical mistakes in causal reasoning have names.

Post Hoc Ergo Propter Hoc

The fallacy known as *Post Hoc Ergo Propter Hoc* is likely the basis for all manner of superstition and superstitious rituals. In simple words, the fallacy is to conclude that one thing is the cause of the other simply because the one follows the other. Visually, we can represent the fallacy on the following timeline.

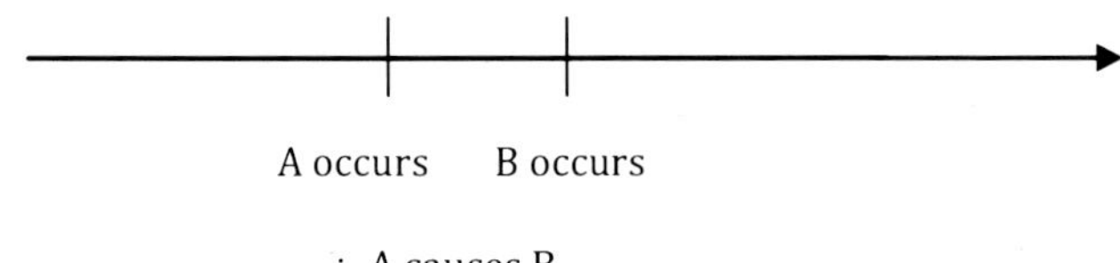
A occurs
B occurs
∴ A causes B

The fact that one event occurs immediately after another, by itself, is not enough to ground the conclusion that the one thing is the cause of the other. The fact that one goes to bed after watching the news doesn't mean that the news was the cause of that person going to bed. The fact that your team lost the game when you didn't wear their jersey when you watched the game is not an indication that your failure to wear the jersey had anything to do with the loss.

Non Causa Pro Causa

We adopt the usage that the *Non Causa Pro Causa* fallacy occurs when one thing is concluded to be the cause of another merely because the things overlap in space or time. We need something more than only an overlap to judge that the one thing is really the cause of the other. Here is a representation of the Non Causa Pro Causa fallacy.

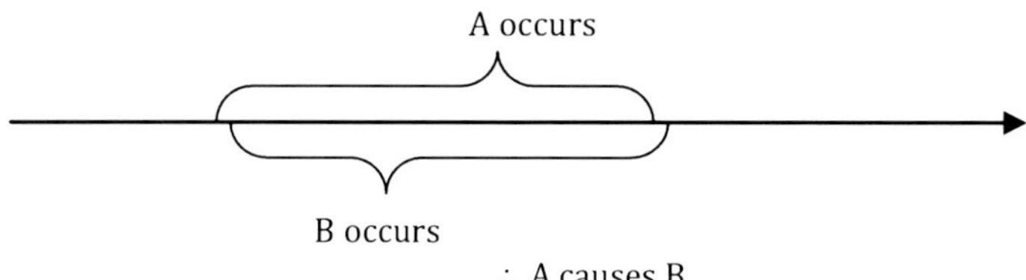

∴ A causes B

An example of this fallacy is the following: Global temperatures have increased from 1980 to 2000, and the output of carbon dioxide by human industries has increased, therefore the output of carbon dioxide is the cause of increasing global temperatures. My point here is not to discount one prominent theory regarding global warming, but only to point out that the argument as stated above is ridiculously inadequate to justify its conclusion. Numerous other things have occurred over the same time period. The argument gives us no reason to think that the output of carbon dioxide is the only one of them that could affect global temperature. Moreover, by itself, it gives us no reason at all to think that the output of carbon dioxide has anything to do with global warming.

In case you are skeptical, consider this: over the same time period, SAT scores have been declining. It would be ridiculous to conclude that therefore, lower SAT scores are bringing about higher temperatures. Of course, the difference is that we have some reason to believe that the output of carbon dioxide could have something to do with the temperature of the Earth. We recognize a certain causal mechanism, the greenhouse gas theory, whereby increased carbon dioxide could have something to do with increased temperatures. My point is that without this information, the argument is wildly fallacious.

Again, to be a strong argument, we would need good evidence, and even with a causal mechanism in place, the argument above would be inadequate. We would need a careful analysis that other things which could plausibly affect the temperature were also considered. Even if the temperature has increased, could solar output cycles, or cycles in the Earth's orbit, or volcanoes, or other forms of pollution, or many other things be the cause? Unless a careful analysis could rule these out, then we have little reason to think that it must be carbon dioxide emissions.

Have these other things been ruled out? Do your own research to find out. One thing to consider on this issue is what the perfect global temperature should be. Perhaps more people would benefit from the temperature being a bit higher than it is now. One could argue that a spike in the global temperature would cause global catastrophe, but that sounds like a causal argument, and we need to examine the argument carefully to make an informed judgment.

Common Cause

I have a barometer on my table, and generally speaking, a little while after the level of the barometer drops, it rains. It can't be the rain that causes the barometer to fall, after all the rain comes after the barometer drops, so my falling barometer must cause the rain.

This bit of fallacious reasoning exhibits the common cause fallacy. One might conclude on some reasonable basis that A causes B, because they seem to have some kind of causal relationship. The problem here is that the reason there appears to be a direct causal relationship is that some underlying phenomena, C, is the cause of both A and B. In the case of the barometer, it is the air pressure. Lower air pressure is associated with storms, and lower air pressure is also the reason the barometer falls.

On the basis of some kind of correlation,

It is concluded that: But in reality:

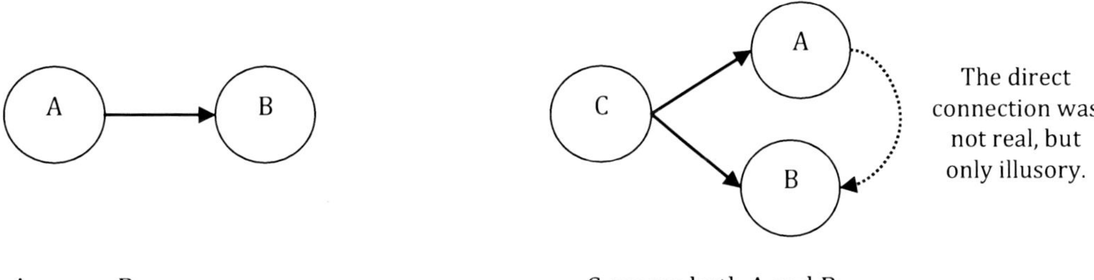

The direct connection was not real, but only illusory.

A causes B C causes both A and B

In order to help identify common cause fallacy, one should attempt to uncover a plausible causal mechanism. If one cannot, then one might begin to suspect a common cause may be the answer. For example, I can't imagine a plausible way for my barometer to directly affect the weather. For this reason, we should look for some other cause for both the phenomena of my barometer lowering and the rain.

Reversed Cause

It appears that causation works in only one direction in time. We cannot cause things to occur in the past, no matter how much many of us would like to do so. At least, although our current physical theories don't seem to rule out backwards causation, it doesn't seem to be possible. This means that if one knows for sure that one event occurs before another, then the second event cannot be the cause of the first. If A occurs before B, then it cannot be the case that B caused A.

For more complicated cases, and perhaps when we are ignorant of the timing, it is possible to commit the fallacy of reversed cause. This fallacy is committed when someone concludes that A is the cause of B, but it is actually B that causes A.

On the basis of some kind of correlation,

It is concluded that: But in reality:

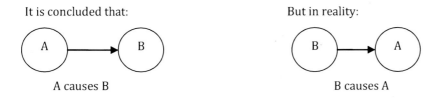

A causes B B causes A

Here is an example of a case which would likely be committing the fallacy of reversed causation. Fred notices that Sandra is depressed. He then finds out that she failed an exam at some point, and concludes that her depression must have been the cause of her failure. If she were only feeling better, she could have studied better and done well on the exam. If Fred had only considered that he might be reversing cause and effect, he might have realized that Sandra was only depressed because she failed the exam.

Slippery Slope

The Slippery Slope fallacy is well-known. In one common form, the fallacy can be seen as a causal fallacy. The general idea of a slippery slope argument is that we should not take one step, because it will inevitably lead to some horrendous consequence. We wouldn't recognize the argument as fallacious if the causal connections really were inevitable, but in a slippery slope fallacy, it is implausible that the supposed causal inevitability will arise.

In this case, someone says that if we do A, whatever A is, then it will lead to B, which will

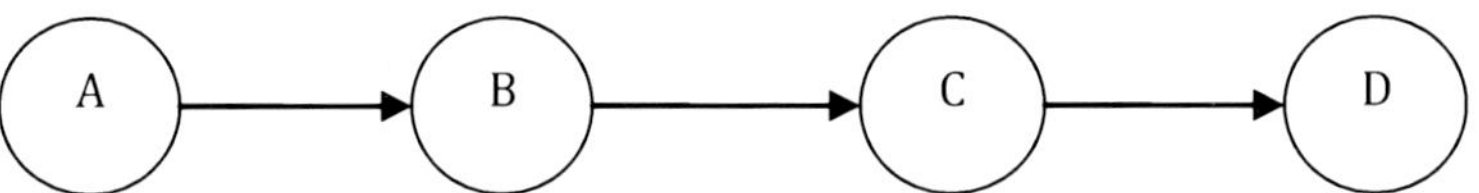

lead to C, which will lead to D, but D is a horribly bad situation, so therefore we should not do A. If we are dealing with a causal chain, and the chain in question has a broken link, then there is no plausibility to the argument. If C will not likely lead to D, or there is any other broken link, then we say that the argument commits a slippery slope fallacy.

Here is an argument which commits a slippery slope fallacy: I better not get a credit card. If I get a credit card, I'll start buying things I really don't need. Then, I won't be able to pay my bill. Pretty soon, I'll be stealing from people just to pay the exorbitant interest on the card. Eventually, I'll find myself in prison, just because I wanted my own flashy credit card.

There are some reasons not to get a credit card, and they do often charge exorbitant interest rates, but there are some reasons to get a credit card, and it is not the case that getting a credit card will lead inexorably to finding oneself in prison. Since the argument above doesn't consider these arguments, but simply relies on an unlikely chain of events, it commits a slippery slope fallacy.

Arguments from Authority

Skill 23.4

Recognizing, Analyzing, and Evaluating Arguments by Authority

In a great many cases, it is impossible, or at least incredibly difficult, for us to evaluate given information on our own. We may have to spend years training in a subject, which we just do not have time to do. In these cases, we generally rely on the word of experts. Every argument by authority takes the following form:

1) <u>Someone says that "p" is true.</u>
2) ∴ "p" is true.

The claim that one person is saying something must be cited in the premise of the argument, or it won't be considered an argument by authority. Anytime someone gives you an argument, though, you can ask what the basis of the premises is. If you don't have any other reason to believe them, or they haven't offered any reason to believe them, then you can accept the premises on the basis of an implied argument by authority by saying "I should believe "x" because this person says "x".

Argument from Authority
An argument whose only premise is that an authority has asserted the conclusion

The question here, as with all inductive arguments, is "when should one believe the argument to be a good one?" What makes for a strong argument by authority? This is, as usual, a complicated question, but we can offer a few suggestions. Put simply, the issue is whether the person has the requisite credibility to be believed.

A person's credibility is affected by a great many things, but here is a cursory list:

1) Background/Experience
2) Studies
3) Degrees
4) Positions
5) Publications
6) Track record
7) Critical thinking

It is easy to see that a person's credibility can be affected by the fact that they have studied in a particular field. If they have earned any degrees in that field, so much the better for their credibility. Of course, a person can study on their own and gain just as much knowledge as someone with a degree, but the fact that they have earned a degree shows that other people in the field have confirmed that the person has the knowledge, which counts for a great deal.

It is also the case that a person who has advanced in his field by attaining any high-ranking position would have more credibility than others. We would trust the legal opinion of a judge over a lawyer, even if they had basically the same experience and training. A person's track record is also a very important factor in determining one's credibility. We all have some friends who seem to say lots of things that turn out to be wrong, and some friends who hardly ever seem to be wrong. They only seem to make assertions when they are confident themselves. Of course, it's easy to know a person's track record when they are your friend, but one can still determine something about an expert's track record. Many lawyers keep track of their win/loss ratio, for example. These sorts of records are not perfect, of course, since some lawyers will take more difficult cases than others, but they are a good place to start.

One last issue, but in my opinion one of the most important, is critical thinking. It is easy for someone to memorize a great deal of information, but if they can't themselves recognize inconsistencies and incongruities, or are incapable of thinking critically, it doesn't bode well for any expert opinions they may share. We expect experts not only to have a great deal of information, but to be able to evaluate that data and clarify discrepancies.

Keep in mind that we can take the word "expert" here very loosely. Eyewitness testimony can be seen as "expert" testimony in the sense that we are believing that something is true solely on the basis that someone says it is. In this case, we can look at factors such as the person's eyesight and other factors. Some people are simply more observant than others, for example. Credibility comes in degrees, and it is important to recognize this fact.

Appeal to Inappropriate Authority
A fallacy which occurs when an authority is relied upon when his credibility is insufficient for the issue at hand

Relying on an improper authority is said to commit the fallacy of **appeal to inappropriate authority**. It can occur for a few reasons. First, there can be a complete lack of expertise, or completely unknown expertise. For example, one might say "I heard a talk show host on the radio who said that the stock market will rise." Concluding that the stock market will rise on this basis would be foolish. We don't have any information about the person who made this assertion, particularly what credibility this person might have on economic issues. If one cannot identify the source of the information, it is impossible to make a judgment as to the source's credibility, and in that case, one has not been given a good reason to accept the information as true.

The second reason is misplaced expertise. We should certainly consult a doctor if we have a rash, and will probably just accept his opinion should he say it is tinea corporis (ringworm). We shouldn't, however, just accept his judgment that we should change our auto insurance. Nor should we ask an insurance agent his opinion about the rash on our arm. Experts generally are experts in a particular area, and when it comes to areas outside their expertise, they have no more credibility than anyone else.

Finally, we must consider the issue of bias. Someone may have advanced degrees and lots of information about a given issue, but if that person has a stake in the issue, it is inappropriate to treat them as any other expert. For example, an owner of a tobacco company might have a medical degree, but even then, when he says that his products are perfectly safe, we can't just take him at his word. Even if he has done studies himself, we just won't take them to be as credible as an independent expert, who doesn't stand to gain or lose by the results of the study.

Chapter Twenty-Three Exercises

For the basic concept exercises, decide whether the argument is an argument by analogy, an inductive generalization, a causal inference, an argument by authority, or some other kind of inductive argument. Record your initial impulse as to the argument's strength.

Basic Concept Exercises

1. We were having a debate the other day about whether global warming is occurring. When I heard that Hillary Clinton accepted it, that was enough to convince me. She's one of the smartest Secretaries of State we've ever had.
2. The Christians say, "Creatures are not bound with desire unless satisfaction for those desires exists." A baby feels hunger: well, there is such a thing as food. A duckling wants to swim: well, there is such a thing as water. Men feel sexual desire: well, there is such a thing as sex. If I find in myself a desire which no experience in this world can satisfy, the most probable explanation is that I was made for another world.

   C. S. Lewis – *Mere Christianity*
3. I keep noticing that tires which come in overinflated tend to have much more wear down the center of the tire. I'll bet when tires are overinflated, the excessive pressure makes the tread wear unevenly, less on the outside and more on the inside.
4. It seems to me that people who are presently in jail were much less likely to attend church regularly before they went to prison than the non-prison population. If the government is interested in getting people to not break the law, which it should be, then it should do everything it can to encourage people to attend church regularly.
5. Of course the defendant is guilty! Mrs. Lee was an eyewitness to the crime, and she testified that she saw the defendant commit the crime.
6. Studies have shown that 73% of college students don't shower every day, so I bet the student reading this book didn't shower today. That's gross!

7. Eighty-two percent of the students on Howzyourprof.com think Mr. Monge is a horrible professor, so about eighty-two percent of his students must think he's horrible.
8. Eighty-two percent of Mr. Monge's students think he's a horrible professor! He must be a really horrible professor!
9. A referee should never be a player in the game in which he is officiating, but the government officiates in the disputes between businesses and individuals. That's why the government should never run businesses or even own them.
10. Almost all of the terrorists who have attacked the United States have been Muslims, so probably most Muslims are terrorists.

Intermediate Exercises

For each of the following arguments, decide what kind of inductive argument it is, then analyze and evaluate the argument using techniques specific to that type of argument. If the argument as stated is weak, state any possible fallacies and decide whether there is a more appropriate conclusion which could be drawn from the given premises.

11. We were having a debate the other day about whether global warming is occurring. When I heard that Hillary Clinton accepted it, that was enough to convince me. She's one of the smartest Secretaries of State we've ever had.
12. I was looking through this jar of coins, and of the ones I pulled out, (and I made sure to pull them out randomly), over three-quarters of them (>75%) were minted in San Francisco. I conclude that, since I pulled out around 40, at least half of the coins in the jar were minted in San Francisco.
13. Almost all of the terrorists who have attacked the United States have been Muslims, so probably most Muslims are terrorists.
14. I plugged my hair dryer into this outlet, and it worked, but the lamp that was plugged in before wasn't working. It must be that the lightbulb is busted, or else there is a problem with the wiring in the lamp.
15. I was getting a cold, and then I took some VitaBlast cold and flu remedy, and sure enough, the next day my cold was gone. I guess that stuff really works.
16. Eighty-two percent of the students on Howzyourprof.com think Mr. Monge is a horrible professor, so about eighty-two percent of his students must think he's horrible.
17. Eighty-two percent of Mr. Monge's students think he's a horrible professor! He must be a really horrible professor!
18. I really want to find a nice girl to settle down with, but every girl I meet at a bar cheats on me after a few months. Seriously, it's happened like five times. I just assume now that most all women are unfaithful.
19. Analogies are very similar to generalizations. Since I understand analogies well, I shouldn't have too much trouble with generalizations.
20. I have one question for people who get all paranoid about swimming in a place where untreated human sewage goes into the water—where do you think fish poop?

Challenging exercises

21. It seems to me that people who are presently in jail were much less likely to attend church regularly before they went to prison than the non-prison population. If the government is interested in getting people to not break the

law, which it should be, then it should do everything it can to encourage people to attend church regularly.

22. A referee should never be a player in the game in which he is officiating, but the government officiates in the disputes between businesses and individuals. That's why the government should never run businesses or even own them.
23. Just as the family should never be put in the hands of the children, the government should never be put in the hands of the people. Democracy only invites mob rule.
24. The bigger one's brain, the smarter one is. In general, men's brains are larger than women's brains. Therefore, in general, men are smarter than women.
25. The wheels of a motorcycle are like gyroscopes. If you try to tilt a gyroscope left or right, it will resist moving in that direction and instead turn at a ninety degree angle to the direction the force is applied. So, if you try to fall over on a motorcycle, the wheels will resist falling over to the right or left, and instead turn to the left or right direction. That's why it's so hard to fall over on a motorcycle.
26. My economics professor said that the Supreme Court decision in favor of Walmart, which held that female employees could not sue as a class action, was a blessing. She said that if the lawsuit were to go forward, it would have had devastating effects on the economy. It looks like the Supreme Court made the right decision.
27. Many of the detainees were released from Guantanamo Bay because there was not enough evidence to detain them, according to the muckety mucks in charge down there. It turns out that a significant number of them went right back to killing, both military targets and civilians. Perhaps we should just draw the conclusion that virtually all of the detainees still at Guantanamo Bay really are terrorists.
28. Abortion consists in killing a living person. So if you believe in capital punishment, you must also be in favor of abortion rights.
29. I've heard that Fox News Channel is conservative, but Chris Wallace, a host on the channel, said that including the conservative side of things only makes the channel look conservative because of the backdrop of other media outlets which regularly exclude conservative views. So, I guess the Fox News Channel isn't conservative after all.
30. Everyone these days crows about the successes of the civil rights movement, especially citing the Supreme Court's ruling in Brown vs. Board of education. That ruling required schools to integrate students of different races, but that is the precise start of the precipitous decline of academic achievement among black students. Think about the fact that black students in all black colleges do vastly better than students at integrated colleges, and you will conclude as I do that the decision of the Supreme Court in Brown v. Board of Education destroyed the hopes of millions of black people in this country.

In-Context Exercises

Evaluate the following arguments.

A. Squirrels and rats are both rodents of similar size and appearance, and while rats cause problems in the city, squirrels cause problems in the suburbs. Since we all agree that rats should be exterminated, it's about time we just exterminated all squirrels.

B. "...I've always reckoned that looking at the new moon over your left shoulder is one of the carelessest and foolishest things a body can do. Old Hank Bunker done it once, and bragged about it; and in less than two years he got drunk and fell off the shot tower, and spread himself out so that he was just a kind of layer, as you may say; and they slid him edgeways between two doors for a coffin, and buried him so, so they say, but I didn't see it. Pap told me. But anyway it all come of looking at the moon that way, like a fool."

Mark Twain—*The Adventures of Huckleberry Finn*

C. A CEO who had sex with an intern would be fired on the spot. A senior officer who slept with a recruit would be court-martialed. That's why Bill Clinton should not have been acquitted by the Senate.

D. Health care plans generally cover pills like Viagra, Cialis, and Levitra so men can get an erection, but they refuse to cover birth control pills. Just goes to show you that men make these decisions, and the old boys club screws women over once again.

E. I don't see why some people have such a problem with universal healthcare, and the government requiring people to buy health insurance. After all, the government requires everyone to buy auto insurance.

F. I don't see why people think Congressmen Weiner should resign for sending pictures of his genitals to women. No one asked Football quarterback Brett Favre to resign for doing the same thing!

G. The Christians say, "Creatures are not bound with desire unless satisfaction for those desires exists." A baby feels hunger: well, there is such a thing as food. A duckling wants to swim: well, there is such a thing as water. Men feel sexual desire: well, there is such a thing as sex. If I find in myself a desire which no experience in this world can satisfy, the most probable explanation is that I was made for another world.

C. S. Lewis - *Mere Christianity*

Logic Puzzle

Since we are dealing with inductive reasoning, this logic puzzle, and the three that follow, will be a little different.

There is one and only one 10-letter word that over 75% of Harvard graduates pronounce improperly. What is it?

CHAPTER

24

Rhetorical Pitfalls

Skill 24.1

Recognizing Rhetorical Pitfalls

Skill 24.2

Avoiding Rhetorical Pitfalls in One's Own Thinking and Writing

In the previous chapter, we briefly learned about recognizing and evaluating a few common inductive argument styles. This introduction is admittedly rather brief, but hopefully enough for the beginning student of logic to use to some degree. No one should think that it is sufficient to address even the majority of inductive arguments. Instead of trying to catalog thousands of different styles of inductive reasoning, we will look at particular patterns of improper reasoning which can take place among many styles of argument.

We will learn more about fallacies in the next chapters. In this chapter we will not learn about fallacies, per se, but rhetorical devices and habits of mind which can very easily lead to fallacious reasoning, or to drawing conclusions which are not warranted.

Whether in one's own reasoning, or that of others, one should always be careful to recognize these rhetorical pitfalls.

Careless Habits of Mind

The first types of rhetorical pitfalls can be labeled careless habits of mind. They are approaches to thinking which are not rigorous, and can easily lead a person to draw faulty conclusions. We should avoid them as much as possible.

Wishful Thinking

Rhetorical Pitfalls
Careless habits of mind or devices which often lead to poor reasoning

Many people seem to think that the fact that they want something to be true counts as evidence that it is true. To engage in wishful thinking is to disregard any actual evidence or reasoning and to believe whatever it feels best to believe. Critical thinkers want to know what is true, and what the best available evidence points to being true.

John is watching television late at night, and he sees a product for sale which he really would like. He knows that often the products purchased on television infomercials are of inferior quality, and he hopes to use the product for a long time. He thinks, maybe, just this once, the product will be of decent quality. John is engaging in wishful thinking.

The point is not that one should never buy items advertised in infomercials, but only that one should not fool oneself into believing that they will be of high quality. If you want a product that is somewhat inexpensive, but not of too high a quality, then perhaps it makes sense, but don't throw away your intellect while doing so.

Wishful thinking can take the form of denial, a refusal to accept something just because its truth would be too painful to consider. The fact that wishful thinking is fallacious, however, does not mean that one can never have hope, or wish for the best. It is a fallacy, however, when allows one's hopes to cloud one's judgment about what is true or what is likely to be true, or false.

Stereotyping

The original meaning of 'stereotype' was a printing device for creating exact duplicates. Stereotyping, as a rhetorical pitfall, is to assume that all members of a group are exactly alike. It is a form of generalization, but presumes that we can universally generalize over all of the members of a group, without any evidence to support that presupposition. Mature individuals realize that it is virtually impossible to make any universal generalizations about all people. No matter what group about which we wish to generalize, there is rarely anything which will hold true of every member of the group, at least for any large group.

There are, of course, statistical differences among different groups of people, and these can be fascinating and important, but the person stereotyping doesn't look for statistical variation, but only a simplistic judgment used to distinguish and differentiate groups of people. Often, a person is said to stereotype not for necessarily believing that all members of a group are the same, but just for not really caring about whether any purported similarity is real, and just assuming that it is. For example, one might think that people with turbans are suspicious. We would still probably think of this as stereotyping, even if one protested that he didn't think all people who wore turbans were guilty, but we should just be suspicious of them. We have a moral duty, most people think, including your author, to treat each person as an individual first, and as a member of a group only secondarily and provisionally.

Moral obligation put aside, it is an intellectual error to engage in stereotyping. If we care about the truth, we won't go around assuming that every member of a group is just like every other member. Whatever our moral duties are, this attitude will too often lead us to make incorrect judgments about people, as well as situations, objects, and most other things.

Scapegoating (and Demonizing)

Yom Kippur, also known as The Day of Atonement, is a Jewish holiday, one of the holiest days of the year. It is a day to ask for forgiveness and to atone for one's sins. In Biblical times, the sins of all the people were believed to have been placed onto a goat, and then the goat would be sent out as an outcast. The goat, through a mistranslation apparently, came to be known as a scapegoat.

Regardless what one thinks about such a practice, the term scapegoating has come to mean heaping blame on someone who doesn't deserve it. It is easy for most people to try to evade their own responsibility for something by finding a particular person or group upon which to place that responsibility, but a person engaging in scapegoating may not be evading responsibility for his own actions. One might scapegoat a person or group for any societal or personal wrong, simply because it is convenient or satisfying to identify a particular villain (perhaps a form of wishful thinking).

Scapegoating does not occur when the person in question is actually guilty of the supposed crime, however, one who engages in scapegoating usually hasn't really stopped to consider the evidence. It just feels too good to identify someone else upon whom to place the blame to stop and carefully consider how blame should actually be apportioned.

Oversimplifying

It is reasonable to want to distill ideas down to their most basic form, and this distillation can help in understanding complex ideas; in fact, teachers must often simplify the material they are presenting so that it can be digested by their students. There is nothing wrong with simplifying complex ideas. A problem can occur, however, when one tries to draw conclusions from these simplified ideas. These conclusions may lack the subtlety or completeness which conclusions could have had if they were drawn from the ideas in all their complexity.

Of course, even when simplifying, it is possible to go too far. Remember, as with paraphrasing, the idea is to produce a simpler statement with the same meaning. When one oversimplifies so that the original idea is distorted and bears little relation to the original, one makes it very likely that bad reasoning will occur.

Causes are often oversimplified. To say that 400,000 people die from smoking-related illnesses every year is an oversimplification which confuses more than it enlightens. Lung cancer is a smoking related illness, and someone who gets lung cancer is counted among those who die of smoking-related illnesses every year, *regardless of whether he ever smoked*. Even saying that smoking causes cancer is probably too oversimplified. Smoking does increase one's chance of getting cancer; it is a causal factor in getting cancer, but so are many other things which are not completely understood.

Many of the rhetorical pitfalls we are learning here may be considered forms of oversimplification. When diagnosing an argument for rhetorical pitfalls, however, one should only identify oversimplifying when a more specific pitfall is not available. Also, if one thinks someone is "over-"simplifying, one should be able to explain what the more complete idea should be, and why and how the way it was presented left out important details.

Rationalizing

Rationalizing is often like reasoning in reverse. The time to think about justifying our behavior is before we engage in it. Even then it can be difficult to maintain an objective standpoint, but afterwards it is even harder. Rationalizing means to attempt to create a rationale for behavior that sounds good, but isn't really the reason for one's action. It often occurs when the real reason is embarrassing, or even immoral.

One might rationalize robbing a store on the grounds that the owners have lots of money. At root, it was one's own greed and lack of planning for one's own life that got someone into a bad situation. The fact that a store has a lot of money (which often isn't even true), really had nothing to do with it.

Rationalizing is a habit of mind that doesn't try to uncover actual reasons, but to substitute what one perceives to be more socially acceptable reasons. A man could rationalize cheating on his spouse by saying that she wasn't paying enough attention to him, when in reality it was his fear to discuss his needs, sexual and otherwise, with his spouse that caused conflict in the marriage.

It is possible to justify behavior, sometimes even what seems to be bad behavior. I might say that I punched someone because he insulted my mother. Whether it counts as justification is an issue for ethics, but it's not rationalizing if it is the actual reason for my action, and not some underlying reason I am too afraid to admit.

Confirmation Bias

Whether our theory is positive or negative, we often tend to remember and make use of confirming instances, and reject or simply forget disconfirming ones. We have all heard the complaint that every time someone washes their car, it rains. Some people have actually come to believe this obvious foolishness. Unless one lives in Seattle, it is far more likely that it will not rain after one washes one's car, but the problem is that we will remember the cases where it occurs far longer than cases where it doesn't. Who would remember the time they washed their car and it didn't rain?

Technically, confirmation bias is the impulse we have to find, remember and even interpret data in ways that confirm our theories or preconceived notions. We sometimes assume that data doesn't take sides, but we forget that we do. We like to be right, and we have the desire to find information which supports our views, and discount evidence which goes against it. A critical thinker will consider this bias and try to counter it.

One way scientists fight confirmation bias is to dispassionately record the data. Write it down. Don't worry about what the data is saying, or what view it is supporting, until after the data collection is complete. Then, one can look back at the data and make judgments about how it functions as evidence for a theory.

Imagine if we had a record book where we recorded every day we washed our car, and the weather the next three days. In most areas, it will most likely show that the old saw is just a result of confirmation bias.

Fadophilia

A fadophiliac is a person who loves fads, someone who jumps on board anything new or different without trying to ascertain whether there are good reasons for making the change. Of course we should sometimes change what we are doing or thinking, but change for change's sake can lead to unwanted results, especially when the consequences and repercussions are not thought out.

A fad is any activity or object which takes on an exaggerated importance, out of line with its inherent worth or value. Some people are all too willing to jump on board the latest fad, without any thought that it is a flash in the pan and will be out of vogue as soon as it came into it. Think about the hot new trendy restaurant that everyone wants to attend, and about which you hear all the buzz. Their food is the best. The best, that is, until everyone realizes it was overpriced and the food wasn't that good anyway.

Then, the fadophiliac will simply latch on to the next restaurant, or hairstyle, or whatever else the gods of fashion and trends tell them they must adore.

Other Rhetorical Pitfalls

Complex Question

Have you stopped cheating on exams? This question is a complex question. It looks like a yes or no question, but answering it by saying simply "yes" or "no" can get you into all sorts of trouble. The question has a built in assumption, namely that you *have* cheated on exams. Answering the question with a "yes" or a "no" can give the impression that one accepts the built-in presumption of the question. If you say "yes" then you admit that you have cheated but not anymore. Answering "no," however, admits that you have cheated and are still doing so.

Any question which has built in assumptions which make it difficult to answer in a straightforward way is a complex question. It has nothing to do with the complexity or difficulty of the question in any other sense. A complex question is not an error in reasoning itself, but the problem is that the way it is answered can easily lead to improper conclusions. When someone answers "No," one might intend to say that one has never cheated, but someone can draw the conclusion that one has never stopped.

The proper way to answer a complex question is to disentangle the assumed aspect of the question. In the question above, one can simply say "I have never cheated on exams", or "Yes, I did cheat on exams in grade school, but I never cheated on anything in college." Or, of course, one can simply say, "No, I never have stopped, and am still doing it today," but your honesty might mean you need to take the exam at the front of the classroom.

Another common type of complex question is a "why" question. Asking for an explanation for something generally assumes that the thing in question is true. So, asking "Why is it so hard for you to answer my questions?" assumes that it is hard for the person being addressed to answer questions. As with all complex questions, the way to handle these questions is to address whether the underlying presumption is true or false, and only give an explanation if the presumption is true.

Euphemisms/Dysphemisms

A synonym for a word is another word with the same meaning. One issue is that it is often very difficult to find a word with the exact same meaning, and often we just settle for one which is close enough for our purposes. A euphemism is a word or phrase used in place of another, where the replacement has a nicer "ring" to it. Technically, the euphemism has a more positive connotation. The euphemism sounds better, or less crude, disgusting, or horrible. A fairly harmless example is the word 'bathroom.' It is often used for a place where no bathing is meant to occur. A dysphemism, on the other hand, is a word or phrase which has a more negative connotation. Sometimes we will call someone a "liar," even when they honestly believed what he was saying. I would say that such usage is dysphemistic.

We worry about euphemisms and dysphemisms when they impede good thinking. We shouldn't allow our minds to be influenced by word choice, but by the underlying reality. So, if we draw different conclusions from a euphemistic or dysphemistic word than we would from a more straightforward term, then we are allowing the selection of words to control our minds. An example is cheating on one's spouse. If we looked less harshly on someone because they had a "dalliance" or a "tryst" than we would if it were reported as having an "affair," then we are probably not thinking clearly.

Realtors often use euphemistic language, as in "cozy" for small. "Lots of possibilities" might mean you'll have to replace most everything. An example of a dysphemism is the term 'date-rape' for sexual contact where force is not used. The word 'rape' has an incredibly powerful negative connotation. To use the term to describe improper sexual conduct which doesn't use force is to try to use some of that negative connotation for rhetorical purposes. This fact does not mean that having sex with a drunken person is morally permissible, but just that the word 'rape' was being used specifically for its rhetorical effect and not because the word was literally correct.

Remember that it isn't necessary that we eliminate all euphemisms. Saying to someone that their loved one "passed away" is generally preferred in place of "died", not because it is more accurate, but because it is cognizant of their feelings. To use euphemisms to manipulate people, however, or to allow oneself to be manipulated by them, is to be taken in by faulty reasoning.

Innuendo

It may seem odd, but sometimes speaking the truth can be more misleading than not saying anything, usually because of expectations about what people will say. Innuendo is when someone says one thing, but people will take what they have said to mean something more.

There is a classic story about a sailing ship where the ship's mate was sometimes too drunk to write in the ship's log. The Captain wanted to drive home the point, and wrote in the ship's log that "The mate was drunk all day." The next day the mate had sobered up, and decided to turn the tables. He added to the log "The Captain was sober all day."

What the mate wrote was literally true, but would lead anyone who read the log to think that perhaps the Captain was drunk most every day. After all, you wouldn't expect anyone to write that the Captain was sober unless it was an unusual circumstance.

The trouble with innuendo is that it can be misleading. We can be led into believing something that is not true, not because we have been given a reason to believe it, but because our expectations have been used against us. Complex questions, and the answers to them, often involve cases of improper innuendo.

Innuendo can also be used for humorous effect, which no one wants to prohibit. One classic use is in the following quote by W. C. Fields: "I did not say that this meat was tough. I just said I didn't see the horse that usually stands outside."

Hyperbole

Hyperbole is overblown exaggeration. We use hyperbole to make our assertions sound important or dramatic, as if that enhances their claim to truth. We could say that a television is very expensive, but we instead throw out "That's the most expensive television ever!" It should be clear that hyperbolic statements are not intended to facilitate careful, calm evaluation of the facts.

There is usually some truth to hyperbolic statements, at least as believed by the utterer, but it is exaggerated or too broad. One may not be led too far astray by hyperbole, even if one doesn't recognize it, but might have one's attitude or expectation affected so that the statement achieves a kind of inevitability about it. One might accept that "Perhaps it's not exactly true, but it must be close."

The misuse of the word "literally" might be seen as hyperbolic. The word "literally" means that an expression is meant to be understood in the plain meaning of the words, and not in a figurative or metaphorical sense. Yet, the word is often used and applied to clearly figurative expressions. When someone says "It was so cold outside, we literally froze to death," it's a safe bet that they are using the expression hyperbolically.

Persuasive Definitions

Definitions play an important role in thinking logically and well. Unless we are using the same definitions for words, we are not really communicating with each other. We should define our terms dispassionately, however, and then make a case for our position. When we try to incorporate our argument into our definitions, then we are creating persuasive definitions.

We can define "abortion" as "the murder of an innocent fetus for the crime of being created", or as "the right of every woman to have control over her own body." Neither of these definitions seeks to accurately and objectively define the word "abortion", but to push the listener to accept a certain view of abortion. A better definition is that "abortion is the intentional termination of a pregnancy before full gestation which is accomplished through the death of the fetus." Although I have seen some students balk at this definition, but if one terminates a pregnancy early, say by inducing childbirth medically, where the fetus lives and is intended to live, no one would call it an abortion. The definitional question of whether terminating a pregnancy while there is only an embryo present still exists, but one can either claim that these do not count as abortions, or take a broad definition of 'fetus.' In any case, given this definition, we can still debate whether abortion is morally right or wrong, but at least we can agree that we are debating the same subject.

Proof Surrogate

Some people seem to believe that unless a study says something, then it can't be true. It seems reasonable to think that many things are true, or false, whether they have been studied or not. We may not know whether they are true, however. We do know that whenever someone cites "a study" to confirm their beliefs, without citing the source of the study, they are using a proof surrogate. Any time someone uses the claim that "there is evidence" or "it has been proven" they are not really offering the evidence or the proof, they are claiming that there is proof out there somewhere, which is a much different claim.

We are comforted by the fact that even though we don't know what the evidence is, it does exist somewhere. The problem, of course, is that there is no way to confirm that the purported evidence actually says what it is purported to say. Unless one knows what the evidence is, or at least where it can be found, we cannot verify that the evidence isn't being distorted or misrepresented.

The possibility of being charged with offering merely a proof surrogate is why it is important to source your information in your papers. When you are using someone else's evidence, it is important to tell your reader what the source of the information is, so they can check it. Claiming that "there is evidence that 'x'" is really no better than saying 'x' is true without any support. Treating it as if it did is to fall victim to a proof surrogate.

Apple Polishing

Most people like having their egos stroked, though not all. Apple polishing, or "buttering someone up" is to tell them something flattering or nice in an attempt to get them to draw certain conclusions, generally to treat the speaker better than they would otherwise, or to buy a product for which they don't have a good enough reason to buy.

Paying someone a compliment is not necessarily a bad thing, even if it comes right before you ask them for something. The real problem is if they allow that compliment to get them to draw different conclusions or make different judgments from what they would if there were no compliment. Of course, if the person realizes what is going on, it often backfires.

When a debater tells the judges that they look good today, or that they are esteemed or wise, then there is an attempt at apple polishing. Let's hope the judges never fall for it.

Misleading Statistics

Statistics are important, but they can be used in inappropriate ways. In this brief presentation, it is impossible to detail all the ways that statistics can be misused, but hopefully this warning will encourage the reader to be more careful when hearing statistics and figuring out what they mean.

One example is the figure reported earlier that 400,000 people die from smoking related diseases. That number sounds very high, but it doesn't tell us how many of those people actually got the disease from smoking and not some other way. Of course, that kind of refinement might be impossible to determine. If someone is a heavy smoker, we would just assume that the smoking caused their disease even though we know it's possible that something else was the cause.

Averages can also be misleading. A tax-cut might result in the "average" taxpayer receiving a $1,000 cut, but this result could be the arithmetical average. It could be that 75% of taxpayers receive no tax reduction whatsoever, and the others average a $4,000 cut. It would certainly be wrong in this case to expect that one will receive around $1,000 from the tax cut.

Also, be on the lookout for statistical comparisons, such as "our product is 25% bigger." Here the issue is that the standard for comparison is not listed. One might assume that the manufacturer means 25% bigger than the product used to be, but it could mean 25% bigger than their new smaller product, or any number of things.

As one might suspect, a lot of the problems with statistics arise from a kind of innuendo, if you call someone on where they are getting their statistics, be careful for proof surrogates. It is good advice that when someone offers precise statistics to ask them what their source is, and to try to consider what information could be left out.

Chapter Twenty-Four Exercises

Examine the following arguments or statements. If they involve any kind of rhetorical pitfalls, identify them. Unless you think it is totally obvious, you should defend your judgment in a sentence or two.

Basic Concept Exercises

1. The time I spend with my family is quality time. Other businessmen forget their families entirely.
2. 90% of U.S. Congressman are lawyers. Since Bob Barr is a U.S. Congressman, it follows that he is a lawyer.
3. Look, I voted for Congressman Sanchez, so I just have to think he's doing a good job.
4. Are you still planning on plagiarizing your friend's work by looking at his notes?
5. The United States is currently involved in three overseas contingency operations, but hopefully, those contingencies will change.
6. Every conservative I know just bashes President Obama every chance they get.
7. I'll tell you what's wrong with our country—feminists! They're ruining everything that used to be American.
8. I'm afraid I can't hire that last applicant. His last name is Sulaiman, which is basically Arabic for Solomon.
9. It's so simple. All we have to do if we want to balance the federal budget is to raise income taxes.
10. I know you're really busy right now, but I think you're smart enough to figure out a way to get my project done before the others.

Intermediate Exercises

11. I was pretty sure that the claim that our government was behind 9/11 was true, and it turns out I was right. I found plenty of evidence for it when I searched for it on the internet.

12. Change will not come if we wait for some other person or some other time. We are the ones we've been waiting for. We are the change that we seek.
    President Barack Obama, Feb. 5, 2008 speech
13. Adam, you're the smartest kid in the room right now whose name is Adam.
14. The Journal of American Studies published their study that says that children raised by homosexual parents are 99.7% as well adjusted as their peers who are raised by others.
15. A professor is someone who likes to profess his beliefs to others, but isn't necessarily so good at listening to them.
16. Yeah, I got a D in chemistry, but it's just because the teacher is so bad at explaining things, and I just couldn't understand the book, so I didn't read it.
17. I know that increasing government spending by at least double has not yet improved the economy, but I just think we need to stay the course. If we just increase government spending even more, I'm sure we will see the economy start moving.
18. Try our new diet potato chips—each serving has only 100 calories!
19. How is it that you always know what I'm thinking?
20. Your traditional views on marriage are positively medieval! Why don't you get with the times.

Challenging exercises

21. Torture is the intentional infliction of intense bodily or mental harm, which is why the United States should never use torture, not even on terrorists.
22. I would say that the President is responsible for the bad economy. He supported healthcare reform, and the version of it pushed through the House has made it much more unlikely that businesses will hire people. The economy can't improve if businesses are not doing any hiring.
23. "In the polls, who is [sic] the most consistently misinformed media viewers? The most consistently misinformed? Fox. Fox viewers. Consistently, every poll."
    Jon Stewart, on Chris Wallace's program "Fox News Sunday"
24. The only thing you need to know is that the mainstream media has a liberal bias and is full of liberals. That explains why they consistently favor Democrats and portray Republicans as idiots or evil.
25. Let me read your palm. Ah, you have a very long life line, and your head line is thick and deep. You must be very intelligent. Come, let me do a complete reading—it's only fifteen dollars.
26. The President is on the verge of passing the largest tax increase ever! It is at least 20% more than any previous tax increase.
27. The second round of quantitative easing is almost over, which is where the Federal Reserve purchases government securities.
28. We just got Boom Blox for the Wii. It's only the best game ever! You'll have more fun than you've had in your whole life.
29. It's a simple fact that science has shown that human beings have evolved, not from monkeys, as is so often thrown out as a straw man, but from some kind of pro-simian creature over 4 million years ago.
30. I totally knew that house was haunted. After we met outside that old house and Billy said he had seen a ghost the night before, we all went inside, and sure

enough, we all heard strange sounds and most of us saw strange shapes and hazy figures. It must have been ghosts alright!

In-Context Exercises

31. Let's think about the issue of evolutionism versus creationism. If you are on the side of the evolutionist, then you are really nothing more than the great-great-great grandchild of a monkey. If you accept creationism, then you were created in the image of God. I see in you the image of God. You have a righteous soul.
32. I heard that most intellectuals are atheists, so if you want to be recognized as intelligent, you should be an atheist, too.

Additional Exercise: Look through a newspaper or magazine, and find examples of people engaging in five of the rhetorical pitfalls from this chapter.

Logic Puzzle

What seven-letter word actually becomes longer when one letter is removed?

CHAPTER

25

Argumentative Fallacies

Skill 25.1

Recognizing Argumentative Fallacies

Skill 25.2

Avoiding Argumentative Fallacies in One's Own Thinking and Writing

In the previous chapter, we briefly learned about how to guard against certain rhetorical pitfalls and bad mental habits. These rhetorical pitfalls were not fallacies, but they strongly encourage fallacious reasoning. In this chapter we will learn about actual fallacies. A fallacy is a particular pattern of bad reasoning, which deceptively appears to be convincing.

In ordinary discourse, the term fallacy is often used to refer to any false ideas, but we are using the term more precisely. A fallacy must have at least one premise, albeit possibly an implicit one, and a conclusion that is purported to follow from the given premise or premises. A fallacy occurs when, either a premise fails in a particular way, or despite appearances the conclusion does not follow from the premises, or the argument fails to provide a reason to accept the conclusion. In some way, the argument is faulty.

The fallacies we are covering in this chapter and the next are informal fallacies. They are not based on the form of the argument, as is the case with affirming the consequent and denying the antecedent. One cannot diagnose these fallacies unless the content of the argument, or the meaning of the component parts, is examined.

Inappropriate Appeal to Emotion (Pity/Anger/Resentment/Guilt/Fear)

Fallacy
A characteristic pattern of faulty reasoning which is often deceptively persuasive

Argumentative Fallacy
A fallacy which generally occurs in a single argument; only one arguer is required

It is important to have emotions. Someone with no emotions is bound to be a sociopath. Some emotions may be appropriate or inappropriate at certain times, and it may even be appropriate that emotions drive some behavior, although usually philosophers hope that the behavior is still backed up by reason. For example, one might love another person and so decide to ask her to marry him. It would seem unlikely that anyone without any emotions would ever decide to marry. Plus, difficulties aside, it doesn't seem that marriage is unreasonable. The point is that emotions can and should guide behavior, which means they can and should guide decisions, which means they can and should influence reasoning.

Yet, far too often, emotion is substituted for reason, where there is no connection. Let's consider an appeal to pity (it is common to drop the "inappropriate" part, but when criticizing a process of reasoning, it is implied). When a student says that he deserves a higher grade because with his current grade he will never get into med school, he is committing an inappropriate appeal to pity.

The premise in this case is that one should feel sorry for the student, and perhaps that is true. But the conclusion, that he deserves a higher grade because of the appropriate pity one should feel for him, simply doesn't follow. It is irrelevant to the grade. Not only is the student trying to impel the professor to engage in a faulty process of reasoning, but also to undermine the integrity of the grading system. Students' grades depend on how well they understand the material and how well they can present the material themselves and apply it, not on how bad we feel for the student. The next time you insult a professor's intelligence and their profession by using such an appeal to pity, you should think again.

Pity, anger, guilt, resentment, fear and many other emotions can be manipulated in order to push people to accept conclusions which they shouldn't accept. In any case of this kind, an inappropriate appeal to emotion has occurred. An appeal to fear is a very common one, and it will help us to make a subtle distinction.

It is always appropriate to vote against a policy because it will have negative consequences. For example, I could argue that one should vote against privatizing social security because without the threat of punishment, many people will not contribute to their own retirement funds, and then they will be bailed out by an irresponsible future legislature. This is probably not an inappropriate appeal to fear. It is an argument that if we vote to privatize social security, there will be negative consequences.

An inappropriate appeal to fear is to play on someone's fears to push them in a way that doesn't engage their intellect, but solely their emotions. Perhaps saying that we should not privatize social security because if we do so we are just putting our futures into the hands of greedy Wall Street types who will lose it all and destroy the country. In this case the appeal to fear could also be diagnosed as a slippery slope fallacy.

If you suspect that someone is pushing you or a larger audience based on an appeal to fear, the appropriate response is to slow down and try to disengage the actual negative consequences and the emotion involved. Yes, perhaps there will be negative consequences, but how drastic are they? Perhaps they are being exaggerated, but even if they are not, we can still think calmly and carefully and not let our emotions run away with us. Even recognizing that there could be negative consequences, we should still compare them to the positive consequences, and if we think about it, perhaps we could do something that will block the negative consequences from occurring. In the case of privatizing social security, perhaps we can mandate that everyone contribute to a retirement account, just not a government run one. This approach was basically the one adopted by President Obama in his healthcare insurance reform measures for healthcare. One might reject this approach for being unconstitutional, but that issue is still being resolved in the courts.

There is one type of appeal to fear that will be specifically mentioned. If an arguer tells you that you should believe or do something, because if you don't they will hurt you, you will likely feel some fear. In this case, the fallacy is specifically called an appeal to force, because the only reason to fear is that the arguer himself is threatening to use force against you, specifically and only because you refuse to accept his "argument".

Inappropriate Appeal to Tradition

One should realize that an appeal to tradition will rarely work with a fadophiliac, but most people do feel a sense that traditions should be maintained. Yet, a naked appeal to tradition, without any other considerations, should be recognized as fallacious.

One response to the question "why should we do something?" is simply "that's the way we've always done it." By itself, this hardly justifies any action rationally. This point is illustrated by the legend about the woman who always cut off the ends of a roast before she put it in the oven. When her husband asks her why she cuts off the ends, she says "that's the way my mom always used to do it." One day, the husband asks his mother-in-law why she cuts off the ends of the roast, and she responds, "The biggest pan we had wasn't large enough."

It is not appropriate to slavishly follow tradition when one doesn't understand the purpose behind it, although it probably also isn't appropriate to abandon a tradition just because one doesn't understand it. It can be appropriate to make an appeal to tradition, but in doing so, one will include information about the purpose of the act or policy, and what it intends to accomplish.

Inappropriate Appeal to Tolerance

In modern America, it seems as if the mere hint of a person being intolerant is sufficient to condemn him. As with naked appeals to tradition, a naked appeal to tolerance is also inappropriate. An inappropriate appeal to tolerance says that we should not condemn a particular person or act the person is committing solely because we should be tolerant of others. Recognizing an appeal to tolerance as fallacious does not mean that we don't value tolerance, but only that tolerance is not the only value we should have.

There are all sorts of things that we don't and *shouldn't* tolerate. We shouldn't tolerate stealing, or cheating, or murder. If the naked appeal to tolerance were enough to forbid any kind of condemnation, then we couldn't have any laws at all. There are of course actions which should not be tolerated, even ones that fall short of illegal. We shouldn't tolerate adultery, for example, or a husband berating his wife in public, or a parent abusing his children. Nor should we tolerate public officials groping their employees. Actually, we shouldn't tolerate anyone groping their employees, or abusing them in other ways.

We can certainly make an appeal to tolerance which is appropriate, but it must include other information, such as the claim that the action doesn't cause direct harm to other people, or that the objectionable action falls within the scope of actions protected by law. Even then it still may be appropriate to shun the person or action individually, although we would not be able to punish them or harm them through the enforcement of laws.

Inappropriate Appeal to Moderation

In many cases, moderation is called for. Moderation is when we avoid extremes and steer toward the middle ground. It can be a good idea to avoid extremes, but the naked appeal to moderation isn't enough to ground a decision to do so. When both extremes have negative consequences, then it can make sense to stake out a position in the middle (as long as that doesn't have worse consequences), but an appeal to moderation must include such information to be reasonable.

Compromise is a form of moderation, and it is often a good idea to compromise, but to just assert that people should compromise without looking at and considering the facts is not to be reasonable, but is actually unreasonable. There is a classic story about an ill-advised compromise which makes this point. A slave trader invades a woman's home and says that he is going to take both of her children and sell them into slavery. She pleads for him not to take any of her children. He says "I'll tell you what, let's compromise…"

In a situation where one cannot get everything that one wants, then it makes sense to give up on some of what you want to get some of what you want, but this just means that in some cases we will have to compromise. But one shouldn't just assume that compromise is the best option before considering the other possibilities. It doesn't make sense to reject conservatism and leftism just because they are the extremes and so think that the moderate ground is necessarily the best one.

Inappropriate Appeal to Ignorance

To simply assert that there is proof for one's point without citing any source is called a proof surrogate, while asserting that because there is a lack of proof and that therefore one's point is right is called the fallacy of appeal to ignorance. To say that it has been proven that 'x' is not the case (a proof surrogate), is not the same as saying that it has not been proven that 'x' is the case (an appeal to ignorance when this lack is used as justification for one's belief). People will often combine a proof surrogate with an appeal to ignorance, but they are conceptually different problems.

The mistake of an appeal to ignorance is that one believes that one has proven a fact by claiming that the fact has not been proven false. This thinking is poor reasoning when presented by itself, as one can always turn the tables. One can say that they will believe that the same statement is false because no one has ever proven that it is true. If there is no proof (or sufficient evidence) one way or the other, then there is no reason to believe either way.

The same point is often put this way: The absence of evidence is not evidence of absence. The lack of evidence is not evidence that something is not the case, nor that it is the case. What we want is evidence, one way or the other.

Although the claim that nothing has been proven by itself does not establish a conclusion, it can be part of a very strong argument. In general, if the burden of proof naturally falls on one side, or if the following conditions are met, then no fallacy occurs.

1) Experts have attempted to prove something
2) They have conducted extensive, well-thought research or experiments.
3) If they were right, we would expect the research to indicate it.
4) They have been unable to prove what they set out to prove.

Under these conditions, then we would be within reason to conclude that the concept or theory they set out to prove is mistaken. An example would be the luminiferous, or light-bearing, ether experiments of Michelson and Morley. They reasoned that if there were an ether, or physical medium for light, and the Earth were moving through it, then light would have different speeds depending on which direction it were headed. After extensive experiments, they were unable to find a difference, which eventually led to the rejection of the concept of an ether.

Here would be another example. Consider the claim that there are contradictions in the Bible. If there were contradictions in the Bible, we would expect that a careful reading would reveal it (barring considerations of vagueness and ambiguity). If experts had conducted a careful search, and they were unable to find any contradictions, then of course we would be entitled to conclude that there were no contradictions in the Bible. The point is that someone throwing out the claim that there are no contradictions because "no one has proved that there are" is completely lacking in justification. Of course, if someone says that there are contradictions, but cannot provide a single one, he is likely engaging in fallacious reasoning himself, although the species depends on exactly how he states the reason for that belief.

The other exception is when there is a burden of proof placed on one side. In general, this occurs in American courts of law, where the burden of proof is placed on the prosecution, so that should the prosecutor fail to make a case, we do not just assume guilt (which we could decide to alter our jury system to do—imagine how awful it would be to have the burden of proof on the accused), we assume that for the sake of punishment the accused person is found not guilty. Another case is that of extraordinary claims. Should I claim that I can jump over a building, and you doubt it, you are perfectly reasonable to reject my claim, even without strong "proof" either way, simply because it is an extraordinary claim. For me to attack you by saying that you are committing an appeal to ignorance in this case would be unreasonable. See also the fallacy of misplaced burden of proof in the next chapter.

Ad Populum (Appeal to the People)

We will see two basic forms of *ad populum* fallacy. One appeals to our desire to be like others, and the other appeals to our desire to stand out from others. Most of us have both of these conflicting desires in varying degrees, sometimes simultaneously. In both cases, we are relying on the claim that other people accept some claim, and so the audience should, too.

The first variety, which depends on a desire to fit in with people in general, is called the bandwagon fallacy. An argument which claims that you should adopt a viewpoint because *everyone* else accepts it, or even that most people accept it, commits the bandwagon fallacy. In past political campaigns, a candidate would hire a wagon full of musicians which would ride through town. People would "jump on the bandwagon", which came to mean accepting a viewpoint merely because it is popular.

The bandwagon fallacy is similar to peer pressure, albeit peer pressure is generally exerted by one's own friends or cohorts. It is also called the fallacy of common practice when it is used to attempt to justify some questionable action. "It's okay for me to do something because everyone else is doing it."

The second basic variety of *ad populum* is Snob Appeal. In this case, the persuasive force does not depend on our desire to fit in with everyone, but some specific group which is considered special, or better, than others. It convinces someone that if they want to be admired, or even envied, by the masses, then one should accept some view or use some product. Advertisements quite often make snob appeals, usually for expensive products, as in an ad for Directv ("Opulence, I has it" said with a thick Russian accent) and the ones for Dos Equis ("The Most Interesting Man in the World").

In all cases of the *ad populum* fallacy, there is no additional reason to believe that the group in question has any expertise or knowledge. If we had any reason to hold that the group in question did have more experience or background, or anything which would give them some kind of expertise, then no fallacy would have been committed.

False Dilemma

A false dilemma takes the form of a disjunctive syllogism. As we have seen, disjunctive syllogisms are valid, but in the case of a false dilemma the connection between premises and conclusion is not in question, but rather the truth of one of the premises. Although most fallacies involve the relevance between the premises and conclusion, in a false dilemma the issue is the truth of one of the premises. This mistake in reasoning is so clearly definable, though, that it has come to be known as fallacious. In a disjunctive syllogism there are two premises, one which is disjunctive, and one which negates one of the disjuncts. In the fallacy of false dilemma, the disjunctive premise is false.

For example, one could argue that one should vote for the Republican candidate, because the Democratic candidate is incompetent. This argument depends on the disjunctive statement that one must vote for either the Republican or Democratic candidate. This premise is false because there are other candidates for which one could vote, and in fact, one could refuse to vote for any candidate altogether. It doesn't spoil one's ballot if one leaves a race blank.

Keep in mind that an argument does not commit a false dilemma if the disjunctive premise is actually true. It is only when one can recognize a third possibility not countenanced in the disjunction that the fallacy is committed. So, in the argument below, there is no fallacy of false dilemma. Is the argument still sound?

> Every natural number is either prime or composite. The number 437 is not composite, therefore it is prime.

Begging the Question

The name "Begging the Question" is a bad translation of "*Petitio Principii*," which is the Latin name for the fallacy we will cover next. We will consider two forms of the fallacy. A better translation of *Petitio Principii* might be a Request for First Principles, which brings us to the first variety of question begging, which is also called circular reasoning.

In an argument where the conclusion is presented as one of the premises, the argument reasons in a circle. Often the circularity is concealed by the use of synonymous language, even when only one premise is given, as in this example: We know that all Americans support freedom of speech, since anyone who didn't believe in the right to express oneself would not be an American. In this argument, the conclusion really says nothing more than the premise does, but someone who is not reasoning carefully may come to believe that the conclusion has been supported in some way.

What we were looking for was an independent reason to believe the conclusion, or a principle which comes prior to the conclusion stated. In an argument which is circular, there is lacking such a prior principle. Even when there are more steps to the argument, as is often the case, an independent reason to enter the circle at any point is required.

The classic example of such an instance is using scriptures in a simple way in order to establish the existence of God. The argument concludes that God exists, and that we know that God exists, because it says in scriptures that God exists, and since the scriptures were written by God, they are completely reliable. The claim that the scriptures were written by God would not be accepted by anyone unless he already accepted the conclusion. Inherently, the reader has not been given a reason to accept the conclusion unless he already accepts the conclusion. What we need is an independent reason to establish the conclusion.

It should be noted that an argument which is circular is a valid argument, at least when every assumption is made clear. Whether there is one step, or more than one, the conclusion does follow from the given premises. Let's exhibit the argument in standard symbolic form.

1) A	1) A
2) ∴ A	2) ∴ B
	3) ∴ C
	4) ∴ D
	5) ∴ A

In either case, the truth of the given premise, A, will guarantee the truth of the conclusion, A. So, the argument is technically valid. It fails to actually provide an independent reason to accept the conclusion, however, and so is considered fallacious. Note that we use the same letter for the premise and conclusion in the first argument form. We do this because the two statements mean the same thing, and so it would be inappropriate to mask that fact by using different letters.

The next kind of begging the question fallacy is exhibited in the following argument:

> The massive emission of carbon dioxide by human industry is causing global warming, Therefore, we should try to reduce our use of such industries.

It may be difficult to see the question-begging here, because for many it is so natural to think that the premises do guarantee the conclusion. Yet, it is important to realize that this argument assumes that we do not want global warming, and that we should reduce it as much as possible. Anyone who rejected the conclusion would probably not accept the truth of this implicit assumption. As such, the argument can be said to commit the fallacy of begging the question, but only by someone who rejected the implicit assumption. Both sides can agree that there is a missing premise; that much is not in dispute. The issue, however, is the underlying hidden premise. A resolution of the current issue depends upon the resolution of the issue regarding the missing premise.

Even here, we can say that the argument is technically valid. Certainly the argument is invalid without the implicit assumption that we should reduce global warming, but it is would be unreasonable not to include this assumption, as it is clearly being relied upon, as is the assumption that we have no other way to reduce global warming. The full argument is as follows:

1) The massive emission of carbon dioxide by human industry is causing global warming.
2) We should reduce global warming.
3) The only way to reduce global warming is to reduce our use of industries which emit carbon dioxide.

---

4) ∴ We should reduce our use of industries which emit carbon dioxide.

The argument as standardized is valid, and this is arguably the only way the original argument can be understood. Once we articulate the argument in this fashion, we can see that someone could still accept the stated premise, but think that the conclusion is not established, not because the argument as fully articulated is invalid, but because he disagrees with one of the assumed premises.

People often leave essential premises out of their arguments, usually because they just assume them to be true without reflection. They think such premises are so obvious that they don't need to be stated. Generally, if they are actually true, then we will simply include them as missing premises and consider the argument to be sound. If they are not true, or if they are in serious question or have just as much controversy surrounding them as the conclusion does, then we will say that the argument commits a begging the question fallacy.

One might note that often the phrase "begs the question" is used to mean nothing more that "raises the question". This usage is no doubt the result of a little intelligence being a dangerous thing and people wanting to make themselves sound more astute.

Perfectionist Fallacy

The advice to "never let the perfect be the enemy of the good" is the motivational idea behind the perfectionist fallacy. One commits a perfectionist fallacy when one says that unless we can achieve a perfect situation, we shouldn't do anything. Technically, a perfectionist fallacy can be construed as a false dilemma, but in some cases it just fits so...perfectly.

To argue that we should abolish the death penalty because it doesn't work—it hasn't stopped murders from occurring—would be an example of a perfectionist fallacy. Although the premise is true, it assumes that we shouldn't continue using the death penalty unless it could eliminate all murders. It could very well be that the death penalty prevents some murders, and certainly it is better to prevent some murders than not to prevent any at all.

(This argument also begs the question that deterrence is the only reason for punishment, but commits a perfectionist fallacy even if that questionable premise is granted).

Note that this argument, if valid, could be applied to all forms of punishment, but it is unreasonable to conclude that we should thus eliminate all forms of punishment. Putting people in prison has not prevented all crimes from occurring, but we should still put criminals in prison, presumably. We should not keep ourselves from achieving some good by holding out for the perfect. To do so often leaves us with neither.

Line-Drawing Fallacy

Consider the following two statements:

1) A person with only one dollar is not rich.
2) If a person is not rich, then the fact that he had another dollar would not make him rich.

Both of these statements seem plausible, and from them we could conclude that a person with two dollars is not rich. Notice, though, that we could then add the second statement to our new statement to support the conclusion that a person with three dollars is not rich. One might think that this conclusion is unproblematic, but it would seem that we could continue the argument ad infinitum, or at least indefinitely, so that we could eventually obtain the conclusion that a person with one million dollars is not rich, which would be absurd.

The issue here seems to involve vague predicates. Any time we have such a vague predicate, there is the potential for a line-drawing fallacy. What is the precise dividing line between someone who is rich and someone who is poor? There doesn't seem to be any. One might respond that there is a middle ground between rich and poor, which we will call being in the middle class. This fact, however, only complicates the issue even more. Now, we have two places which call for lines, where we only had one before! After all, we can ask what the precise dividing line is between poor and middle class, as well as between middle class and rich.

That such arguments are invalid is not at issue, but exactly what the metaphysical reason for it is in dispute. In any case, when we have vague predicates, it suffices to combat a line-drawing fallacy by recognizing it, and arguing that even though there is no precise dividing line, there is a difference in kind between the two extremes and not merely a difference in degree.

For example, someone might argue that the day before a person turns twenty-one, he or she is no different from the day he turns twenty-one, and so should still be allowed to drink alcohol, and by a similar process of reasoning, eventually we could get to the conclusion that any child should be allowed to drink alcohol. To combat the argument, one would point out that although there is a gradual change that takes place in maturing, a child is different from an adult in significant enough ways to mark them as distinct. One could point out that alcohol might affect one's growth, and that in that regard, a twenty-one year old has reached the extent of their growth, at least physically. One could also point out that twenty-one year olds have reached a level of maturity where we hold them responsible for their actions, whereas we don't think children have reached that level of maturity.

One could still bicker about where exactly the line should be drawn, as it was in the case of voting, until the voting age was lowered to eighteen. Yet, it is still reasonable to think that there is generally an important difference between adults and children, even if there is no precise point at which a child turns into an adult.

Red Herring

Imagine you are training a bloodhound. You teach him to follow a scent trail, and then to test his ability, you drag a salty, smelly, cured fish (a red herring) across the trail of the scent. If the bloodhound turns from the scent and instead follows the red herring, he obviously was not trained very well or else was not attentive to his task.

In reasoning, a red herring is a side-track: a topic introduced as if it addresses an issue, but really distracts attention from that issue. It is always permissible to switch topics, but to do so in a sneaky, underhanded way which appears as if one is addressing the main issue is to throw out a red herring. An inattentive audience will often fall for it, but only by reasoning poorly. When the arguer himself has no idea that he has moved on to a logically irrelevant side issue, the mistake in reasoning is even more egregious.

Consider the argument in the following passage:

> I'll tell you why I think aliens are visiting Earth. The universe is incredibly vast, approaching infinite. There are millions of stars just in our galaxy, and billions of other galaxies in the universe. It seems like most every star we have the technology to examine has at least one planet. It seems likely that a great number of those planets will be within the habitable range from their planets, and it is completely unreasonable to think that with all those millions upon millions of planets where life could possibly evolve, it occurred on only one of those planets.

The original issue appears to be whether aliens are visiting the Earth. This arguer has not addressed that issue, but instead side-stepped it by addressing the question of whether there is life at some other point in the universe. It is true that aliens cannot be visiting Earth if they don't exist, but if someone thinks they have offered a reason to believe that aliens are visiting the Earth because they have argued that life exists at other places in the universe, they are fooling themselves.

If someone else doesn't recognize that the original issue has gone unsupported, then he has been distracted by a red herring. If you haven't already heard someone call out a red herring in a debate or argument, you will. It is one of the most common fallacies, as well as the one which with most people have heard and can diagnose.

Non Sequitur/Jumping to Conclusions

A *non sequitur* is a conclusion which simply doesn't follow from the given premise. In Latin, *non sequitur* means "it does not follow", and that is basically what it means in English. A *non sequitur* often refers specifically to the conclusion which is purported to follow from premises which can in no way support it. A person who asserts a *non sequitur* is said to be "jumping to conclusions", although a non-sequitur often involves an even larger jump than usual.

The traditional Latin name for a similar fallacy is *ignoratio elenchi*, which roughly translates to ignorance of refutation. The exact taxonomy of this fallacy, and several others, including irrelevant conclusion, missing the point, and even red herring, have inspired some debate among logicians, and every student is encouraged to explore it, but it is a bit technical for the average beginning logic student.

We will say here that in a *non sequitur* fallacy, there must always be a conclusion drawn from some premises which do not support it, often in a grossly obvious way. In a Red Herring fallacy, it is not necessary that the distraction offered be in the form of premises; it can be any kind of information. A *non sequitur* in a logical sense always involves an inference, although a bad one.

In ordinary language, however, sometimes the phrase is used more loosely, and refers to any statement that comes "out of left field". If someone is talking about politics, and someone throws out some information about what he ate for breakfast, one might sheepishly say "that was a *non sequitur*." This use of the term is not fallacious, as no argument was being presented.

Technically, most any fallacy can be said to be a *non sequitur*. After all, every fallacy fails to follow from the premises given in support of it; Begging the Question and False Dilemma being notable exceptions. It is de rigueur, however, to only describe an argument as being a *non sequitur* when it doesn't fit any other common fallacy type.

Accent

The last few fallacies we cover in this chapter are fallacies of ambiguity. We could with some reason include these fallacies in the next chapter, as disputational fallacies. Many times the reason the ambiguity is fallacious is because it is one person misunderstanding what another person has said. But there are far too many cases where a single person can fall prey to the ambiguity of language on his own for us to treat them as only disputational fallacies, especially equivocation, composition and division.

The fallacy of accent is in fact often applied in cases where no mistaken reasoning has yet occurred, and so could even be placed as a rhetorical pitfall, but, again, it made some sense to put all the issues involving ambiguity together in the same section. Technically the fallacy of accent occurs when someone mistakenly inferred some conclusion because of the way information is presented and the emphasis placed on parts of it.

As an example, consider this announcement:

You have won $10,000! if you send in this ticket
and it matches the number on file.

If someone reads this announcement and thinks that he has won $10,000, he has fallen victim to the fallacy of accent. There may be millions of people who got the announcement, but only one ticket that matches the number on file (let's assume the sender is not completely corrupt). One should always read the fine print.

Another case where this fallacy might occur is in the subtleties of vocal expression. It might be difficult to really understand this point in written form, but we will try. Imagine someone says "Don't tell your friend lies". How is this statement to be understood? In written form, it seems so dry and clear; don't tell your friend lies. When spoken, however, the sentence can take on multiple meanings. Imagine that we stress the word tell: "Don't *tell* your friend lies." With a certain inflection, this sentence may seem like it is offering permission to text your friend lies, just don't *tell* them lies. Similarly, different nuances of meaning can be suggested by emphasizing different words.

Don't tell *your* friend lies: because your friend is nice, but lie to mine.
Don't tell your *friend* lies: but lie to everyone else.
Don't tell your friend *lies*: but fudging the truth and fallacies are okay.

This statement is ambiguous in that it can be interpreted many ways, depending on how and what is being stressed or accentuated. It is fallacious to interpret an ambiguous statement in a way in which it wasn't intended, and when one draws faulty conclusions from it, the fallacy of accent has been committed.

One other common way the fallacy is committed is by out of context quotes. The context does not always need to be provided for every quote, but in some cases, words can be taken out of context in a way which is completely manipulative. Technically, one cannot be sure that there is any fallacious reasoning being fostered unless one knows the original context, but any time the context for a quote is missing, one should be wary of a potential accent fallacy.

For example, a Presidential candidate declares "My opponent said 'we should go to war,' that's a direct quote." Obviously, people will draw all sorts of conclusions from this assertion, but if the original statement was "If they attack us, then we should go to war," then those conclusions are all fallaciously drawn. It is rare for a misquote to be as manipulative as in this example, but sometimes the more subtle examples can do more damage, as they can be much more difficult to fully refute.

Equivocation

The fallacy of equivocation always involves semantic ambiguity, which is when a single word or term can have more than one meaning. When a single word is used with two different meanings in an argument, then the argument commits the fallacy of equivocation. The word "cold" when applied to a person can mean either having a low temperature, or being distant. An argument equivocates if it uses the word with one meaning in a premise, but a different meaning elsewhere in the argument.

Here is a simple example. Everything that runs has legs, and all rivers run, thus all rivers have legs. The word "run" is being equivocated in this example. In one sense, it means a form of animal locomotion, and it the other it simply means moving or flowing. Notice that if we just formalized the argument and used R for running, we might symbolize the argument in such a way that it is valid. The problem is not a formal one, but a conceptual one, which is why equivocation is an informal fallacy.

As one may have guessed, puns are basically humorous examples of equivocation. At least they are intended that way. Here is one: "Did you hear about the crime that occurred in the parking garage? It was wrong on so many levels." You'll have to decide for yourself whether the humorous intention was achieved.

Amphiboly

The fallacy of amphiboly also depends on ambiguity, but in this case it is an ambiguity in sentence structure or grammar. Unfortunately, people don't always speak clearly, and when their ambiguous sentences are misinterpreted so that a different meaning is understood than was intended, an amphiboly is bound to occur.

Someone might say "I saw that my house was on fire, so I grabbed my dog and then sprayed it with the hose." It would seem odd that someone would spray his dog with a hose when his house was on fire. Presumably, the speaker meant that he was spraying the house, but the way it is stated seems to indicate that he was spraying the dog. In this case, the issue is pronoun agreement, which is a grammatical issue.

One way to distinguish equivocation from amphiboly is to see whether the sentence can be disambiguated by replacing a single word with a synonymous word. If so, then there is a potential equivocation. If the only way to disambiguate the sentence is to reword the sentence, then you are dealing with a potential amphiboly.

Dangling modifiers are also common ways for an amphiboly to come about. Consider this wanted ad:

> Wanted: Someone to take care of a cow that doesn't smoke or drink.

The adjectival phrase "that doesn't smoke or drink" most likely should be modifiying "someone", but in this sentence it looks like it is modifying "cow". I should hope that the cow doesn't smoke or drink.

Amphiboly can be difficult for some students to diagnose. It is easy to get locked into a certain reading, and not consider alternative meanings. Learning more about grammar and how language works will help, as will becoming familiar with rhetorical pitfalls and fallacies in general.

Composition

Individuals have properties, but so do groups. Sometimes the properties of the individuals can be transferred to the whole group, but not always. For example, if every thread in a shirt is blue, then the shirt is blue. This inference is reasonable. It does not follow, however, to say that a shirt is long because every thread in the shirt is long. This argument commits the fallacy of composition.

The fallacy of composition occurs when someone transfers a property from the parts of a thing to the whole thing for a property which does not transfer in this way. Thinking that someone's backyard is square based on the fact that it is composed of many tiles, each one of which is square, is to commit a composition fallacy. The property of being square can be true of the parts of a thing, but not be true of the whole.

It is easy to confuse the fallacy of composition with hasty generalization. Remember that in a hasty generalization, we are taking a sample of the members of a group, and deriving a conclusion about each of the members of the group. We are not saying anything about the group as a group. In composition, one argues that because each of the members of a group has a certain property, then the group itself must have that same property.

For example, saying that I tried one tomato, and so I would like all tomatoes, is a hasty generalization. To say that "I like tomatoes, and I like ice cream, and therefore I would like tomatoes on top of my ice cream," would be a composition fallacy, and horribly so.

Division

Division is simply the opposite of composition. In division, one concludes something about the parts of a thing, based upon a property of the entire thing as a whole. When we say that a person must be over 300 years old because he belongs to a society which is older than 300 years old, we are committing the fallacy of division.

We must emphasize that some properties do transfer from whole to parts. The fact that an object has mass indicates that the things which make up the object (atoms), also have mass. But to say that an object is visible to humans does not indicate that atoms are visible. The property of mass does transfer from whole to parts, but the property of visibility does not, or at least not always.

If one is unsure whether an argument is committing division or composition, one need only determine what the conclusion of the argument is. If the conclusion regards the parts, then the argument potentially commits a division fallacy. If the conclusion is about the whole, then a composition fallacy must be considered.

Chapter Twenty-Five Exercises

Determine which fallacy or fallacies, if any, are committed in each of the following passages. Unless you think it is totally obvious, you should also provide a sentence or two defending your judgment.

Basic Concept Exercises

1. A dog eats more than an insect, so all dogs eat more than all insects.
2. Of course you should buy a life insurance policy! Why shouldn't you?
3. We know Chinese green tea is good for you because if it weren't, how could it be so beneficial to drink it?
4. We have a simple choice. Saving Social Security is a lot more important than giving people a tax cut. So write your representative now and let him or her know how you feel.
5. One union member has little political power, so a whole union has little political power.
6. I've come before you to ask that you rehire Professor Johnson. I realize that Mr. Johnson does not have a Ph.D., and I am aware that he has yet to publish his first article. But Mr. Johnson is over forty now, and he has a wife and two high-school aged children to support. It will be very difficult for him to find another job at his age, I'm sure you will agree.
7. The Ayatollah speaks truly because he is not a man who would ever lie.
8. If you don't believe what I believe, you'll go to hell, where the fire is not quenched and the worm dieth not.
9. Dear Editor—If Christians do not participate in government, only sinners will.
10. Year round schools? I'm opposed. Once we let them do that, there's nowhere to draw the line. The next thing you know they'll be cutting into our vacation time and asking us to teach in the evenings and on weekends and who knows where it will end. We teachers have to stand up for our rights.

Intermediate Exercises

11. You say that smoking causes all these diseases. But people are mortal. Wars kill lots of people. We should be trying to stop wars.
12. I was once engaged to a wonderful man, but when I found out he had a wooden leg, I had to break it off.
13. The argument we are analyzing is unsound, because we don't know whether the premise is true or false.
14. "Are you saying that I'm crazy?"—"I would never *say* that you're crazy."
15. Did you know that over 93% of the entire world's population believes in some kind of God? I'd say that's a pretty strong consensus.
16. A poll shows that overall, 90% of black people think President Obama is doing a good job. So, if you're black, you should be about 90% on Obama's side yourself.
17. There no reason for me to take a reasoning class unless I'm going to get an A.

18. It takes a lot of time and effort to write a textbook. Obviously, you'd have to be very smart in order to accomplish it.
19. I am totally against gay marriage. We have never allowed it before, not even before we achieved our own independence.
20. I hate it when people treat homosexuals poorly. We should be open to things that are different. Something isn't wrong just because it's new or different.

Challenging exercises

21. I believe that the mind and the brain are different, because the brain is a physical thing, and the mind is not a physical thing.
22. I heard that poor people are having a hard time paying their medical bills. We should use government money to help them out.
23. It's just silly to think that the mainstream media have a liberal bias. They have a sensationalistic bias and a commercial bias.
24. The Democrats say we should raise taxes, and the Republicans say we should lower spending. I don't see why we don't just split the difference and do a little bit of both.
25. They said on the radio that if we increase taxes on the ultra-rich, it will bring in 100 billion dollars, which would reduce the deficit by 20%. That means that we should have a balanced budget in a mere five years.
26. We know that the Bible is unreliable, because it was written by men, and not God.
27. My brother says that organic food is better than non-organic food, but he's an idiot. There's no such thing as non-organic food; everything we eat is organic.
28. I can't believe my brother. He said that he was breeding chickens and pigs. I think that's totally immoral to try to mess with nature like that.
29. I don't understand why the Republicans would concede to raising the debt limit. They generally support having a balanced budget. If the government can't borrow any more money that doesn't mean the government can't spend at all, but it can only spend what it takes in. So, refusing to raise the debt limit is in effect forcing the government to operate a balanced budget.
30. Our Constitution was a completely racist document. It held that a black person was only worth three-fifths as much as a white person.

In-Context Exercises

In his essay "Utilitarianism", John Stuart Mill makes the following argument:

The only proof capable of being given that an object is visible, is that people actually see it. The only proof that a sound is audible, is that people hear it: and so of the other sources of our experience. In like manner, I apprehend, the sole evidence it is possible to produce that anything is desirable, is that people do actually desire it. If the end which the utilitarian doctrine proposes to itself were not, in theory and in practice, acknowledged to be an end, nothing could ever convince any person that it was so. No reason can be given why the general happiness is desirable, except that each person, so far as he believes it to be attainable, desires his own happiness.[7]

G. E. Moore accuses Mill of equivocating in his *Principia Ethica*, where he says:

> The first step by which Mill has attempted to establish his Hedonism [which is the view that happiness is the only intrinsic good] is simply fallacious. He has attempted to establish the identity of the good with the desired, by confusing the proper sense of "desirable," in which it denotes that which it is good to desire, with the sense which it would bear if it were analogous to such words as "visible." If "desirable" is to be identical with "good," then it must bear one sense; and if it is to be identical with "desired," then it must bear quite another sense. And yet to Mill's contention that the desired is necessarily good, it is quite essential that these two senses of "desirable" should be the same.[8]

Do you agree with Moore that Mill is equivocating?

Logic Puzzle

Dr. Loki states that Logic begins with an 'L' and ends with an 'e'. Is there any possible way he can be right?

---

[7] John Stuart Mill, *Utilitarianism*, Hackett, Indianapolis, 1979, p. 34, originally published 1861.

[8] G. E. Moore, *Principia Ethica*, Cambridge University Press, London, 1903, pp. 67-68.

CHAPTER

26

Disputational Fallacies

In the previous chapter, we learned a bit about several argumentative fallacies. What distinguishes them from the fallacies in this chapter is that argumentative fallacies can occur in a single argument presented by a single person. Disputational fallacies, on the other hand, only occur in the context of a debate, or disputation. When people are debating an issue, there are a few more fallacies which can also be committed and/or identified.

Skill 26.1

Recognizing Disputational Fallacies

Skill 26.2

Avoiding Disputational Fallacies in One's Own Thinking and Writing

Ad Hominem Abusive

When someone offers a position, whether they defend it or not, we can respond reasonably by criticizing the position, or the argument presented to support it. If instead we aim our criticism toward the person, we are committing an *ad hominem* fallacy. An *ad hominem* abusive is a straightforward personal attack.

Technically, no fallacy is committed unless one thinks that the attack does anything to show that the position or conclusion is false. Consider the following dispute:

Ricky: I think Fidel Castro should release all of Cuba's political prisoners.
Lucy: I think you're an idiot.

Whether Lucy's comment counts as *ad hominem* fallacy depends on what she meant. If she meant that Ricky has an indefensible position, and therefore he is an idiot, she hasn't engaged in an *ad hominem*. It may not be nice, and she can be accused of begging the question, since she hasn't independently defended her premise, but her personal attack is not an *ad hominem*. If her thought is the other way around, so that she is concluding that Ricky's position is mistaken *because* he is an idiot, then she has committed an *ad hominem* fallacy.

Disputational Fallacy
A fallacy which generally occurs in a dispute; multiple arguers are required

In the real world, it may be very difficult to distinguish exactly what is meant, especially when there is another audience to the debate. For this reason, any personal attack launched during a debate is likely to be classified as an *ad hominem* fallacy unless the person making it states clearly that they do not intend for people to draw the conclusion they are likely to draw.

Ad Hominem Circumstantial

An *ad hominem* circumstantial is also an attack on the arguer or person and not what he is saying. The difference is that a circumstantial *ad hominem* is not just a straightforward attack on the person's intelligence or character. Instead, it holds that the person's viewpoints are mistaken because of the person's circumstances or situation, often because they stand to gain should their viewpoint be correct.

Here is an example of a fallacious *ad hominem* circumstantial:

Melanie: I think that women should be paid just the same as men.
Tony: You would think that way; you're a woman.

If Tony thinks he has undermined Melanie's position, or justified his disagreement, he is reasoning poorly. Notice, though, that it is not a personal attack to call someone a woman. There is nothing wrong with being a woman, and it is not a personal attack. But Tony is using the fact that Melanie is a woman to dismiss or delegitimize her viewpoint.

There is a fine line between recognizing an arguer of committing an *ad hominem* circumstantial and committing the fallacy of inappropriate authority oneself. Recall that relying on an expert when that expert has some kind of bias is to commit an appeal to inappropriate authority, yet dismissing a person's view because of that person's bias commits an *ad hominem* circumstantial. These positions may seem inconsistent, but they are not.

Recall that in an argument from authority, we are treating someone as an expert, such that we recognize that their credibility on an issue is elevated from others without any expertise. If it is revealed that they have some kind of bias, such that they might stand to profit from the truth of their assertions, it would be inappropriate to continue treating them as an expert upon whom one will simply rely.

The fact that an expert has some bias *does* mean that we should not simply accept what she says, as we might with an unbiased expert. It *does not* mean, however, that we can summarily dismiss what she says either, nor does it imply that what she says is necessarily false, or even likely to be false. In order to undermine her argument, we need to find a flaw in it, and if we want to show that her conclusion is false, we need to bring some evidence or reasoning of our own to the debate.

Tu Quoque

While I wrote the first version of this textbook, there was a substantial ongoing controversy involving raising the debt limit for the United States. The issue was postponed by passing a continuing resolution with a small increase, which means we will probably face the issue many times in the future. If the debt limit is not raised when we reach it, then the United States won't legally be able to borrow any more money, which could have disastrous consequences. Of course, all of the borrowing and spending beyond revenue can have disastrous consequences as well.

In any case, President Obama is strongly behind raising the debt ceiling. Yet, right-leaning commentators are wont to point out that when President Obama was a Senator, he voted *against* raising the debt ceiling. The question is, what this information is supposed to imply. If it is a subtle innuendo that we should not now raise the debt ceiling because President Obama has taken both positions, then it is a *tu quoque* fallacy.

Tu quoque can be translated as "You, too", and it has come to mean pointing out an opponent's hypocrisy as if one is providing reasons in support of one's position. The fact that Barack Obama once was opposed to raising the debt limit should not be used as evidence that we shouldn't support the raise, unless we want to consider him an expert, in which case we should probably accept what he is telling us now. The fact of the matter is that someone's hypocrisy, inconsistency, or switching of their position should not be used as evidence for or against the issue, we need independent reasons to make a decision.

If one only wants to point out the Barack Obama had a different position in the past, but not as support for one's own position, then there is no *tu quoque* fallacy, but often it is difficult to tell. Don't immediately assume either that because some right-leaning commentator intimates that Barack Obama is a hypocrite that it is true (what fallacy would that be?). It could be that the situations are significantly different, such that at the time the best view was not to raise the limit, but that now we should. We shouldn't make a judgment in that regard unless we did at least a little research.

Poisoning the Well

The forms of *ad hominem* about which we have been learning require a person to actually have a position, or to have made an argument. Poisoning the well can be considered an *ad hominem* in advance. Personally attacking a person before they have even opened their mouths can be quite effective, but a critical thinker will avoid prejudging what a person has to say just because they have been smeared beforehand.

Remember that there is no poisoning the well occurring unless there is an anticipation that someone will be making an argument or staking out a position. It is the attempt to poison's one mind against any argument that makes poisoning the well fallacious.

So, if you said that you just subscribed to the Long Beach News of the World, and I said "Don't read that tabloid piece of junk", my comment would be an attempt at poisoning the well. I could, however, calmly explain that I had seen the newspaper, and that my judgment of their credibility was low, and that would not qualify as poisoning the well. Just keep in mind that a critical thinker will generally want to see the source for themselves before they make any final judgment.

Genetic Fallacy

The genesis of something is its origin, and the genetic fallacy is to reject a view because of where it originated. In that sense, the genetic fallacy is similar to an *ad hominem* fallacy. The difference, however, is that in a genetic fallacy one is relying on a pre-existing negative attitude, whereas in an *ad hominem* fallacy, one is attempting to create the negative attitude.

There are always plenty of people or groups which will have a pre-existing negative association for most people: Nazis, communists, racists, murderers. These groups generally deserve the negative association people have for them, but that is not the issue. The point is that even a person or group who deserves a bad reputation for something can have a decent position or argument in another area. Hitler is famous for treating his dogs well, but that is no reason for us to treat dogs poorly.

Here is an argument which commits the genetic fallacy:

> We should stop trying to confiscate people's guns; that's what the Nazi's did!

I would agree that we should not confiscate law-abiding citizen's guns, but not because the Nazi's did it. After all, they made sure the trains ran on time, and did lots of other things that we should continue doing. We don't need to drag in the Nazi's to make our case, if we really have a case. We shouldn't confiscate people's guns because people have the right to have guns, as recognized in the Second Amendment. Should anyone complain that we are begging the question, we can point out that guns are useful in self-defense from criminals and from tyrannical governments which might try to violate people's rights. Whether people agree with this point or not, it is still actually making a case for the conclusion, and not just trying to associate the opposite conclusion with people of whom our audience will disapprove.

Straw Man

Imagine that you must fight against a famous boxer, let's say Muhammad Ali in his prime. You've got two choices. You can either fight the real boxer, or you can step into the ring with a cardboard cutout of Muhammad Ali. It makes sense from a prudential point of view to fight the cardboard cutout—it's much easier to beat up.

Think of a straw man as a kind of scarecrow—a dummy or cardboard cutout, which is easy to beat on and win. In the realm of reasoning, a straw man is a distorted version of an opponent's argument, one which is easier to defeat. Instead of presenting the argument or position in an accurate way, a person presenting a straw man argument is stating their opponent's argument in a simplified, exaggerated or extreme way, so that it sounds ridiculous or inane. It is considered very bad form.

"Did you hear that the Republicans were trying to destroy Medicare?" They were not, of course, but only trying to modify it in order to extend its solvency. Yet, presenting their viewpoint in an extreme fashion will easily push people who don't think carefully into opposing the Republicans plan, without even really knowing what it is. There may be reasons to oppose the Republican plan, but one should oppose the actual plan of the Republicans. Most people are opposed to the deceitful straw man argument portrayed above as the Republican plan, even the Republicans.

Good critical thinkers are not interested in winning an argument. What they care about is finding out which viewpoints have the best arguments behind them, even if they are someone else's. This goal cannot be met unless we are willing to confront the actual arguments our opponents make. A confident critical thinker will even strengthen his opponent's argument when possible.

Shifting Ground/Definitional Sulk

Although shifting ground may not strictly be a single fallacy, it is a strong indicator of poor reasoning. In general, when a person commits a fallacy in their reasoning, it is appropriate to continue reasoning with that person. Point out what you think is fallacious in someone's reasoning, and see how the person responds. Should the person consider your criticism and either defend his view, point out how you are mistaken, accept your view, or try to find some middle ground, then it is perfectly appropriate to continue the conversation.

On the other hand, if the person continues on as if you hadn't said anything, or switches topics without acting as if your point had mattered, then you probably should get the heck out of dodge. If the person shifts their view around, so that no criticism you make seems to hit home, then you probably won't gain anything by continuing in the conversation. It is the response of a person who doesn't know much about what they are discussing, and who doesn't much care. There is little point in debating such a person, unless one wants to test the limits of one's patience.

The following interchange exemplifies the fallacy:

> Thuong: It was such a colossal waste of time for us to invade Iraq, and it just made everyone in the world hate America.
>
> Julio: Really, I thought there was good reason for the invasion.
>
> Thoung: That's ridiculous. The whole justification for the war was that there were WMD's, and there weren't any. I'd say that is pretty much case closed.
>
> Julio: I don't know, I recall that George W. Bush said that even if Iraq and Hussein were not an imminent threat, which would be the case if he had no

> WMD's, that we could not wait for him to become an imminent threat. It seems perfectly clear that Bush contemplated the possibility that there were no WMD's, but judged that we should still invade anyway.
>
> Thuong: Bush couldn't even spell the word "contemplate" much less engage in it.
>
> Julio: Okay...that's...funny, I guess, but what about the point?
>
> Thuong: No one ever found any WMD's, so that just proves that we shouldn't have gone in.
>
> Julio: But that's a bit of a distortion. There were no stockpiles of usable WMD's, that's true, but there was plenty of evidence that he had WMD's at one point and had a program in place to try to reconstitute them as soon as he could.
>
> Thuong: Bush was just trying to get revenge because Saddam Hussein embarrassed his daddy.
>
> Julio: Wasn't part of the justification for the Iraq war the fact that Hussein's armies were continually firing missiles at our airplanes?
>
> Thuong: But he never hit one!
>
> Julio: So we should allow our enemy to try to kill our military members, until he actually succeeds, before we can invade?
>
> Thuong: Why is it that Republicans always want to solve problems by using the military?
>
> Julio: What does that have to do with anything? I'm not even a Republican!

I think Julio did an admirable job keeping his cool. It was pretty clear that Thuong wasn't really interested in finding out whether we were justified in invading Iraq. He had already made his mind up, and wasn't going to let any reasons get in the way. It is probably a good idea for Julio to stop trying to reason through the issue, at least with Thuong.

A person engaging in shifting ground will not defend their assertions, but will just keep throwing new thoughts out, whether they are relevant or not. One might think of the shifting ground fallacy as a series of red herrings, but each step need not count as a red herring. It just needs to be the case that they continually jump to something new without really considering either their own points or the points of their conversational partner.

One particular form of shifting ground, although brief, is the definitional sulk. To sulk is to retreat into one's own mood. A definitional sulk is also a retreat in a way which is careless. Here is a simple example:

> Mitt: The hallmark of being a Republican is being against abortion.
>
> Rudy: I know a Republican who is pro-choice.
>
> Mitt: Well, then, he's just not a real Republican.

If a property is truly definitional, then it can admit of no exceptions: That is what it means to be a definition. In defining a word, one is capturing the meaning of the word itself, and not just offering a generalization about the things being defined.

Misplaced Burden of Proof

The fallacy of misplaced burden of proof is related to the appeal to ignorance. For someone to say that I will believe that you cannot jump over a building until you can prove that you can jump over a building is appropriate. In this case, the burden of proof is rightly placed upon the person making an extraordinary claim. For that person to turn the tables, and say that you should believe the claim unless you can prove otherwise is to shift the burden of proof inappropriately. It is a sure sign that they are telling tall tales. Part of the issue here is that the level of proof required is so disproportionate. In order to prove that someone can jump over a building, they need only do it. How can one prove that a person cannot jump over a building? One can appeal to general experience, but that is not proof in a strong sense. Since one side has such an easy burden, and the other has such a difficult one, it is appropriate in this case to side against the position with a trivially light burden.

Existence claims follow this model, especially about things which are unusual. In order to prove that something exists, it suffices to produce one. Proving that something doesn't exist is far more challenging. It is quite difficult in cases like these to prove a negative. As such, it is sometimes reasonable to reject the existence of something very odd and uncommon even when neither side meets their corresponding burdens of proof.

False Charge of Fallacy

One very important thing to remember is that many people with whom the average student converses will not know the names of most fallacies. It will do no good to throw out the claim that "You just used an amphiboly!" It may even solidify the image that you are an arrogant elitist. Instead, when someone with whom you are debating commits what you think is a fallacy, explain what the mistake in reasoning is, and ask the person whether he thinks his reasoning fits that pattern. It may take more time, and it may not feel as good immediately, but in the long run it will save a lot more relationships.

Another related issue is that it is easy to accuse someone of committing a fallacy, even when he has done no such thing. In a room full of students who have just learned a little about fallacies, but haven't solidified their understanding, it is easy to manipulate them into rejecting a viewpoint simply by accusing it of committing a fallacy. The technique is so powerful that it is appropriate to classify a false charge of fallacy as a fallacy in its own right.

The fact that one person accuses another person of engaging in fallacious reasoning does not mean that it is occurring. Of course, if one doesn't understand fallacious reasoning oneself that well, it may be appropriate to accept the judgment of someone who is an expert. But one shouldn't do so unreflectively. The point of learning about fallacies is that one doesn't have to rely on the judgments of others.

Even when someone claims that a given argument or person is committing a fallacy, it is always appropriate to carefully consider the charge. Hopefully, one can ask the arguer to defend his argument or point, but at the very least, one should apply the definition of the fallacy to see whether the fallacy fits. The fact that it doesn't fit does not mean the reasoning is good (that would be a fallacious appeal to ignorance), but it does mean that the argument should be evaluated on its own merits.

Missing the Point

If you have ever heard someone say "you're missing the point," then you have a basic idea of the fallacy of missing the point. When one misses the point, one draws an improper conclusion from a given piece of information. It is not necessarily a bad conclusion, but it is not the one which is intended by the other arguer.

This fallacy is similar to the fallacy we identified as a *non sequitur*, except the fallacy involves multiple people. Technically, even when it occurs within a debate, this mistake in reasoning is still sometimes called a *non sequitur*, but the term "missing the point" is probably more common.

Here is an example of a missing the point fallacy:

> Angelina: I think that it's wrong that colleges are canceling male sports programs because of Title Nine, just because not as many women are interested in sports.
>
> Jennifer: So, you're saying that we should cancel women's programs instead?
>
> Angelina: What?! No. I'm saying that a college spending more on male sports programs than female sports programs is perfectly fine, as long as it is spending as much money as is needed for all those women interested in playing sports.

Angelina was trying to make one point, but Jennifer drew a different conclusion—she "missed the point." One cannot engage in careful reasoning if one doesn't understand the point someone is making. Angelina tried to clarify her point, but hopefully a careful reader would have realized that Jennifer was missing the point even before Angelina corrected her. For one to assert that an arguer has missed the point, it is important that one can state what the point really is. If one doesn't know what the point is, one can't really be sure that the point was missed.

This fallacy is often confused with the fallacy of straw man, for an understandable, though not excusable, reason. Both fallacies involve a distortion of what someone is saying. Whereas in straw man, one distorts the statement the person is making itself, in missing the point one distorts the point the arguer is trying to make. The confusion sometimes arises because the language we use can be ambiguous. When one says "what you mean is..." or "what you're saying is..." one sometimes refers to the statement the person actually makes, and sometimes one refers to the conclusions implied by what the person is saying.

Straw Man involves distorting what the person actually says, and in missing the point, one distorts the implication that follows from what the person is saying. The difference is often subtle, and can be especially difficult when the arguers themselves are unclear and ignorant of the distinction. In these contexts it may not be as important to clearly distinguish whether a given passage commits straw man or missing the point as it is to listen carefully to what the person is saying and presenting it as accurately as possible.

Some Advice

You have now learned a great number of fallacies, but remember that a little knowledge can be a dangerous thing. Learning about fallacies isn't a magic bullet to win arguments. Hopefully, when you reason better, you will form better judgments and will be better able to protect yourself from manipulation, but the point is not to win arguments. The point is to determine what views have the best, or least fallacious, arguments behind them.

What logicians hope students will take from studying fallacies is to avoid using them, and to recognize them when others use them. When one uses fallacies, not only will one be fooling oneself, one will come to be considered irrational, uncredible, and someone to whom it is not worth listening. We don't want to just *think* we have good reasons to believe something; we want to *have* good reasons, if possible.

One must be careful, however, in accusing another person or argument of committing a fallacy. One doesn't want to be fooled by a fallacious argument, but nor does one want to ignore a good argument because one has too quickly condemned it. We want to judge arguments carefully and accurately.

One must also be aware that just asserting that an argument commits a fallacy often does little to nothing. If one's contender is unaware of the fallacy, he may consider you to be evading the discussion, and potentially guilty of a red herring. But even if the person is aware of the fallacy, he may not agree, and think one is making a false charge of fallacy. Either way, it is a good idea to be able to explain what the faulty process of reasoning is, and why it fails to provide a good reason. My hope is that you are now in a better position to do so.

Chapter Twenty-Six Exercises

Determine which fallacy or fallacies, if any, are committed in each of the following passages. For the Intermediate and Challenging Exercises, look also for argumentative fallacies and other rhetorical pitfalls. Unless you think the fallacy is totally obvious, you should provide a sentence or two justifying your decision.

Basic Concept Exercises

1. Fred: Every liberal believes in the right to choose.
   Sue: My friend Elisa is a liberal, and she is opposed to abortion.
   Fred: She can't be a real liberal.
2. The mayor's argument is that the developers' fee would reduce the number of building starts, and ultimately the city would lose more money than it would gain through the fee. But I can't go along with that. Mayor Tower is a member of the Board of Realtors, and you know what they think of the fee.
3. Horace, you're new to this town, and I want to warn you about the local newspaper. It's in cahoots with all them left-wing environmental nutcakes that are wrecking the economy around here. You can't believe a thing you read in it.
4. Look, maybe you think it's a good idea to legalize tribal casinos, but I don't. Letting every last group of people in the country open a casino is a ridiculous idea, bound to cause trouble.
5. I know you think that women are better at handling stress than men, but don't you think you might be saying that just because you're a woman.
6. My parents gave me a lecture on not smoking marijuana because it's bad for you, but forget them! I overhear them talking all the time about how they smoked it when they were younger.
7. My professor said the other day that my paper was bad, but what does he know. I heard that his wife cheated on him. Obviously he can't even make his wife happy.
8. Do you know who was behind the effort to get Proposition 93B on the ballot? It was a group of child-molestors, that's who! There's no way I'm voting for that monstrous bill.
9. My professor told us that we shouldn't worry about the upcoming exam as long as we study. I guess that means it will be very easy.
10. Ha! You said that Professor Laurie's Intro to Philosophy class was totally different from his Logic class. You don't even know what you're talking about. Both classes had around 40 students, and that's a clear similarity.

Intermediate Exercises

11. Democrats and President Obama accused the Chamber of Commerce of using foreign money to influence the 2010 election. The New York Times reported that there was no evidence of this claim. Bob Schieffer of CBS News asked David

Axelrod, an advisor to President Obama, about the story: "Do you have any evidence that it's anything other than peanuts?" Axelrod responded "Well, do you have any evidence that it's not, Bob?"

12. The only reason humanities professors like Rawls so much is that he offered them a pretense that their socialist dream world could be justified by liberal principles.
13. I have a simple solution to the problem of poverty. The government should just give every person in the country one million dollars, even if they have to print it.
14. I can't believe you threw your wife on the ground and kicked her! You're nothing but a violent beast. You can't control yourself and are so insecure that you have to use other people as punching bags to feel good about yourself.
15. I think we can agree that people have inconsistent views. Since you believe that the Earth orbits the Sun, in order to be inconsistent, you must also believe that the Sun orbits the Earth. Or do you claim that you are better than everyone else?
16. If the color red is in the object which is viewed, then there must be some mode of transport which contains the color red and moves it from the object to the eye, but if it is not in the object, then the world really has no color. So, either the world as it truly is has no color, or else light picks up tiny pieces of redness from the object seen and transports them to the eye.
17. If I enjoy drinking one beer a small amount, then it must follow that I would enjoy drinking the entire case a whole lot more!
18. Professor Stickler said that "the time in the classroom is not where learning is supposed to occur; it is supposed to occur outside the classroom." I guess he intends for us to just sit around in class and do nothing.
19. Nothing good can be found in Reggae music. It's created by nothing but potheads and stoners.
20. The Twin Towers could not have been taken down by an airplane. I saw on the internet that it would have been impossible to melt steel like that. It would have had to have been some kind of explosion.

Challenging exercises

21. The G.I. Bill is just another way for academics to have government subsidize their employment. Our soldiers, airmen, seamen, and marines should be able to take their G.I. Bill money and invest it in a business of their own choosing.
22. When the scribes and Pharisees asked Jesus whether they should stone a woman accused of adultery, Jesus said, "He that is without sin among you, let him first cast a stone at her." John 8:7
23. Abraham Lincoln didn't really care about the slaves. He even said "My paramount object in this struggle is to save the Union, and is not either to save or to destroy slavery. If I could save the Union without freeing any slave I would do it, and if I could save it by freeing all the slaves I would do it."
24. Brothers and sisters have way more of a right to get married than homosexuals do. After all, a brother and sister can still produce offspring, even if there is a higher chance of birth defects. Homosexual unions cannot produce children, whether deformed or not.
25. Most slaves were treated very well. Each slave was an investment, and you only made money off your slaves if you kept them well-fed, healthy, and as much as possible, happy.

26. Every mile driven by car is more dangerous than every mile flown in a plane. So, plane travel is safer than travel by automobile.
27. I read your article, and I conclude that it is too biased. You have twelve criticisms of liberal arguments, but only four criticisms of conservative ones.
28. I heard former Congressman Tom Tancredo say that all illegal immigrants should be deported. He is such a disgustingly ignorant racist. He seems to be completely unaware that our country is founded on immigration and built on the backs of immigrants.
29. **Holier-than-thou:** Would you say that facts and opinions are completely different, or that they can sometimes be the same?

    Oblivious: No, they're completely different.

    Holier-than-thou: And opinions are the same as beliefs?

    Oblivious: Of course.

    Holier-than-thou: Okay, so do you believe that the moon orbits the Earth?

    Oblivious: Duh? Obviously it does.

    Holier-than-thou: So, you believe it does?

    Oblivious: Yes.

    Holier-than-thou: So, you believe it is true, and beliefs are just opinions, and opinions and facts are completely separate, so it is not a fact that the moon orbits the Earth.

    Oblivious: Exactly, it is not a fact that the Moon orbits the Earth.
30. It is absurd to claim, as a few have done, that the New Deal, the basis of what we now know as "liberalism," was identical to either German Nazism or Italian fascism. But it is equally absurd to ignore, as all our textbooks do, the fact that the New Deal and European fascism grew from the same ideological roots, produced strikingly similar policies, and fostered national cultures that, if not identical, bore the resemblance of siblings. Though we think of Hitler's and Mussolini's regimes as pathological, even psychotic, and entirely alien to our political tradition, in fact, they were organically connected to the most influential American political movement of the twentieth century.

    Thaddeus Russell, *A Renegade's History of the United States*, p. 240

In-Context Exercises

Identify at least 10 fallacies or rhetorical pitfalls in the following dialog. Defend your judgment for each one in a sentence or two.

Richard: I'm so tired of Christians trying to use the Bible to justify their ethical views. It's just a book, after all. And yet they feel totally justified in imposing their views on others.

Alvin: So you don't think it was inspired by God.

Richard: Of course not, it's full of contradictions.

Alvin: Could it be written by men, but inspired by God?

Richard: Now you're just quibbling. What does any of this have to do with the fact that Christians try to use the government to impose their moral views on others?

Alvin: It just seems to me that if the Bible were inspired by God, then we should turn to it for guidance. Don't you think so?

Richard: That is ridiculous. Only an idiot would get their morality from the Bible.

Alvin: I get my morality from the Bible.

Richard: Yeah, but you don't go around telling everyone else how to live.

Alvin: Perhaps, but I do think that I use the morality I get from the Bible to inform my votes on candidates. For example, I wouldn't vote for any candidates who fundamentally disagreed with my morality.
Richard: Oh, that's fine, but it would be wrong if you were actually in Congress to use your Biblical morality.
Alvin: I don't see what the difference is.
Richard: How can you not see what the difference is? For a Congressman to use Biblical morality to decide on legislation would violate the First Amendment, which says that no politician can use his religious views to pass legislation.
Alvin: What?! It does no such thing.
Richard: Of course it does, which you would know if you ever read it.
Alvin: I have read it, and all it does is forbid the establishment of a state religion, and protect the free exercise of religion.
Richard: Exactly. How can one practice their own religion if the legislature tells you what religious beliefs you can have?
Alvin: Wait, isn't there a difference between religious beliefs and moral beliefs?
Richard: You yourself said that you get your moral beliefs from the Bible.
Alvin: I did, and I do, but I can separate the two. I can distinguish my moral views from the theological views I have. If I were in the legislature, why shouldn't I be able to use my moral views, even when they are based on the Bible?
Richard: Because that would be imposing your religious views on other people.
Alvin: But if I vote for people solely because I think they will vote in accord with a Biblical perspective, then I am not imposing my religious views?
Richard: No. That doesn't violate the Constitution.
Alvin: Really? Are they effectively the same? Aren't you quibbling?
Richard: The two are totally different, and again, one violates the Constitution and the other doesn't. Are you saying that we should put limitations on how people cast their vote? Do you want to go back to the days of Jim Crow?
Alvin: I don't want to have poll taxes, if that's what you're asking. But I am suggesting that if we have limits on how legislators can vote on legislation, those same limitations should apply to citizens when they are voting for candidates.
Richard: That's ridiculous, and would violate the First Amendment.
Alvin: Exactly—But I think it would violate the First Amendment rights of legislators, too. Let me ask you this. When you started, you criticized all Christians for imposing their views on others. Have you changed your view, or do you still think that all Christians try to impose their moral views on others?
Richard: I still think it, because it's so obvious.
Alvin: So, how are all Christians trying to impose their moral views on others?
Richard: They do it all the time, by judging people, and supporting legislation based on Christian views, like laws against abortion and laws punishing homosexuals.
Alvin: Didn't you just say that my voting for candidates, even when guided by my religion, was not an imposition of moral views because it didn't violate the Constitution?
Richard: But it's possible to impose one's moral views without violating the Constitution.
Alvin: That's my view, but maybe I misunderstood you. Let me just put it this way. I believe that abortion and homosexuality are morally wrong, and I believe so at least in part on my understanding of the Bible.

Richard: How can you possibly.... You know, that's the position of all kinds of tyrants throughout history, including the Nazis. And you know that prohibiting abortion is just a way for men to control women.
Alvin: I don't know what any of that has to do with anything, but let me ask you this: If there were a proposed law banning homosexuality, why shouldn't I vote in favor of it?
Richard: Because there is nothing morally wrong with homosexuality! That's just bigotry and discrimination.
Alvin: And how should you vote on such a bill?
Richard: I say everyone should vote against it.
Alvin: So, you're saying that I should vote in accord with your moral views.
Richard: Exactly.
Alvin: Apparently, you think that your moral views are better than mine.
Richard: What? I never said such a thing!
Alvin: But you don't think I should vote based on my views, but should vote the way you say I should vote. Doesn't that imply that your views are better than mine?
Richard: You're always trying to twist my words. You don't think you should be able to violate the Constitution, do you?
Alvin: No, but I think we have different understandings of the Constitution, at least when it comes to what violates the First Amendment. Is discrimination wrong?
Richard: Of course.
Alvin: Why is it wrong?
Richard: It's unconstitutional, that's why.
Alvin: So, you get your moral views from the Constitution then?
Richard: Let's say I do.
Alvin: Okay then. Do you think that the Constitution was inspired by God?
Richard: No, not at all. I don't think God gets his hands dirty with human beings.
Alvin: So, why should I accept the Constitution?
Richard: What do you mean? Aren't you an American?
Alvin: Yes I am, and I accept the Constitution because I think it comports well with my Biblical morality. I suspect that it was inspired by God, inasmuch as it was inspired by Christians and the Christian worldview.
Richard: There you go again. You know, not all Americans are Christians.
Alvin: That's absolutely true, but it doesn't follow that the Constitution was not inspired by Christian philosophy. Shouldn't people get to decide their own moral views, and vote accordingly, and then we should let the majority rule, or are you now against democracy.
Richard: Hey, just as long as they don't try to use some archaic book written long ago to justify their votes, I'll be just fine with that.
Alvin: Isn't that completely hypocritical?
Richard: Why?
Alvin: Don't you want to force me to abide by the Constitution, which is a piece of writing written long ago? And you don't even think it was written or inspired by God? You're such a blatant hypocrite, my views look brilliant in comparison.
Richard: You are ridiculous. The Constitution isn't full of contradictions.
Alvin: Are you saying that if a document doesn't have contradictions, then we have to believe it?
Richard: No, but then it can be rational to believe it.

Alvin: So, then why do you accept the Constitution? Does it comport with your moral views or does it create them?
Richard: I would say it comports with them.
Alvin: So, then where do you actually get your moral views?
Richard: I just have them. I just know it in my heart that there is nothing wrong with homosexuality, and that it is wrong to discriminate against people.
Alvin: So, you're saying that it's perfectly fine for you to impose whatever you feel on others, but I can't use my religious views which have been perfected over thousands of years by many brilliant people, to pass legislation. Isn't that anti-religious bigotry and discrimination against religious views. Besides that, are you saying that "your heart" never has any fluctuations, and that it always says the same thing.
Richard: You don't know what you are talking about.
Alvin: For example, if I'm religious and against abortion, your view says that I have to keep it to myself, but if I'm an atheist, then I can pass legislation against abortion.
Richard: That's crazy. Why would an atheist be against abortion? You can't even imagine that it is possible for someone to have a different view than you. That's the textbook definition of closed-minded.
Alvin: I don't...what? I'm just saying *if* an atheist were against abortion. I know that there are atheists who are in favor of abortion, but isn't it closed-minded to think that no atheist is opposed to abortion. Look, I don't think we're making any progress, maybe we should start again.
Richard: Maybe we should just agree to disagree.
Alvin: Oh brother, do you even know what you are saying?

Logic Puzzle

What always occurs once in April, and once in September, but never in October?

Probability and Monty Hall

We have seen that inductive reasoning involves probability and not absolute certainty, but what is probability? The simplest answer is that it is a measure of the likelihood of an occurrence, yet this simple definition masks a lot of challenging issues. One can argue, after all, that all events either happen or they don't, based upon natural laws. So, if something is going to happen, then it is definitely going to happen. For example, a die when thrown. One might say that there is a probability or 1/6 that it will end up on 2, since there are six possibilities and only one of them is a 2. Yet, given an understanding of physics in which objects mechanistically follow the laws of gravitation, friction, compression, etc. there is a matter of fact about which die face will land up. It, then, is certain to occur, and all the others were certain not to occur.

This result seems troubling, partly because it collapses measurements of probability to either one (certain) and zero (certainly not). There does seem to be some sense in saying that something is 75% likely to occur. Furthermore, if everything is either certain or certain not to occur, then it would seem like inductive reasoning would be impossible, and all reasoning would be deductive.

One way to avoid this troubling result is to think of probability in terms of imperfect epistemological states. Sure, if one knew everything about the universe and everything in it, one would not need probability (on one metaphysical view of the world), but none of us is in such a state. We only have limited knowledge. So, one might ask given only what we know to be true, what is the probability that something will occur.

This understanding might take us a little further, but it still leads into interesting issues. One debate is whether the universe works in mechanistic ways, or whether, as quantum mechanics suggests, there are built-in probabilistic outcomes in physical reality.

In any case, anyone who desires to understand inductive reasoning can hardly do so without learning a great deal about probability. And interestingly, most people have some real problems in their intuitive understanding of probability. One way of seeing this often called the Monty Hall problem.

Monty Hall was the host of the original "Let's Make a Deal" television program. You will understand why the problem has his name once you hear the way is it framed, if you have ever seen the show. Here is is:

> Before you are three doors. Behind one of the doors is a car. Behind the others there is nothing. If you select the right door, you get the car. It would seem that you have a 1/3 chance of picking the right door. Let's say you pick the left-most door. The host then opens the middle door, and reveals that there is nothing behind it. Then he asks you if you want to change your mind, a switch to the right-most door. Should you switch, and perhaps more importantly, does it make any difference if you do?

Most people seem to intuitively think that is makes no difference whether one switches or not. The reasoning seems to be something along the lines of "now that there are only two doors, there is a 50/50 shot either way. So, although one could switch, it doesn't really make any difference.

Unfortunately, it seems that most people are wrong. The right answer, according to probability theory and experimental science, as well as Mythbusters, is that one should switch. Switching gives you a 2/3 chance to win, whereas sticking with your original door gives you only a 1/3 chance to drive home in a new car!

If you are convinced by these proof surrogates and an appeal to authority, we will go through the argument. You originally had a 1/3 chance of selecting the door with the car behind it. That means that there is a 2/3 probability that the car was behind another door. This is the key to the problem. Imagine that the host, before opening the middle door, had said "Do you want to switch to the other 2 doors?" most of us would switch, right? Even those of us who trust our gut more than others would probably admit that from the cold view of statistical reasoning, getting the two doors would have a probability of 2/3.

In effect, that is what the host is doing. He is giving you the choice of the other two doors, only he is indicating that one of them is empty. After all, if one of them hides a car (which we have 2/3 probability of being the case) he is not going to open that door. So, he really has two doors he can open, he just will necessarily open the one which doesn't reveal the car.

This argument has not convinced many people, but it really is the case that every door the host reveals (knowing that it is empty) really does lend its probability to the other door. The following revised argument should convince anyone who is balking. Imagine that there were actually one hundred doors, and you chose one. It should be clear that I chose the correct door with a probability of 1/100. That means, however, that I chose the wrong door with a probability of 99/100. Now, imagine the host opens up ninety-eight of the other doors, and leaves only the door you chose, and one other. In this case, it seems far more obvious that we should switch doors.

Again, the reason is that the host knows which door has the car behind it, and only opens doors which do not have the car behind them. All that 99/100 probability gets moved to the one other door. It would be foolish not to switch at this point. No one could believe that the door chosen at the beginning would have a 50% chance of being the right door. It's probability was fixed, just like the selection was fixed. The door which remained closed was fixed as well, since it was chosen each time not to be opened because it was the right door. Really think about it. Could you really think the door you chose would still have a 50% of being the right door after you see the host open up 98 other doors.

The only difference in this case is the number of doors, but the principle is the same. The added probability of the door which is opened shifts over to the door which you didn't choose. The last argument I can make is that one can run the test over and over, and see what the results are. Take two people, one whose strategy is to keep the first door, and the other whose strategy is to switch. The experimental results confirm the switching strategy which winning approaching to 2/3 of the time.

The lesson to learn from this is that most of us are not really that good at probability. Our intuitive notions, from wherever they come, are not perfect, and in many cases give us the wrong answer. One shouldn't despair at this, however, as many of our intuitions or impulses can be wrong or problematic for other reasons. All it means is that we have to be much more careful about just relying on those intuitions in such cases. We can do that by learning a bit more about probability, which can be done at nearly every college in the country, if not the world.

CHAPTER

27

Logic Puzzles

Skill 27.1

Solving Logic Puzzles

In this chapter we will learn about some techniques to solve logic puzzles. The second edition of this textbook has logic puzzles included throughout, so hopefully the reader has picked up a few techniques already. There is an unlimited variety of such puzzles, and we could never provide a comprehensive approach to all of them. Hopefully, the interested student could take the few techniques learned here and adapt them to apply to cases which are not mentioned here.

One reason to do logic puzzles is to practice and hone our logical skills, particularly those dealing with deductive logic. The sort of logic puzzle envisioned here is where deductive reasoning can solve the puzzle with one specific answer. Solving the puzzle means finding that solution, not by luck, but through a step by step process of reasoning. In this sense, a logic puzzle with more than one solution is poorly designed.

Let's start with a simple puzzle, one which we will choose specifically because it is amenable to the truth-functional symbolization which we have already learned.

Use the statements below, each of which is true, to determine who is guilty of the murder, and what weapon was used.

1) If Abraham is guilty, then the murderer used a gun.
2) If Brad is guilty, then the murderer used a rope.
3) If a knife was used, then the killer was not Carmine.
4) If a knife was not used, then Abraham is not guilty.
5) If a rope was used, then Abraham is guilty.

Based on these statements, we should be able to solve the puzzle. Perhaps the precocious student can figure it out quickly using only intuition, but we will use this example to develop a technique which can be used in much more challenging cases.

The first thing we can do is to rewrite each statement using symbols. This puzzle relies on straightforward statements which can easily be symbolized. I don't think it is even necessary to make a key.

1) $A \supset G$
2) $B \supset R$
3) $K \supset {\sim}C$
4) ${\sim}K \supset {\sim}A$
5) $R \supset A$

Each statement is a conditional. So far, so good. Next, it is usually a good idea to consider what the possible solutions are. Hopefully, we can use the information given to rule out the possible solutions. Once we get down to one solution, and all of our statements remain true, then we know the solution which remains must be correct.

We can list the solutions in many different ways, but one technique is to put them on a grid. In this case, we have two dimensions to our solution: A person and a weapon. We can put one dimension along one side of the grid, and another dimension along the other, as in the example below.

	G	K	R
A			
B			
C			

As we can see visually, there are nine possible solutions. As we said, we could list those possible solutions in other forms, and perhaps one of those might work better for some students. Each student will have to determine their preference for themselves. Here is a list of each of the nine possible solutions:

A • G A • K A • R B • G B • K B • R C • G C • K C • R

Abraham could be guilty, and he could have used a gun, knife or rope. Brad also could be guilty, and he could have used a gun, knife or rope, and Carmine as well could have used one of the three weapons.

Each one of these solutions is represented on the grid from above, although it is easy to miss it. Each box represents a solution, which depends on the values in the index columns. Let's see the table again, with each solution labeled.

	G	K	R
A	A • G	A • K	A • R
B	B • G	B • K	B • R
C	C • G	C • K	C • R

The next step is to use the statements given to rule out possible solutions. Let's see the first statement again:

1) A ⊃ G

This statement asserts that if A is one of the conjuncts in the solution, then so is G. It does not say that A is true, but only that if A is true, then so is G. Implicit in the context of this puzzle is that only one person is guilty, and only one weapon was used. So, this statement tells us that If A were true, then K and R would be false. This reasoning allows us to rule out two possible solutions, as shown in the grid below.

	G	K	R
A		X ①	X ①
B			
C			

We include the circled '1' to show that it was statement one, by itself, which allowed us to rule out these possible solutions. One rule which must be followed is that for conditional statements, we can never cross out a possible solution which does not make the antecedent true—To do so would be to commit a denying the antecedent fallacy. So, for conditional statements, one identifies the possible solutions associated with the antecedent, and then cross out all solutions which would make the consequent false. Those solutions would give the conditional statement a true antecedent and a false consequent, which would make the conditional false, contra our instructions. In this case, the grid makes it easy. The solutions which make the antecedent true can be found along the row across from the A, and in that row, K and R would make the consequent false, so we can rule those solutions out.

Our next statement is:

2) $B \supset R$

Using the same reasoning as we used for the first statement, we identify those solutions where B is true, which are simply the solutions in the second row, and we rule out any solutions which would make the consequent false. Then we mark them with a circled two.

	G	K	R
A		X ①	X ①
B	X ②	X ②	
C			

3) $K \supset \sim C$

We can identify the possible solutions where K is true, which are the three in the middle column. We can then eliminate those solutions which make the consequent false. Any solution which made C true would make ~C false, so we can rule out K • C. As always, we mark the statement we used to rule the solution out. Technically, this is not required, but it is incredibly useful for others to confirm that our diagram proves what we assert that it proves, and it is very helpful if we get stuck and need to backtrack.

	G	K	R
A		X ①	X ①
B	X ②	X ②	
C		X ③	

The fourth statement is unlike the others.

4) $\sim K \supset \sim A$

In this case, the antecedent is a negation, but it really should pose no more difficulty. In this case, we still look to all those cases where the antecedent is true, or in this case, where K is false. So, we must consider the G and R columns, as those are the ones where K is false. Then we must rule out those solutions where the consequent is false. Since the consequent is that A is false, we can cross out any solution which includes A, again, as long as it is in the G or R columns.

	G	K	R
A	X ④	X ①	X ①
B	X ②	X ②	
C		X ③	

5) $R \supset A$

The last statement says that if R is true, then A is true, which would mean that B and C couldn't be true (again, only in the case that C is true, which includes all those solutions in the last column). So, we can rule out those solutions in the last column which would make A false.

	G	K	R
A	X ④	X ①	X ①
B	X ②	X ②	X ⑤
C		X ③	X ⑤

There is only one solution remaining, so if we have not made any mistakes, and the puzzle is designed properly, this must be the correct solution. So, it looks like Carmine is guilty, his weapon was a gun. The last thing we can do is go through and check to ensure that each of our statements remains true. All we do is recall that the conditional is true as long as it is not that case that the antecedent is true and the consequent is false. So let's write in the truth values and check.

1) $A \supset G$
F T T
2) $B \supset R$
F T T
3) $K \supset {\sim}C$
F T FT
4) ${\sim}K \supset {\sim}A$
TF T TF
5) $R \supset A$
F T F

Every statement is true, so our results check out. It's time to go arrest Carmine.

Let's just see how a different approach would have worked out. This time, we will simply list the solutions, and use the statements in the same way we did earlier to rule out solutions. We will put the statements and reasoning on the left, and the solutions on the right, just so that everything is presented all at once.

1) $A \supset G$
   So we can rule out any solution which includes A, but not G.
2) $B \supset R$
   So we can rule out any solution which includes B, but not R.
3) $K \supset \sim C$
   So we can rule out any solution which includes K and C.
4) $\sim K \supset \sim A$
   So we can check any solution which does not include K, and make sure it does not include A.
5) $R \supset A$
   So we can rule out any solution which includes R, but not A.

~~A • G~~ ④
~~A • K~~ ①
~~A • R~~ ①
~~B • G~~ ②
~~B • K~~ ②
~~B • R~~ ⑤
C • G
~~C • K~~ ③
~~C • R~~ ⑤

Again, we get the same solution as we did earlier, as we would expect. It doesn't matter what method we use, as long as we employ it correctly, we will get to the same right answer.

The next technique is often one that is used in conjunction with other techniques, though it can sometimes be used alone. The trick is to use the forms of reasoning which we learned previously, especially in this case hypothetical syllogism. Let's see the statements again:

1) $A \supset G$
2) $B \supset R$
3) $K \supset \sim C$
4) $\sim K \supset \sim A$
5) $R \supset A$

Look at the first and the fourth statements. We know from the first statement that if A is true, then G is true, but we know that if the gun was used, then the knife was not. But, according to the fourth statement, if the knife was not used, then the murderer was not Abraham. So, if A is true, then A is not true, which tells us that A cannot be true. Using hypothetical syllogism, and statements one and four as premises, we obtain $A \supset \sim A$. The only way for this statement to be true is for A to be false (check for yourself!), which tells us that A must be false.

Now that we know that A is false, we can use that information, along with the fifth statement and *modus tollens*, to assert that R is false. We can use this information, along with statement 2 and *modus tollens*, to conclude that B is false. With both A and B being false, we know that C must be true.

Knowing that C is true allows us to assert that K is false, by statement 3 using *modus tollens* again. Finally, since we know that K and R are both false, we can conclude that G must be true. Again we get to the same conclusion, that Carmine is guilty and he used a gun.

One last technique is to use a proof line, along with possible *reductio ad absurdum* arguments. We will assume that something is true, and hopefully we will end up with a complete solution, which we can then check to ensure it makes all the statements are true. Another good possibility is that we end up with a contradiction, because at least then we know the assumption is false. If neither of these events occur, then we need to try another assumption, or use some other technique.

We will take advantage of the fact that we know that one of three people is guilty, so we will assume each one is guilty in turn, and see if two of the three run into contradictions. Hopefully, this will allow us to also figure out the murder weapon, otherwise, we may have to run the test over using each of the weapons. Let's start with Abraham:

| A | We are assuming A, and put this at the top of our proof line.
| ~B | From the assumption of exclusivity (only one murderer).
| ~C | From the assumption of exclusivity (only one murderer).
| G | from 1) and *modus ponens*
| ~K | from exclusivity (only one weapon).
| ~R | from exclusivity (only one weapon).
| ~A | from 4) and ~K
| A • ~A
| ⊥ | We obtained a contradiction.

~A So, we know that A is false.

Let's try it again with B. We will list the statements again for ease of reference.

1) $A \supset G$
2) $B \supset R$
3) $K \supset \sim C$
4) $\sim K \supset \sim A$
5) $R \supset A$

| B | We are assuming B, and put this at the top of our proof line.
| ~A | from our previous proof. We have already proven that it is true.
| ~C | From the assumption of exclusivity (only one murderer).
| R | from 2) and *modus ponens*
| ~G | from exclusivity (only one weapon).
| ~K | from exclusivity (only one weapon).
| A | from 5) and R
| A • ~A
| ⊥ | We obtained a contradiction.

~B So, we know that B is false.

As long as we didn't mess up somewhere, then C must be correct. We still don't know what the murder weapon is, and it can increase our confidence that we didn't mess up if we don't get a contradiction for C. If we did get a contradiction, then either the logic puzzle was poorly designed, or else we made a mistake somewhere and will need to go over our work. Let's start.

| C | We are assuming C, and put this at the top of our proof line.
|---
| ~A from our proof and exclusivity
| ~B from our proof and exclusivity
| ~K from 3) and *modus tollens*
| ~R from 5) and ~A
| G since all other weapons are ruled out.
| a last look at all the statements just to make sure no other information can be garnered—it can't.

So, we do not run into any contradiction, and we have determined that the weapon must be the gun. As with all the other techniques, we have proven that given the information in the statements, Carmine must be guilty, and he used a gun.

Different puzzles may be more amenable to solution using certain techniques, but often multiple techniques will work just as well, and it just depends on personal preference. We will try one more puzzle before turning to the exercises. We will solve it using the grid technique, but every reader is welcome to try to solve it using a difference technique.

There are three children, each with a different birthday. Determine which child has which birthday from the statements below, each of which is true.

1) Albert was not born in March.
2) Either Bert or Cassandra was born in November.
3) The child born in January was born on the first.
4) The child born on the twenty third was not Cassandra.
5) The child born in November was born on the fifteenth.

The solution may seem to call for two dimensions, a child and a birthday, but the birthday can be divided into a month and a day. There are several ways we can construct a grid for this puzzle. One involves placing two dimensions along one side of the grid, as in the following example:

	J	**M**	**N**	**1**	**15**	**23**
A						
B						
C						
1						
15						
23						

This grid simplifies certain steps, and is perfectly acceptable to use. One other technique would be to place the extra dimension inside each solution box.

	J	M	N
A	1 15 23	1 15 23	1 15 23
B	1 15 23	1 15 23	1 15 23
C	1 15 23	1 15 23	1 15 23

One could also leave the dates out and simply write them in the appropriate box when they are discovered. This is the technique I will use. It often takes some ingenuity in order to determine how to conceptualize the solutions, but with experience, it becomes much easier.

Unfortunately, it is difficult to symbolize these statements using the propositional logic symbols we have learned. For the sake of foreshadowing what may be coming, we will use Predicate Logic symbolization. Keep in mind that this step is not technically necessary. One can solve the puzzle just by reading the statements in English. Still, we will present a way to symbolize them. The basic idea is that we will use capital letters to represent properties, and lower case letters to represent people. So, Albert is *a*, Bert is *b*, and Cassandra is *c*. For any person, say p, we will write that *p* was born in March by using a capital M, like so: *Mp*.

1) $\sim Ma$
2) $Nb \vee Nc$
3) $Jx \supset 1x$ no matter who is *x*.
4) $\sim 23c$
5) $Nx \supset 15x$ no matter who is *x*.

Feel free to examine each of these symbolizations of the original English statements. The important thing is to see what can properly be ruled out. The first statement allows us to rule out one box, or solution, as shown here:

	J	M	N
A		✕ ①	
B			
C			

The second statement tells us that the child born in November had to be *b* or *c*, so it couldn't be *a*, which means we can cross off that possibility.

	J	M	N
A		✕ ①	✕ ②
B			
C			

So, we know by exclusivity that Albert was born in January, which we can combine with the third statement to conclude that Albert was born on the first. Since Albert was born on the first of January, we know that no one else can be, so we can rule out January from each of the others (The circled 'x' indicates that we ruled out the solution based upon exclusivity).

	J	M	N
A	1	X ①	X ②
B	X ⊗		
C	X ⊗		

The fourth statement says that Cassandra was not born on the twenty third. Since we know that Albert was born on the first, the only possibility left is that Cassandra was born on the 15th, which tells us that Bert must have been born on the 23rd. We still don't know who was born in what month though, so let's examine the fifth statement. It says that whoever was born in November was born on the fifteenth. We should be careful here. We cannot think that $Nc \supset 15c$, and $15c$ is true, so Nc is true. To do so would be to commit an Affirming the Consequent fallacy. Instead we have to think this way: $Nb \supset 15b$, but $\sim 15b$, so $\sim Nb$. We know that no matter who it is, if a person is born in November, he must be born on the fifteenth. Supposing that Bert was born in November, he would have been born on the fifteenth, but we already know that he was not born on the fifteenth, so, by a *reductio* argument, he cannot be born in November. It follows that he was born in March, and Cassandra was born in November from the exclusive nature of the solution dimensions.

	J	M	N
A	1	X ①	X ②
B	X ⊗	23	X ⑤
C	X ⊗	X ⊗	15

So, we have found out that Albert was born on January 1st, Bert was born on March 23rd, and Cassandra was born on November 15th. The last thing we should do is check our answer. Go back and make sure that all the statements are indeed true.

One should also notice that this grid did not result in one box being checked, but one box in each column and one box in each row. Each child had his or her individual birth month. Make sure you fully understand what the solution requires, or it is easy to make mistakes.

Chapter Twenty-Seven Exercises

Basic Concept Exercises

Using the grid supplied, mark which squares are ruled out by each of the following statements. If you do each statement correctly, there should be only one open box. What is it?

1. $A \supset \sim J$
2. $A \supset J$
3. $K \supset D$
4. $B \vee C$
5. $\sim K \vee C$
6. $D \vee \sim M$
7. $B \vee L$
8. $(C \vee D) \supset \sim J$
9. $B \supset (\sim K \bullet \sim L)$
10. $\sim D \supset L$

	J	K	L	M
A				
B				
C				
D				

Intermediate Exercises

Complete the logic puzzles in the Adventures of Kentucky Jones series.

The Adventures of Kentucky Jones

11. The Mummy

Kentucky Jones felt like his life was being overshadowed by his more famous brother, so he decided to go exploring himself. His first destination was an ancient pyramid in Central America. Upon exploring the ancient pyramid, Kentucky encountered a mummy. Determine the outcome of his encounter and the location of the pyramid by analyzing the statements below, each of which is true.

1. If the mummy arose and chased Kentucky, then the pyramid was in Mexico.
2. If the pyramid was in Honduras, then the mummy never moved.
3. If the pyramid was in Mexico, then the mummy grabbed Kentucky and held him until he died.
4. If Kentucky died, then the pyramid was in Honduras.

12. Further Travels

After his last adventure, Kentucky had to decide what to do next. Based upon the following true statements, determine what choice he made.

1. Kentucky decided to go on to either Nicaragua or Costa Rica, or else he decided to return for reinforcements.
2. If he went on to Nicaragua directly, then he traveled by car.
3. If he went on to Costa Rica directly, then he traveled by bus.
4. If Kentucky did not return for reinforcements, then he did not travel by car or by bus.

13. Tennessee and Rhode Island

On the next leg of his journey, Kentucky was accompanied by his brothers, Tennessee and Rhode Island. They traveled many miles until they came to a wide body of water. There was a boat on their side, and they decided to takes turns rowing across the water. From the statements below, determine the order of rowing.

1. If Kentucky was not the first to take a turn rowing, then he was third.
2. If Tennessee was the first to take a turn rowing, then Rhode Island was the second.
3. If Tennessee was the third to take a turn rowing, then Kentucky was second.
4. If Rhode Island was second to take a turn, then Tennessee was third.
5. Rhode Island was not the first to take a turn.

14. The Belly of the Beast

The three men rowed for many hours, but before they could make it to the other side, an enormous creature came along and swallowed them up, boat and all. None of them got a good look at the creature, but from the statements below, decide what the creature was, and how big.

1. If the creature was 100 feet long, then it was not a fish.
2. If the creature was not a squid, then it was not a whale.
3. If the creature was a squid, then it was 150 feet long.
4. If the creature was 200 feet long, then it was a whale.
5. If the creature was 150 feet long, then it was a whale or a squid.

15. Escape

Kentucky and his brothers were quite surprised by what had happened, and quickly began to plan their escape, if they could. Kentucky wanted to start a fire, thinking the smoke would cause the creature to cough them up. Tennessee thought the more prudent course was to tickle the creature's stomach, until it couldn't take any more and spit them out. Rhode Island, who wasn't very creative, said they should just wait and see if the creature would find them indigestible and simply regurgitate them. From the statements that follow, determine how the travelers escaped, and whether they escaped into the middle of the sea or if the creature carried them all the way to the land on the opposite side of the body of water.

1. They either started a fire, or they ended up on the land, but not both.
2. If they ended up on the land, then they either started a fire, or they were simply regurgitated.
3. If they tickled the creature's stomach, then they ended up on the land.
4. If they were simply regurgitated, then they ended up on the sea.

16. Capture

Once the three brothers made it to land they followed a stream up into the jungle. Before too long, they were captured by a primitive tribe. The chief of the tribe intended to put them to death. The chief had a wife, a sister, and a daughter, and before the chief could act, one of the women saved the Jones brothers. Based on the statements here, figure out which woman it was, and how she did it.

1. If the brothers were saved by the wife, then she untied the ropes holding them to an anthill.
2. If the brothers were not saved by the sister, then the rescuer soaked the logs under the pot so they would not be lit.
3. If the daughter was the rescuer, then she did it by lowering a branch so the brothers could pull themselves free of the quicksand.
4. If the rescuer soaked the logs or lowered the branch, then she was either the wife or the daughter.

17. Rescue

The three brothers, at the direction of their rescuer, ran down toward the beach. They saw three ships on the water, and they were rescued by one of them when they swam out to it. One ship had three masts and two had four masts. One ship was black, one was green, and one was white. Which of the three ships rescued the brothers, and how many masts did it have?

1. If the brothers were not rescued by the white ship, then the rescue ship had four masts.

2. If the rescue ship was black, then it did not have four masts.
3. If the rescue ship had four masts, then it was green.
4. If the rescue ship had three masts, then it was not white.

Challenging exercises

Complete the logic puzzles in the Saga of the Superheroes series.

The Saga of the Superheroes

18. Beginnings

Aquaman, Batman, Captain America and Daredevil were discussing their latest encounters. Two of them had each recently battled one bad guy. One of them had battled two villains, and the last one had battled three. Determine the number of villains each superhero battled from the statements below.

1. If Captain America did not confront three villains, then Daredevil battled one.
2. If Daredevil did not battle two villains, then Aquaman did.
3. Batman fought three villains, if he did not battle two.

19. The Super Olympics

Batman, Captain America, and Daredevil all decided to enter the Super Olympics, where they competed in different event. Two of them won the gold medal, while one of them won the bronze. Which superheroes won which medals?

1. Batman won the gold, if Daredevil won the bronze.
2. If Daredevil won the gold, then Captain America won the bronze.
3. Batman won the bronze, if Captain America won the gold.

20. Murder in the Hall of Justice

The superheroes had captured Two-Face and the Joker and they were being held in the Hall of Justice. One night, three of the superheroes were staying in their rooms. That night, a murder was committed! You don't know the culprit, but oddly, you don't even know who the victim was. The Hall of Justice was sealed all night, so you do know that both culprit and victim must come from one of the five people who were inside it the night before. Based on the clues that follow, determine both victim and culprit.

1. If the superhero in room 1 was the culprit, the one in room 3 was the victim.
2. If the superhero in room 2 was the victim, then the Joker was the culprit.
3. If the superhero in room 3 was the victim, the superhero in room 2 was the victim.
4. If the Joker was the culprit, then the victim was the superhero in room 3.
5. The Joker was in his cell in the morning, but there is no way to know he was in it all night.
6. If the superhero in room 3 was the culprit, the superhero in room 2 was the victim.
7. If the superhero in room 2 was the culprit, then the Joker was the victim.

21. The Mysterious Masked Mischief Maker

For quite some time, Batman had been unable to catch a Mysterious Masked Mischief Maker. The Mischief Maker had committed numerous minor crimes, but had always managed to escape before Batman arrived at the scene. One day, however, Batman did get to the scene of the crime while the Masked Mischief Maker was still making his getaway. Batman managed to pull off the mask and reveal one of his worst enemies. Based on the statements below, find out who the Mysterious Masked Mischief Maker was, as well as the time of day.

1. If the Mischief Maker turned out to be the Riddler, then it was midnight.
2. If the Mischief Maker was actually Catwoman, then it was noon.
3. If it was midnight, then the Mischief Maker was the Penguin.
4. If it was evening, then the Mischief Maker was Catwoman.
5. If it was noon, then the Mischief Maker was the Riddler.

22. Eyewitness

Wonder Woman, the Invisible Woman, and Storm were patrolling the streets one night when they witnessed a crime being committed. Unfortunately, they were called away to battle Doctor Doom. Before they left, however, each of them was able to give the local police a description of the criminal. Unfortunately, the descriptions weren't exactly the same. The police brought in two suspects, but they need your help to catch the right one. Using the statements below, determine which suspect is guilty.

1. If suspect number one was guilty, then Wonder Woman's description was accurate.
2. If the Invisible Woman's description was inaccurate, then suspect number two was guilty.
3. If Storm's description was accurate, then the Invisible Woman's description was inaccurate.
4. If Wonder Woman's description was accurate, then Storm's description was accurate.

23. Spiderman's Most Challenging Enemy

Spiderman has had many encounters with supervillains throughout his crime-fighting career. Each of them was challenging, but Spiderman always prevailed. The statements below should help you determine which one of Spidey's enemies was the most challenging.

1. If neither Doc Oc nor the Hobgoblin was the most challenging, then neither was the Scorpion.
2. If the Scorpion was not the most challenging, then neither was Electro nor the Green Goblin.
3. If neither Doc Oc nor the Green Goblin was the second most challenging, then either the Hobgoblin or the Scorpion was the most challenging.
4. If the Green Goblin was the second most challenging, then Electro was the most challenging.

24. Heeding the Call

Aquaman, Batman, Captain America, Daredevil, Flash, and the Green Lantern were all at the Hall of Justice when a distress call came in. Only two of the superheroes were dispatched to investigate. Use the clues below to find out which two were sent.

1. If neither Aquaman nor the Green Lantern were sent, then Daredevil was.
2. If either Daredevil or the Green Lantern investigated the signal, then Batman did not.
3. If neither Batman nor Aquaman went, then Flash did.
4. If neither Captain America nor Batman was sent, then the Green Lantern was.
5. If Aquaman went, then either Daredevil or Flash accompanied him.
6. If the Green Lantern was not sent to investigate, then neither was Batman nor Flash.

25. The Strongest Superhero

The superheroes decided to hold a contest to see who was the strongest. Aquaman, Batman, Captain America, Daredevil, and Flash all decided to compete. Three of the superheroes were eliminated quickly, and the last two lifted more and more weight, until they both stopped at the same point. They decided to declare a tie. Use logic to determine which two superheroes won the contest.

1. If Captain America was victorious, then Daredevil was not.
2. If Aquaman was a winner, then Captain America was defeated.
3. If Daredevil was defeated, then so was Batman.
4. If Flash was a victor, then so was Aquaman.
5. If Batman was one of the champions, then Aquaman was not.
6. Flash was one of the strongest superheroes, provided that Daredevil was too.

CHAPTER

28

What's Next?

Just as the students who enter a logic class will have diverging levels of skills in logic, so will the students who leave one. Yet, it is hard to imagine that any student who really understood the class could leave it thinking that their logical skills were sufficient (was that a definitional sulk?). Hopefully, each of our logical skills will improve as we traverse the course of our lives.

This textbook has focused on logic in a very general sense. We have tried to apply the general principles to many different areas, both academic and in life. Yet, no introductory textbook can offer more specific epistemological principles, or principles of reasoning, which apply to every specific field of study. As one moves into particular fields of study, one will learn more specifically the form that proper reasoning will take in those particular fields. Often, one can rework those principles back into the general framework, but it is not generally necessary.

For example, learning the logic of engine repair may involve numerous pieces of information about the relationships between terms, like "All combustion automobiles without gasoline are automobiles which will not run", and "No automobiles which have starter motors without electricity supplied are automobiles which will run." Yes, a car mechanic could learn Venn diagrams much better, and put much of the reasoning he does into a syllogistic form, but I've never heard of one. The forms of reasoning which are applicable to repairing cars can be internalized and understood without appealing to the general patterns of reasoning we have learned in this textbook. Yet, it can be enlightening to realize that they often can be.

Should one have caught the bug, so to speak, and actually enjoy logical reasoning in the style we have been using, one might be happy to know that there is a lot more to learn. There is not enough space to cover all areas of the study of logic even briefly, but in this chapter we will cover a few of the major areas which the student who continues to pursue the study of logic will encounter.

Quantificational Logic

Here is a seemingly pretty basic argument:

1) All philosophers are absent-minded.
2) <u>Mr. Monge is a philosopher.</u>
3) ∴ Mr. Monge is absent-minded.

Notwithstanding the apparent falsity of the first premise, and the unsoundness of this argument, it seems pretty clearly to be valid. It can be shown to be valid using categorical logic, using the rather odd term "people identical to Mr. Monge." It seems difficult, however, to show that the argument is valid using truth-functional logic. We could come close using the following form:

1) $P \supset A$
2) $\underline{P\quad}$
3) $\therefore A$

In this argument, P represents "Mr. Monge is a philosopher", and A represents "Mr. Monge is absent-minded." This argument is thus represented as a *modus ponens*, and so is valid. Yet, the first premise didn't say that if Mr. Monge were a philosopher, then Mr. Monge would be absent-minded. It said that if *anyone* were a philosopher, then *that person* would be absent-minded.

Logicians were not really happy with trying to force a kind of symbolic form onto such arguments. They would not be satisfied unless they had a logical way to represent the argument precisely. It wasn't until the late nineteenth century and Gottlob Frege, however, that quantificational theory really became systematized.

Quantificational logic allows us to symbolize general statements using the concept of predicates applied to individuals and quantifiers. In a way, it is a melding of categorical and truth-functional logic.

In basic truth-functional logic, one represents simple statements by single capital letters. The genius of predicate logic is to pull apart a simple statement into its components: an individual and a predicate that tells us something about that individual. So, the assertion that Mr. Monge is a philosopher will be separated out into "Mr. Monge" as an individual subject, and the predicate "...is a philosopher." Traditionally, individuals are represented by lower-case letters, and predicates are represented by capital letters. So, we represent Mr. Monge is absent-minded by *Am*.

So far, we can represent the second premise and conclusion, but we still don't know how to represent the first premise. We want to be able to say that any person who is a philosopher is absent-minded. How can we say that without having a name for any arbitrary individual? The secret is to not use a name, but instead a variable. Just as in mathematics, if one doesn't know the specific number being discussed, or one wants to discuss any arbitrary number, one uses a variable.

We can say this: for anything in the universe, if that thing is a philosopher, then that thing is absent-minded. This means exactly the same thing as the first premise in the argument. We can symbolize this way: For every x, $Px \supset Ax$. So far, so good. The only thing to add is that logicians prefer to symbolize the phrase "for every x", generally using what is called the universal quantifier: $\forall x$. Students should know that there are other ways to symbolize universal quantification, such as enclosing the variable in parentheses, as (x). Putting everything together, we get the following symbolic form:

1) $\forall x\ (Px \supset Ax)$
2) $\underline{Pm\qquad\qquad}$
3) $\therefore Am$

This form is an exact representation of the original argument, and this argument form can be proven to be valid using natural deduction, although we would have to supplement our system with a few more rules dealing with quantification. Unfortunately, there does not appear to be any decisive procedure for settling whether an argument using quantificational logic is valid. In the early to mid-twentieth century, numerous philosophers mathematicians, and other sought such a decisive technique, only to find a strong argument that such a procedure is impossible. This proof is beyond the scope of this textbook, but hopefully some of its readers will continue on to learn it.

One might notice the individualistic emphasis of quantificational logic. In contains no groups, per se, but only individuals and properties. Groups are "created", in a sense, by quantifying properties over individuals. Groups are conceptually dependent on the fact that individuals have properties, and some of those individuals share the same properties. This emphasis is arguably the decisive feature of the modern era, in the Western world, at least.

The only addition required for the basic apparatus of quantificational logic is the existential quantifier: $\exists x$. Consider the following argument:

1) All athletes are coordinated individuals.
2) Some coordinated individuals are wealthy people.
3) ∴ Some athletes are wealthy people.

Hopefully, every student can at this point tell us whether this argument is valid. The answer is that it is not. The conclusion does not follow from the argument. The issue here, though, is simply how to represent the argument using quantificational symbolism. We will need a universal quantifier for the first premise, but the universal quantifier will not do for the second premise or conclusion, at least not in a straightforward way.

We can, however, use the existential quantifier, which can be understood as "for some *x*". The second premise asserts that there is some x who is both coordinated and wealthy. Putting it all together we get the following:

1) $\forall x\ (Ax \supset Cx)$
2) $\exists x\ (Cx \bullet Wx)$
3) $\therefore \exists x\ (Ax \bullet Wx)$

It may not appear as obvious as the previous example, but this argument form can be proven to be invalid using other techniques, such as the finite universe method, not covered in this textbook. It is basically like using a truth table for a universe with only a limited number of members. It can be used to prove that an argument is invalid (though not always feasibly), but not valid. Combined with natural deduction, which can only prove an argument to be valid, we can generally prove a quantificational argument to be valid or invalid. Quantificational logic is essential in modern mathematical proofs and many other areas. Plus, it's just cool.

Quantificational logic can be extended to the logic of Relations, such as Mike is the brother of Troy, symbolized as *Bmt,* as well as the relation of being equal, which is usually written not $=xy$, but in the regular way, $x = y$. It can also be extended to second order logic, where quantification can be applied not only to individuals, but also to predicates. If one wants to pursue logic further, one must learn about quantificational logic.

Metalogic

Once one has learned Quantificational Logic, the next thing one should learn is a little metalogic. The prefix 'meta-' means something like 'above' or 'beyond'. When added to 'logic' it refers to the study of logical systems to determine their usefulness. A few distinctions are in order.

First is the distinction between semantics and syntax. Consider the following groups of symbols: '$p \bullet (q \vee r)$.' No doubt most readers are already thinking "p is true and q implies r." You have learned to immediately interpret the symbols in this way. Strictly speaking, however, the formula is just a string of symbols and letters, which we could interpret in many different ways. I could say that the dot means "is speaking to" so that the formula above means that "p is speaking to q or r." The point is that we can separate the meaning of the symbols from the symbols themselves. Technically, the rules we have learned are rules to manipulate the symbols themselves, and we can apply them regardless of what the symbols mean. In this sense, we would be dealing with the syntax of the formulas. The syntax is the rules involving the structure of the symbols. I can teach you the rules completely independently of what the symbols mean. In fact, one could learn the rules on their own, without learning any meaning to the symbols. It might be harder, but one can learn the syntax of formulas without knowing anything about what the symbols mean.

Semantics involves the meaning of our symbols. Obviously, different people could assign a different semantic value to the same symbols. It may be hard to see now, but in the next section, on Modal Logic, we will learn about the box operator, and in one system the box means 'necessity' and in another it means "morally obligatory". The symbols may be the same, but the meaning behind the symbols is different. The trick is to make sure that the rules one uses for inferring conclusions, or the rules to derive formulas, matches the semantic value one is using for the symbols.

The distinction between semantics and syntax is considered very important in logic. A logical system, such as truth-functional logic, is a system regarding the manipulation of symbols on paper. Of course, we have given each symbol a meaning, and this has guided our choices as to what rules to accept, but the distinction still exists. We can still ask, however, whether the rules we have chosen are acceptable. We can ask whether the system of symbol manipulation we have chosen is the best one for the semantic meaning we have given those symbols.

In particular, logicians will ask two things of a system of logic. First, is the logic system being employed sound, and is it complete? By 'soundness' we mean something a little different than we learned in evaluating deductive arguments. Our system of rules for truth-functional logic is sound when every argument which can be proven valid in the system (or where a statement matching the conclusion is derivable from statements corresponding to the premises by mechanically applying the rules) is valid in reality. It would do no good to have rules which could derive statements which would not result in valid arguments.

As an example, I could have a rule that said that every time one sees the formula 'p ∨ q' one can derive p. Adding this rule to our system would make the system unsound for the standard semantic value of the wedge. If the wedge means "or," this rule would allow us to derive statements which are not logically implied by the original statement. If I know that today it is "either Monday or Tuesday" then it does not follow that today is Monday.

So it is very important that our system of rules be sound. We would also like for our system to be complete. A logical system is complete when every logically valid inference can be shown to be valid in our system. In a complete system, if an argument is valid, then our system, given the premises, can derive the conclusion. A system which was not complete might not be able to prove that an argument is valid, even though it is valid. Obviously, we would much prefer a complete system to one which was incomplete.

Generally, proving the soundness of a system is much easier than proving completeness, but both are beyond the scope of this text. Any student who wishes to advance in studying logic from an academic point of view should look forward to seeing these proofs eventually.

Modal Logic

Modal logic is another extension of truth-functional logic which is separable from quantificational logic, although the two are generally combined. Modal logic, in its basic form, deals with the concepts of necessity and possibility.

Obviously, to say that something is true is different than saying that it is possibly true, or necessarily true. To say that it is possible that I am rich is not the same as saying that I am rich. To say that it is necessarily the case that ten dollars is more than five dollars (of the same kind) is to say more than it happens to be the case on this one occasion that ten dollars is more than five dollars.

Modal logic introduces two new operators, the box and the diamond. The box represent "It is necessary that..." and the diamond represents "it is possible that...." Using modal logic, we can accurately and completely capture an argument such as the following:

It is necessarily the case that if and only if a number is prime, then it cannot be divided by any number less than it (besides one). It is not possible to divide the number 143 by any number smaller than it, thus it is necessarily the case that 143 is prime.

This argument may not be overly challenging, but hopefully seeing it in symbolic form will familiarize the student with the use of modal operators:

1) $\Box\forall x[Px \equiv {\sim}\exists y > 1\ (y < x \bullet Dxy)]$
2) $\underline{{\sim}\Diamond\exists y > 1\ [y < 143 \bullet D(143)y]}$
3) $\therefore \Box P(143)$

This conclusion holds not only that the number 143 is prime, but that it is necessarily prime. It may not appear that there should be too much controversy around the issues of necessity and possibility, but there are incredible debates about the proper system for modal logic. In some sense, there is ambiguity about what we mean by necessity and possibility, which has resulted in a series of systems of modal logic, each of which includes different axioms.

Modal logic can be challenging, but very rewarding for the student who pursues it.

Deontic Logic

Deontic Logic is the logic of obligation, or duty. In some sense, it is intended to capture the idea of morally necessary actions, and so can be seen as an extension of modal logic. The same symbols are even sometimes used, but with different meanings. The box operator can be interpreted as "It is morally required that..." and the diamond interpreted as "It is morally permissible that...."

So, in order to say that it is morally wrong to lie, we could write $\Box{\sim}L$, which we can read as "It is morally required that one not lie." To say that an action is morally permissible, we can say that it is not required that one not do the action. So, to symbolize the statement that one may get divorced, one would write ${\sim}\Box{\sim}D$. One might also use the diamond to write $\Diamond D$, which is equivalent, and means that "it is morally permissible to get a divorce."

There are similarities between deontic and basic, or alethic, modal logic, but there is one important distinction which has driven many logicians who deal with it to refrain from using the box and diamond operators in favor of other symbols, often O for Obligatory and P for permissible. The distinction hinges around the following proposition:

$\Box p \supset p$

This proposition is eminently reasonable for modal logic. To say that it is necessary that *p* is true does establish that *p* is true. Perhaps it is unfortunate, but the fact that something is morally required does not mean that people will actually do it. So, this proposition does not seem to hold for deontic logic. Expect quite a few logicians who engage in deontic logic to use the alternative symbols. Some may include the operator F to represent forbidden, which can be defined simply as O~*p*. One benefit of using letters for deontic logic is that it can then be added to modal logic more cleanly. Otherwise one would have to somehow distinguish when a box is deontic and when it is alethic.

Other Logics

There is a lot more to the field of academic logic, including epistemic logic, temporal logic, relevance logic, and intuitionistic logic. We will give just a brief statement about each of these.

Epistemic Logic is a system which it is hoped can model our understanding of the logic behind belief and knowledge. We write *Bap* to say that Person *a* believes proposition *p*, and *Kap* to say that person *a* knows proposition *p*. Here are a few potential theorems of epistemic logic. Which of them seems plausible?

Kap ⊃ Bap
Bap ⊃ Kap
~Bap ∨ Bap
Kap ⊃ p
Bap ⊃ Ka(Bap)
~(Bap) ≡ ~Bap

Many of these statements are debated in the philosophical community. The mere ability to devise a system to more clearly articulate these sorts of statements may not immediately settle any of the perennial issues of logic, but it can be useful to see the issues more clearly.

Epistemic logic is very different from the Classical logic upon which we have focused in this textbook. Classical logic deals with extensional contexts, which deal with the world as it exists, whereas epistemic logic involves the world of the mind. It is a variety of intensional logic, which involves contexts where the meaning of terms plays a substantive role. In intensional logic, symbols are not generally truth-functional.

For example, *p* is either true or false, but for any person *a*, *Bap* can be true or false completely independently of the truth of *p*. Some other phrases which seem to require an intensional logic are "It is surprising that…" and "It is trivial that…."

Classical logic is often assumed to take place in a sort of timeless state, which may be quite appropriate for mathematical concepts and arguments which don't rely on any change in time or state. Yet, some arguments rely on changes which can take place over time, and thus arose temporal logic. Temporal logic, sometimes called tense logic, adds several operators relating to truth over a time period. *Fp* mean that *p* is true at some time in the future, while *Pp* means that *p* was true at some time in the past. *Hp* means that *p* has always been true in the past, and *Gp* states that *p* will always be true in the future.

Dynamic logic is a term applied to a sort of logic which is often applied to computer programs, though it can be extended to other areas. It has the operator $[a]$, where $[a]p$ is read as "executing program *a* now will result in *p*." As with all of the systems of logic included here, there have been many developments in dynamic logic over the past forty years or so since it was developed.

Relevance logic generally attempts to capture a more intuitive sense of implication. We learned earlier about some odd features of material implication in classical logic, namely that $p \supset q$ is true when p and q are true, even if p and q have nothing to do with each other. So the sentence "If Mr. Monge teaches Logic, then the Earth orbits the Sun" is true in classical logic, even though most every person who hasn't learned classical logic, and even most who have, think that such a statement is false. The problem seems to be that the antecedent is not properly relevant to the conclusion. Any system which attempts to require antecedents to be relevant to their consequents will be referred to as a relevance logic.

Second-order logic refers to a logic which allowed variables over predicates, and not only individuals. As such, most any of the logics we have covered can be extended to a second order logic by allowing quantification on predicates. In the basic quantificational predicate logic, we might express a principle such as $\forall P \exists x(Px)$, which asserts that for every property there must exist at least one individual object which has that property (Is that true? Can you think of any counterexamples?).

The point of this section has not been for introductory students to be able to understand these different logics enough to actually use them, but only to point out a few areas which students interested in logic might be able to study further. Should that apply to you, then I wish you all the best on your journey. For the large majority of readers for whom that description does not apply, I hope that this textbook hasn't been too painful. I also hope that you have learned a great deal from your reading, and that in the future, you are always careful to reason well, and avoid sophistry.

APPENDIX

A

Answers to Odd Exercises

Chapter One Exercises

1. Statement
3. Non-statement, command
5. Non-statement (unless uttered in a context)
7. Statement
9. Non-statement
11. Statement
13. Non-statement (unless uttered in a context)
15. Non-statement
17. Statement
19. Non-statement (fragment)
21. Statement
23. Probably a statement (technically a command, but it sounds like the kind of command which will be supported, so is best seen as an ought imperative)
25. Non-statement (This sentence contains several category mistakes. It is probably best to treat it as a non-statement. It is certainly not true, but it doesn't seem right to call it false either).
27. Non-statement, suggestion?
29. Probably a non-statement. It has the form of a statement, but it is not generally meant literally. In most contexts is means something like make yourself at home, which is an imperative or command.
31. Non-statement, it is unlikely that someone would provide a reason to back up this imperative statement
33. Non-statement. It seems unlikely that one would try to justify this sentence as an ought imperative. How would your mother respond if you asked "why?"
35. Probably a statement, but it depends on how the sentence is stressed (see Fallacy of Accent, Chapter 25). It probably just means "You should drop the class in which you are getting an 'F'". We could also possibly interpret this utterance as an argument (see chapter 2)
37. Probably a rhetorical question, which means we should treat it as a statement. It is possibly a real question, if the person asking it is actually unsure and is eliciting information or confirmation.
39. The first line of Hamlet's soliloquy could be put into the form of a question, as: "Should I continue living or kill myself?" Hamlet doesn't really seem to be asking himself a straightforward question, though. It is probably best seen as rhetorical, and could be treated as a statement. Perhaps we could capture it as "the statement "The most fundamental question each of us faces is whether we should continue living."
41. Probably a real question, actually asking "you" if you've noticed the same thing. The "not" here seems to indicate that the speaker is open to you disagreeing.

Chapter Two Exercises

1. Non-argument
3. Argument, Conclusion: The Pledge of Allegiance is Unconstitutional.
5. Non-argument
7. Argument, Conclusion: If you do something and it makes you unhappy, then it is immoral.
9. Argument, Conclusion: The *Star Wars* movies are the best movies ever.
11. Argument, Conclusion: No one needs logic.
13. Non-argument, explanation
15. Argument, Conclusion: One should never pour any ammonia-based cleaner into a toilet when there is [chlorine] bleach present.
17. Argument, Conclusion: Smoking marijuana without a filter is far more dangerous than smoking tobacco with a filter.
19. Argument, Conclusion: You should rewrite the first paragraph in your essay.
21. Argument, Conclusion: something like "Republicans should not give in too easily on the debt ceiling issue."
23. Non-argument, explanation
25. Argument, Conclusion: You have Lyme disease.
27. Probably best interpreted as an argument, although technically a single statement. The author almost certainly believes that we ought not burn witches (he says "no better"), and with this added premise, the conclusion would be "We ought not tell children that they better believe the Earth is round because we say

it is and we know better and people who disagree with us are ridiculous."

29. Argument, Conclusion: Something like "Children today are no more out of control than they have ever been." There is an indication of an anterior claim (you have been saying...) so that this seems like a counter to the original claim.

Chapter Three Exercises

1.
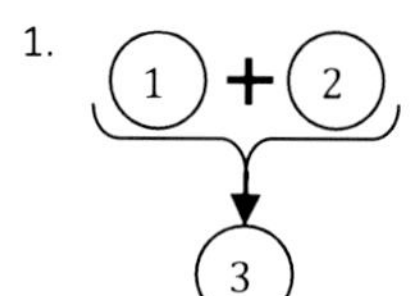

3.
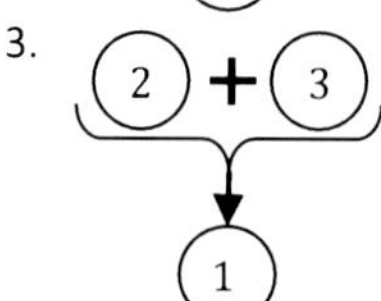

5.
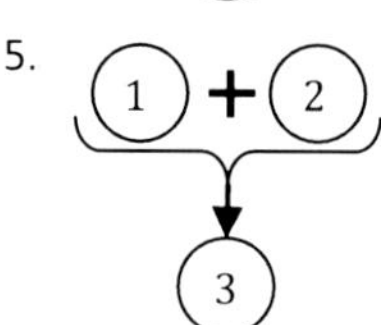

7.
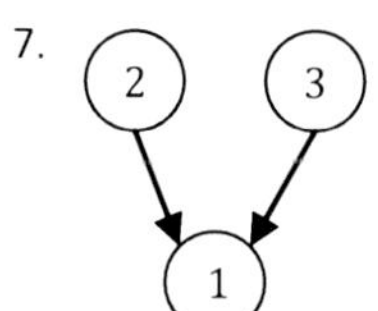

9.
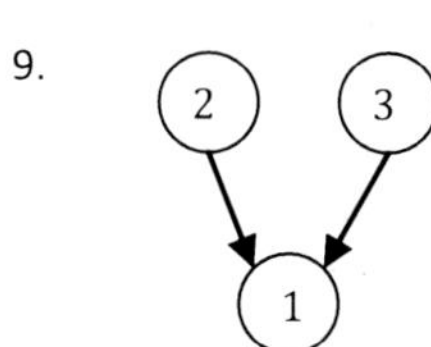

11.
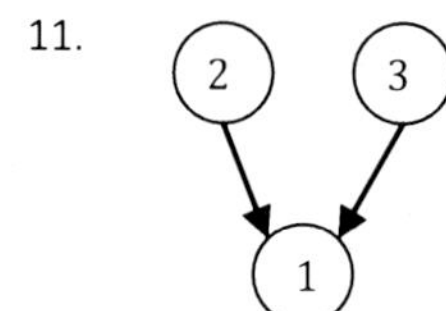

13.
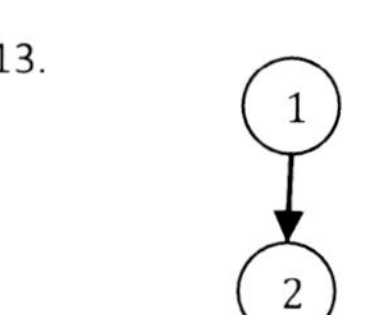

15.
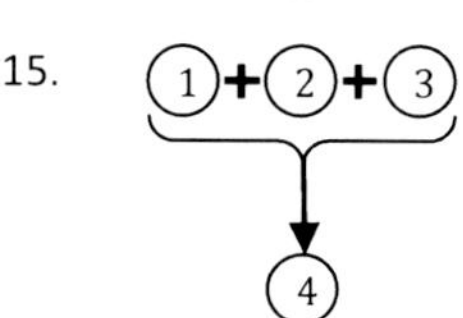

17.
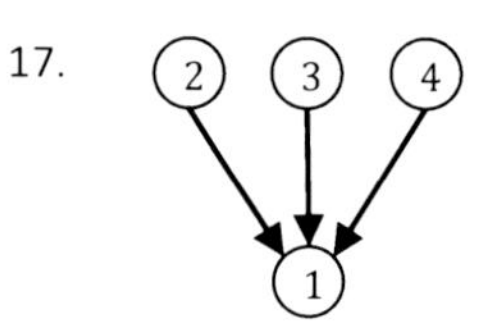

19.
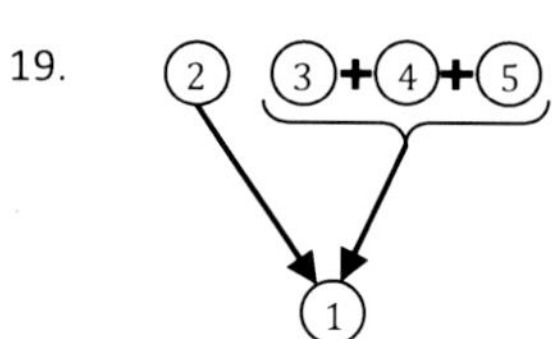

21.
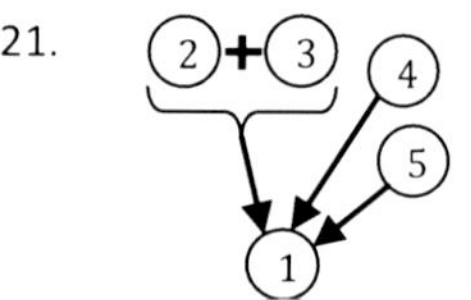

23.
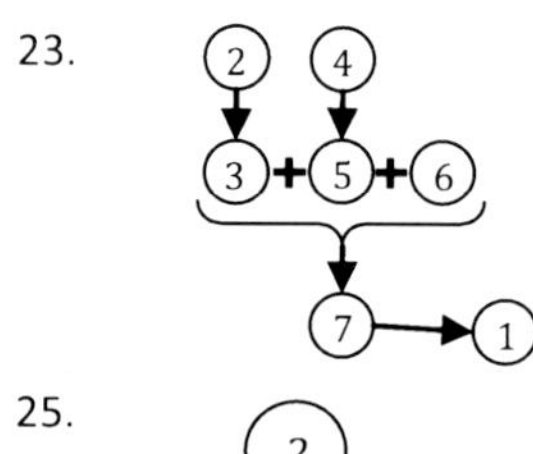

25.
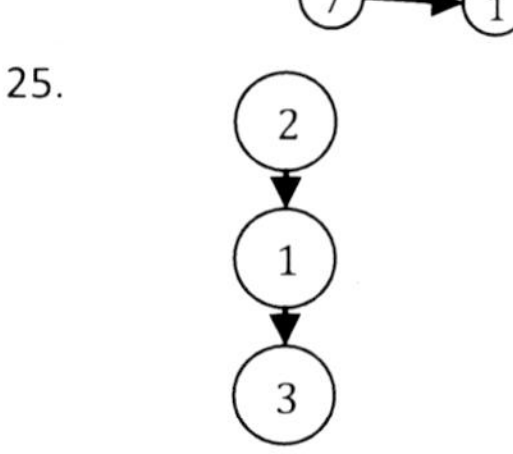

27.
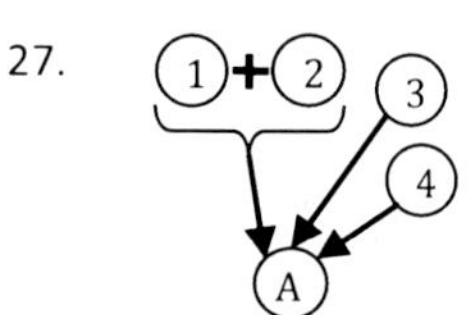

A = "The government should not ban gambling."

29.

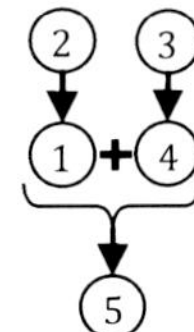

Chapter Four Exercises

1. 1) The suspect's fingerprints were on the murder weapon.

 2) ∴ The suspect committed the crime.

3. 1) The Constitution forbids the establishment of religion.
 2) To include the words "under God" in the Pledge of Allegiance is an establishment of religion.

 3) ∴ The Pledge of Allegiance is unconstitutional.

5. 1) All repeating decimals can be written as fractions.
 2) All repeating decimals are rational numbers.

 2) ∴ All rational numbers can be written as fractions.

7. 1) If you do the right thing, it will make you happy.

 3) ∴ If you do something which make you unhappy, then it is not right (moral).

9. 1) The *Star Wars* movies include an incredible story of freedom and fighting against tyranny.
 2) The *Star Wars* movies inspired generations of movies after them.

 3) ∴ The *Star Wars* movies are the best movies ever.

11. 1) The Constitution forbids cruel and unusual punishment.
 2) (Assumed) The death penalty is cruel and/or unusual.

 3) ∴ The death penalty is unconstitutional.

13. 1) Without lawyers, big businesses and unions would be able to do whatever they want.
 2) Big businesses and unions want to consolidate power and control everyone.

 3) ∴ It's a good thing we have lawyers.

15. 1) Figurative language causes all sorts of confusion and miscommunication.
 2) The point of logic is to eliminate the confusion of language.

 3) ∴ One studying logic should not use figurative language .

17. 1) The distance between galaxies has been accelerating.
 2) It is impossible for the distance between galaxies to accelerate unless there is some repellent force operating on them.
 3) The only repellent forces that are currently accepted in physics are the electromagnetic force and maybe the weak nuclear force.
 4) Neither the electromagnetic force nor the weak force can explain the acceleration of galaxies.

 5) ∴ Either there is some previously unknown mysterious force in the universe, or else Newton was wrong.

19. 1) People in jail were much less likely to attend church regularly before they went to prison than the non-prison population.

 2) (Implied) ∴ Attending church regularly causes people to commit fewer crimes.

 3) ∴ If the government is interested in getting people to not break the law, then it should do everything it can to encourage people to attend church regularly.
 4) The government should be interested in getting people to not break the law.

 5) ∴ The government should do everything it can to encourage people to attend church regularly.

21. 1) President Obama has kept the same policies in Iraq as President Bush.

 2) ∴ President Obama thinks President had the right policies in Iraq.
 3) President Obama is more divisive than President Bush.
 4) You voted for Barack Obama because you thought President Bush had bad policies and was divisive.
 5) ∴You voted against someone who had good policies because of those very policies.

 6) ∴ (Implied?) Your vote was foolishly cast.

23. 1) Democrats favor same-day voter registration.
 2) Same-day voter registration makes it more difficult to ensure people are entitled to vote.
 3) Democrats are opposed to voter I.D. requirements.
 4) Not having voter I.D. requirements makes it easier to commit voter fraud.

 5) ∴ Democrats actually favor same-day voter registration and reject voter I.D. requirements so that they can engage in voter fraud of various kinds.

25. 1) Poor people are the most desperate to play state-sponsored lotteries, turning over large portions of their income to the state.

2) The state redistributed this money to a few people, who are then part of the mega-rich.

---

3) ∴ State-sponsored lotteries are a very regressive method of income for the state.

---

4) ∴ State- sponsored lotteries take advantage of poor people.

---

5) ∴ Leftists should not support state-sponsored lotteries.

27. 1) The laws of thermodynamics hold that the entropy of a closed system always increases.

---

2) ∴ The order in a closed system always decreases (the natural state of the universe is decay).
3) According to evolutionists, life is evolving from less ordered creatures to more ordered creatures.

---

4) ∴ Evolution violates the laws of thermodynamics.
5) The only entity which could violate the laws of thermodynamics is God.
6) ∴ God must be the driving force behind evolution.

---

7) ∴ God exists.

29. 1) There are four different categorical syllogistic standard forms with eight possible arrangements.

---

2) ∴ There are 32 different categorical assertions which can be made.
3) Assertions can be made positively or negatively (asserted as false).

---

4) ∴ There are 64 things we can say using two terms and their complements.
5) If we use one premise and one conclusion, then for each possible premise there are 64 possible conclusions.

---

6) ∴ There are a total of 4096 possible arguments involving two terms and their term complements using one premise and one conclusion.

Chapter Five Exercises

1. Inductive – based on causal reasoning – good argument from the standpoint of logic, although NOT strong enough by itself to convict someone.
3. Deductive – categorical syllogism
5. Deductive – categorical syllogism
7. Deductive – categorical syllogism
9. Inductive – causal reasoning
11. Deductive – categorical syllogism
13. Deductive – categorical syllogism
15. Inductive – involves causal and analogical reasoning
17. Deductive – categorical syllogism
19. Deductive – categorical syllogism
21. Deductive – disjunctive syllogism
23. Inductive
25. Inductive – analogical reasoning
27. Deductive – categorical syllogism
29. Inductive

Chapter Six Exercises

1. Invalid, unsound (a smaller, more dense object could weigh more than a larger one)
3. Invalid, unsound
5. Invalid, unsound
7. Valid, unsound, we would at least need to add "rightly" to the first premise
9. Valid, unsound (there is very likely at least one person for whom either premise is false)
11. F
13. F
15. T
17. T
19. F
21. Invalid, unsound
23. Valid, ??
25. Invalid, unsound
27. Invalid, unsound
29. Valid, unsound (the area of a circle is πr^2)

Chapter Seven Exercises

1. Strong, Unknown
3. Strong, though the cogency is questionable (one may be engaging in confirmation bias (See Chapter 24)
5. Strong, uncogent (the poll is entirely fictional)
7. Strong, probably cogent (the conclusion is true today, though it wasn't when the first edition of this textbook was written. It is cogent either way, IF most Democrats are in favor)
9. Strong, uncogent (I've never done this, have you?)
11. F
13. F
15. T

17. F
19. F
21. Strong?, Cogent? For most of these challenging exercises, I would expect a paragraph defending your judgment either way.
23. Strong, uncogent (for me and I hope for you)
25. Strong, probably uncogent
27. Weak?, uncogent (the first part of the argument is probably strong, but we would need more information to confirm that it is cogent).
29. Strong?, cogent?

Chapter Eight Exercises

1. Some diseases are not curable illnesses.

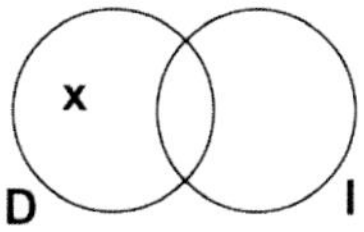

x
D I

3. No diamonds are rubies.

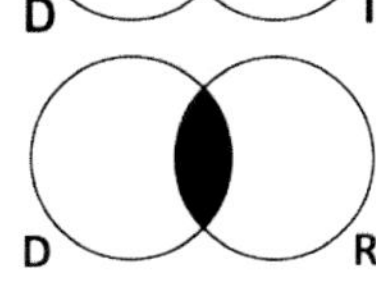

5. Some clowns are funny people.

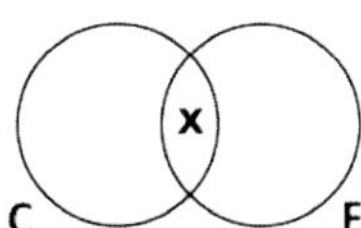

7. All diamonds are hard substances.

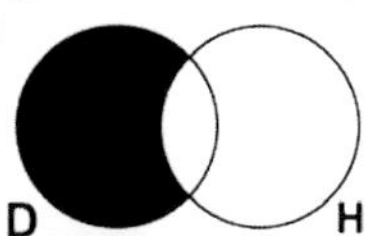

9. All categorical statements are true statements.

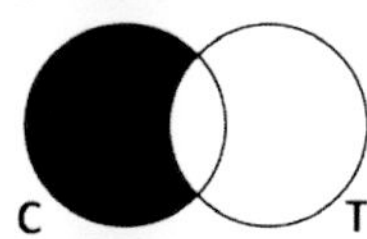

11. All bats are mammals.

13. Some marriages are happy institutions.

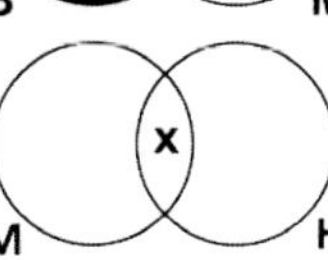

15. Some fast food restaurants are places that serve burgers.

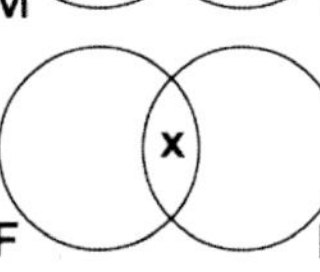

17. All times I travel are times I lose my luggage.

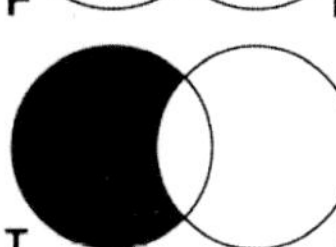

19. Some Presidents are left-handed people.

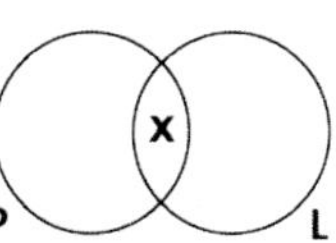

21. All students who want to pass are students who must learn to do proofs.

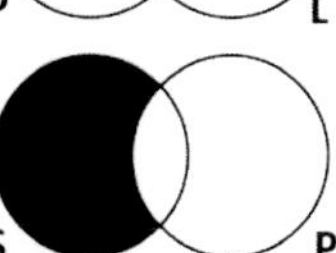

23. All people who are allowed to vote are citizens.

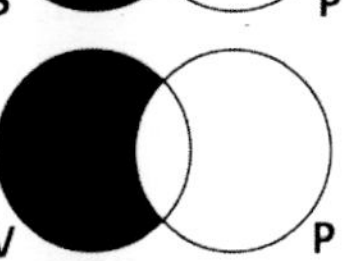

25. All pollutants are things we should remove from our water.

27. Some nephews of mine are fans of Justin Bieber.

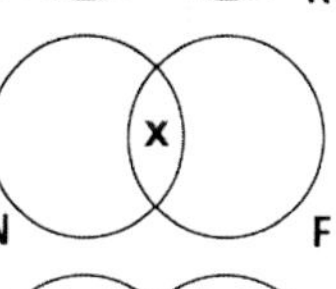

29. Some teachers are not professors.

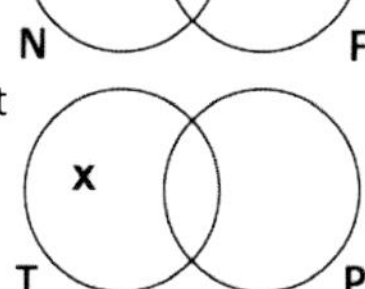

Chapter Nine Exercises

For these answers, 'und.' indicates a statement of undetermined truth value. Note that one might have independent information about the truth of one of these statements.

1. Some frogs are amphibians. I (True statement)
   All frogs are amphibians. A (und.)
   No frogs are amphibians. E (F)
   Some frogs are not amphibians. O (und.)
3. Some spiders are hairy creatures. I (True statement)
   All spiders are hairy creatures. A (und.)
   No spiders are hairy creatures. E (F)
   Some spiders are not hairy creatures. O (und.)
5. All spiders are scary creatures. A (False, for me)
   No spiders are scary creatures. E (und.)
   Some spiders are scary creatures. I (und.)
   Some spiders are not scary creatures. O (T)
7. Some students are smart people. I (True statement)
   All students are smart people. A (und.)
   No students are smart people. E (F)
   Some students are not smart people. O (und.)
9. Some apples are red fruits. I (True statement)

All apples are red fruits. A (und.)
No apples are red fruits. E (F)
Some apples are not red fruits. O (und.)

11. invalid, illicit contraries fallacy. A true A statement actually guarantees that the corresponding E statement is false.
13. Contradictories, invalid
15. Invalid, illicit contraries
17. Invalid, illicit sub-contraries
19. Invalid, illicit contraries
21. All P are M, therefore Some P are not M. Invalid, contradictories used improperly.
23. No F are T, therefore F: Some F are T. Valid, contradictories.
25. F: Some A are R, therefore Some A are not R Valid, sub-contraries (apples do exist)
27. F:Some P are not M, therefore F: No P are M. Subalternation, used properly. P exists, so it is appropriate to add this premise to make a valid argument
29. Some A are R, therefore Some A are not R Invalid, illicit sub-contraries

Chapter Ten Exercises

1. Obversion, yes
3. Conversion, no
5. Obversion, yes
7. Obversion, yes
9. Contraposition, yes
11. Valid, obversion
13. Invalid, illicit conversion
15. Valid, conversion
17. Valid, use conversion and then obversion
19. Invalid, illicit conversion
21. Invalid, illicit conversion, unsound
23. Valid, contraposition, sound
25. Valid, use conversion and then obversion, UNSOUND!
27. Valid, conversion, unsound
29. Valid, sound. One proof will use conversion, then obversion, then contradictories.

Chapter Eleven Exercises

1. Red
3. Pink
5. Green
7. Brown
9. Pink
11. Valid, Red 1 to Red 2
13. Invalid, there is no path from Brown to Purple
15. Valid, Green 2 to Green 4
17. Valid, Orange 4 to Orange 1
19. Invalid, there is no path from Green to Orange
21. Valid, Green 1 to Green 4
23. Valid, Red 1 to Red 3
25. Valid, Brown 1 to Brown 4
27. Valid, Pink 1 to Pink 3 (both false)
29. Valid, true Orange 4 to false Blue 1

Chapter Twelve Exercises

1. AEA-1: invalid

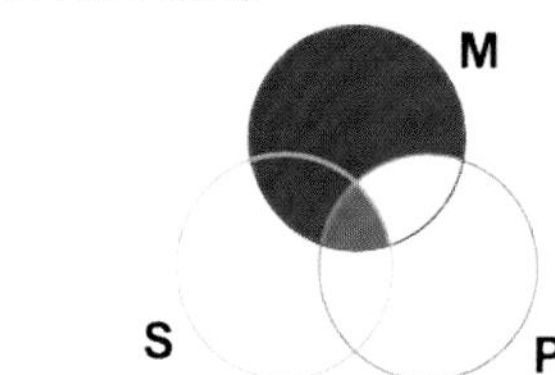

3. IEO-2: invalid

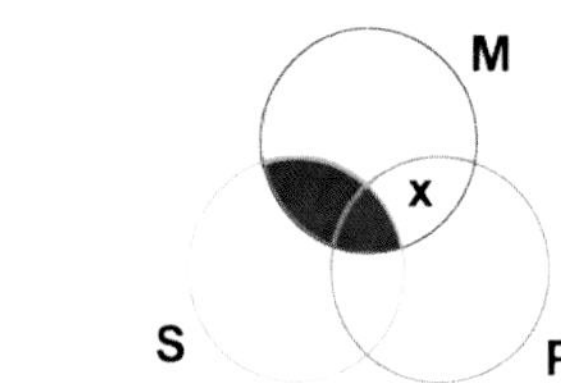

5. EAE-2: valid

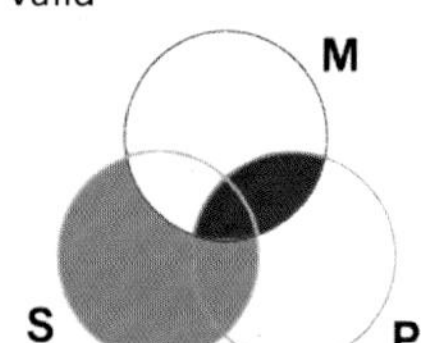

7. AEE-3: invalid

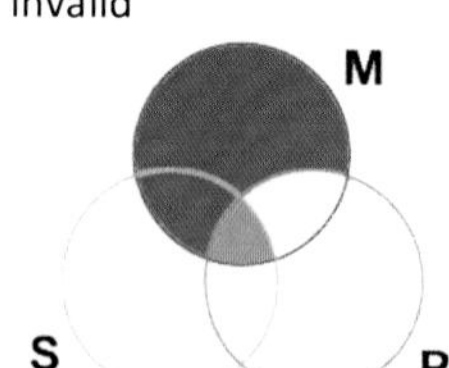

9. EIO-4: valid

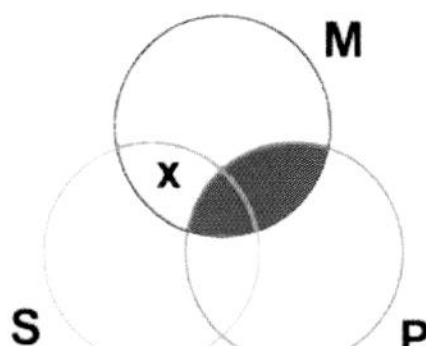

11. No C are W
Some D are not C
∴ Some D are not W

EOO-1: invalid

13. Some D_7 are D_4
No P are D_7
∴ No P are D_4

IEE-1: invalid

15. All D are F
Some D are R
∴ Some R are F

AII-3: valid

17. Some E are D
No D are P
∴ Some P are E

IEI-4: invalid

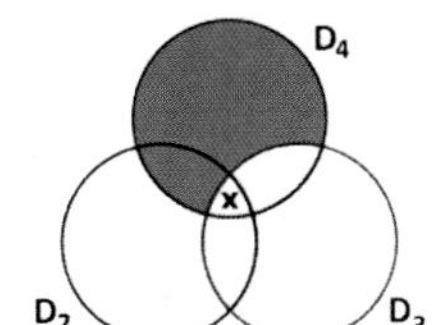

19. Some D_4 are D_3
All D_4 are D_2
∴ Some D_2 are D_3

IAI-3: valid

21. Conclusion: All marsupials are warm-blooded creatures.
All R are M
All M are W
∴ All R are W

AAA-1: valid

23. Premise: All philosophers are teachers.
All P are T
No T are M
∴ No P are M

AEE-4: valid

25. No human activities are actions governed by free will.
All H are M
No M are F
∴ No F are H (reworded above using conversion)

AEE-4: Valid

27. None.

All D are M	All D are M
All J are M	Some J are M
∴ ? none	
AA_ -2: none	AI_ -2: none
	IA_ -2: none

29. No footprint impressions attributed to bigfoot are footprints created by humans walking.
All F are T
No H are T
∴ No H are F (reworded above using conversion)

AEE-2, Valid

Chapter Thirteen Exercises

1. All stars are objects with planets
3. All citizens who are not allowed to vote are felons.
5. All sentences imposing the death penalty are unconstitutional punishments.
7. All places where lightning is present are places where thunderstorms are present.
9. All times one has been drinking are times one should not drive.
11. Valid
13. Valid
15. Valid (but unsound)
17. Valid
19. Valid
21. Invalid
23. Enthymene, conclusion: Johnny will not go to the beach today, valid
25. There may be some issues involving "should" but there is a basically valid syllogism at the heart of the argument.

27. Enthymeme, conclusion: All apologies are insincere. Hopefully unsound.
29. Valid. This argument is perhaps impossible to capture using standard form categorical syllogisms, but it can be proven to be valid using Venn diagrams.

Chapter Fourteen Exercises

1. C
3. S ⊃ ~J
5. ~C ⊃ ~P or P ⊃ C
7. E • S
9. W ⊃ C
11. (S ⊃ C) ∨ G
13. P_8 • (D_2 ∨ D_3)
15. D • (G ⊃ R)
17. (D ⊃ M) • ~(D ⊃ S)
19. S ('P • J' would not work)
21. D ⊃ (H • B)
23. (R ⊃ D) • (M ⊃ D)
25. F could work, but F ⊃ Q is better
27. (B_1 • B_2) • (M ⊃ C)
29. [~B ∨ (F • M)] ∨ (~N • S)

Chapter Fifteen Exercises

1. T
3. F
5. T
7. T
9. F
11. W • V True
13. C ∨ (V ∨ A) True
15. F ⊃ (R ∨ E) False
17. C ⊃ [R • (V • F)] ?
19. (R ⊃ F) • ~R ?
21. undetermined
23. T
25. undetermined
27. undetermined
29. undetermined

Chapter Sixteen Exercises

1.

P	P ⊃ ~P
T	F
F	T

contingent

3.

P	P ∨ ~P
T	T
F	T

tautology

5.

A	B	A ⊃ (B ⊃ A)
T	T	T
T	F	T
F	T	T
F	F	T

tautology

7.

S	T	~(S ∨ T)	~S ∨ ~T
T	T	F	F
T	F	F	T
F	T	F	T
F	F	T	T

consistent

9.

S	T	~(S ∨ T)	~S • ~T
T	T	F	F
T	F	F	F
F	T	F	F
F	F	T	T

logically equivalent

11.

S	R	(S • ~R) • (S ⊃ R)
T	T	F
T	F	F
F	T	F
F	F	F

self-contradiction

13.

P	Q	(P ≡ Q) ⊃ (~Q ∨ P)
T	T	T
T	F	T
F	T	T
F	F	T

tautology

15.

A	B	C	[(A • B) ∨ C] ∨ [(A ∨ B) • C]
T	T	T	T
T	T	F	T
T	F	T	T
T	F	F	F
F	T	T	T
F	T	F	F
F	F	T	T
F	F	F	F

contingent

17.

A	B	A • B	(B ⊃ A) ≡ ~(~B ∨ A)
T	T	T	F
T	F	F	F
F	T	F	F
F	F	F	F

Inconsistent

19.

P	Q	R	P ⊃ (Q ⊃ R)	(P • Q) ⊃ R
T	T	T	T	T
T	T	F	F	F
T	F	T	T	T
T	F	F	T	T
F	T	T	T	T
F	T	F	T	T
F	F	T	T	T
F	F	F	T	T

logically equivalent

21.

D	E	F	D ⊃ (E ≡ F)	(D • E) ⊃ (D • F)
T	T	T	T	T
T	T	F	F	F
T	F	T	F	T
T	F	F	T	T
F	T	T	T	T
F	T	F	T	T
F	F	T	T	T
F	F	F	T	T

consistent

23.

R	S	V	(R • S) ∨ V	(R ∨ V) • (S ∨ V)
T	T	T	T	T
T	T	F	T	T
T	F	T	T	T
T	F	F	F	F
F	T	T	T	T
F	T	F	F	F
F	F	T	T	T
F	F	F	F	F

logically equivalent

25.

A	G	H	[A ⊃ (G ≡ H)] ⊃ [(A • G) ⊃ H]
T	T	T	T
T	T	F	T
T	F	T	T
T	F	F	T
F	T	T	T
F	T	F	T
F	F	T	T
F	F	F	T

Tautology

27.

M	N	O	{[(M ⊃ N) • (M ⊃ O)] • ~(N ∨ O)} • M
T	T	T	F
T	T	F	F
T	F	T	F
T	F	F	F
F	T	T	F
F	T	F	F
F	F	T	F
F	F	F	F

self-contradiction

29.

	A	B	C	D	(A ⊃ B) ∨ (C ⊃ D)	(A • ~B) • (C • ~D)
1	T	T	T	T	T	F
2	T	T	T	F	T	F
3	T	T	F	T	T	F
4	T	T	F	F	T	F
5	T	F	T	T	T	F
6	T	F	T	F	F	T
7	T	F	F	T	T	F
8	T	F	F	F	T	F
9	F	T	T	T	T	F
10	F	T	T	F	T	F
11	F	T	F	T	T	F
12	F	T	F	F	T	F
13	F	F	T	T	T	F
14	F	F	T	F	T	F
15	F	F	F	T	T	F
16	F	F	F	F	T	F

contradictory

Chapter Seventeen Exercises

1.

P	P ⊃ ~P	~P
T	F	F
F	T	T

valid

3.

A	B	A ∨ B	A • B
T	T	T	T
T	F	T	F
F	T	T	F
F	F	F	F

invalid

5.

A	B	A ∨ B	B ∨ A
T	T	T	T
T	F	T	T
F	T	T	T
F	F	F	F

valid

7.

R	P	R ≡ P	~(R • ~P)
T	T	T	T
T	F	F	F
F	T	F	T
F	F	T	T

valid

9.

A	B	A ⊃ B	A	B
T	T	T	T	T
T	F	F	T	F
F	T	T	F	T
F	F	T	F	F

valid

11.

G	M	G ⊃ ~M	~M ⊃ G	G ≡ M
T	T	F	T	T
T	F	T	T	F
F	T	T	T	F
F	F	T	F	T

invalid

13.

G	M	D	G ⊃ (M ∨ D)	G ∨ (M • D)	M ∨ D
T	T	T	T	T	T
T	T	F	T	T	T
T	F	T	T	T	T
T	F	F	F	T	F
F	T	T	T	T	T
F	T	F	T	F	T
F	F	T	T	F	T
F	F	F	T	F	F

valid

15.

G	F	D	G ⊃ ~(F • D)	G ∨ F	D
T	T	T	F	T	T
T	T	F	T	T	F
T	F	T	T	T	T
T	F	F	T	T	F
F	T	T	T	T	T
F	T	F	T	T	F
F	F	T	T	F	T
F	F	F	T	F	F

invalid

17.

M	N	O	M ⊃ ~(N ⊃ O)	N ∨ O	M ⊃ ~O
T	T	T	F	T	F
T	T	F	T	T	T
T	F	T	F	T	F
T	F	F	F	F	T
F	T	T	T	T	T
F	T	F	T	T	T
F	F	T	T	T	T
F	F	F	T	F	T

valid

19.

A	B	X	Y	(~A ∨ B) ≡ (X • ~Y)	~B ∨ ~X	Y	~A
T	T	T	T	T F F	F	T	F
T	T	T	F	T T T	F	F	F
T	T	F	T	T F F	T	T	F
T	T	F	F	T F F	T	F	F
T	F	T	T	F T F	T	T	F
T	F	T	F	F F T	T	F	F
T	F	F	T	F T F	T	T	F
T	F	F	F	F T F	T	F	F
F	T	T	T	T F F	F	T	T
F	T	T	F	T T T	F	F	T
F	T	F	T	T F F	T	T	T
F	T	F	F	T F F	T	F	T
F	F	T	T	T F F	T	T	T
F	F	T	F	T T T	T	F	T
F	F	F	T	T F F	T	T	T
F	F	F	F	T F F	T	F	T

invalid

21. It is false that if a thing is a disease then it is a curable illness.
If a thing is a curable illness, then it is not something to be worried about.
∴ It is false that if a thing is a disease, then it is not something to be worried about.

D	C	W	~(D ⊃ C)	C ⊃ ~W	~(D ⊃ ~W)
T	T	T	F	F	T
T	T	F	F	T	F
T	F	T	T	T	T
T	F	F	T	T	F
F	T	T	F	F	T
F	T	F	F	T	T
F	F	T	F	T	T
F	F	F	F	T	T

invalid

23.

R	S	R ⊃ S	~S	~R
T	T	T	F	F
T	F	F	T	F
F	T	T	F	T
F	F	T	T	T

valid

25.

R	H	R ⊃ H	~H ⊃ ~R
T	T	T	T
T	F	F	F
F	T	T	T
F	F	T	T

valid

27.

C	L	~C ⊃ L	~C	L
T	T	T	F	T
T	F	T	F	F
F	T	T	T	T
F	F	F	T	F

valid

29.

M	W	K	C	M ⊃ W	K ⊃ M	C ⊃ K	C ⊃ W
T	T	T	T	T	T	T	T
T	T	T	F	T	T	T	T
T	T	F	T	T	T	F	T
T	T	F	F	T	T	T	T
T	F	T	T	F	T	T	F
T	F	T	F	F	T	T	T
T	F	F	T	F	T	F	F
T	F	F	F	F	T	T	T
F	T	T	T	T	F	T	T
F	T	T	F	T	F	T	T
F	T	F	T	T	T	F	T
F	T	F	F	T	T	T	T
F	F	T	T	T	F	T	F
F	F	T	F	T	F	T	T
F	F	F	T	T	T	F	F
F	F	F	F	T	T	T	T

valid

Chapter Eighteen Exercises

The numbers below the truth values indicate the order the truth values were entered.

1.

R	P	R	≡	P	~	(R	•	~	P)
T	F	T	T	T/F	F	T	T	T	F
5	8	9	1	⊥	2	4	3	6	7

valid

3.

A	B	A	⊃	B	A	B
		T	T	T/F	T	F
		4	1	⊥	2	3

valid

5.

P	Q	P	⊃	Q	~	Q	⊃	~	P
		T	T	T/F	T	F	F	F	T
		7	1	⊥	3	4	2	5	6

valid

7.

L	P	L	≡	~	P	~	P	⊃	~	L	~	L
		T/F	T	F	T	F	T	T	F	T	F	T
		⊥	1	10	9	7	8	2	6	5	3	4

valid

9.

D	E	F	D	∨	(E	•	F)	~	E	D
			F	T	F	T	T/F	T	F	F
			5	1	7	6	⊥	2	4	3

valid

11.

M	N	O	M ⊃ ~(N ⊃ O)	N ∨ O	M ⊃ ~O
			T T T F ⊥	T T	T F FT

valid

13.

A	B	X	Y	(~A ∨ B) ≡ (X • ~Y)	~B ∨ ~X	Y	~A
T	F		T	FT F F T F FT	TF T	T	FT

At this point, we can go no farther, but the only item left without a truth value is X. We can break the truth table in two, one for X=T and one for X=F, as those are the only two possibilities. You should confirm for yourself that either one will complete the truth table, making the argument invalid. There are two lines on the direct truth table which would prove the argument to be invalid: A=T, B=F, X=T, Y=T, and A=T, B=F, X=F, Y=T

15.

F ⊃ G	G ⊃ H	H ⊃ I	I ⊃ J	J ⊃ K	K ⊃ L	F ∨ ~L
F TT	TTT	TTT	TTT	TTT	TTT	F F FT

invalid

We could split the truth table into three lines, but we can quickly see that G in the first premise can be true or false, and K in the last premise can be true or false. If we assign all the other letters T, we will have all true premises and a false conclusion, which is sufficient proof that the argument is invalid.

17.

Q ⊃ (P • R)	S ⊃ (P • T)	U ⊃ (R ⊃ ~T)	S ⊃ (U ⊃ ~Q)
T T T T ⊥	TT TTT	T T F T FT	TF T F FT

valid

19.

G	F	D	G ⊃ ~(F • D)	G ∨ F	D
T	T	F	TT TTF F	T TT	F
				T TF	F
				F TT	F

invalid

21.

W	V	~W ⊃ ~V	~V ⊃ ~W	W ∨ V	W • V
		T	TF T F⊥	T T F	T F F
		TF T F⊥	T	F T T	F F T
		T	T	F T ⊥	F F F

valid

23

A	B	C	D	A ⊃ ~B	B ⊃ ~C	C ⊃ ~D	~(A ⊃ D)
T	F	F	T	T T TF	F T TF	F T FT	F TTT
							F FTT
							F FTF

invalid

25.

A	B	C	G	D	A ∨ (B • C)	G ⊃ ~B	D ⊃ ~C	A • (G ∨ D)
F	T	T	T	F	F T TTT	T T TF	F T FT	F F T T F
						F T TF		
						F T FT		

invalid

27.

(B ⊃ N) • (C ⊃ O)	B ∨ C	N ∨ O	~C ⊃ ~O	~B ⊃ ~N	(B • C) ∨ (N • O)
T T T T T T T	T T T	T T T	T	T	T F ⊥ F F
T T T T F T F	T T F	T T F	TF T TF	FT T FT	T F F F T F F
	F T T				T F ⊥ F F

invalid

29.

K	C	F	O	K ⊃ C	C ⊃ ~F	O ⊃ ~~K	F ⊃ ~O
				T T T	T T T⊥	T T TFT	T F FT

valid

If the future is knowable, then our actions are caused. If our actions are caused, then we do not have free will. If God is omniscient, then it is not the case that the future is unknowable. Therefore, if we have free will, then God is not omniscient.

Chapter Nineteen Exercises

1. *Modus Ponens* (MP), valid
3. Pure Hypothetical Syllogism (HS), valid
5. Denying the Antecedent, invalid
7. Presidential Fallacy, invalid
9. Affirming the Consequent, invalid
11. Disjunctive Syllogism (DS), valid
13. *Modus Tollens*, (MT), valid
15. Denying the Antecedent, invalid
17. Presidential Fallacy, invalid
19. Destructive Dilemma (DD), valid
21. Presidential Fallacy, invalid
23. Pure Hypothetical Syllogism (HS), valid
25. Pure Hypothetical Syllogism (HS), valid
27. Affirming the Consequent, invalid
29. *Modus Ponens* (MP), valid

Chapter Twenty Exercises

1. MP
3. 1, Simp
5. ~(A ⊃ B)
7. A, MP
9. 2, 3, Conj

11. 1) (R ≡ S) ⊃ L
2) ~L //~(R ≡ S)
3) ~(R ≡ S) 1,2, MT

13. 1) (D ⊃ P) ∨ W
2) ~(D ⊃ P) //W
3) W 1,2, DS

15. 1) J ⊃ (K ∨ P)
2) J
3) ~K // P
4) K ∨ P 1, 2, MP
5) P 4, 3, DS

17. 1) B ⊃ (A ∨ C)
2) (A ∨ C) ⊃ D
3) ~D // ~B
4) B ⊃ D 1, 2, HS
5) ~B 4, 3, MT

19. 1) (H ⊃ Q) • (S ⊃ D)
2) H ∨ S
3) ~Q // ~D
4) Q ∨ D 1, 2, CD
5) D 4, 3, DS

21. 1) L ⊃ M
2) M ⊃ G
3) ~G // ~L
4) ~M 2, 3 MT
5) ~L 3, 1, MT

23. 1) (D ∨ W) ⊃ P
2) [D ∨ (A ≡ L)] ⊃ R
3) D // P • R
4) D ∨ W 3, Add
5) P 1, 4, MP
6) D ∨ (A ≡ L) 3, Add
7) R 2, 6, MP
8) P • R 5, 7, Conj

25. 1) O ⊃ (M ∨ N)
2) ~M ⊃ (O • G)
3) ~M // N
4) O • G 2, 3, MP
5) O 4, Simp
6) M ∨ N 1, 5, MP
7) N 6, 3, DS

27. 1) ~D
2) ~R ⊃ G
2) (D ⊃ B) ∨ (R ⊃ D)
3) ~(D ⊃ B) // G
4) R ⊃ D 2, 3, DS
5) ~R 4, 1, MT
6) G 2, 5 MP

29.

1)	L ⊃ (W ⊃ G)	
2)	(D ∨ B) ⊃ R	
3)	R ⊃ V	
4)	L	
5)	(D ∨ B) ∨ W	// V ∨ G
6)	W ⊃ G	1, 4, MP
7)	(D ∨ B) ⊃ V	2, 3, HS
8)	[(D ∨ B) ⊃ V] • (W ⊃ G)	7, 6, Conj
9)	V ∨ G	8, 5, CD

Chapter Twenty-One Exercises

1. Impl
3. 1, Equiv
5. (E • A) ⊃ B
7. 1, DM
9. 2, Exp

11.

1)	(B ≡ D) ⊃ M	// ~(B ≡ D) ∨ M
2)	~(B ≡ D) ∨ M	1, Impl

13.

1)	~F ⊃ ~E	// F ∨ ~E
2)	~~F ∨ ~E	1, Impl
3)	F ∨ ~E	2, DN

15.

1)	C ⊃ G	
2)	(C ∨ D) • (D ⊃ M)	// M ∨ G
3)	(D ⊃ M) • (C ∨ D)	2, Com
4)	D ⊃ M	3, Simp
5)	(C ⊃ G) • (D ⊃ M)	1, 4, Conj
6)	C ∨ D	2, Simp
7)	G ∨ M	5, 6, CD
8)	M ∨ G	7, Com

17.

1)	(L • K) ∨ (L • I)	
2)	L ⊃ M	// M
3)	L • (K ∨ I)	1, Dist
4)	L	3, Simp
5)	M	2, 4, MP

19.

1)	R ⊃ (L ⊃ P)	
2)	~R ⊃ ~M	// M ⊃ (~L ∨ P)
3)	M ⊃ R	2, Trans
4)	M ⊃ (L ⊃ P)	1, 3, HS
5)	M ⊃ (~L ∨ P)	4, Impl

21.

1)	(P • M) ∨ (L • N)	
2)	~P	// L
3)	~P ∨ ~M	2, Add
4)	~(P • M)	3, DM
5)	L • N	1, 4, DS
6)	L	5, Simp

23.

1)	(R ⊃ S) • (B ⊃ ~D)	
2)	D ∨ ~S	// ~R ∨ ~B
3)	(~S ⊃ ~R) • (D ⊃ ~B)	1, Trans (x2)
4)	~S ∨ D	2, Com
5)	~R ∨ ~B	3, 4, CD

25.

1)	K ⊃ (L ⊃ P)	// L ⊃ (~K ∨ P)
2)	~K ∨ (~L ∨ P)	1, Impl (x2)
3)	(~K ∨ ~L) ∨ P	2, Assoc
4)	(~L ∨ ~K) ∨ P	3, Com
5)	~L ∨ (~K ∨ P)	4, Assoc
6)	L ⊃ (~K ∨ P)	5, Impl

27.

1)	M ∨ C	
2)	M ⊃ C	// C
3)	~~M ∨ C	1, DN
4)	~M ⊃ C	3, Imp
5)	~C ⊃ ~M	2, Trans
6)	~C ⊃ C	5, 4, HS
7)	~~C ∨ C	6, Impl
8)	C ∨ C	7, DN
9)	C	8, Taut

29.

1)	E ⊃ (S • N)	// E ⊃ (S ⊃ N)
2)	~E ∨ (S • N)	1, Impl
3)	(~E ∨ S) • (~E ∨ N)	2, Dist
4)	(~E ∨ N) • (~E ∨ S)	3, Com
5)	~E ∨ N	4, Simp
6)	(~E ∨ N) ∨ ~S	5, Add
7)	~E ∨ (N ∨ ~S)	6, Assoc
8)	~E ∨ (~S ∨ N)	7, Com
9)	E ⊃ (S ⊃ N)	8, Impl (x2)

Chapter Twenty-Two Exercises

1. ACP, CP
3. CP
5. ~A • B
7. (A • B) ⊃ R
9. AIP, (A • B) • ~(A • B), [5, 2, Conj], ~A, 3-6 IP

11.

1)	A ⊃ M	
2)	B ⊃ M	// (A • B) ⊃ M
3)	A • B	ACP
4)	A	3, Simp
5)	M	1, 4, MP
6)	(A • B) ⊃ M	3-5, CP

13.

1)	L ⊃ ~G	// ~(L • G)
2)	L • G	AIP
3)	L	2, Simp
4)	~G	1, 3, MP
5)	G • L	2, Com
6)	G	5, Simp
7)	G • ~G	6, 4, Conj
8)	~(L • G)	2-7, IP

15.

1)	H ⊃ ~E	
2)	G ⊃ E	// H ⊃ ~G
3)	H	ACP
4)	G	AIP
5)	~E	1, 3, MP
6)	E	2, 4, MP
7)	E • ~E	6, 5, Conj
8)	~G	4-7, IP
9)	H ⊃ ~G	3-8, CP

17.

1)	D ⊃ (P • V)	
2)	(V ∨ W) ⊃ A	// ~A ⊃ ~D
3)	~A	ACP
4)	D	AIP
5)	~(V ∨ W)	2, 3, MT
6)	~ V • ~W	5, DM
7)	~V	6, Simp
8)	~V ∨ ~P	7, IP
9)	~P ∨ ~V	8, Com
10)	~(P • V)	9, DM
11)	~D	1, 10, MT
12)	D • ~D	4, 11, Conj
13)	~D	4-12, IP
14)	~A ⊃ ~D	3-13, CP

19.

1)	(J ⊃ H) • (K ⊃ L)	
2)	J ∨ K	
3)	(H ∨ L) ⊃ E	// E
4)	~E	AIP
5)	~(H ∨ L)	3, 4, MT
6)	H ∨ L	1, 2, CD
7)	(H ∨ L) • ~(H ∨ L)	6, 5, Conj
8)	~~E	4-8, IP
9)	E	8, DN

21.

1)	(A ∨ B) ⊃ (N • M)	
2)	(M ∨ B) ⊃ (G • ~A)	// ~A
3)	A	AIP
4)	A ∨ B	3, Add
5)	N • M	1, 4, MP
6)	M • N	5, Com
7)	M	6, Simp
8)	M ∨ B	7, Add
9)	G • ~A	2, 8, MP
10)	~A • G	9, Com
11)	~A	10, Simp
12)	A • ~A	3, 11, Conj
13)	~A	3-12, IP

23.

1)	D ⊃ (E ⊃ L)	
2)	L ⊃ ~L	// ~D ∨ ~E
3)	D • E	AIP
4)	D	3, Simp
5)	E ⊃ L	1, 4, MP
6)	E • D	3, Com
7)	E	6, Simp
8)	L	5, 7, MP
9)	~L	2, 8 MP
10)	L • ~L	8, 9, Conj
11)	~(D • E)	3-10, IP
12)	~D ∨ ~E	11 DM

25.

1)	G ⊃ [(H • P) ⊃ ~G]	
2)	(H • G) ⊃ P	// H ⊃ ~G
3)	H	ACP
4)	G	AIP
5)	H • G	3, 4, Conj
6)	P	2, 5, MP
7)	(H • P) ⊃ ~G	1, 4, MP
8)	H • P	3, 6, Conj
9)	~G	7, 8 MP
10)	G • ~G	4, 9, Conj
11)	~G	4-10, IP
12)	H ⊃ ~G	3-11, CP

27.

1)	P ∨ K	
2)	(P • ~K) ⊃ (S • G)	// K ∨ S
3)	~(K ∨ S)	AIP
4)	~K • ~S	3, DM
5)	~K	4, Simp
6)	K ∨ P	1, Com
7)	P	6, 5, DS
8)	~S • ~K	4, Com
9)	~S	8, Simp
10)	~S ∨ ~G	10, Add
11)	~(S • G)	11, DM
12)	~(P • ~K)	2, 11, MT
13)	~P ∨ ~~K	12, DM
14)	~P ∨ K	13, DN
15)	K ∨ ~P	14, Com
16)	~P	15, 5, DS
17)	P • ~P	7, 16, Conj
18)	~~(K ∨ S)	3-17, IP
19)	K ∨ S	18, DN

29.

1)	D ⊃ (S ⊃ N)	
2)	D ⊃ S	
3)	G ⊃ (N ∨ D)	// ~G ∨ N
4)	G	ACP
5)	N ∨ D	3, 4, MP
6)	~N	AIP
7)	D	5, 6, DS
8)	S ⊃ N	1, 7, MP
9)	S	2, 7, MP
10)	N	8, 9, MP
11)	N • ~N	10, 6, Conj
12)	~G	6-11, IP
13)	H ⊃ ~G	4-12, CP

Chapter Twenty-Three Exercises

1. Argument by authority
3. Causal inference
5. Argument by authority
7. Inductive Generalization
9. Analogy
11. weak, fallacy of inappropriate authority, probably no appropriate conclusion
13. Inductive generalization, very hasty and weak. Perhaps we can conclude that there is some faction of Muslims who hate the United States.
15. Causal inference, weak, *Post Hoc Ergo Propter Hoc*
17. Appeal to authority. In general, I think that it is a bad idea to have students judge the competence of a professor, however, given the truth of the premise, we should consider the conclusion more likely to be true, putting the argument on the strong side. It might to important to see how the sample was gathered. Perhaps it just means that the professor grades strictly.
19. Analogy, strong.
21. I would like to see far more information before I accepted the premises with any degree of certainty, but I might say the first part of the argument leans toward the strong side. Even if we accept that there is some causal link between church attendance and criminal activity, however, the argument is incredibly vague. The government can't do anything that is unconstitutional.
23. Weak analogy. There are significant disanalogies between children and adults, including maturity level, self-sufficiency and responsibility.
25. This is a strong analogy.
27. Hasty generalization. The conclusion is stated too strongly. We might be able to draw the conclusion that a large number of the people held in Guantanamo Bay are terrorists.
29. Inappropriate authority. Although Wallace may have a point, he has an obvious bias, and so we cannot accept without question his assertions.

Chapter Twenty-Four Exercises

1. It sounds to me like rationalization. If we thought ahead, would we really plan on spending less time with are children, as long as it was filled with "quality" activities, whatever that means. One could say that is a hint of a euphemism.
3. Wishful thinking, perhaps rationalization
5. euphemism
7. scapegoating, stereotyping
9. oversimplification, wishful thinking
11. confirmation bias
13. innuendo
15. persuasive definition
17. wishful thinking
19. complex question
21. persuasive definition?
23. proof surrogate. Perhaps hyperbole.
25. apple polishing
27. euphemism

29. proof surrogate

Chapter Twenty-Five Exercises

1. composition
3. begging the question
5. composition
7. begging the question
9. false dilemma
11. red herring
13. appeal to ignorance
15. bandwagon
17. perfectionist fallacy
19. inappropriate appeal to tradition
21. begging the question
23. false dilemma
25. composition – 20% each year won't add up to 100% in five years.
27. equivocation
29. non-sequitur? Although it would force the government to operate with a balanced budget, that could have all sorts of devastating effects which are worse than raising the debt limit (conceivably)

Chapter Twenty-Six Exercises

1. definitional sulk
3. poisoning the well
5. *ad hominem* circumstantial
7. *ad hominem*? Red herring
9. missing the point
11. appeal to ignorance
13. oversimplification, the issue of hyperinflation is not even considered
15. division, appeal to guilt?
17. composition
19. *Ad hominem* abusive, genetic fallacy?
21. The first line seems to include a subtle *ad hominem* circumstantial. Maybe the G.I. Bill should be amended, but the fact that academics stand to profit from the G.I. Bill as it stands is not a good reason to do so.
23. False Dilemma. Lincoln said that his highest concern was the unity of the country, but that doesn't mean that he cannot also care about slaves. They could be his next concern. Here he is emphasizing the rank of his concerns, but the fact that he puts national unity above freeing the slaves, does not mean that he wasn't deeply concerned for slaves. We was dedicated to freeing the slaves, but he didn't want to do it by ripping apart the nation.

I could also see a case for definitional sulk as well as perfectionist fallacy.

25. non-sequitur? Equivocation? It is true that slave owners fed most of their slaves well and provided medical care they might not otherwise have had, but I'm not sure that most of us would call that decent treatment, considering the fact that they could also be cruelly punished for any disobedience. We should note that slave owners were not generally interested in the happiness of their slaves, but in their productivity, which often was achieved through fear and not happiness.
27. This argument seems to beg the question that an unbiased article will always have equal amounts of criticism for both liberals and conservatives. This is a ridiculous claim, and is based on the further assumption that liberals and conservatives always present equally good or faulty arguments. It is certainly possible that liberals present more faulty arguments than conservatives, or vice versa, and to recognize it does not automatically make one unbiased. Of course it might, but we cannot be sure based solely on the numbers of criticisms.

All biased people will criticize one side more than another.

Therefore, all people who criticize one side more than the other are biased.

(that's the fallacy of illicit conversion)

29. This might have been an opportunity to see some shifting ground, but Oblivious doesn't do so. He instead he bites the bullet and rejects the claim that "It is a fact that the Moon orbits the Earth." Instead there is probably a False Dilemma here. If we understand "opinion" to just mean "belief" then it can be the case that an opinion is a fact, and there is no dilemma. We could also interpret this as equivocation, as there may be a shift in meaning on the word "opinion".

Chapter Twenty-Seven Exercises

Statements 1 through 10 are shown in the table below, in each box which is ruled out by the statement.

	J	K	L	M
A	1,4,7,10	2,3,4,5,7,10	2,4	2,4,6,7,10
B	10	3,5,9,10	9	6,10
C	7,8,10	3,7,10		6,7,10
D	4,7,8	4,5,7	4	4,7

So, the only remaining solution is C • L.

Tennessee and Rhode Island

1. $\sim K_1 \supset K_3$
2. $T_1 \supset R_2$
3. $T_3 \supset K_2$
4. $R_2 \supset T_3$
5. $\sim R_1$

	1	2	3
K	✓	① ╳	⊗ ╳
T	⊗ ╳	✓	③ ╳
R	⑤ ╳	④ ╳	✓

$(K_1 \bullet T_2) \bullet R_3$

A

B

C

D

E

Q

R

S

T

U

V

W